Appositions
of Jacques Derrida and
Emmanuel Levinas

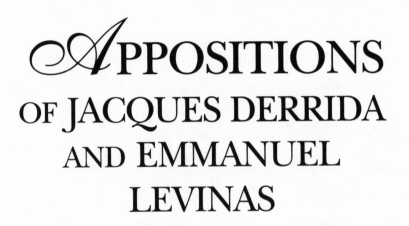

APPOSITIONS
OF JACQUES DERRIDA
AND EMMANUEL
LEVINAS

John Llewelyn

INDIANA UNIVERSITY PRESS

Bloomington & Indianapolis

This book is a publication of

Indiana University Press
601 North Morton Street
Bloomington, IN 47404-3797 USA

http://iupress.indiana.edu

Telephone orders   800-842-6796
Fax orders   812-855-7931
E-mail orders   iuporder@indiana.edu

© 2002 by John Llewelyn

The paper used in this publication meets the minimum requirements of American National Standard for Information Sciences—Permanence of Paper for Printed Library Materials, ANSI Z39.48-1984.

Manufactured in the United States of America

Library of Congress Cataloging-in-Publication Data

Llewelyn, John.
   Appositions of Jacques Derrida and Emmanuel Levinas / John Llewelyn.
      p. cm. — (Studies in Continental thought)
   Includes bibliographical references and index.
   ISBN 0-253-34018-7 (cloth : alk. paper) — ISBN 0-253-21493-9 (pbk. : alk. paper)
   1. Derrida, Jacques. 2. Lévinas, Emmanuel. I. Title. II. Series.
   B2430.D484 L555 2002
   194—dc21

                                                                      2001002816

1   2   3   4   5   07   06   05   04   03   02

For Charles Bigger

The Other measures me with a look incomparable with that by which I discover him. The dimension of *height* in which the Other is placed is like the primary curvature of being on which turns the privilege of the other, the altitude of transcendence. The Other is metaphysical.

. . . Welcome of the Other—the term expresses a simultaneity of passivity and activity—which places the relation with the other outside the dichotomies valid for things: the *a priori* and the *a posteriori*, activity and passivity.

But we wish to show also how, from knowledge identified with thematization, the truth of this knowledge leads back to the relation with the other—that is to say, to justice.

—EMMANUEL LEVINAS (*Totality and Infinity*, pp. 86–87)

. . . this necessity, that is not a constraint, but a very gentle force that obliges, and obliges not to bend otherwise the space of thinking in its respect for the other, but to give oneself to that other heteronomous curvature which relates us to the wholly other (that is to say, to justice, he says somewhere, in a powerful and formidable ellipse: the relation to the other, he says, that is to say, justice), according to a law that therefore calls one to give oneself to the other infinite precedence of the wholly other.

—JACQUES DERRIDA (*Adieu à Emmanuel Lévinas,* p. 22)

CONTENTS

PREFACE

The Oxford English Dictionary says that to appose is "to put or apply one thing *to* another, as a seal to another." As a seal or signature. To another.

This volume applies *to* one another chapters primarily concerned with the writings of Derrida or Levinas, with emphasis on the preposition *to*, as in the definition from the OED. My emphasis of that preposition is motivated by my wish not to emphasize the meaning of parallelism that the dictionary gives for "apposition," unless this meaning is taken along with the thought that parallel lines meet at Infinity. I wish to focus attention on the meaning of apposition as "being in close contact." The close contact between the writings of Levinas and of Derrida in question here is one that the dictionary might call "juxtaposition" and "close proximity," but their proximity does not exclude the further force of apposition which the dictionary gives, that of a "public disputation by scholars; a formal examination by question and answer." (The entry goes on to say that "Apposition" is applied to the Speech-Day at St Paul's School, London.) This is part of what Levinas means by "critique."

The reader is advised that in my discussion of the work of Levinas "the Other" usually translates his "Autrui," "Others" his "les Autres," "other" his "autre," and "others" his "les autres."

Speaking in *Proper Names* of the disputation between Derrida and himself, he says: "Our crossing of paths is already very good, and it is probably the very modality of the philosophical encounter. In emphasizing the primordial importance of the questions raised by Derrida, I have desired to express the pleasure of a contact at the heart of a chiasmus." In "The Word of Welcome" spoken on the first anniversary of Levinas's death, Derrida speaks of the hypothesis of a messianicity that would not be ahistorical, but whose historicalness might be called structural and would be without any particular empirically determinate incarnation. This hypothesis would not be Levinas's quite, "but it seeks to advance in his direction—perhaps to cross his path again. 'At the heart of a chiasmus,' as he once said."

This then is the mode of intercrossing that readers of the present volume will find between any one of the chapters in it treating primarily the writings of Derrida and any one of them treating primarily the writings of Levinas; they will find this relation further articulated in the chapters in which the writings of both of them are discussed. The chiasmic typography of this relation is not simply that of the upper-case version of the Greek letter *chi*, the symmetrical X. This monogram is complicated by having interwoven with it the asymmetrical lower-case χ, where the foot apposed to one of the legs may be taken to stand for the way in which Derrida and Levinas advance upon each other in turn. This "reciprocal surpassing" (JD), without entertaining "the ridiculous ambition of 'bettering'" (EL), repeats the backward and forward translation between Athens and Jerusalem, and between Hebrew and Greek, that goes on in the texts to which are apposed the signatures of Jacques Derrida and Emmanuel Levinas. I leave to the reader the intriguing questions whether aleph, א, and, if not, which other Hebrew letter might be laced into the Greek diplogram in order to do justice to this circumstance, and what watermark, marking the crossing of rivers and seas, might be supposed from Arabic, and so on.

After an introductory text concerned with writings of both Derrida and Levinas there follow three that are concerned mainly with writings of the former, then four concerned mainly with writings of the latter. Chapter 8 (which prepares the way for the second section of chapter 12) is an appendix apposed to chapter 7. Together they announce chapter 9, which, remembering the dedication and dedicatees of *Otherwise than Being and Beyond Essence,* is a watershed between the chapters chiefly concerned with the writings of only one of the two signatories and a series in which the work of both signatories is discussed. Chapter 14, "halfway between commentary and translation" (JD), and chapter 15 bring threads together without entertaining the ridiculous ambition to tie up all loose ends (see the end of chapter 5). That would be like wanting to hold back the ebb and flow of the tide with which Derrida compares the insistance of Levinas's paragraphs. Thanks to this break, break, break, one gets another chance to catch what may have passed one by earlier in his book. In my book too there is repetition. For example, some of the events performed in the brief chapter 11— an unavoidably difficult and perhaps exasperating chapter because it adds yet another pronoun of uncertain gender to Derrida's polylogical play on Levinas's play on pronouns—are repeated in reported speech in the section entitled "Pronouns and Pronunciation" in chapter 12 and the section "In Touch" in chapter 15. If, therefore, I have here and there failed to be as clear as it is possible to be, I urge the reader to read on to my succeeding attempts. If they are no more successful, let the reader take cheer, as I do, from the knowledge that the nine years Horace advised writers to postpone publication have elapsed since in another preface I described as forthcoming a book on Levinas and Derrida by Robert Bernasconi.

ACKNOWLEDGMENTS

I am grateful for the support of Janet Rabinowitch, Dee Mortensen, Rebecca Tolen, Jane Lyle, Drew Bryan, and Tony Brewer at Indiana University Press; of the Faculty of Arts computer service at the University of Edinburgh; of my wife Margaret and all our kin who even when at a distance were always at hand. I thank the editors and publishers, copyright holders of the following papers, for kindly granting permission to use abbreviated, expanded, or otherwise adapted versions of them here.

"Levinas and Language," in Robert Bernasconi and Simon Critchley, eds., *The Cambridge Companion to Levinas* (Cambridge: Cambridge University Press, 2001).

"What Is Orientation in Thinking? Facing the Facts," in Melvyn New, Robert Bernasconi, and Richard A. Cohen, eds., *In Proximity: Levinas and the Eighteenth Century* (Lubbock: Texas Tech University Press, 2001).

"The Impossibility of Levinas's Death," in Mark Robson, Mark Smith, and Joanne Morra, eds., *Death and Its Concepts* (Manchester: Manchester University Press, 2000).

"sELection," in Alan Milchman and Alan Rosenberg, eds., *Postmodernism and the Holocaust* (Amsterdam and Atlanta: Rodopi, 1998).

"Approaches to Semioethics," in Hugh Silverman, ed., *Cultural Semiosis: Tracing the Signifier* (New York: Routledge, 1998).

"In the Name of Philosophy," *Research in Phenomenology* XXVII (1998).

"Amen," in Adriaan Peperzak, ed., *Ethics as First Philosophy: The Significance of Emmanuel Levinas for Philosophy, Literature and Religion* (New York: Routledge, 1995).

"At This Very Moment . . . ," a translation of "En ce moment même . . . une répétition qui n'en est pas une," in *Le passage des frontières. Autour du travail de Jacques Derrida* (Paris: Galilée, 1994).

A section of "Meanings Reserved, Re-served and Reduced," *The Southern Journal of Philosophy* XXXII, Spindel Conference 1993 Supp. vol., *Derrida's Interpretation of Husserl,* 1994.

"Responsibility with Indecidability," in David Wood, ed., *Derrida: A Critical Reader* (Oxford: Blackwell, 1992).

"Derrida, Mallarmé and Anatole," in David Wood, ed., *Philosophers' Poets* (London: Routledge, 1990).

"The Origin and End of Philosophy," in Hugh J. Silverman, ed., *Philosophy and Non-Philosophy since Merleau-Ponty* (New York: Routledge, 1988).

"Thresholds," in David Wood and Robert Bernasconi, eds., *Derrida and Différance* (Evanston: Northwestern University Press, 1988).

"Levinas, Derrida and Others vis-à-vis," in Robert Bernasconi and David Wood, eds., *The Provocation of Levinas: Rethinking the Other* (London: Routledge, 1988).

"Jewgreek or Greekjew," J. Sallis, M. Moneta, and J. Taminiaux, eds., *The Collegium Phaenomenologicum: The First Ten Years* (Dordrecht: Kluwer, 1987).

"The 'Possibility' of Heidegger's Death," *Journal of the British Society for Phenomenology* 14 (1983).

KEY TO ABBREVIATIONS

Publications referred to by abbreviation in the text are as follows:

WORKS BY JACQUES DERRIDA

A   (with Pierre-Jean Labarrière) *Altérités* (Paris: Osiris, 1986).

Ad   *Adieu à Emmanuel Lévinas* (Paris: Galilée, 1997).

Ap   *Apories: Mourir—s'attendre aux "limites de la vérité"* (Paris: Galilée, 1996).

Ap tr. *Aporias: Dying—awaiting (one another) at the "limits of truth,"* trans. Thomas Dutoit (Stanford: Stanford University Press, 1993).

CP   *La carte postale de Socrate à Freud et au-delà* (Paris: Aubier-Flammarion, 1980).

D   *La Dissémination* (Paris: Seuil, 1972).

D tr.   *Dissemination,* trans. Barbara Johnson (Chicago: University of Chicago Press, 1981).

DG   *De la grammatologie* (Paris: Minuit, 1967).

DTA   *D'un ton apocalyptique adopté naguère en philosophie* (Paris: Galilee, 1983).

E   *De l'esprit: Heidegger et la question* (Paris: Galilée, 1987).

ED   *L'écriture et la différence* (Paris: Seuil, 1967).

F   "Fors: les mots anglés de Nicolas Abraham et Maria Torok," Introduction to Nicolas Abraham and Maria Torok, *Cryptonymie: le verbier de l'homme aux loups* (Paris: Aubier-Flammarion, 1976).

F tr.   "Fors," trans. Barbara Johnson, *The Georgia Review,* 1977, vol. 31, 64–116.

FC   *Feu la cendre* (Paris: Des femmes, 1987).

FH	"D'un ton apocalyptique adopté naguère en philosophie," in Philippe Lacoue-Labarthe and Jean-Luc Nancy, eds., *Les fins de l'homme: à partir du travail de Jacques Derrida* (Paris: Galilee, 1981).
FL	"Force of Law: The 'Mystical Foundation of Authority'," *Deconstruction and the Possibility of Justice, Cardozo Law Review*, 1990, vol. 11.
G2	*Glyph* 2 (Baltimore and London: Johns Hopkins University Press, 1977).
G2S	*Glyph* 2 Supplement (Baltimore and London: Johns Hopkins University Press, 1977).
G7	*Glyph* 7 (Baltimore and London: Johns Hopkins University Press, 1980).
Gl	*Glas* (Paris: Galilée, 1974 (Paris: Denoel/Gonthier, 1981))
Gl tr.	*Glas,* trans. John P. Leavey, Jr., and Richard Rand (Lincoln: University of Nebraska Press, 1986).
HO	Edmund Husserl, *L'origine de la géométrie,* trans. and introduction by Jacques Derrida (Paris: Presses Universitaires de France, 1962).
HO tr.	*Edmund Husserl's Origin of Geometry: An Introduction,* ed. David B. Allison, trans. John P. Leavey, Jr. (New York: Nicolas Hays, Brighton, Harvester, 1977).
Ja	"Ja, ou le faux-bond," *Digraphe,* 1977, no. 11, 83–121.
LI	*Limited Inc,* trans. Samuel Weber and Jeffrey Mehlman (Evanston: Northwestern University Press, 1988).
M	*Marges de la philosophie* (Paris: Minuit, 1972).
M tr	*Margins of Philosophy,* trans. Alan Bass (Chicago: University of Chicago Press, 1982).
MPM	*Mémoires pour Paul de Man* (Paris: Galilée, 1988).
OA	*L'oreille de l'autre* (Montreal: VLB Editeur, 1982).
OG	*Of Grammatology,* trans. Gayatri Chakravorti Spivak (Baltimore and London: Johns Hopkins University Press, 1974).
P	*Positions* (Paris: Minuit, 1972).
P tr.	*Positions,* trans. Alan Bass (Chicago: University of Chicago Press, 1981).
Par	*Parages* (Paris: Galilée, 1986).
PC	*The Postcard: From Socrates to Freud and Beyond,* trans. Alan Bass (Chicago: University of Chicago Press, 1987).
PG	*Le problème de la genèse dans la philosophie de Husserl* (Paris: Presses Universitaires de France, 1990).
Ps	*Psyché: inventions de l'autre* (Paris: Galilée, 1987).
S	*Of Spirit: Heidegger and the Question,* trans. Geoffrey Bennington and Rachel Bowlby (Chicago: University of Chicago Press, 1989).
SM	*Spectres de Marx: L'état de la dette, le travail du deuil et la nouvelle Internationale* (Paris: Galilée, 1993).

SM tr. *Specters of Marx: The State of the Debt, the Work of Mourning, and the New International,* trans. Peggy Kamuf (New York and London: Routledge, 1994).

SP *Speech and Phenomena,* trans. David B. Allison (Evanston: Northwestern University Press, 1973).

T *Le toucher, Jean-Luc Nancy* (Paris: Galilée, 2000).

VP *La voix et le phénomène* (Paris: Presses Universitaires de France, 1967).

WD *Writing and Difference,* trans. Alan Bass (Chicago: University of Chicago Press, 1978).

WORKS BY EMMANUEL LEVINAS

ADV *L'au-delà du verset: lectures et discours talmudiques* (Paris: Minuit, 1982).

AE *Autrement qu'être ou au-delà de l'essence* (The Hague: Nijhoff, 1978).

AHN *A l'heure des nations* (Paris: Minuit, 1988).

BV *Beyond the Verse: Talmudic Readings and Lectures,* trans. Gary D. Mole (London: Athlone, 1994).

CPP *Collected Philosophical Papers,* trans. Alphonso Lingis (The Hague: Nijhoff, 1987).

DE *De l'existence à l'existant* (Paris: Vrin, 1981).

DF *Difficult Freedom: Essays on Judaism,* trans. Seán Hand (Baltimore: Johns Hopkins University Press, 1990).

DL *Difficile liberté: Essais sur le judaïsme* (Paris: Albin Michel, 1976).

DMT *Dieu, la mort et le temps* (Paris: Grasset, 1993).

DVI *De Dieu qui vient à l'idée* (Paris: Vrin, 1982).

EaI *Ethics and Infinity,* trans. Richard A. Cohen (Pittsburgh: Duquesne University Press, 1985).

EDE *En découvrant l'existence avec Husserl et Heidegger* (Paris: Vrin, 1967).

EE *Existence and Existents,* trans. Alphonso Lingis (The Hague: Nijhoff, 1978).

EeI *Éthique et infini* (Paris: Fayard, 1982).

EN *Entre nous: Essais sur le penser-à-l'autre* (Paris: Grasset, 1991).

GCM *Of God Who Comes To Mind,* trans. Bettina Bergo (Stanford: Stanford University Press, 1998).

HAH *L'humanisme de l'autre homme* (Montpellier: Fata Morgana, 1972).

HLR *The Levinas Reader,* ed. Seán Hand (Oxford: Blackwell. 1989).

HS *Hors sujet* (Montpellier: Fata Morgana, 1987).

II *L'intrigue de l'infini* (Paris: Flammarion, 1944).

ITN *In the Time of the Nations,* trans. Michael B. Smith (London: Athlone, 1994).

LBPW *Emmanuel Levinas: Basic Philosophical Writings,* ed. Adriaan T. Peperzak, Simon Critchley, and Robert Bernasconi (Bloomington: Indiana University Press, 1996).

NP   *Noms propres* (Montpellier: Fata Morgana, 1976).

NTL   *Nine Talmudic Lectures,* trans. Annette Aronowicz (Bloomington: Indiana University Press, 1990).

OB   *Otherwise than Being or Beyond Essence,* trans. Alphonso Lingis (The Hague: Nijhoff, 1981).

OS   *Outside the Subject,* trans. Michael B. Smith (London: Athlone, 1993).

PN   *Proper Names,* trans. Michael B. Smith (London: Athlone, 1996).

QLT   *Quatre lectures talmudiques* (Paris: Minuit, 1968).

RRL   *Re-Reading Levinas,* ed. Robert Bernasconi and Simon Critchley (Bloomington: Indiana University Press, 1991).

SMB   *Sur Maurice Blanchot* (Montpellier: Fata Morgana, 1975).

TA   *Le temps et l'autre* (Paris: Presses Universitaires de France, 1983).

TaI   *Totality and Infinity: An Essay on Exteriority,* trans. Alphonso Lingis (The Hague: Nijhoff, 1969).

TeI   *Totalité et Infini: Essai sur l'extériorité* (The Hague: Nijhoff, 1961).

TEL   *Textes pour Emmanuel Lévinas,* ed. François Laruelle (Paris: Jean-Michel Place, 1980).

TO   *Time and the Other,* trans. Richard A. Cohen (Pittsburgh: Duquesne University Press, 1987).

TrI   *Transcendance et intelligibilité* (Geneva: Labor et Fides, 1984).

Appositions
of Jacques Derrida and
Emmanuel Levinas

INTRODUCTION: LEVINAS, DERRIDA, AND OTHERS VIS-À-VIS

> He is Greek, and he speaks Greek, does he not?
>
> —Socrates

ETHICAL METAPHYSICS

Heidegger frequently links the notion of the physical to a certain Greek conception of what it means to be. He also links it to the idea of emergence into the open and coming to light (*phôs*). So the study of being, ontology, at the time of *Being and Time*, is a phenomenology, a description of appearing (*phainesthai*) and dis-appearing.

Husserl's phenomenology is no less an ontology, a study of essences, than Heidegger's fundamental ontology is a phenomenology. Both Heidegger and Husserl describe what the Greeks called the physical, in the wide sense that Heidegger finds this word to have had for them. If we understand the word in this wide sense, we understand why Levinas says that the main topic of his thinking is metaphysical. It is metaphysical because it is ethical. And it is ethical not because he aims to present a code or a metaphysics of ethics. Kant's groundwork of the metaphysics of ethics suggests an analogy between Kantian respect and Heideggerian letting be. But it is being that is to be let be according to Heidegger, and it is the moral law that is to be respected according to Kant. The other person is to be respected, according to Kant, only because the other person is a rational agent, and he is a rational agent only insofar as he personifies the moral law and is capable of exercising a freedom to refrain from following rules of behavior that could not be universally followed or willed. By the same standard, the agent is entitled and obliged to respect himself. He respects the law which transcends the laws of physical nature, without of course suspending them. Kant's metaphysics of ethics describes the structure of interpersonality, a structure for which his analogy is that of the lawfulness of nature. It describes the foundation of justice.

The ethical, as Levinas describes it, is "older than" justice as conceived by Kant. It is a condition which is not a foundation of justice as conceived by Kant; so it is, more strictly speaking, an un-condition which is pre-original and prior to the *intér-esse-ment* which is no less a feature of Kantian deontological morality than it is of the teleological morality of self-interest and general interest. Both of these models of morality are styles of being and

1

being-with, *Mitsein,* notwithstanding the criteria they provide for distin-guishing the immoral from the moral and the inauthentic from the authen-tic. They are both ontological.

The ethical as Levinas would have us understand it is deontological, dis-ontological, *ent-ontologisch.* It is prior to all structures of being-with. It is prior to all structures, whether these be the categories of Greek philosophy, of Kant, of Hegel, of Husserl, or the structures of structuralism and of linguis-tic or economic exchange. It is prior to all system, to Symmetry, to correla-tion, to the will, to freedom, and to the opposition of activity and passivity. It is the superlation of passivity. Because it is prior to the third person.

Without yet knowing what is prior to the third-personal point of view according to Levinas, it is not difficult to see how he stands vis-à-vis certain of the other authors whose work has been influential in recent European thinking. The surrationalistic structures of the natural sciences as con-ceived, say, by Bachelard are third-personal objectivated systems. The disil-lusioning techniques prescribed in the critical theory of Habermas call for the same objectivation in the social sciences. This third-personal scientific objectivity is demanded by the theories and methods of interpretation advocated by realist critics of Gadamer like Emilio Betti and E. D. Hirsch. As for the structuralist theories which Lévi-Strauss and others have developed from the teaching of Saussure, these are predicated on a concept of lan-guage as a system of opposed terms regarded in isolation from the particular speech acts performed by users of that system. *Langue,* as described by Saussure and his adaptors, fulfills the description that Levinas gives of a system as a coexistence or agreement of different terms in the unity of a theme (AE 210, OB 165).

So is Levinas in the lineage of those who deny the primacy of *langue* over *parole?* And is he a champion of diachrony against synchrony? The answer to both of these questions is that he is, but in a way that sets him apart. When Merleau-Ponty and Ricoeur re-emphasize the dependence of instituted language upon *parole,* they are stressing the intentionality of creative, sense-giving speech acts. When, following Husserl, Merleau-Ponty underlines the importance of anonymous, centripetal intentionality, he is proposing noth-ing that transcends the general sphere of significance to which the structur-alists apply their theories. He, like them, is talking about the universe of discourse in which one thing stands for another, the system of signifier and signified (AE 188, OB 148). When the system of one thing with another and one thing standing for another is supplemented by the significative inten-tionality of a speaker, we are still short of the nonintentional, pre-inten-tional or, as Levinas sometimes calls it, reversed intentional, *significance* which, he says, is presupposed by semantic signification. And the diachrony of the speech act is but a difference in the same time in contrast with the radical diachrony Levinas ascribes to my responsibility for the Other, *Autrui,* to whom I address my words and myself. In the essentialist phenomenology of Husserl, utterance and all other signifying gestures are noetic-noematic, an intentional projection of subjectivity toward an accusative. This is because for Husserl

> all acts generally—even the acts of feeling and will—are "objectifying" acts, original factors in the "constituting" of objects, the necessary sources of different regions of being and of the ontologies that belong therewith.[1]

For Husserl the prototype of even non-theoretical acts is perception and the correlation of subjectivity and objectivity, the co-relation of being-with.

Levinas discerns very much the same sort of auto-affection at work in this prototype as is posited by the Kantians and Neo-Kantians from whom Husserl was hoping to move away. These and Husserl are all inheritors of the Cartesian tradition in which consciousness is egological. Another heir of this tradition is Sartre. Although in his existential phenomenology intentionality is interpreted as the for-itself's refusal of the in-itself with which it is correlated, a kind of "othering," consciousness remains a free recuperation. Its ideal is that of assumption, consumption, digestion, though, in contrast with the Hegelian phenomenology of the concept, fulfillment of the ideal is condemned never to be achieved. In Husserl's essentialist phenomenology the other, although my alter ego and an analogue of myself, resists assimilation because he is only ever appresented: I have no adequate consciousness of his consciousness. Sartre, for different reasons, agrees with this, yet he continues to see the for-itself as consciousness projected toward assimilation.

Somewhat the same assimilative character is ascribed by Gadamer to our efforts to understand each other and the texts and works of art and artifice that others have produced. Understanding is at the same time self-understanding and an interfusion of horizons. It is true that with Sartre cognition is secondary to consciousness and that with Gadamer and Heidegger consciousness is secondary to understanding (*Verstehen*) as a structure of being. However, the Husserlian notion of horizon persists in the accounts that Sartre, Gadamer, and Heidegger give of situation or environing world, *Umwelt*. This, Levinas maintains, is incommensurable with the for-the-other, which, far from being the mere contingency that is Sartre's being-for-the-other, is an unavoidable and unvoidable human responsibility. Levinas would say that this ethical responsibility is also neglected in the hermeneutic co-responsibility of Gadamer's interpretation of understanding. He does say that it is beyond the reach of the ecstasis of *Verstehen* as this is described in *Being and Time*. It cannot be comprehended by comprehension. Like the infinite of Descartes's third Meditation, it cannot be comprehended. Levinas agrees with readers of the *Meditations* like Martial Gueroult, one of his teachers at Strasbourg, who take as provisional and artificial Descartes's distinction between the consciousness he has of his self and the consciousness he has of his finitude. "My nature is not only to be a thinking being, thinking itself as thought, but a being thinking itself as finite and consequently thinking the infinite."[2] The thought of the infinite is implicit in and logically prior to the thought of myself, to the *cogito*.

In thinking the infinite—the self at once *thinks more than it can think.* The infinite does not enter into the *idea* of the infinite; it is not grasped—this idea is not a concept. The infinite is the radically, absolutely other. (EDE 172, CPP 54)

Whereas Descartes employs causal and ontological arguments to demonstrate that there is a God, the descriptions Levinas gives purport not to be ontological. They take as their cue the axiological function that Descartes attributes to the idea of God's perfection, although, as Gueroult observes, Descartes does not make as clear as Malebranche does the distinction between judgments of truth or reality and judgments of value or perfection.[3] What Levinas refers to as the most high (*altus*) is the radically other (*alter*). The Other, *Autrui,* is not simply an alter ego, an appresented analogue of myself. He and I are not equals, citizens in an intelligible kingdom of ends. We are not relatives. We are not different as chalk and cheese. There is between us, in the Hegelian phrase that Levinas adapts, an absolute difference. The Other is he to whom and in virtue of whom I am subject, with a subjectivity that is heteronomy, not autonomy, and hetero-affection, not auto-affection. The Other is not the object of my concern and solicitude. Beyond what Heidegger means by *Sorge* and *Fürsorge* is my being concerned, *con-cerné,* obsessed by the Other. He is not the accusative of my theoretical, practical, or affective intentionality or ecstasis. He is the topic of my regard (*il me regarde*) only because I am the accusative of his look (*il me regarde*) (AE 147, OB 116). The subject is an accusative, *me,* which is not a declension from a nominative, but an accusative absolute like the pronoun *se* for which, Levinas says, Latin grammars acknowledge no nominative (AE 143, OB 112). This latter accusative is not a case of the I that accuses itself. The accusative in question is beholden to the Other, but not for any services rendered. He is subpoenaed by the Other, pursued and persecuted, but not on account of any crime or original sin (AE 156, OB 121). The persecuted is himself responsible for the persecution to which he is subjected, but his responsibility is beyond free will; and the accusation is not one that he can answer or to which he can respond with an apology, for "Persecution is the precise moment in which the subject is reached or touched without the mediation of the logos."[4] It is beyond the spoken word, and beyond or before Christian and Hegelian mediation.

The accused self is categorized beyond free will and beyond the opposition of freedom and non-freedom, where by freedom is understood freedom to choose and initiate. Original ontological freedom, according to Sartre, although prior to deliberation and will, is nonetheless an unreflective choice. It is also ontological because it is the choice of a way to be. Levinasian ethical responsibility is preoriginal and beyond ontology. Sartrian fundamental choice founds the agent's situation. It is a descendant of Fichtean self-positing. Levinasian responsibility is non-foundational and an-archic. It deposes, ex-poses and de-situates the self. This does not mean, however, that the self is alienated, "Because the Other in the Same is my substitution for the other

4

through the *responsibility* for which I am summoned as the one who is *irreplaceable*" (AE 146, OB 114). This substitution is not a derivative of the intersubstitutability of *das Man.*

> Through substitution for others, the oneself escapes relations. At the limit of passivity, the oneself escapes passivity or the inevitable limitation that the terms within relation undergo. In the incomparable relationship of responsibility, the other no longer limits the same, it is supported by what it limits. Here the overdetermination of the ontological categories is visible, which transforms them into ethical terms. In the most passive passivity, the self liberates itself ethically from every other and from itself. Its responsibility for the other, the proximity of the neighbor, does not signify a submission to the non-ego; it means an openness in which being's essence is surpassed in inspiration. It is an openness of which respiration is a modality or a foretaste, or, more exactly, of which it retains the aftertaste. Outside of any mysticism, in this respiration, the possibility of every sacrifice for the other, activity and passivity coincide. (AE 146, OB 115)

Since what Levinas here calls "the most passive passivity" and elsewhere "the passivity of passivity" is said to be a passivity that coincides with activity, it might be expected that he would refer to this also as a most active activity or the activity of activity. That he never does this marks off the superlative emphatic passivity he does refer to not only from Cartesian freedom, the Kantian rational will and Sartrean originative choice, it marks it off too from any respect and *Seinlassen* such as would lend itself to articulation in the middle voice construed as the expression of a neutral state between or a mixture or compound of activity and passivity taken as opposites. Levinas's beyond of passivity and activity is beyond being, whether being be expressed by a noun, a verb, or by a verbal noun; insofar as it can be expressed by a word, it is more correct to call it a passivity than an activity. It follows that this passivity must not be construed as the taking on of suffering, suffering to suffer either a useful passion or a *passion inutile.* It is a passivity that is presupposed by any such assumption or undertaking: assumed by assumption. Contract, engagement, and commitment, whether entered into altruistically or from egoistic motives, are still at the level of egoity, and egoity has absolute passivity as its un-condition. Entering into a commitment is subscribing to a project, not something to which the accused is subjected.

For Sartre, even the adversity of that which limits my freedom is a function of my freedom,[5] as for Fichte is the resistance, *Anstoss,* of the not-I. He devotes several paragraphs of *Being and Nothingness* to describing the paradoxes of passivity.[6] These paradoxes arise, he says, from the supposition that passivity is a mode of being-in-itself, whereas both passivity and activity presuppose human beings and the instruments they use: "man is active and the means which he employs are called passive." So activity and passivity presuppose being-for-itself, hence non-being. The self-consistency of being-in-itself is beyond both the active and the passive. The absolute passivity of which Levinas writes is indeed subjectivity, but sub-jectivity of the for-others, not of the for-itself. Absolute passivity is also beyond being and nothingness. Levinas agrees with Hegel that meontology is the mirror image of ontology. They occupy the same logical space, the space of the Same. So too does the neutral third value between being and nothingness for which Levinas employs the expression *il y a,* the there-is. In *De l'existence à l'existant* this expression carries some of the force carried by the notions of facticity and thrownness in *Being and Nothingness* and *Being and Time.* But this sheer anonymous fact of one's existence is prior to the notion of world or situation. And prior to both the *il y a* and worldhood, availing an exit from them and an exile, is the absolute passivity of passivity (DE 26, EE 21).[7]

FACIAL EXPRESSION

The absoluteness of my passivity answers the infinitude of the absolutely other. It fills the place that Descartes gives to the infinitude of the freedom of my will, which for him is "that above all in respect of which I bear the image and likeness of God." For Levinas and Descartes, infinitude is the positive notion in terms of which the notion of man's finitude is understood. Instead of this positive notion of infinity, Kant substitutes a regulative idea required to give sense to man's always unfinished search for more knowledge. This notion of infinity is an ideal "ought." Heidegger applauds what Kant has to say about human finitude, though where Kant interprets this as man's limitedness by the given, Heidegger interprets it as man's being toward death. Hegel opposes a good infinite to the interminable bad infinite of the Kantian "ought." To the finitude of man's being toward his term he opposes the negation of this finitude, the infinity of the end of history. Against this, Levinas says:

> We recognize in the finitude to which the Hegelian infinite is opposed, and which it encompasses, the finitude of man before the elements, the finitude of man invaded by the *there is,* at each instant traversed by faceless gods against whom labour is pursued in order to realize the security in which the "other" of the elements would be revealed as the same. (TeI 171, TaI 197)

That is to say, Hegel's good infinite is an infinite of goods. It is an economic infinity of need and the war of each in competition with all where my freedom is limited but also consummated by that of the other. Levinas argues that room must be found also for an infinite of goodness, a peaceful infinite of Desire which, instead of limiting and enhancing my freedom, extends my responsibility and exalts it the more I respond to the other's call: "the absolutely Other does not limit the freedom of the Same. In calling it to responsibility it renews and justifies it." This renewal, *instauration,* is inspiration, the Levinasian incomingly affective counterpart to the Husserlian outgoingly intentional animation of the body of the corporeal signifier. Husserl's egological sense-giving *Beseeling* is what Levinas doubtless has in view when he introduces his notion of heteronomous "psychism." In

Levinas's account of Husserl's semiology, signs express meaning only within a horizon against which they are presented, much after the manner of objects in a visual field. He gives a similar account of the ready to hand, which is accorded priority over the present at hand in Heidegger's analysis of the everyday world as well as in the semiology of *Being and Time*. For Heidegger and Husserl, "To comprehend the particular being is to grasp it out of an illuminated site it does not fill" (TeI 164, TaI 190). For them there is no aspect of a being that is transcendentally foreign to being and comprehension, even if it may be temporarily hidden.

For Levinas the face of the other is beyond being and comprehension. Beyond Husserlian expressive meaning and presupposed by it is the expression of the other's face. This expression is not the expression that is seen. It is heard expression that is the discourse of the Saying (*Dire*) that is presupposed by the Said (*Dit*). The face is not the countenance. It cannot be contained. Like the infinitude of Descartes's God, it cannot be comprehended. Unlike the Look of Sartre's being-for-the-other, the other's face is not a threat to my freedom before which I shrivel. It increases my responsibility and is welcomed.

> Under the eye of another, I remain an unattackable subject in respect. It is the obsession by the other, my neighbour, accusing me of a fault which I have not committed freely, that reduces the ego to a self on the hither side of my identity, prior to all self-consciousness, and denudes me absolutely. To revert to oneself is not to establish oneself at home, even if stripped of all one's acquisitions. It is to be like a stranger, hunted down even in one's home, contested in one's identity. . . . It is always to empty oneself anew of oneself, and to absolve oneself, like in a haemophiliac's haemorrhage. (AE 117, OB 92)

The internal hemorrhage in my universe which on Sartre's analysis results from my being seen by the other is the foundation of my unreflective consciousness of myself.[8] The hemorrhage to which Levinas refers is not in the zone of self-consciousness, *Selbstbewusstsein,* or in any other region of consciousness, unconsciousness, or being, *Sein*. It is an emptying out of my consciousness, a *kenôsis* commanded by the ethical word of the other which inflicts a wound that never heals (TeI 171, TaI 197; AE 162, OB 126).

The first traumatic word which is the pre-original expression of the face is "thou shalt commit no murder."

> The epiphany of the face is ethical. The struggle this face can threaten *presupposes* the transcendence of expression. The face threatens the eventuality of a struggle, but this threat does not exhaust the epiphany of infinity, does not formulate its first word. War presupposes peace, the antecedent and non-allergic presence of the Other; it does not represent the first event of the encounter. (TeI 173–74, TaI 199)

By war Levinas means a resistance and counter-resistance of energies, an allergy which is an opposition of powers analogous to the reciprocity of forces in the system of Newtonian mechanics. The ethical resistance is "the resistance of what has no resistance," since it is the weakness of the other which commands me. The other is the poor, the widow and the orphan mentioned in the Book of Job. Paradoxically, it is the vulnerability of the other, the nakedness of the face, which wounds me. The ethical "thou shalt not" dominates the economic and political "I can." The "I can" and the philosophies of "I can" are no less egocentric than the philosophies of "I think," notwithstanding that the ego is correlated with an other. Although Levinas recognizes that in his later writings Husserl explores the limits of the correlation of subject and object, he insists that Husserl never relinquishes the idea that the ego—which Levinas equates with the same—always has its correlative *cogitatum;* that is to say, although, in the track of Brentano, Husserl holds that all intentionality, even non-theoretical intentionality, is the intending of a noematic Object, this other is assimilated into the same. It is the object of my active or passive concern. But this concern is not ultimate since it presupposes a concern beyond activity and passivity. For Heidegger and for Husserl, on Levinas's reading of them, my ultimate concern is the unconcealing of the truth of being (DVI 239). For Hegel and for Husserl, the other is assimilated to the same, to the identity of identity and difference. Hegel, Husserl, and Heidegger are all three philosophers of possibilities and powers. They are philosophers whose logics of canceling-uplifting-preserving (*Aufhebung*), memorial interiorizing (*Erinnerung*), and hermeneutic recycling recollect Plato's recollection but forget the *epekeina tês ousias,* which for Levinas is the singular plural *Autrui* rather than the neutral Good of the *Republic.* They forget that ontology presupposes metaphysics (TeI 18, TaI 48).

PARADOXICAL PROXIMITY

In his essay "Violence and Metaphysics," Derrida asks whether Levinas forgets the ontological difference. He makes the suggestion that Heidegger's notion of letting be may amount to an acknowledgment of the radical alterity which Levinas assigns to the ethical and metaphysical, and that this acknowledgment is perhaps implicit also in Husserl's conception of phenomenology.

In *Speech and Phenomena,* Derrida plots the interplay between two themes of Husserl's phenomenology. On the one hand is the principle of all principles which demands that knowledge of any principle be based on "a primordial dator act" which is an intuition of essence analogous to perception."[9] This theme would lead us to expect an adequation of the act and its object. It is this theme that Levinas has in mind when he says that the model with which Husserl's phenomenological ontology works is that of satisfaction, hence of need rather than of desire in Levinas's sense.

On the other hand Husserl develops the theme that apodicticity of evidence is possible without its being adequate. Derrida cites Husserl's allusions to the countless profiles of physical objects that are not presented to the person looking at the object but are appresented with those that are presented. More specifically, there are the retentions and protentions involved in my perception of the object, the immediate echo and pre-echo that perception entails. The consciousness directed to my past and to my future is an analogue, Husserl says, of my consciousness of other selves. Which of these, if either, is prior to the other is a question on which Husserl seems to have had different views at different times. In the *Cartesian Meditations*, he takes the view that the consciousness of my past self is presupposed by my consciousness of other selves. He also takes the view there that the latter presupposes consciousness of physical things, in particular the other's body. But he insists that my consciousness of the other is different in principle from my consciousness of physical things in that whereas I cannot have presentations of all of the profiles of the physical thing (although those that I do have will be presentations of profiles that the other person has or could have), I can have no presentations of his presentations. Is not this, Derrida asks, recognition of the infinite transcendence of the other, recognition of his positive infinitude, as against the negative infinitude of my inability to experience the totality of profiles of the physical thing? And is not this recognition of the infinite transcendence of the other possible only if, like Husserl, we conceive the other on analogy with the ego? If we do not, are we not conceiving the other on analogy with a stone? Does not the radical alterity of the other depend on his being another ego? And does not this otherness depend on his sameness, this dissymmetry on this symmetry? The dependence of his otherness on his being another ego does not make the other's ego a dependency of mine. It does not make him part of my real economy, because Husserl is describing a transcendental, not a real, economy.

Derrida is here saying about Levinas what has to be said about those who hold that Husserl embraces metaphysical idealism and those who say that he embraces metaphysical realism. What he calls transcendental phenomenological idealism is neutral in the debate between these alternatives. The transcendental phenomenological reduction aims to suspend matters of empirical and metaphysical factuality. That is why it would be naive to equate Husserl's appeal to analogical appresentation with the argument from analogy to the existence of other minds. This would be a naivety comparable with that of supposing that there could be in phenomenology an ontological or causal proof of the existence of God. This would be the naivety of the natural attitude in favor of the world and its Creator which the successful reduction suspends.

Of course, Levinas is no more intent than Husserl on producing ratiocinative proofs of the existence of other minds or of God. We have seen however that this talk about others is at the same time talk about God. It draws less on Descartes's fifth Meditation than on the third, but it abstracts from the causal terminology of the latter and from the theologicality of both. It abstracts from causality because a cause and an effect are terms within a system. Their causal relation is their way of being together. But the proximity of the face to face is a "relation" of speaking (*langage*). This is why it can be neither theological nor analogical, hence not a topic of a theology of *analogia entis* or a *theologia negativa*. It is not logical. It is paralogical and paradoxical. That is to say, this strange speech act is beyond the possibility, ascribed by Husserl to all theoretical and non-theoretical acts, of being made the topic of doxic positing.[10] It cannot be named or nominalized. It cannot be said. It would seem then that it cannot be the topic of a phenomenology of the Husserlian kind, despite the indebtedness Levinas acknowledges to Husserl. This is the source of one of the difficulties Derrida warns us we shall find facing Levinas, difficulties of which Levinas himself warns us, for example in his title *Difficult Freedom*.

What sort of discourse can this be which is somehow beyond the scope of logic, exterior to what Derrida calls the logical and phenomenological *clôture*? How can there be any saying where what is said is not said within the framework of a language as systematic as that of cause and effect? And would not the description of the structure of that language be a science or a *logos* of the appearing of meaning: a semiology, to employ Saussure's word, a phenomenology, to employ Husserl's, a phenomenological semiology or semiotics? Although part of the subject matter of phenomenology is the essence of facthood or facticity, empirical and any other factuality is excluded by reduction. Yet Levinas, Derrida suggests, seems to want to combine phenomenology with empiricism. A comparison with Descartes is again relevant. The idea of infinity for Descartes is not adventitious. It is not based on a sensible impression. Nor is it something I make; it is not a fiction, not inventitious. It is innate. But the innateness Descartes attributes to this idea goes along with a sort of adventitiousness in that it comes to me from my Maker—and insofar as Descartes and Malebranche allow that the idea is made by Him, it is to that degree also a fiction. Levinas's account of my idea of the other draws upon Descartes's account of his idea of the infinite. Hence it is not surprising that on Levinas's account the idea of the other is also a hybrid, an unstable amalgam of the phenomenological and the empirical. It is somewhat as though Aristotle, having told us that there is no science of the singular, nevertheless proceeded to present one. Somewhat as though only, because according to Levinas, "the neighbour concerns me with his exclusive singularity without appearing, not even as a *tode ti*. His extreme singularity is precisely his assignation: he assigns me before I designate him as *tode ti*" (AE 109, OB 86). Levinas himself often says that by the standards of formal logic the instability and difficulty of his account would amount to contradiction.

As when "the Lord spake unto Moses face to face" (Exod. 33: 11), and as when the Lord called Samuel and the latter replied, "Speak, Master, for thy servant heareth," so does the Other command *me,* and I am ethically and religiously bound to answer, "Here am I," "Lo, here am I," "*me voici,*" "*hineni*" (Exod. 3: 4, 1 Sam. 3: 4, 6, 8; cf. Gen. 22: 1,7, 11). I am beholden. I am the

One, as Levinas puts it, using the language of the first hypothesis of the *Parmenides*. I am (On) It, as children say when playing hide-and-seek. I am uniquely responsible (AE 124,126, OB 159,161). Levinas thinks that this empirical—or, as he would prefer to say, ethical—lopsidedness is in conflict with the symmetry Husserl ascribes to the relationship of the ego and the alter ego in the *Cartesian Meditations*. We have seen that Derrida questions whether there is a conflict here. Is not the so-called empirical dissymmetry possible only because of the transcendental symmetry? Levinas seems to forget that the ego described in the *Cartesian Meditations* is the transcendental ego, the ego in general. But *qua* philosopher Levinas wants to say something about the essence of the face to face. Perhaps there is little that can be said about this, and what one succeeds in saying appears to leave out what is important. What is important in the discourse of the face to face either does not enter or slips through the net of the said, the *dit*. What is important is the *Dire*, the infinite calling, which is never said. Whatever is said about it calls to be unsaid or, better, dis-said, *dédit*. What is significant in the discourse of the face to face is not what is semantically signified. It is not the meaning or the referent of a sign. Nor is it a sign. It is not and never was present and cannot be represented. To call it a trace is to give it not a name but a pro-name.

Maybe a trace of this pronominal trace can be picked up in the signature, and in the call sign a signaler transmits before his message begins. The call sign and the prefatory "I say" that beckons the person with whom one wants to speak are no more part of the message than is the autograph with which the author signs himself off. Even so, call signs and signatures can be faked, and no single one of them is indubitably authentic. The same applies to them as applies to any pronoun.

> The absolutely other [*Autre*] *is* the Other [*Autrui*]. He and I do not form a number. The collectivity in which I say "you" or "we" is not a plural of the "I." I, you—these are not individuals of a common concept. . . . Alterity is possible only starting from *me*. (TeI 9–10, TaI 39–40. Cf. AE 202, OB 159)

That the most idiosyncratic of token reflexives is essentially imitable is something that has been maintained by philosophers as different as Hegel and Russell. Although "I" and "this" and "you" and "that" are not common names, they are universal in their use. This is what Derrida demonstrates in his meditation on the various moments in *Otherwise than Being or Beyond Essence* when Levinas refers to what he is doing in that book "at this very moment."[11]

THE BACK OF BEYOND

In his very philosophizing about what is beyond being, the author is responding to an ethical call in the face to face with his reader. His reader is therefore, ethically speaking, at that moment his *magister*, his teacher and master. One reader, Derrida, comments on the difficulty of philosophizing about what is otherwise than being and beyond essence. Levinas himself comments on this difficulty. Is it a difficulty that amounts to paradox or incoherence? There is nothing paradoxical or incoherent in the idea of philosophical discourse about, say, incoherence or the illogical. The meta-language may be perfectly coherent and logical. However, Levinas's pre-dicament is different. His philosophical discourse purports to be about all discourse. So there is a self-referentiality that Levinas compares with that of the arguments for skepticism regarding reason. These arguments depend on that very reason regarding which it is skeptical. Levinas's predicament is comparable too with Heidegger's embarrassment at having to assert propo-sitions in order to distinguish the assertoric propounding of thoughts from monstrative saying. Heidegger needs to make this distinction in order to bring into the open the difference between the beingness of beings and the truth of being, in order, that is, to reveal that traditional metaphysics conceals the ontological difference. He sees that this difference is con-cealed again by its name and by his stating that his aim is to return metaphys-ics to fundamental ontology. Levinas states that his aim is to return so-called fundamental ontology to ethical metaphysics. It is to penetrate beyond the *logos,* beyond the propositional comprehension of metaphysical ontology, beyond the hermeneutic understanding of Heidegger's fundamental ontol-ogy, beyond maieutics, and beyond the coherent discourse of reason to the emphatic rationality of the teaching that makes possible the rationality of the said (TeI 178, TaI 203). Nonetheless, in seeking to achieve this aim

> one must refer—I am convinced—to the medium of all comprehension and of all understanding in which all truth is reflected—precisely to Greek civilization, and to what it produced: to the *logos,* to the coherent discourse of reason. . . . One could not possibly . . . arrest philosophical discourse without philosophizing. (DL 230, DF 176)

Levinas's discourse illustrates this. Whereas Heidegger, without denying that being is always being of a being, believes there is need to remind ourselves of the priority of being, Levinas aims to show "The philosophical priority of the existent (*étant*) over being" (TeI 22, TaI 51). That surely means that Levinas's discourse is ontic, discourse about beings. It has at least that in common with traditional metaphysical discourse on the being of beings and, despite their declared intentions, with the essentialist ontology of Husserl and the existentialist ontology of Sartre.

However, Levinas's metaphysics is ethical. The ethical would be a mode or region of the ontic as Heidegger uses this term, other modes being the psychological, the biological, and so on. But the ethical in Levinas's sense is not even remotely comparable with any natural or human science. And it is "more original" than fundamental ontology. Yet because the ethical "dimen-sion" in which man ceases to be the measure of all things is a dimension of a being, albeit a dimension in which that being transcends himself, one cannot help thinking of this as an ontological mode, as, using a phrase to which Levinas often has recourse, a way of being (*manière d'être*), as, using Heidegger's word, a *Seinsweise*. Hence, notwithstanding Levinas's declared intention to convince his reader that "to exist has meaning in another dimension than that of the perduration of the totality; it can go beyond being" (TeI 278, TaI 301), he says "Being is exteriority" (TeI 266, TaI 290). That is, not only does Levinas, as Derrida observes, appear to confirm Heidegger's assertion that one tends to forget the ontological difference, it appears to confirm Heidegger's assertion that language is the house of being. Levinas does not wait for Derrida to tell him that the discourse of the face to face is inscribed within what they both call, following Bataille, the "general economy" of being.

Of the many other examples of statements one could cite that, like "Being is exteriority," show that Levinas assumes a fore-understanding of being, here is but one:

> A relation whose terms do not form a totality can hence be produced within the general economy of being only as proceeding from the I to the other, as a *face to face*, as delineating a distance in depth—that of conversation (*discours*), of goodness, of Desire—irreducible to the distance the synthetic activity of the understanding establishes between the diverse terms, other with respect to one another, that lend themselves to its synoptic operation. (TeI 95, TaI 39)[12]

This is not a Levinasian version of the question whether "ought" can be derived from "is." It is a denial that the *being* of alterity can be comprehended. So it is a further contribution toward the destruction of the epistemological and perceptual tradition of metaphysics to which those Greek-speaking philosophers, Parmenides, Plato, Aristotle, Descartes, Kant, Hegel, and Husserl, all belong, according to Martin Heidegger. What the philosopher Emmanuel Levinas says seems unable to make the step beyond being and beyond Heidegger announced in the title of the book *Otherwise than Being or Beyond Essence* and previously in a title of a section near the end of *Totality and Infinity*. If the words just cited from the first section of *Totality and Infinity* can be taken at their face value, how can these titles be taken at theirs? If, as his essay "Is Ontology Fundamental?" makes clear, Levinas is unhappy with the ontology of *Being and Time*, how can this enable him to get outside the thinking of being to which Heidegger himself moved when he became dissatisfied with his earlier stress on fundamentality and put more stress on the thinking of *Ab-grund* and anarchy? True, Levinas stresses a different, ethical, kind of anarchy. But how does this anarchy escape being an anarchy in being rather than exterior to it, *epekeina tês ousias,* and how does this exteriority escape being an exteriority interior to being? Levinas's response to these questions lies in his statement that

> the relation of the face to face is not only dreamed of by philosophers because, forgetful of Being, they have cut off "objective thought" from its

deep roots. This relation is accomplished in the welcome of the Other, where, absolutely present, in his face, the Other—without any metaphor— faces me. (EDE 186)

This response leads Derrida to ask whether it is not the indulgence of the "etymological empiricism" that he calls, with studied irony, the hidden root of all empiricism (ED 204, WD 139). Exteriority, space, respiration, inspiration: these are all well-worn metaphors for being. Levinas uses them as metaphors for alterity. He uses them also, we have seen, as metaphors for and of being. And they are ontic metaphors which are liable to prevent philosophers from remembering the ontological difference, including, Derrida suspects, the philosopher who would have us remember the naked face of the Other.

> If to understand Being is to be able to let be (that is, to respect Being in essence and existence, and to be responsible for one's respect), then the understanding of Being always concerns alterity, and par excellence the alterity of the Other in all its originality: one can have to let be only that which one is not. (ED 207, WD 141)

Levinas would reply that respect for radical alterity is accorded only when it is acknowledged that I am ethically responsible to the Other. But could it not be said that this acknowledgment is implicit in Heidegger's inclusion of conscience in his table of existentials? Implicit, because although the voice of conscience in *Being and Time* is the call to responsibility for being, that responsibility is nothing outside the responsibility for existents. Indeed, Derrida remarks, it is precisely because being is nothing outside the existent that being cannot be articulated in language without the resource of ontic metaphor (ED 203, WD 138).

What do we find when we turn from the remarks Derrida makes about Levinas in "Violence and Metaphysics" to the remarks Levinas makes about Derrida in "Tout autrement"? There Levinas writes:

> What stays constructed after de-construction is surely the severe architecture of the discourse which deconstructs and which employs in predicative propositions the present tense of the verb "to be." Discourse in the course of which, at the very moment when it is shaking the foundations of truth, in face of the evidence of a lived present which appears to offer a last refuge to presence, Derrida still has the strength to say "Is that certain?," as if anything could be secure at that moment, and as if security and insecurity should still matter.
>
> It would be tempting to appeal to this use of logocentric language against that very language as an objection to the resulting de-construction. An approach often made in the refutation of skepticism which, nevertheless, having been knocked down and trampled underfoot, gets up again to become once more the legitimate child of philosophy. An approach which perhaps Derrida himself has not always disdained to follow in his polemics.
>
> But in following this approach there is a risk of failing to recognize the signification effected by the very inconsistency of this procedure, of failing

14

to recognize the incompressible non-simultaneity of the Said and the Saying, the dislocation of their correlation: a minimal dislocation, but wide enough for the words of the skeptic to pass through without being strangled by the contradiction between what is signified by what is *said* in them and what is signified by the very fact of uttering something *said*. As if the two significations lacked the simultaneity needed for contradiction to be able to break the knot in which they are tied. As if the correlation of the *Saying* and the *Said* were a dia-chrony of what cannot be united; as if the situation of the *Saying* were already a "memory of retention" for the *Said,* but without the *lapsed* moments of Saying allowing themselves to be retrieved in this memory. (NP 85–86, PN 58–59)

Otherwise said: Derrida has a keen ear for the diachrony of the said. He locates that diachrony in the dead time of writing with which the living present of the spoken word is engraved. But beyond this diachrony and/or supplementary to it is a radical diachrony that Derrida runs the risk of failing to recognize: a diachrony that is due to the paradoxical tie between the said and the fact of someone's saying something. The paradoxicality is the recalcitrance of the uttering to formulation as a proposition that is said. It is because the saying and the said are in this way "refractory to the category" that it and the said are *inassemblable*—even if the factuality referred to in Levinas's very words "the very fact of uttering something *said*" suggests assemblability! The saying and the said are so incomparable that they resist every attempt to bring them together. They resist even the limit case of togetherness of logical contradiction. Statements that contradict each other logically are *mutually* contradictory. They are contradictory only because they are posited together in the same time. The contradiction can sometimes be resolved by asserting them at different times. But the saying and the said are neither at the same time nor at different times. They are in different times. So the saying cannot be retrieved in the said. And this says something about beyondness and the retrieval of hermeneutic circularity.

The hermeneutic circle is, we are told, the ontological condition of understanding. More precisely, it is the priority of the existential over the apophantic, the recalcitrance of the existential to the category. Assuming that saying is existential and the said categorial, Heidegger, Gadamer, and Levinas will be in agreement that the categorial cannot retrieve the existential without a residual existential trace, and they will be in agreement with Merleau-Ponty's judgment that the lesson that the reduction teaches us is the impossibility of a complete reduction.[13] But the Heideggerian existentials are ontological conditions of understanding, whereas saying, Levinas wants to say, is somehow beyond ontology and beyond understanding. Further, the Heideggerian existentials are constitutive of temporality, and although this is not to be confused with the time of the categorized objects and states of affairs about which we assert propositions, the latter is in the former, which is somehow prior. Admittedly, there remains the difficulty of giving an account of this inclusive priority, the difficulty with which Heidegger is occupied in his extrapolation of Kant's doctrine of schematism. This difficulty has not been resolved. It is not resolved by Heidegger, nor has it been resolved in the deconstruction of Heidegger's doctrines undertaken by Derrida and Levinas. Indicative of this difficulty is Levinas's need to have it both ways: to affirm the radical alterity of the time of the other's saying while granting that irretrievable moments of saying are nonetheless, as it were, immemorial memories retained in the same memory with the said. Metaphorically speaking, so to speak.

The difficulty is the difficulty with metaphor. If, as Derrida says, all metaphors are ontic, they will present a difficulty for anyone, like Heidegger, who is trying to get beyond ontic metaphysics to fundamental ontology, and for anyone, like Levinas, who is trying to get beyond ontology to ethical metaphysics. "The extraordinary word *beyond*" transmits an ontic metaphor (AE 16, OB 19). No wonder Levinas rings the changes on *au-delà,* "on the thither side," and *en-deçà,* "on the hither side." Totality *is* Infinity if we erase this verb "to be" or raise it, not by *Aufhebung,* but by *emphasis.* When Derrida and Levinas have begun deconstructing the ontic metaphors of priority and transgression we can expect to have difficulty deciding what or who is prior to what or whom. The apparently secure notion of logical priority will begin to quake, and we may consequently fail to find our feet with Levinas when he says, "The neighbour concerns me outside every *a priori*—but perhaps *prior to every a priori*" (AE 109 n20, OB 192 n20). When faced with the question whether ontology is beyond metaphysics or metaphysics is beyond being, we may be at a loss for words.

1

RESPONSIBILITY WITH INDECIDABILITY

> There is even a more radical responsibility
> before questions, on the subject of ethics for
> example, that are not intrinsically ethical.
>
> —JACQUES DERRIDA (A 70)

The topics—or utopics—of responsibility and undecidability have been prominent in Derrida's writings from the beginning. Perhaps it is because the second of them is treated more explicitly than the other in his earlier publications, for instance in his introduction to Husserl's "The Origin of Geometry," that in his more recent ones express attention is given increasingly to the first, though Husserl's obsession by "radical responsibility" is also already treated at some length in the introduction (HO 38, HO tr. 52). Derrida is no less aware than some of his critical readers are that undecidability is *prima facie* incompatible with responsibility. The one seems to exclude the other. How can one respond responsibly to a question unless there is a criterion, rule, or law by reference to which the validity of the answer can be judged? Surely, one cannot. How can a response to a command be responsible and taken seriously unless it is guided by a determinate criterion, principle, or law? Surely, it cannot, unless it is in this sense critical, as defined by *krinein*, to divide and decide.

USE AND MENTION

Despite what some of his readers have too quickly concluded, Derrida is not (in principle?) against principle, against (the) law:

> I see well the risk there is, I wouldn't say in going beyond law, which I believe to be impossible . . . , but in subordinating law. What I am saying here is not said against law in the ethical sense of the term. (A 72)

Nonetheless, wherever we find him using or mentioning principles we also find him busy demonstrating that what is allegedly a first principle is never really first. This is the revised version of Husserl's "principle of all principles." This is the law of all law.

"Necessarily," "law," "never," "all"? By what right, it must be asked, does Derrida use these expressions? Is he not entitled to use them only if they are used in inverted commas—mentioned, not used, or, if used, used with a trepidation to mark which inverted commas, "scare quotes," should also be used? At the very least, should he not admit that inverted commas are there

17

invisibly? But, will be his response, where is "there"? Alongside a token of the word? That cannot suffice. Because Derrida's general practice is being called into question, because what is being challenged is what he is meaning to say when he lays down the law about the law of the law, our concern must be with the word as type. Only thus can what is being challenged be what he says or what he means to say. His words and what he says with them cannot be unrepeatable. So the "there" is wherever he or anyone else says what he means to say, in the space of statements, propositions, or thoughts.

What Derrida means to say is that although someone can mean what he says and say what he means, and although we can understand him when he does so, his doing so and our understanding him are possible only by the grace of the repeatability of marks or sounds in circumstances which we cannot predict. Such successful communication occurs, as it does more often than not, because we have acquired a mastery of words. However, that mastery is for any given speaker or community of speakers counterpoised against and sometimes unbalanced by a mastery that words have over us. The most familiar experience of this shortfall in our power over words is the so-called unintended pun, the pun we discover we have made after we have uttered it. Derrida, following Freud, wonders whether such puns are as unintended as they seem. He also observes that the punster is someone who turns the lucky find into an opportunity to enjoy and enjoy showing off a particular linguistic gift. Hence, if that is what it is to pun, there are no puns in *Glas*. *If* that is what it is to "make" a pun, there are no puns in *Glas* since *Glas* is an analysis of the formation and deformation rules of puns and other suchlike displays of verbal wit. Note the conditionality of this statement made by Derrida in his "Proverb" in *Glassary*.[1] It is designed to open the question of the relationship of the making of a statement to the making of a pun, or, more precisely—since one can be making a statement in making a pun and vice versa—it is designed to test that assumption that the pun is sheer free play with no other motivating force than the pleasure of exhibiting one's verbal address or *Geschicklichkeit,* as we may provisionally say.

However, even after all of Freud's labors to demonstrate that the mechanisms of what we call abnormal behavior are operative in what we call normal everyday life, it still has to be asked how an analysis of puns and other tricks with words can tell us something general about language, its use, and its users. If playing with words is ploying with words we can see through the joke once we have tracked the deception to its source. Take the one about the painter of pub signs who made a mess of a job by putting commas between Fox and and and and and Goose. To turn this apparent gibberish into good sense all we need do is insert some inverted commas. The addition of inverted commas also straightens out the sense of the piece of advice we are being given when we are told "Wenn Sie brauchen gebrauchen, müssen Sie brauchen mit zu gebrauchen, sonst brauchen Sie brauchen überhaupt nicht zu gebrauchen." As Hegel asks the defender of sense-certainty, we just need to ask our adviser to write it down, employing the conventional signs to distinguish the mention of an expression from its use or at least to indicate this distinction by varying the tone of his voice or by raising his fingers as is sometimes done when a speaker wants his audience to remark the quotation marks he has in his script. These examples are made up. How can our views of natural language functioning as it does in ordinary everyday life be upset by a setup? Or by a send-up, a carrécature, of the Le Carré style of spy story like Tom Stoppard's where "In the beginning the idea was that if they thought Purvis was their man, they would assume that the information we gave Purvis to give them would be the information designed to mislead, so they would take that into account and thus, if we told Purvis to tell them we were going to do something, they would draw the conclusion that we were not going to do it, but as we were on to that, we naturally were giving Purvis genuine information to give them, knowing they would be drawing the wrong conclusions from it . . . "?[2] Can these double takes and double binds be resolved? One might think that, precisely because the examples we have given are fictions, nothing could be easier. All we have to do is ask the author or work out from the *dénouement* of his story what the characters in it decided as a matter of empirical or literary fact. But this does not show that the author or his story can provide us with a decision procedure by which undecidability can be avoided. It shows only that decisions can be made that leave an undecidability in its unlocatable place. Decisions can be made by tossing coins, but not all the coins in the vaults of the Royal Mint will resolve a double bind.

TYPES AND PERFORMANCES

Other ways of deciding some classes of apparent undecidability have been proposed. One such proposal is Russell's theory of types—a "theory," it should be noted in passing, which is no less a prescription for practice. Now many of Derrida's examples of undecidables appear to be of the sort for which Russell's theory would offer the most appropriate solution. Like the semantic paradoxes generated by "This sentence is false" and "'Heterological' is heterological," they involve self-reference and the dyad mention-use. To avoid the paradoxes to which sentences like these give rise all it seems necessary to do is decide to prohibit self-reference by ordering classes and propositional functions hierarchically according to the arguments they can take and by asserting that no propositional function can meaningfully take itself as argument. Hence both the statement that a class is a member of itself and the statement that a class is not a member of itself will be neither true nor false, but meaningless. However, as F. P. Ramsey observes, although the theory of types thus formulated may serve to protect a logical or mathematical system from the paradox of the class of all classes which are not members of themselves, this is so only because in the absence of such protection the contradiction would occur inside the system and so would show that there is something wrong with it.[3] On the other hand, of the paradoxes which are not as he sees them internal to a mathematical or logical system since they invoke the empirical notions of language or symbolism or thought, we are not at liberty to say that they can be prevented by noting that a propositional function cannot significantly take itself as argument; for the paradox may arise because there is something wrong with our beliefs about these empirical notions.

Ramsey is perhaps too sanguine in his belief that a mathematical and formal system can be protected in this way. Does the idea of such a system make sense in isolation from the non-formal language in terms of which it is set up and understood? If not, it may be vulnerable to the paradoxes that crop up in that non-formal language, the so-called semantic paradoxes. Whichever of the two kinds of paradoxes we have in mind, the theory of types, at least in the informal formulation Ramsey gives it, succumbs to semantic paradoxicality. For if the assertion of the theory of types itself refers to all assertions, it refers to itself. If a qualifying clause is embedded in it purporting to exclude itself from the range of its reference, it refers to itself in excluding itself from its range of reference; it includes itself in excluding itself.

Ramsey is not sanguine enough, however, in his belief that non-formal discourse cannot be protected from paradoxes simply by pointing out that a proposition or propositional function cannot significantly take itself as argument. We can agree with this denial and go on to assert positively that propositions outside formal logical and mathematical systems can refer to themselves while retaining significance, and this significance is not restricted merely to the meanings of the words in the sentence or sentences in which they are affirmed. An example of this maybe is the quotation from Francis Ponge analyzed by Derrida in "Invention de l'autre":

> Par le mot *par* commence donc ce texte
> Dont la première ligne dit la vérité,
> Mais ce tain sous l'une et l'autre
> Peut-il être toléré?

> With the word *with* then begins this text
> Of which the first line tells the truth,
> But this foil beneath the one and the other
> Can it be tolerated?

This is a text that refers to itself. Since "text" is what Ramsey calls a semantic term, any paradox to which this self-reference may give rise will not be a paradox of the kind peculiar to a mathematical or logical calculus. That this is so is confirmed by Derrida's statement in the introduction to *Parages* that the undecidables analyzed in the pieces collected under that title and elsewhere are not of the kind that may be anticipated in a calculus (Par 15). This statement taken in isolation echoes Ramsey's optimism over our ability to separate mathematical and logical systems off from non-formal discourse and any paradoxes that may arise there. Such optimism about this separability assumes a greater degree of optimism than we are perhaps entitled to about our ability to distinguish the analytic from the synthetic. However, earlier in his introduction to *Parages*, Derrida has agreed that there is at least an indirect and analogical relation between the paradoxes of set theory and the paradoxes of which he treats (Par 12); and that he is alert to the problems posed by forms of optimism analogous to Ramsey's is already made plain by his comments in his introduction to *The Origin of Geometry* on Husserl's handling of the distinction between what is intra-mathematical and what is not (HO 38ff., HO tr. 52ff.).

Are the paradoxes of which Derrida treats to be included in the set which Ramsey calls semantic? Is the par-adox Derrida cites from Ponge and re-cited above, if we may take that as an example? That at least an analogical relationship between them can be expected is suggested by the fact already mentioned that Ponge's and Derrida's text makes use of the semantic notion of text. This expectation is strengthened by the further fact that this text talks about truth. Semantic paradoxicality is an undecidability as to which, if either, of the values True and False, Yes and No, should be ascribed to a given statement. But it is of particular interest in the Ponge case that instead of an undecidability as to the truth-value of a given statement there is an undecidability as to what act is being performed in making the statement in question. The second line claims that what the first line says, namely that this text begins with the word "with," is true. What makes it true, however, is not some independent state of affairs constated by this statement. What makes the statement true is the making of the statement itself. Rather as of "I am making a statement" or *cogito ergo sum* we may ask whether it is constative or performative and find it not at all easy to decide, so with "With the word *with* then begins this text," Derrida says that it is both performative and constative. It is performative in the sense that it produces, institutes, or invents the state of affairs, namely a text's beginning with the word "with." On the other hand, this practical producing is performed at one and the same stroke or in one and the same breath as the theoretical constatement. Ponge's lines, constructed in strict conformity with the conventions of grammar and syntax, deconstruct two contrasts made by some proponents of the theory of speech acts, the contrast between constative and performative speech acts and the contrast between use and mention. We cannot decide whether Ponge's text is performative as opposed to constative, and this is because we cannot decide for every word in it whether it is mentioned or used. Our endeavors to decide this are foiled by the tin or silver retina backing of the looking glass in which the first "with" in the sentence looked at as performatively producing a state of affairs is reflected in the same sentence looked at as constating that state of affairs, and thus becomes second because there will be no sentence or text produced in which it can be truly reported that it begins with the word "with" until this report is made.

21

The point here is not that constative statements are *made* and are for that reason performative. Whatever may be the case with other proponents of the theory of so-called speech acts, the deeds done with words that primarily interest John Austin are not necessarily acts of speech or writing as such in the way that any employment of words is the performance of an act, a locutionary act, whether this be merely the utterance of phonemes (a "phonetic" act), the utterance of phonemes belonging to and as belonging to a vocabulary, according to grammatical conventions, with a certain tone of voice, etc. (a "phatic" act), or also the performance of a phatic act in which the constituents are given sense and reference (a "rhetic" act). He introduces the word "performative" because although the word "operative" as used by lawyers covers what he has in mind, they use it in other senses as well. A performative utterance as understood at least in Austin's consideration of the subject early on in *How to Do Things with Words* is one that is "operative" in the sense appropriate to that part of a legal instrument which, unlike its preamble, effects a transaction, brings about a conveyance or a bequest or, more ceremonially, a marriage, a baptism, or the opening of a new town hall, by using certain forms of words in certain appropriate circumstances. This is part, but only part, of the explanation for Derrida's fondness for the word *effet,* as in the title of the series in which some of his own writings appear, *La philosophie en effet.* From those writings, for instance those collected in that series under the titles *Psyché: Inventions de l'autre* and *Parages,* it is plain that Derrida does not limit the label "performative" to utterances that are operative in the legal or quasi-legal sense for which Austin at first reserves the word. As with *effet* in the title of the series, "performative" gets used not just for a putative kind of utterance, but also for a style of philosophizing, a practice which calls for analytic labor, experiments on given texts that test their mettle in a fashion not utterly remote from what goes on in a laboratory where apparatus is set up and experiments are performed. Derrida does not agree with Heidegger that in doing science you cannot as such be doing any philosophical thinking, a view Derrida challenges on the grounds that it depends on notions of science and thinking that fail to recognize that the constitutive laws of both of these are derivatives of deconstitutive laws whose workings are displayed by the science of graphematics, which is a science of the impossible conditions of the possible. Among the findings that Derrida's performative philosophizing with a *hama* comes up with (see below) is that performative and constative utterances, as some speech-act theoreticians purport to define them, do not constitute two distinguishable classes. This is what Austin himself eventually comes to suspect, but his reasons for doing so are different from Derrida's reasons for questioning whether the distinction can be maintained.

Austin's *Kehre,* assuming that it is not just a pedagogical device, comes about after the failure of a dogged attempt to discover either a semantic or a simple or complex grammatical or verbal criterion that would mark off performative from constative utterances. The semantic test would demarcate the performative from the constative on the grounds that utterances of the latter but not of the former kind are true or false. This test does not work, he says, because on the one hand questions of fact have to be answered before we can be in a position to appraise the fairness, validity etc. of advice, warnings, arguments, and other utterances we would not be inclined to call constative. This is a bad argument because there being questions of truth and falsity to be answered before we can properly appraise a piece of advice, warning, or an argument does not imply that the advice, warning, or argument can, without raising eyebrows, be called true or false—even if as a matter of fact, since advice (*avis*) can be information or an observation offered as counsel, there may be nothing odd in saying at least of a piece of advice that it is true or false. However, this last fact, if it is one, supports Austin's main point. And this is supported by the second part of his argument, a mirror image of the first, that the terms of appraisal we naturally use of utterances we would not be inclined to regard as constative, terms like "good," "bad," "valid," "fair," are terms we quite naturally use of utterances we would regard as typically constative or descriptive. "France is hexagonal" is a good, bad, or rough description, rather than true or false. (Still, "France is roughly hexagonal" is true, isn't it?)

Of the various grammatical or verbal hypotheses Austin puts through the hoops, the most promising to his mind is the proposal that a performative utterance either is or is expressible in the form "I x that . . . ," "I x to . . . ," or "I x," where x is a grammatically present indicative active verb, and where to make an utterance of one of these forms in certain circumstances (e.g., I own a watch when I say "I bequeath my watch . . . ," I am the Lady Mayoress or some such authorized personage when I say "I declare this building open") is thereby to x. Because "I state . . ." passes this test, Austin comes round to offering it not as a way of demarcating performatives from constatives, but as a way of making explicit the illocutionary force of an utterance, that is, the act that is performed in making it. We must therefore give up the idea of a dichotomy of performative and constative utterances each with sufficient or sufficient and necessary defining conditions. We must turn instead to the task of drawing up a genealogy of speech acts related only by family resemblances allowing one kind of speech act to overlap another. This overlap permits not only the same sentence to be employed on different occasions in what before his *Kehre* Austin distinguishes as performative and constative utterances.[4] It would seem to permit this on one and the same occasion. "'I class' or perhaps 'I hold' seems in a way one, in a way the other. Which is it, or is it both?"[5] "With the word *with* begins then this text." Which is it, or is it both? We can now see how different are the considerations leading Austin to admit that an utterance may be simultaneously constative and non-constative from those leading Derrida to affirm a simultaneity in his citation from Ponge. Austin's reasons have to do with the semantic property of open texture. Derrida's are such as to disrupt, as Einstein did, the very notion of simultaneity. The "open texture" of the

Ponge sentence, its sponginess, is such that the simultaneity, without being altogether abandoned, is holed by an altertaneity, by the different occasion marked by the "then" and tol(le)d by Ponge's *donc*, which is not only chronological and campanological, but at the same time a logical "therefore" related by more than a family resemblance to the *ergo* of Descartes and the *igitur* of Mallarmé and others. The combination of both illocutionary forces in one syllogism is more than the psyche can bear. The psyche—which is also a revolving cheval mirror such as might reflect the *Psyche* that in the verso running head of the collection of that name at the same time reflects the title of one of the essays it collects—is split. The "at the same time" (*hama*) of the flip between the performative or constative citation and the constative or performative recitation is not the "at the same time" of the classical formulation, criticized by Kant, of the principle of non-contradiction which permits that both *p* and not *p* may be true provided that they are asserted of different respects and different times—always assuming (an assumption Kant was perhaps unwilling to make) that given these differences "*p*" would not be equivocal. The strange logic of the relation between the two faces of the mirror exceeds classical logic. Its non-Euclidean space-time is the space-time of the eyelid of the momentary ironic wink (*Augenblick, clin d'œil*) which, in blacking out the light of day, thereby effects a syncope in which the "hereby" implicit in "*Par le mot* par *donc commence ce texte*" vanishes into the otherwhere and otherwhen of a dislocated, allo-temporally illocutive otherwise said.

THE PARADOX OF QUASI-ANALYSIS

There is something eccentric about the example of otherwise saying with which we have been occupied up until now. Surely (*ergo* unsurely, for, as Derrida remarks, "surely" is a sure sign that one is unsure) the undecidability it exemplifies is overdetermined in comparison with the examples of undecidability that suffice in some of Derrida's other writings to demonstrate the dividedness of the moment? To shake our confidence in the self-containedness of an act of speech is it not enough to have our attention drawn to the necessary possibility of the whole and any part of what we say being said again, by someone else or by ourselves? Nothing is said unless it can be resaid. Its identity as something said consists in the possibility of its being said on a different occasion by the speaker or writer or someone else, for instance the reader of a note he wrote, who may be the same person as the author. This is a necessary feature of language. But is it the feature that Derrida has uppermost in his mind? If it is, it is what has been uppermost in the minds of all those philosophers before him who have distinguished universals or concepts from particulars falling under them and linguistic tokens from types. One of the aims of Derrida's philosophical practice is to bring out how text after so-called philosophical or so-called non-philosophical text works against its own assumption that the repeatability implied in the notions of the universal, the concept, the type, the class, meaning and the notion is at least in principle delimitable, where by this is meant that a line can be drawn defining the logical or semantic space occupied by these notions, even if this definition may often have to be less strict than a specification of necessary and sufficient conditions. Derrida tries to show that delimitations have a tendency to become de-limitations. The question we are now asking is whether, in order to show this, he has to come up with paradoxes as mind-boggling as the one to which we have confined our attention so far, the one from Ponge. That paradox has us turning in a circle, it would seem, with no hope of breaking out, whereas for Derrida (*pace* Heidegger, *Being and Time* p. 153) what is decisive is to break out of the circle: *Das entscheidende ist . . . , aus dem Zirkel heraus- . . . zukommen*—or, more exactly, what is decisive is to realize that the circle is inscribed in an ellipse. This sense of claustrophobic aporia is not diminished by the words of "Limited Inc a b c . . . ," "There would thus be two speech acts in a single utterance. How is this possible?" (LI 75), the tone of which words might seem to suggest that the occurrence of two simultaneous speech acts in one utterance is impossible, notwithstanding the suggestion that this is possible that appears to be made in the words cited above from Austin. Of course, tones of voice and appearances, like duck-rabbits, depend on how we hear or see what surrounds them, for the surroundings are also internal to the figure of which they are the ground. So when we pan out from the words we have cited from Austin and Derrida, they may come to make on us the opposite impression to that which they made in close-up. Let us now take into account another aspect of the Ponge text.

The Ponge text is entitled "Fable." A fable, from *fari*, to speak, is a fabulation, a fabrication, a fiction, even a fib, a "story": the Ponge paradox could turn out to be a liar paradox of sorts. So Ponge's fable, one might say, bears to statements of fact a relation similar to that in which stand the formal logical and mathematical systems we touched on earlier. Hence anyone who was worried by the paradox Derrida elicits from that text can stop being so worried. He need not feel, like Frege did on learning of Russell's paradox, that the entire world is crumbling around him. There are more things on earth than literary fictions, so, it would seem, those other things, like well-behaved schoolchildren sitting up properly in the class where they belong, could be kept quite safe from the dizzying dilemmas contrived in literary artifacts. What would Derrida say about this sigh of relief?

The title of the Ponge piece, "Fable," is but one of the many devices indicating a literary genre. In "The Law of Genre" Derrida cites other ways in which this indication is made. "A Novel" or "A Play" on the cover or the title page serves the same purpose. So too does the line length or verse form in the case of a poem. The mark of a literary genre may be fairly complex, and especially in modern writing the genres may be more or less artfully mixed. After granting that this indicator of genre may not be explicitly before the mind of the author or the reader and may even be at variance with the genre as stated in or under the title or elsewhere, Derrida writes "If I am not mistaken in saying that such a trait is remarkable, that is, notice-able, in every aesthetic, poetic or literary corpus, then consider this paradox . . ." (Par 264, G7 185 and 212). If I am not mistaken, Derrida believes that he is not mistaken. A page earlier he says unreservedly: "this re-mark . . . is absolutely necessary for and constitutive of what we call art, poetry or literature." That is what interests him at this point. And all he says at this point about other kinds of text is that it is always possible for them to bear such a mark, whether they be oral texts, like a speech for the defense in a court of law, or written, like an editorial in a newspaper. Whereas the literary text is necessarily re-marked, other kinds of text are necessarily re-mark-*able*. Note therefore that there still seems to be a loophole through which we can evade the apparently paralyzing dilemma of "Par le mot *par*. . . ." Derrida seems to be interested so far only in a special theory of undecidability, one concerned with literary texts. "What interests me" at this stage, he stresses, is a paradox resulting from the fact that all literary texts carry a genre marker. Note secondly, therefore, that whatever this paradox may turn out to be, it too may be avoidable if Derrida is mistaken in his belief, asserted here without argument, that what for simplicity's sake we are calling literary texts must have such markers. Must he not prove this if we are to be bound to accept his paradox? Whether or not he must is something we shall find out in finding out what this paradox may be.

The paradox is that at the very same moment that the mark of the genre of a literary text marks off that genre it marks itself off from the genre. Russell proposed that the paradox of the class of all classes not belonging to them-selves should be avoided by a theory of types from which it follows that no class can belong to itself. Derrida's paradox of the genre-clause has to do not solely with class inclusion and class membership or participation, so the theory of types is of no avail to avoid it. The paradox of the genre-clause has to do with the distinctive feature marking the membership of a text in a genre, for example the explicit proclamation "A Novel," "Fable" or *Un récit,* as on the cover and elsewhere of Maurice Blanchot's *La folie du jour,* or the less explicit traits which amount to declarations in which the text mentions itself, such as "Hey presto, I am a poem." This prosopopoeic mention is not poetic.

To anticipate the objection (to which we shall return) that the titular or subtitular announcement of the genre of a text does not even begin to look like a part of the text itself, consider just the features, for instance the rhyming or rhythmic character of the lines or the tone of voice in which the lines are read, that vindicate the classification of the text as a poem but would usually be presumed to disqualify its classification as a piece of philosophic or scientific prose. These marks tell us "This is a poem" and so, like an operative clause in a legal instrument, constitute the text's member-ship in that particular genre. However, because remarks like "This is a poem" are not poetic, at one and the same time they exclude the text from its genre. The text both belongs and does not belong. The condition of its possibility is at the same time the condition of its impossibility.

But, it must be asked, is a mark or index of the genre of a text a part of the text itself? If it is not at least partly a part of it we shall be without a clue as to whether the text is to be taken as a literary product or as a piece of philosophical or scientific prose.

But, it must also be asked, what about "I am prose," which seems to be a bit of unpoetic prose? And what about "I am taxonomic" or "This (this taxonomic text) is taxonomic"? Do not these belong to the genre of text they mention and do not the texts they mention belong entirely to them-selves, without any disruptive residue? Not if we accept that these markers are makers, that is to say, are operatively constitutive in their function, as signaled (operatively?) by their allowing themselves to incorporate a "Hey presto," "voilà," or "hereby."

But now it must be asked whether such recognizably operative markers do not belong fairly and squarely, *carrément,* within the class of the text whose class they define in the case where the text is operative. In that case do not both the constituting marker and the text constituted by it belong to the class of operative texts without not belonging to it? What casts doubt on this is the fact that for our classificatory purposes the marker which makes or constitutes the text a text of its kind is required at the same time to make a statement constating that kind. Hence the text's kind is deconstituted. Let us name this predicament the paradox of quasi-analysis.

The paradox of quasi-analysis is distantly related to the paradox of analysis provoked by the philosophy of G. E. Moore. According to the paradox of analysis, an analysis of a statement is trivial if the sentence expressing the analyzing statement means the same as the sentence expressing the statement analyzed, and incorrect if it does not. The remoteness of the relationship of this paradox to the paradox of quasi-analysis is due to the fact that the latter excludes the possibility of a division down to self-contained logical elements and includes a pragmatic element, the illocutionary deed done in saying the words, which confers upon the paradox of quasi-analysis a kinship with another notion germane to the philosophy of G. E. Moore, the notion of pragmatic or, as Austin has since taught us to say, performative contradiction. If the paradox of quasi-analysis may be looked on as a hybrid of Moorish and Austinian lines of thought, it should not be overlooked that it also has a connection with the predicament that confronts, among others, Heidegger (and, though otherwise, Levinas): how to combine the prose of the lecture which talks about its topic with the poetry without which there would be no topic to be talked about and threatened. Where, if anywhere, do *poiêsis, praxis,* and *theôria* meet? That is one of the topics or utopias in plotting the geography of which Derrida discovers the paradox of quasi-analysis.

What are we to make of this paradox? Does not Derrida make too much of it? Would it not dissolve if he made less of the vagueness of the idea of telling, took this idea less literally? We can sex chickens by their distinctive features without those features literally telling us "I am a male," so is it not only in a manner of speaking, a *façon de parler,* that the verse form, meter, and rhymes tell us "I am a poem," even if we can allow that the title or subtitular gloss "Poem" may say this? Surely it is only the chicken sexers and the literary theorists who say something here, not the shape of the sexual organs or the length of the text's lines. The degree of relevance of this objection depends in part on whether it is legitimate to draw an analogy with non-literary classification according to gender in view of the fact that Derrida's analysis in "The Law of Genre" begins with, even if it is not ultimately confined to, the question of classification according to literary genre. The relevance of this objection decreases dramatically if, as idealists of one stripe or another and non-idealists like Heidegger have in their different ways held, we cannot make sense of the notion of something's constituting the membership of a class and the notion of something's being of this or that gender independently of the notion of beings who are users of and used by language through which and through whom constitution itself is constituted—and, Derrida would have us add, deconstituted. Assuming that Derrida, with this important supplement, shares this point of departure, as is implied for example by his remark "the things themselves are marked in advance by the possibility of fiction" (LI 100), it makes little difference whether we say prosopopoeically that the verse form or rhyme says unpoetically "I am a poem" or say prosaically, as in a lecture, that on the basis of the verse form or rhyme we say "This is a poem." In either case we are left with the problem of how to understand the relationship between what is taken to make something a member of a class and our making about it the statement that it belongs to that class. That is to say, we are left with the paradox of quasi-analysis.

What difference does the paradox of quasi-analysis make as regards our purposes here? The Ponge paradox seemed to be an especially special and eccentric case insofar as it looked as though its apparently sheerly aporetic and negative outcome had no stultifying implications for our thinking about what is beyond the range of such artfully devised examples. Now, however, we have been given reason to believe that we have to say good-bye to the possibility of classification across the entire field of literature, to give it up as lost, *en faire son deuil.* As far as literature is concerned, all genre suffers from a congenital degenerative disease. We are listening to the death knell of classification in this field, the *glas* of the class of its classes. Its field is a field of burial. The only firm ground left to stand on can be that of its complementary class, the class of non-literary texts of which Derrida states at one point of "The Law of Genre," it will be recalled, that it is not what at that point interests him.

What was it that at that point did not interest him? Whatever was to be opposed to the literary genre, e.g., the mode *récit,* which Gérard Genette considers to be a category not of literature but of the anthropology of verbal expression. Derrida unravels and reravels Blanchot's "*récit*" *La folie du jour* with a view to questioning whether we or Genette understand what we mean by a mode and, more generally, what we are doing when we distinguish literary texts and their genres from other texts. For any text is haunted as

28

much as any other by the possibility of its becoming literature. "The Bible as Literature," for example. It is not only such parts of the Bible as the Psalms and the Song of Solomon that are susceptible to being read as literature; so too are those parts that started off as factual genealogical records of the tribes of Israel, as factual in intent as, to give another example, the Anglo-Saxon Chronicle. Of course, what is at stake here is the very idea of example. If the class falls so does the case or example that falls under it. We now see why we had to be so cagey earlier on in our employment of this word "example," and why Derrida refers so frequently to what is an example "maybe," *peut-être*. *Peut-être* may be construed as Derrida's graft onto the *Seinkönnen* of *Being and Time*, the concept onto which, after writing that book, Heidegger himself grafts the concept *Vermögen*. The possibility denoted by Derrida's *peut-être* shares with Heidegger's *Seinkönnen* at least the negative characteristic of not being a potentiality whose actualization is the unfolding of a definable self-contained essence. But if it is not what expresses itself with the analytic necessity of a Leibnizian essence, neither is its realization the sheerly empirical contingency of a historical event that befalls something from outside. The possibility of this *peut-être* is the necessary contingency that the so-called normal, standard, or paradigm case, for example the statement of fact, may turn out to be abnormal, non-standard, parasitized, fictive, or fake, and vice versa. *Peut-être*, intrinsically, the insider has it in him to be an outsider and the outsider to get outside his disreputable, pocket-picking, un-self-contained self to be acknowledged as an honest citizen. Apropos: "Purvis was acting, in effect, as a genuine Russian spy in order to maintain his usefulness as a bogus Russian spy." "Apropos: in what sense did Nixon pretend to be Nixon, President of the United States up to a certain date? Who will ever know this, in all rigor? He himself?" (G2S 79, G2 251, LI 106)

Peut-être is one of the marks of the deconstructive genre, as too are "almost," "not quite," and "up to a certain point." It is the mark that commemorates and announces the deconstruction of deconstruction. So are we to put the flags at half-mast or hoist them to the top of the pole? We began by supposing that the cancer could be contained, because its victims seemed to be only eccentric fictions. Then we discovered that any fictions are vulnerable, any literature, if we agree with Derrida that every literary genre has a mark, however complex and unobvious it may be. Should we agree with this? I am inclined to think that we should, because not only is literature woman- or man-made, so too are literary theory, criticism, and rhetoric which see to it that its subject matter gets classified, however much overlap there may in some cases have to be. Anyway, it is enough that a putatively non-literary text be capable of becoming literary. That is also enough to diminish our confidence in the sharpness of the distinction between the literary and the non-literary, and so to dampen our hope of stopping the degenerative rot.

SURSUM CORDA

The degeneration of classification is also its regeneration. When in the Proverb of *Glassary* Derrida calls what is going on in *Glas* analysis we can see this as a name for the renaming and reclassification to which the law of law gives rise. Searle is right to say, as Derrida says, that a distinction must be made between citation in which quotation marks are used and whatever it is that Derrida means by the iteration which makes citation possible. But further distinctions must be made between such citation and citation in which the quotation marks are mentioned or quoted. And still further distinctions must be made among the varieties of mention and use, and their subvarieties or rather grafts. Thus do our ears get finer. The tain of the mirror is corroded by iterability, by the remarkability of the mark. However, the mirror can be retained so as to reflect with greater power of resolution, that power thanks to which things are called by their names, and called to be renamed interminably. Iterability is not an it or a namable being. Beyond the opposition of being and non-being, and beyond the ontological difference, iterability defeats the inclination of the *es* of *es gibt Sein* and the *ça* of the unconscious to become reified. A quasi-transcendental rather than a transcendental condition, iterability is a condition not simply of the possibility of class as effect but also of its impossibility as a logically self-contained entity. For according to the generalized law of genre, every class is necessarily outside itself, declassified by the very condition of its identity, deconstructed by its own structure.

Nevertheless, to reiterate, deconstruction is an affirmative force, transstructuration, *perestroika,* invention of the other, its own other included, as displayed in the history of its many pseudo-names: differance, supplement, *pharmakon, hymen,* restance, trace, archi-writing . . .

theography

(neither just title or subtitle nor text or subtext as opposed to title or subtitle).

Iterability is another name for what theology calls God (Ps 561). Not "the church's one foundation," and older than "the old old story" of hymnography, not quite the creative spirit or the maker of the new, iterability's entitlement to be compared with the incomparable and uncompèrable God of negative theology is considered in "Comment ne pas parler" (1986). This essay takes further the question raised in the Differance essay (1968) of the distance between graphematic alterity and the *totaliter aliter* of so-called negative onto-theology. It is also, in passing, a comment on the theory of placing, exemplification, and classing which Austin outlines in "How to Talk—some simple ways," though Derrida's essay (whose title could be translated perhaps as "How not to talk—some not-so-simple ways" or "How to undo things with or without (*'sans'*) Words") does not mention Austin's piece or its author. Austin is more than mentioned in "Signature Event

Context." Not every reader of this piece notices however that God gets more or less of a mention there. As "Limited Inc a b c" points out, the title of the penultimate section of "Sec" (What sort of a mention or use is this, and is it a different sort from *Sec?*) mentions or uses or abuses the title of Descartes's penultimate Meditation, before going on to a series of *Objections et réponses.* Descartes's title, "On the Essence of Material Things; and once more of God, that He Exists," *De essentiâ rerum materialum; et iterum de Deo, quod existat,* is parodied as "Parasites. Iter, Of Writing: That It Perhaps Does Not Exist," where the English translation of Derrida's parasitizing traduction of Descartes, *Les parasites. Iter, de l'écriture: qu'elle n'existe peut-être pas,* demolishes the pyramid of *essentiâ,* as the French already does, though the circumflex accent of its *être* re-erects the resting place which commemorates the loss of the disseminative letter *s* and the death of the metaphysical being of matter and its sustaining God. It also loses the suggestion that writing and the God inscribed in it are perhaps feminine. On the other hand, it gains the hint of a promise or a threat that it may remain to be discovered that our path leads nowhere in particular, *partout et nulle part,* to no decidable site, and that the It of iteration is not an identifiable item and *idem,* but paradoxically participates in the indefiniteness of the status of the definite article-cum-pronoun in what Derrida calls Jean-Luc Marion's "magnificent title" *Dieu sans l'être* (Ps 540).[6] Without being the God of "negative" theology, without being the being of the God of onto-theology, the theographematic heir and ancestor of God, far from being a *Dieu sans lettre,* is not just, as Bishop Berkeley and others say, the Author of the book of nature set for humanity to read, but is already Text inventing Him-Her-It-self and the other. God of the old old story becomes Archi-Secretarial scriptance of a still older story, becomes without quite being and without quite becoming either a being or a non-being.

Despite the magnificence of the title of this book, in his earlier publication *L'idole et la distance,* Marion does not allow sufficiently for the supplementary logic Derrida ascribes to the little (dis)connecting word *sans.* The "negativity without negativity" (Ps 575) of the withoutness intended in Derrida's Blanchotian employment of *sans* means that it is misleading to say, as Marion does, that the writing of differance "contests" the ontological difference or tries to "pass beyond" it,[7] hence commits itself dialectically to the ontological difference no less than does Levinas who, according to Marion's judgment, which Levinas contests, simply inverts the order of priority Heidegger gives to being over beings. This is in both cases to suppose that the first step is the only one each of them makes. It is to forget that in the case of both Levinas and Derrida the first step is first only pedagogically. It is not true here that the first step is the only step that counts, for when the second step has been taken it takes with it the firstness of the other. This is the nature of the negativity of the *pas.* The trace will have retraced the distance covered by the first step before it was ever made. Therefore, perhaps both Levinas and Derrida are asking the question that

Marion poses as follows: "Would distance overstep the ontological difference and Being that figures metaphysically in it, hence also their idol, not in
leaving it, but in remaining in it—as not remaining in it?"[8] This sounds very
like the question Levinas asks at least in *Totality and Infinity*. And it is not
difficult to hear this question being asked in a Derridian tone of voice so
long as allowance is made for the paradoxicality of the class inclusion
"exemplified" earlier in this chapter and quite felicitously captured, if that
is not too strong a word, in Marion's ruptured (self-de-constructing?) phrase
y demeurant—comme n'y demeurant pas.

Marion's second objection is that Derrida facilitates the passage to a
differance beyond onto-theology by drawing "an astonishing equivalence"
between onto-theology, "negative theology," and philosophy.[9] Marion aims
to show that so-called negative theology, in particular that of the (according
to some authorities pseudonymously named) Pseudo-Dionysus, can be rescued from this equation, thereby opening up room for a non-idolatrous
because non-ontological God. He believes that this room is left by what he
calls, with Kierkegaardian and Barthian overtones, Levinas's "vertical" alterity, the infinite alterity of *Autrui*. Can we not now say that this room is left
also by the "horizontal" alterity of differance, insofar as we are entitled to
rename it theographematics on the basis of the remark in "Comment ne pas
parler" that the talking or "parlance" (*langage*) has already begun without
us, in us, before us, that it is what theology calls God and that we are and will
have been obliged to speak (Ps 561)?

In view of what is up to a certain point a Heideggerian element in the
ancestry of this remark, one cannot avoid wondering whether Derrida
would be able to imagine a dialogue involving himself arising from it
analogous to the one that, in the last few pages of *De l'esprit*, he imagines
Heidegger having with persons whom we may call, remembering again the
above-mentioned historical objections and replies, diverse theologians.
What would Derrida say to these theologians? This question is particularly
relevant to the second of Marion's objections. A clue to what Derrida might
say is provided by his comment that what he sees as Heidegger's attempt to
save Trakl's conception of *Geist* from a Christian interpretation is prejudiced by an extremely narrow conception of Christianity (E 178, S 108–9).
Does Derrida think this undermines or reinforces the theologians' right to
say, as they do in his not entirely imaginary conversation, that Heidegger,
with the help of his poets, is putting into words what they, diverse Christian,
maybe Jewish, and even Muslim theologians, have been trying to say all
along? *De l'esprit* refuses to conclude. And its readers must make do with a
long-range forecast of how the breezes of *ruah, pneuma,* and *spiritus* eventually may blow. That forecast will have to recognize that Heidegger's later
thinking follows two paths. It has no "common root," or if it has it is one that
is two-fold. There are at least two Heidegger mark IIs . There is the one who
says that *Geist,* of which he finally brings himself to write without the inverted
commas that earlier protected him from it, is the "common root" of *spiritus,*

pneuma, and (on second thoughts) *ruah* from which these subsequently spring. This is the Heidegger of the origin. Then there is the Heidegger of what is heterogeneous to the origin, heterogeneous perhaps both because it is at the origin and although it is at the origin (E 177, S 108). Derrida says that in his outlining of these two paths he is highlighting "what, I imagine at least, can still tell us something about *our* steps, of a certain crossing of *our* paths. About an *us* who are maybe not *given*." Would the theologians who in the *Zwiesprache* with Heidegger welcome his word *Zuspruch* as another name for God be equally welcoming to Derrida's theographematics? This depends on their belief as to how well Heidegger's word is translated by Derrida's word *provocation* and, no less, on how they translate the word "translation."

BEFORE THE QUESTION

Provocation provokes us to return to the beginning and before: before the question with which this text failed to begin, before the question, to pro-vocative address. In the *Grundbegriffe der Metaphysik* (*The Fundamental Concepts of Metaphysics*) of 1929–1930, Heidegger thinks of *Zusprechen* still as true or false affirmation, opposing it to true or false denial, and opposing both to the prior possibility of the neither true nor false and of the both positive and also negative (§ 73).[10] This possibility, he says, not—as Aristotle and he himself in *Being and Time* had supposed—the true affirmative proposition, is what puts us on the way to understanding the essence of logic. Does this put us on the way to understanding why Derrida begins his texts again and again by citing not just literary fictions, but mind-bogglingly paradoxical ones, like "Par le mot *par* . . ."? Of the dozens of stingrays Derrida nets, one of the most numbing is the behest of the angel of the Revelation, whose logic is explored in "*D'un ton apocalyptique* . . .": "Seal not the sayings of the prophecy of this book." If the sayings are not sealed, i.e., signed or endorsed, this saying is endorsed, and if it is, it isn't. We do not know what to do or say. Now being told something that tells us that we do not know what to do or to say could well have the perlocutionary effect that we reflect on fundamentals. That is to do something, and to do it is to shoulder a fundamental responsibility. This is a Socratic way of bringing out the tie between responsibility and undecidability. A semantic or pragmatic paradox that helps us see more particularly the Derridian way of conceiving this tie is the one unfolded from the title of his earlier mentioned essay "Comment ne pas parler."

In addition to reminding us that there are several monstrous species of stingray, species to which they do not quite belong, the words "Comment ne pas parler" take us further through the looking-glass of language than do the words from Heidegger just paraphrased. They not only take us to the unde-cided alethic modes, true-or-false, true-and-false, and the undecided assertive modes, affirmation-or-denial, affirmation-and-denial, that are modes of the powers (*Vermögen*) that are prior to and enabling conditions of the decided values truth, falsity, affirmation, and denial ascribable to (con)statements.

They bring to our attention that also on the scene is performance or production, whether we think of this in the way Austin comes to think of it in the later parts of *How to Do Things with Words,* as an illocutionary act of which constating is one kind, or in the way Derrida continues to do, as a non-constative act. Heidegger himself takes a step in this direction in "The Nature of Language" (1957–1958). Early in these lectures Heidegger wonders whether they should be entitled "The Nature (?)—of Language?" in order to indicate that the nature of language and of nature and the language of "nature" and of "language" are being put into question. The experimentally inserted question marks are removed, however, when it emerges that the question itself, the point of departure of *Being and Time,* is discovered to be a point of departure only in the *ordo inveniendi.* On the page on which Heidegger admits that this idea of adding question marks was not such a good one after all, and that they should be crossed out, *gestrichen* (which is not quite the same as removed), he explains that this is because to think is to listen to language. We must let language avow its nature to us, *uns zusprechen.* This *Zusprechen* is the enabling condition of the *Zusprechen* of which Heidegger writes nearly thirty years earlier in the *Grundbegriffe der Metaphysik.* There it is affirmation as opposed to denial. Here it is affirmation presupposed by such assertive acts: unassertive affirmation that is the affirmation not of language users but of language itself. Heidegger speaks of this *Zuspruch* also as *Zusage,* promise. Derrida says yes to this, up to a certain point. Hear hear, he says, *ouï ouï, oui oui.* Before I can ask "Comment ne pas parler?" I am already engaged in language. *Langage* is *l'engage.* The words "Comment ne pas parler," with the question mark not inserted, mark my pre-predicative predicament of being already provoked by the quasi-transcendental double affirmation between any "I" who says yes, for example Derrida or Nietzsche or Rosenzweig, and the quasi-transcendental absolute performative yes inscribed in it as *l'engage* is performed in *langage.* The say-so of my *dire oui* is predicated upon the hear-say of an unpredicative *ouï-dire.*

Why yes only up to a certain point? Perhaps because of the first path Derrida discerns *du côté de chez* Heidegger. And because of Heidegger's inclination to think that that first path and the second have a common source or *souche.* And because of the reliance Heidegger puts on reliance, *Verlässlichkeit,* in "The Origin of the Work of Art" and other writings dating from the 1930s, of which Derrida writes in *La vérité en peinture, De l'esprit,* and other pieces, anticipating some of the stories told in the Farias affair.[11] Also in *De l'esprit* however, as we saw, Derrida states that there is a crossing of Heidegger's two paths. Further, no one has been more insistent than he on the revolution that takes place in Heidegger's thinking between *Being and Time* and "Time and Being" when attention moves not only from *Dasein* to *Sein,* but to *Ereignis, es gibt* and (the focus of our own attention now) *Zusage* and *Zuspruch.* It is not without significance that Derrida's partial endorsement of parts of what Heidegger writes about promise and engagement, shifting the force of this last word from what it was made to mean in France immediately after the Second World War, is given in paragraphs of the essay "Nombre de oui" following some paragraphs on Eckhart's notion of *Gelâzenheit*. Heidegger's adaptation of this notion must be such as to let it be without (*sans?*) *Seinlassen* being any longer at its base. Heideggerian ontological responsibility must falter and give way, *il faut,* to responsibility otherwise said.

If Heidegger's paths cross each other, Derrida says, they also cross ours. The "*us* who are maybe not *given*" includes Derrida and Levinas. And their paths cross, as Levinas says at the end of the essay on Derrida entitled "Tout autrement":

> The ridiculous ambition to "improve on" a true philosopher is certainly not part of our aim. To cross him on his path is already a good thing and is probably exactly what meeting in philosophy means. In stressing the primordial importance of the questions Derrida puts we have wanted to express the pleasure given by an encounter at the heart of a chiasmus. (NP 89, PN 62)

And here is one way in which Derrida returns the compliment, without it being necessary to give Levinas's name:

> Command or promise, this injunction engages (me) in a rigorously asymmetrical fashion even before I have managed, myself, to say *I* and to sign such a *provocation*, in order to reappropriate it and reconstitute symmetry. That attenuates my responsibility not one whit. On the contrary. There would be no responsibility without this *prevenience* of the trace, and if autonomy were primary or absolute. Autonomy itself would not be possible, nor respect for the law (the sole "cause" of this respect) in the strictly Kantian sense of these words. To escape this responsibility, to deny it, to attempt to efface it by means of an absolute retreat, I must countersign it again or already. When Jeremiah curses the day he was born, he must once more or already *affirm*. (Ps 561–62)

If as well as complimenting each other Derrida and Levinas also complement each other, it is only because the completion implied by this word is simultaneously an unlimited overbrimming. The analysis of the pun that, in the Proverb for *Glassary,* Derrida says he is doing in *Glas* and elsewhere is not analysis in the usual sense of division down to simples. It is quasi-analysis the end of which is after a fashion a beginning, but a beginning that has already begun (Ps 648). The complexity of the crossing of the traces of Derrida and Levinas and Heidegger is the complexity of the crossing of responsibility or obligation or religion in Levinas's non-dogmatic sense with the undecidable double bind. It obliges us to ask, for example, how pre-predicative affirmation stands to the *Verlässlichkeit* of what Derrida calls Heideggerian hope, how both of these relate to the religious faith that according to Heidegger is not compatible with thinking, and whether Derrida's response to Heidegger and to Heidegger's question *Was heisst Denken?* is that a certain faith, *foi,* without any assumptive act of commitment, and religious only in Levinas's sense, is necessary, *inévitablement,* as the last word of *De l'esprit* affirms, if we are to respond responsibly: a certain loyalty, *loi, une certaine fidélité à la venue, chaque fois, de l'autre singulier* (A 71), an already pledged, affirmed, "Come," a *Bienvenue* that "marks in itself neither a desire, nor an order, nor a prayer, nor a request," but crosses the grammatical, linguistic, semantic, and pragmatic categories.[12] It binds us to ask at least this: What happens where the professedly "horizontal" other of Derrida meets Levinas's "vertical" *Autrui?* What or who takes precedence when their unparallel lines meet at Infinity? Derrida writes:

> Suppose a first *yes,* the archi-original *yes* that engages, promises, acquiesces before all. On the one hand, it is originarily, in its very structure, a reply. It is *from the beginning second,* coming after a request, a question, or a *yes.* On the other hand, as engagement or promise, it must *at least* and in advance bind itself to a confirmation in a neighbouring *yes. Yes* to the neighbour(ing), otherwise said to the other *yes* that is already there and yet remains to come. *Oui* au prochain, autrement dit à l'autre *oui* qui est déjà là mais reste pourtant à venir. (Ps 648–49)

There is no comma after the words *autrement dit* here. Even if there were, we should still be bound to ask: Does the "prochain" say a who or a what? A sayer or a constative said? Neither or both? Neither and both? Or a constative or performative saying, *dire,* that is other than either? In any case, the *in-venire* of the other is the invention *of* the other where the genitive is both subjective and objective and where the invention is at the same time advent and address, the *Geschick* of a *Geschenk* that is never an entirely present gift, never an entirely given present, but always promised, presently to come. So maybe we have here yet another undecidability, another not-quite-either-and-not-quite-both, to add to the manifold overlapping quasi-classes of undecidability of which this chapter has only begun to sketch the (u)topography: illocutionary undecidability as to the performative or constative status of a speech act (e.g., "Par le mot *par . . .*"); alethic undecidablity as to the truth or falsity of a constatation (e.g., a Gödelian sentence, "This sentence is false," "This is a poem"); semantico-pragmatic undecidability as between the affirmation and denial of apparent contra-*dictory* responses to a question (e.g., "Comment ne pas parler?"); pragmatico-semantic undecidability as between responses to a command (e.g., "Seal not . . ."); undecidability as to genre (e.g., *Glas, Feu la cendre* and the dangerous liaisons of *La carte postale*), as to style (e.g., *Spurs*), as to tone of voice (Hölderlin: *Wechsel der Töne*) or gesture or both (e.g., the *chanson de geste* of "D'un ton apocalyptique . . . ," especially: "the difference between one 'Come' and another . . . is tonal. . . . It is the gesture in the utterance (*parole*), that gesture which does not allow itself to be recaptured by the analysis—linguistic, semantic or rhetorical— of an utterance."[13] Compare Austin's reference to the difficulty of reproducing tone and gesture analytically,[14] a difficulty to which Derrida's style of quasi-analytic negotiation may be seen as an inevitably interminable, hence both unsuccessful and maybe at the same time and for the same reason up to a point successful, response); and so on.

None of these quasi-classes of undecidability implies irresponsibility, notwithstanding the suspicions to the contrary expressed in the first paragraph of this chapter. Undecidability increases responsibility in that it obliges us to make finer and finer distinctions—for example, as we have seen, between quasi-kinds of undecidability and, as we shall begin to see in a moment, between classes and quasi-classes of responsibility—and to recognize that the order of priority of classes, for example that between human beings and chimpanzees, is no more grounded in the nature of things than is the distinction between the nature of things and culture or convention. Older than nature and culture or convention is the immemorial trace inviting and welcoming alterity, calling for the responsiveness of a responsibility *toward* without which the responsibilities *for* of my station and its duties are irresponsible. The price of justice is indeed eternal vigilance, but the recollection of pre-judicial undecidability prevents the vigilance of blind justice turning into the vigilantism of the totalitarian *polis* and its panoptical police, which insist either that a distinction is guillotine-sharp or that where there appears to be a difference there is monolithic continuity.

Undecidability is not exclusively opposed to responsibility any more than is seriousness to frivolity or necessity to chance—or responsibility to an essential pre-ethical irresponsibility, a pre-requisite of ethical responsibility: for there is an "essential irresponsibility of the promise and response" in that these are not made unless made in the language of the other, a language for which I lack full responsibility, because it is a language I cannot make entirely my own (Par 197–98). As Derrida writes in "La guerre de Paul de Man," precisely because the experience of undecidability seems to make responsibility impossible, the one calls for the other and the other for the one. Responsibility is beyond being. It cannot be. It can only be denied. But to deny it is to affirm it (MPM 210–11, Ps 561).[15] In his demonstrations of how entrenched hierarchical oppositions within nature and without (The Great Chain of Being) reconstrue themselves, theographematic undecidability, the *coup de Dé-ité*, is shown to be not the sworn enemy of responsibility, but pre-ontological and pre-ethical responsibility's inseparable friend. If Searle, Austin, Derrida, Levinas *et al* belong to a *Société à responsabilité limitée*, Sarl, and if in the deconstruction of the *archê* one does not make a choice (DG 91, OG 62), this does not mean that anything goes. It means that the range of choice over which we can be either ethically responsible or ethically irresponsible is opened more widely than we are normally allowed to discover when we take up our position on the apparently "firm ground of prejudice," to use Austin's phrase, that supports a certain metaphysical conception of conception, classification, and critique. The quirky quasi-French spelling of the word by which quasi-transcendental undecidability is alluded to in the title of this chapter marks not only the difficulty of deciding whether a title is outside or inside its text. It not only names what the text is about. It is also operative within it, performing a deconstrual of the simply negative and oppositional "un-," de-capitating both capitation and decapitation. It de-marcates it and effaces it by tracing it back to a mark which is not exclusively negative or privative but is at the same time an "in" (*donc dans*). Where responsibility is responsibility to the singularity of the other, respect for whom and for which must not be sacrificed to respect for the universality of the law, that is to say, where responsibility is critical co-respondence of reflective judgment and determinant judgment, *responsabilité limitée* is at the same time *responsabilité illimitée*. Therefore, indecidability is not necessarily without responsibility, for, indecidably limited and unlimited, before the law in both senses of the preposition, responsibility within decidability is responsibility with indecidability.[16]

2

DERRIDA, MALLARMÉ, AND ANATOLE

Parmi le long regard de la Seine entr'ouverte.

—PAUL VALÉRY (*Valvins*)

FIRST AFFIRMATION

A parenthetical codicil appended to his article on Mallarmé in a *Tableau de la littérature française* lists various other questions of which Derrida says he "should no doubt have spoken."[1] Among them is the question of Anatole.

Anatole, Mallarmé's only son, died in the autumn of 1879 at the age of eight. To have spoken of him would therefore have been to begin to speak of Mallarmé's griefs and of the work of mourning which Derrida says his article also no doubt ought to have treated. Mourning is a topic Derrida does treat elsewhere, most explicitly in "Fors" and in *Glas,* which refers to his own father's recent death. To mourn—*se douloir,* as the obsolete French form puts it—is to live with the pain (*douleur*) of a death. Mourning (*deuil*) is therefore a topic of which I no doubt should have spoken when, after listening to a paper in which I had referred to *Glas* and "Fors," Ruben Berezdivin asked how I supposed that Derrida could regard pain as anything other than something negative. The time lost in giving my lame excuse for not giving a direct answer would have been better spent hearing Derrida speak for himself. When asked after the period set for discussion what he himself would have said, his reply, if I recall aright, was that pain itself involves a regarding, an evaluation, and is not a sheer datum. Hence it is not negative if by that is meant something other and over against me. Derrida might agree with Nietzsche that "one does not *react* to pain. . . . Pain itself is a reaction," the natural reaction being the value judgment "harmful!" and aversion, moving away.[2] And to the extent that a reaction is an action, pain is as much action as passion. That is one reason for thinking that pain is not something merely received or reacted against. But the reaction which consists in judging something harmful does not entail the reaction which consists in shunning that thing. Different things are harmful in different ways, and what is harmful in one respect may nevertheless be sought after. We are not conceptually bound to say No to it. We can say Yes. This is a second sense in which a pain, meaning by that what is painful, need not be valued negatively. This brings us up against the question whether this valuing can be a feeling, and how such a feeling, in particular the feeling of a felt loss, is to be construed and deconstrued. That question would call for consideration of the question as to how a "pleasure" can be felt as a pain (F 44, F tr. 93).[3] Nothing will be said about these questions here. What can be said however is that whatever Derrida's response might be to the remarks cited from Nietzsche and to the questions these remarks raise, we can be sure that his fine ear picks up the difference Nietzsche makes between two sorts of Yes. Although Zarathustra's Yes, cited by Derrida in "Ja, ou le faux-bond" and toward the end of *Glas,* is "tremendous and unlimited," it is an affirmation that is laced with negation. For it says No to the Yes which merely endorses whatever is, including whatever is painful, as does the big-eared donkey, the camel, and the Christian (OA 70), and it says No to the determinate double negation of dialectic. With Nietzsche classical being becomes becoming, becoming becomes revalued being, revalued being is affirmation, and affirmation is creative revaluation, not the affirmation which takes being as its object and burden.[4] It would be ingenuous to say that Derrida simply endorses this view, but I have a hunch that it is the kind of thing he would say he would like to like. Witness the aforementioned references to "das ungeheure unbegrenzte Ja" of Zarathustra and the paragraphs at the end of "La Différance" where Derrida writes of *différance* that it must be *"affirmed,* in the sense in which Nietzsche puts affirmation into play, in a certain laughter and a certain step of the dance" (Ja 100; Gl 291 (365), Gl tr. 262; M 29, M tr. 27).[5]

Is this "certain *pas* de la danse" a terpsichorean No? It is not, for sure, a dialectical negation. It is precisely from that and its dialectically affirmative partner that Derrida and Nietzsche want to dance, laughing, away. Not from negativity as such, such as might or might not characterize the pain of grief, and is not to be laughed away. But from a philosophical thesis of *determinacy* resulting from negation and the negation of negation. Not toward some indeterminacy, back, say, to an indeterminate Being or Nothingness. But toward an undecidability for which Being and Nothingness are misnomers and which has no proper name. And not because it is a noumenon or is unmentionably numinous. But because it is the *affirmation jouée,* the played, worked, operated, gambled affirmation that is the condition of the possibility of determinacy, indeterminacy, naming—and misnomers. And "undecidability" is a misnomer at least in the sense that it has the disadvantage of suggesting something neutral or repressively negative. Perhaps "indecidability," although or because it is not standard English, would be nearer what Derrida's *indécidabilité* would mark. But then we should lose the implication that Derridian undecidability is an ana-logical take-off of the neutral third value of Gödelian *Unentscheidbarkeit,* an effect similar to that which Derrida gains by pouring new wine into the old bottle of "condition of possibility" to summon the bouquet of what is *before* the law, *Vor dem Gesetz.*

How can Derrida's reiteration of Nietzsche's Yes be squared with the way he reads Mallarmé? Despite the recourse both Nietzsche and Mallarmé have to the throwing of dice, despite the priority they both give to art, despite the proclamation they both make that God is dead, and despite the fact that they both address their words only to the few who have ears fine enough to hear, surely Mallarmé's outlook is the epitome of that of the man of resentment, morbidity, and melancholia rather than, like Nietzsche's, that of the lover of strength, health, and life? Does not a brief perusal of the Contents pages of Mallarmé's *Oeuvres complètes* suffice to show that he is in love with death? Among the poems of his earliest years are two entitled *Sa fosse est creusée!* . . . and *Sa fosse est fermée.* . . . The third part of *Hérodiade* is a poem on the death of John the Baptist. *Remémoration d'amis belges* speaks of the "Pierre veuve" and the "canal défunt" of a town commonly known as Bruges-la-Morte. The prose poem *Réminiscence* begins "Orphan, I wandered in black."[6] It is as though a drowning takes place in *Un coup de dés.* The section of *Igitur* printed last in the Pléiade edition carries the title "Il se couche au tombeau." There is a poem in memory of Gautier called *Toast funèbre* and a series of elegies called *Hommages et Tombeaux.* One of the *Contes indiens,* the one entitled *Le mort vivant,* begins under "un nuage de tristesse" which brings darkness at noon: "Le deuil regnait." And there is a *Deuil* on Maupassant. Furthermore, in a letter dated 3 May 1868, Mallarmé mentions that he is rereading *Melancholia.* Of this collection of poems, which his friend Henri Cazalis published that year, Mallarmé says that it is "une de mes lectures favorites en mon état."[7] In other words, throughout Mallarmé's life and works there sounds what Baudelaire calls, in the introduction to his translation of Poe's "The Philosophy of Composition," an essay in which Mallarmé found much to admire, "un glas de mélancolie." *Le glas* (*le glas, le glas*) is heard as one turns page after page. Mourning and melancholy. *Trauer und Melancholie.* If there is a theme that pervades Mallarmé's works, can it be anything but death? And if there is a theme that pervades the works of Nietzsche, what else can that be but life? What pervades the works of both Nietzsche and Mallarmé on Derrida's reading of them is lifedeath. Not however as theme, but as trace. Wake. Wake!

Consider first some of the comments Derrida makes about Nietzsche in *L'oreille de l'autre.* On the "date" of his forty-fifth anniversary, Nietzsche writes, at what it is reasonable to count as the midpoint of one's life, under the eye of *Midi là-haut,*

> On this perfect day, when everything is ripening and not only the grape turns brown, the eye of the sun just fell upon my life: I looked back, I looked forward, and never saw so many and such good things at once. It was not for nothing that I buried my forty-fourth year today; I had the *right* to bury it; whatever was life in it has been saved, is immortal. The first book of the *Revaluation of All Values,* the *Songs of Zarathustra,* the *Twilight of the Idols,* my attempt to philosophize with a hammer—all presents of this year, indeed of its last quarter! *How could I fail to be grateful to my whole life?*—And so I tell my life to myself.[8]

"Und so erzähle ich mir mein Leben." What is meant by "mir"? Kaufmann translates it "to myself." Derrida gives "je me raconte," which allows both for "to myself" and for the "for myself," "pour moi," that Derrida also gives.

Nietzsche affirms his life. He apposes his signature, his *firma,* his mark. Nietzsche's autobiography, Derrida says, is *auto*biography not, or not just, in the sense that it is his life that it tells, but in the sense that he is telling it to himself, its first, though not its only, addressee. The I, *ich* (a chiasmic *chi,* χ, pronounced by French speakers as *qui,* who) who recites the life is not its first addressee, prior to the recitation of that life. It is the eternal return that reaffirms, repeats "Hear, hear." But where is the ear of this repetition? What is the position of the apposition? Where is its here? Where does it take place? It does not take place, not at any definable here and now. As Mallarmé writes, nothing takes place except the place which is not a location that is simply *fort* or *da,* but is instead an unhomely *loc. cit.,* like that of the above-cited exergue of *Ecce Homo,* between the title and Nietzsche's text, after his preface but before his story, before history, neither inside nor outside the life and the work, yet both.

Entre, between, in the way that the writer Friedrich Nietzsche and the writings to which he appended his name are between the father who died before him and the mother who died after him. Not only is the person who signs himself F. N. their heir, the heir of two sexes, their two laws (the civil law that Creon obeys and the law of the family followed by Antigone), but the heir of life and death. Because he signs for them, not just for their sakes but on their behalf, they have a say in what he says. The deed he performs in signing and what he subscribes to depend, as that Anglish Nietzschean John Austin would say, on their uptake (M 383, M tr. 322). They are co-signatories of recorded deliveries, both senders and receivers. They are correspondents with political responsibility, for if Nietzsche's *enseignement,* i.e., his mark and his message, are opened up in this way, the question as to his and our heirs becomes a question of general interest where it is no easy task to determine who's who and who bequeaths what to whom. This is not only Nietzsche's problem. It is a problem for us his interpreters, whoever we are, for the interpreters of Mallarmé, for Mallarmé and his mother and father. And for his only son, Anatole.

LAST TESTAMENT

The testamentary structure that Derrida uncovers in Nietzsche's writing is discernible also in Mallarmé's. Mallarmé himself says that nowadays to write a book is "faire son testament," to make one's will.[9] Or, rather, the will of more than one, since the signature is, as Villiers de L'Isle Adam's title has it, an intersign. Mallarmé says too that a book is a tomb.[10] Among the notes for his Tombeau d'Anatole we find the following: "mère identité/de vie mort/père reprend/rythme pris ici/du bercement de/mère/suspens—vie/mort —/poésies—pensée."[11] The mother rocking the child dictates the rhythm of the poetry in which the father gives posthumous life to the son who carries the father's name to the grave. But as well as this hymen between mother and father and life and death, there is a hymen of the father, who is already the legatee of his deceased mother and father, and the son, who is also the father of the man in that he gives his life for his father to help him write the work: "il fallait—/héritant de cette/merveilleuse intelli/gence filiale, la/ faisant revivre/—construire/avec sa (nette)/lucidité—cette/oeuvre—trop vaste pour moi/," a work so vast that the father has had to sacrifice his own life to and for it.[12] Having made this sacrifice he need have no qualms that he is exploiting the death of his son, particularly if he is *encrypted* in a tomb-tome engraved in language that is not language of the tribe and the market-place (forum), not language that is *profane*. In the "claustration" of this book father and son give their lives for each other: "je me sens couché en la tombe à côté de toi."[13] They also give their lives to each other. For in the book, in the poem, death is thought. Anatole's physical extinction is an undeniable event, but as such it belongs to the world of contingencies in which, since the crisis of 1866, Mallarmé sees nothing but nothing. If however one thinks that one is dying, death is no longer sheer waste. But in realizing it one makes it all the more real, all the more painful. This is a dilemma that Mallarmé's mourning of his son attempts to resolve. In *Igitur* he writes: "Je pense que je meurs—donc je meurs." In the notes toward a Tombeau d'Anatole, from this swift syllogism, as J.-P. Richard calls it,[14] thereby distancing it from the Cartesian nonsyllogistic *cogito*, Mallarmé hopes to derive on behalf of his son a denial of the consequent from a denial of the antecedent. Formally, this is as invalid as the "therefore" of the hypothetical in *Igitur* is hasty. But perhaps it is out of place to apply formal principles here. It is not the mortality of Caius that Mallarmé has in his mind or heart. As we have already said, Mallarmé does not deny his son's physical extinction. His hope is that he can die for his physically dead son, really die the death that requires realization. At first suffering pangs of guilt at the thought of concealing from his son that he is dying, of depriving him of his death in order to save him from the pain of its realization, the father comes to hope that he and his son may attain to the best of both worlds through a mourning in which the son's unconsciousness of his dying is compensated for through the father's consciousness of his dying, his son's and his own: "je veux tout souffrir/pour toi/qui ignores—/rien ne sera/soustrait (qu'à/toi) du deuil inouï."[15] Death is deceived if it thinks it can inflict on Anatole the thought that he is dying: "mort—ridicule ennemie/—qui ne peux à l'enfant/infliger la notion que tu es!"[16] But is not Stéphane Mallarmé deceiving himself if he thinks he is not deceiving his son? Let him who would cast the first stone remember that the son is an eight-year-old child, that the father's conscience may nevertheless remain unclear over whether he is deceiving his son or not, and that there also remains another thought that gives him anguish: the thought that the disease from which the son is dying may be congenital. So there remains something for which the "tombeau idéal" would be a compensation and an atonement in a quite precise sense if indeed Anatole is its co-author—and co-reader, in that one writes also for and to the dead, including the bearer of one's name and, since every name is testamentary, the name he bears. The name of Mallarmé. The name of Derrida (OA 74).

So the ideal tomb-tome that snatches the dead from death would seem to be the complete writing cure. A *pharmakon*. Could a more "successful," "normal" mourning be imagined? But could it be more than imagined? Could it, when we understand what we are asking this *Denkmal* to do, even be imagined? Could the ideal Tombeau ever be real?

The Tombeau d'Anatole was never constructed. It is no more than a handful of fragments, a handful of dust. Like the *Livre* projected in the little pile of notes while the shadows gathered to wipe away his thoughts of death (to spit into the eye of the "ridicule ennemie" is to spit into the wind), Mallarmé requested it to be burned, for "there is no literary inheritance there, my poor children."[17]

Is Anatole still waiting to be buried, then, still not sublimed, "resorbé,"[18] into eternity, still waiting for his father to transmute him into himself? Yes and no. In the so-called autobiography sent to Verlaine, Mallarmé says that the present time is an interregnum, a time of obsoletion in which the poet can do no more than work "avec mystère" preparing for what will come "later or never."[19] This reference to the present time echoes the "nowadays" of the previously cited observation that "Aujourd'hui écrire un livre, c'est faire son testament." The implication seems to be that the *Livre* with a capital *L* or the *Oeuvre* with a large, fully-rounded *O* is not impossible in principle, however much the literary efforts of Mallarmé and his contemporaries are destined to fail because they live at a time of catastrophe (F 56, F tr. 102), a bordertime of *Crise de vers*, crisis of towardness, between the desire and its consummation, the performance and its memory, "between desire and fulfilment, perpetration and remembrance: here anticipating, there recalling, in the future, in the past, *under the false appearance of a present*" (D 201, D tr.175).[20] But is it only at the present time that the present is a false appearance? Is it only the late nineteenth century that is a tunnel leading from Hugo up into the light that streams through the glass canopy of "the almighty station of the virginal central palace, that crowns," the station dedicated to Saint Lazarus? Or are the only stations we can expect to reach always underground stations, like the Gare des Invalides? Mallarmé's "indication," as I read it, is that the "integrity of the Book" does not presume a Present. The glass crown of the Gare St. Lazare is multifaceted, like the diamonds in the poem that crown the writer's scrupulous labor. The totality of the Book is a totality of glittering fragments, a "représentation fragmentaire."[21] The Book explodes "diamantairement," "in our time and for ever." If we mean by the Book what Mallarmé had been preparing in the manuscript he asked to be committed to the flames, we learn from the fragments of it published by Scherer that the "integrity" of the Book was to combine an extraordinary level of organization with an extraordinary degree of flexibility. Nothing and everything was to be left to chance. Its volumes were to be designed so that they fitted together to form a monumental block like a deconstructible Rubik's cube. The 320 pages of each of the twenty volumes would be folded in such a way that no paper knife would be needed to make the text visible, and since the pages would not be sewn or glued, there would be a wide range of orders in which they could be read. With the result that "the volume, although giving the impression of being fixed, becomes by this play, mobile—from death it becomes life."[22] Some of the preliminary papers calculate meticulously the mathematics and dynamics of the Book, the contrapuntal and harmonic permutations open to its operator. The Book, for which everything in the world exists,[23] would be a word processing machine for translating chance into necessity.[24] And this is why it is destined to remain unrealized. The Book is bound to *faire faux-bond,* as Derrida says, not simply because Mallarmé lacked energy, ingenuity, or time, but because the twenty years he told Aubanel he would need to complete the work would still not be enough, for the reason he himself gives in *Un coup de dés.* If a throw of the dice will never abolish chance and writing is a throw of the dice, Mallarmé has good reason to expect that his project of the Book will be considered an "acte de démence." When he describes this project as his "tapisserie de Pénélope" he is forgetting that she did eventually complete Laertes' shroud.[25] Mallarmé's task, like Igitur's, is a *folie* and, like the task of the old man in *Un coup de dés,* an absurdity. When finally the old man raises his arm, with the dice in his still-clenched fist, his gesture is no more than the mime of a throw from someone who (not waving, but drowning) is overwhelmed by the paralyzing thought that he who wins loses and he who loses wins. Since "Toute Pensée émet un Coup de Dés," even that desperate, demented last deed in which the arm effects a circuit between the sea of chance and the fixed constellations of the sky, writes a momentous, *augenblicklich,* remark to the effect that writing is aboriginally absurd.

The absurdity of writing is, if not the message or the theme, perhaps a motif of Mallarmé's project toward the *Grand Oeuvre.* The *Grand Oeuvre* is in principle incompletable and therefore in a sense not even begun. Yet in another sense it has extant provisional parts: the programmatic notes published by Scherer and maybe *Un coup de dés* and other "exercises" included in the Pléiade *Oeuvres complètes;* maybe also the sketches for a Tombeau d'Anatole. In this sense the unrealized Book, fated to be forever *unterwegs,* already exists, as *débris de. . . .* Mallarmé recognizes this when he says to Verlaine:

> I shall perhaps succeed, not in finishing this work in its entirety (I do not know who one would have to be to be capable of that!), but in producing a completed fragment, in making the *glorious* authenticity of a portion of it scintillate, only hinting at all the rest for which a lifetime would not be enough. To prove by the parts that have been executed that this book exists, and that I have known what I shall not have been able to accomplish.[26]

Thirteen years earlier he had written, of a word he himself uses again and again: "I predict it: the word *authentic,* which was, for many years, the sacramental term of antiquarians, will soon no longer have any meaning."[27]

As for the glory, this is the glory of a Lie. In the tunnel of the "night of Tournon" he had learned the lesson of Plato's cave. All matter is illusion. All is lies. Except for Poetry—and, he later adds, friendship and love. Poetry itself is a lie, but a glorious lie. Man may be a reed, but he is a thinking reed whose most sublime achievement is that of having invented God and the soul and works of art in which the poet sings "en désespéré"[28] his "explication orphique de la terre":[29]

> I have every admiration for the great Magus who searches inconsolably and obstinately for a mystery that he knows does not exist, and which he will pursue for ever precisely on account of his lucid despair, since *that would have been* the truth![30]

When he speaks of the poet's orphic explication of the earth, Mallarmé knows that Eurydice is led forth no further than the exit from her grave. As Anatole remains at the mouth of his. Neither above ground nor below, *subjectile*, "entre le dessus et le dessous, le visible et l'invisible, le devant et le derrière, l'en-deçà et l'au-delà. Entre gésir et jeter." On the subtle threshold between transitive *iacere* and intransitive *iacêre*—(c)I-gît-(t)ur.[31]

LIMITED INCORPORATION

"Introjection/incorporation: everything is played out on the threshold which divides and opposes the two terms" (F 15, F tr. 70). Ashes to ashes, dust to dust. But Derrida elicits from Mallarmé and from elsewhere an explication why the project for an orphic explication of the earth was bound to fall short, *faire faux-bond,* and hence why no book could be a spiritual instrument in which the soul of the departed could be safely entombed, if by safe entombment is meant what some psychoanalysts mean by introjection. Mallarmé himself says that we have *invented* the soul, and this invention plays no little part in the definition of introjection that Maria Torok develops from Ferenczi. Introjection, as this is held to take place in "normal" mourning, is conceived as the inclusion in oneself of the lost object and the drives it occasions,[32] the lost loved one and one's love, the love and friendship that Mallarmé excepts from his principle that all is lies. Introjection is a last supper, a cannibalistic ingestion of the loved one's spirit.

How, as Hegel would have asked, can introjection succeed if what it aims to include is the loved one's free spirit? This question is all the more pertinent in view of the fact that Mallarmé, as so many of his commentators insist, had learned something about Hegel from Villiers de L'Isle Adam and others,[33] if not directly from the writings of Hegel. What we may provisionally call the Hegelian moment in Mallarmé's thinking is evinced in his assertion that Literature suppresses "le Monsieur qui reste en l'écrivant."[34] At Igitur's midnight, which is a "milieu, pur" between night and day, at the zero hour at which the old man of *Un coup de dés* is expected to throw the dice, in the decisive *clin d'oeil* when the flashing blade brings to John the

Baptist deepest darkness and at the same time brightest light, at the dead of Mallarmé's own long "night of Tournon" whose "nuit" suggests the brightness of the day whose "jour" suggests the somberness of night,[35] at such critical epochs *cogito* is phenomenologically reduced to *cogitatur.* At the "instant spécial" there is, as Heidegger says in "What is Metaphysics?," no I or you, only one, the authentic counterpart of the inauthentic *das Man* ("Daher ist im Grunde nicht 'dir' und 'mir' unheimlich, sondern 'einem' ist es so"). As Mallarmé himself says, "my thought thought itself," "I am now impersonal, and no longer the Stéphane you knew—but an aptitude that the spiritual universe has to see itself and develop itself through what was once me,"[36] to develop itself in the Book, "the Text speaking there for itself and without the author's voice."[37] Not that the text speaks with the "voiceless voice" of what Levinas calls the *il y a* or of what Blanchot calls "nothingness as being, the idling (*désoeuvrement*) of being,"[38] The voice is a middle voice, neither simply active nor simply passive, that is incomprehensible (*inouïe*) within the categories of nothingness and being. It does not even *belong* to a person,[39] and the personage through which the voice speaks has no self-consciousness. The depersonalization (*Śunyāvadā*) [40] here in question is a kind of death. Mallarmé writes: "I am dead," "I am perfectly dead." This is not the kind of death of which Igitur says "I think that I am dying—therefore I am dying," since for want of a mirror the self-consciousness of the I has died. The "personage whose thinking is not conscious of him"[41] has died into the poem or the book which is now not only the tomb of the ancestors of Igitur, the Tombeaux of Poe, Baudelaire, Verlaine, and Anatole, but of him who is no longer Stéphane. "L'objet perdu-moi."[42] All that survives is the objective-subjective, subjectile, "operator" of the spiritual instrument— as with the performer of *sean-nós* (old song) in the southwestern corner of Ireland who faces away from the mirroring looks of the listeners as she or he sings—so that *il s'agit.* It is a question of, *es geht um,* my death, the "idiomatic mode of 'I am dead' that maneuvers me or with which I ruse,"[43] a ruse that is not an act of will and war performed by a Mr. So-and-so; rather a calculus that operates itself.[44] *Wo ich war . . . il s'agit* (Ça *gît, Sa gît*) (F 23, F tr. 76).

But *il s'agit* thanks to the voice (*glas*) and the black on white, the black and the blank. And the black is not just the simple opposite of the white, any more than writing is the opposite of speech. Speaking/writing: everything is played out on the threshold that divides and opposes the two terms. Somewhat as writing is to speaking and hypomnesis is to anamnesis,[45] so incorporation is to introjection and melancholia to "normal" mourning. That, at any rate, is how I take Derrida's hint that so-called normal introjective mourning may be no more than a dream:

> The question could of course be asked as to whether or not "normal" mourning preserves the object *as other* (a living dead person) inside me. This question—of the general appropriation and safekeeping of the other *as other*—can always be raised as the deciding factor, but does it not at the same time blur the very line it draws between introjection and incorporation, through an essential and irreducible ambiguity? (F 17, F tr. 71)

The line is blurred, as hinted in Abraham and Torok's heading "Deuil *ou* mélancolie, Introjecter-incorporer."[46]

What is incorporation? To incorporate is to mimic introjection. While introjection speaks, incorporation is, to use the words of the title of a series of letters and articles by Poe that Mallarmé perhaps knew, Secret Writing. Incorporation is cryptography. It encrypts the lost object whose loss it pretends not to acknowledge, by hiding it in a tomb that is simultaneously inside and outside the self that has the gaol of introjection for its goal. In *Cryptonymie: le verbier de l'homme aux loups* Nicolas Abraham and Maria Torok apply to the case of Wolfman this distinction made in earlier papers between two kinds of appropriation.[47] There is no question of pursuing that application here, or indeed Derrida's analysis of it in "Fors." The most we can do is approach some of the implications it might have for a reading of Mallarmé.

"Fors" is subtitled "Les mots anglés de Nicolas Abraham et Maria Torok." It treats of words that fish for complements and is subtended sideways on from Mallarmé's *Les mots anglais*. It is related to it *diamantairement* (F 63, F tr.108).[48] Neither is introjected in the other. Mallarmé and Derrida both say that introjection is no less a deception than incorporation appears to be. Indeed, incorporation, regarded as *maladie du deuil*, invalid, *invalide*, grief, is the place to look for the key to the structure of "normal" grief and of what is called introjection. Somewhat as Sartrean *mauvaise foi* is the place to look for the key to the structure of what he calls good faith. Somewhat as what is ordinarily understood by writing conceals the key to the structure of speech. The operation of this structure or, better, substructure or, still better, destructure, is forcefully caricatured by Mallarmé as he is read, say, in "La double séance" and the essay on Mallarmé mentioned in the opening sentence of the present chapter. Mallarmé is continually taking calculated risks with his readers. For instance, of *Igitur* he writes: "Ce Conte s'adresse à l'intelligence du lecteur qui met les choses en scène, elle-même." This is borne out by the title, namely *Igitur ou la Folie d'Elbehnon,* that has preceded and by the synoptic note that soon follows. "Igitur" can be "therefore," *ergo,* the "donc" of "je pense donc je suis" and the "donc" of "je pense que je meurs—donc je meurs," of the "il faut" of the proof of the patronymic title that Igitur's ancestors foolishly expect him to provide. "Igitur" can also be the first word of Genesis 2: "Igitur perfecti sunt coeli et terra et omnis ornatus eorum."

One commentator questions this reading on the grounds that "there seems to be little if any relationship between this summing up of Creation and Mallarmé's prose-poem."[49] But there is a close relationship surely if Igitur is being asked to vindicate his race and declare that "it was good." The same commentator is reluctant to accept the suggestion that Elbehnon is El behnon, the son of the Elohim,[50] because Semitic grammar would call for the "el" to come second. I suspect that Mallarmé would have said "Let it call," and welcomed Richard's suggestion "El be none" or, come to that, Butler's anglish Erewhon and Dylan Thomas's Anglo-Welsh Llareggub.

Only one word ago he has hazarded an anagram, *folie*, of *fiole*, the glass vial containing the *pharmakon* that would give Igitur his quietus. Anyway, it is often as much for its sound as for its sense that Mallarmé uses a name. Rather, he purports to show that they cannot be separated at least in the language "remedied" by the poet,[51] and in the English language as he found it and described it in *Les mots anglais*. If we are allowed an anglish extrapolation from English to French, we can say that in the sentence "L'infini sort du hasard," in what in the Pléiade edition is the Argument section of *Igitur*, the s of "sort" represents "le jet indefini"[52] and—perhaps its "principle sense"—*incitation*.[53] This extrapolation is warranted by Mallarmé's adherence to the notion that sound and sense are intimately connected at the origin of language, and by his statement in *Diptyque*, where he is not thinking of one language in particular, that the letter s is "la lettre analytique, dissolvante et disséminante, par excellence."[54] What Mallarmé is dissolving here is the opposition of speaking and writing, oral value and purely hieroglyphic value, *grimoire*, by appealing to an occult space of forces and forcings (*forçage?*)[55] that are not simply forced meanings, not purely semantic values, nor purely syntactic or grammatical ones (*grimoire* has the same root as "grammar"), but "une secrète direction confusèment indiquée par l'orthographie et qui concourt mystérieusement au signe pur général qui doit marquer le vers," where, I dare say, in "vers" sounds not only a verse or a line of poetry, but also the divagating approach of the serpent in the garden and the worm in the ground. "L'infini sort du hasard" is indecidably-undecidably "The infinite emerges from the throw of the dice" and/or "The infinite destiny of chance." A monstrous offspring of a hymeneal interlude between semantics and syntax, where "infini" is not simply an adjective or simply a noun, where "sort" is not simply a noun or a verb, and where the fragment "or" may be an adjective suggesting the color of innumerable Mallarméan sunsets and/or the noun that names the metal of political economy (D 198, 318, D tr. 172, 286)[56] and/or the orchestra's sonorous brass and/or the temporal adverb "now" at this fatal hour of "Le vierge, le vivace et le bel aujourd'hui" and/or the conjunction[57] that suggests the "or" of the to-be-or-not-to-be of *vie/mort*, for instance the life and/or death of Anatole.

For Igitur, whether the dice (*assahar*) are cast or not, *kif-kif*, "il y a et il n'y a pas le hasard." As the poem with its rhymes that toll a hymen of sound and sense "réduit le hasard à l'infini," so the poetic afterlife of Anatole is infinite if by that is meant the unfinished "bad" infinity of "le jet indéfini"; but it is not infinite if by that is meant a "good" infinity safe from risk. This is because his entombment is not introjection, but "deep" incorporation, the archi-incorporation, both *vicieuse* and *sacrée*, the *introjecter-incorporer* that is the abyssal "condition of the possibility" of the opposition introjection/incorporation, of the bad *Erinnerung* which is incorporation and the good *Erinnerung* which is introjection; it is what makes these possible only as scenic, *forcené* effect, *crayonné au théâtre*. The elegy would be an appropriation of the death of the loved one that gives him or her new life. In the poem the one who is lost would be resurrected "Tel qu'en Lui-même l'éternité le change." But this new life turns out not to be the Platonic or Hegelian eternal truth of Anatole or Poe. The poem is a fabrication which is, as in Mallarmé's reading of the story of Penelope's weaving of the shroud, never complete— although the shroud may appear to be finished, the weaving of it is not. Its thread, the thread between life and death cut by Iris—the iris being the flower that Mallarmé *says,* the flower that is, as Derrida says, "l'absente de tous bouquets,"[58] the flower whose varicolors make up the colorlessness of white light—is rewoven with a shuttle that eternally returns. And although, after being worked by day and unworked by night, Penelope's shroud appeared to reach completion, this completion was never more than ap-pearance. If the *hymne* to Anatole had been finished, it would still have been unfinished, a hymen of the undone and the done. If we imagine that Anatole could have been laid to rest in his poetic grave, we are forgetting that the black letters are inscribed "parmi le blanc du papier"[59] whose white is not whiteness, but the blank *entre* between perversely dark "jour" and perversely bright "nuit," a perverse deception for whose remuneration through verse one may harbor a hope, a *souhait* that may turn out to be no less a deception, *mon songe,* than that for the stone *dite philoso-phale* (D 198, 318, D tr. 172, 286) otherwise known as the *Grand Oeuvre.* Nevermore.

No more than Mallarmé's literary progeny is Anatole *hermetically* en-crypted. He remains "captif solitaire du seuil," "the threshold never crossed" (D 243, D tr. 214),[60] at the pale of the blank between Mallarmé's whites, the *blanc de blancs*: of, as Derrida conjugates them, the snow, the cold, death, marble, and so on; the swan, the wing, the fan, and so on; virginity, purity, hymen, etc.; the page, the veil, the sail, gauze, milk, semen, the milky way, the star . . . ; and the white of Pierrot's face. But also the *entres* between "entre" (mentioned) and *entre* ("used") and *antre* and *autre,* the unreadable cryptic space between meaning and the mark, sense and sound, life and death, the *milieu, pur, de fiction,* that calls to be recited indefectibly forever-more, *à jamais* " . . . le perpétuel suspens d'une larme qui ne peut jamais toute se former ni choir . . ." (" . . . the perpetual suspense of a tear that can never be entirely formed nor ever fall . . .") (D 206, D tr. 180).[61]

3

THE ORIGIN AND END OF PHILOSOPHY

L'anneau de cette réflexion
Ne se fermera peut-être pas.
Du moins ne reviendra-t-il pas
Où on l'attendait, à son origine,
Avant d'y avoir laissé,
S'y affectant, s'y infectant,
Quelque venin fort peu philosophique:
Ébauche ainsi d'un serpent, parmi l'arbre,
Tirant sa langue à double fil,
De qui le venin quoique vil
Laisse loin la sage ciguë!

—M 330, M TR. 278

SOLID SENSE

Let us not be in too great a hurry to break into the broken circle of Derrida's reflections. Let us approach it at a tangent. Since we are to be attempting to understand as far as is possible something so unfamiliar that it appears to defy traditional modes of philosophical understanding, let us begin with something familiar, the bridge of which Heidegger[1] and Valéry write or the one you cross every day, the table on which philosophers have been writing since Plato, words and the printed page.

Presence in the page proofs is no proof that a word will survive when the printed book finally comes back to its author. But there is an incompleteness that affects every book, however carefully composed and composited, the incompleteness that leads Valéry to compare a word with a plank that will enable us to cross a ditch only if we do not loiter (C 29, pp. 58–59, O II, p. 237).[2] Valéry's plank may be compared in turn with Eddington's, and with Eddington's table: "The plank has no solidity of substance. To step on it is like stepping on a swarm of flies. . . . My scientific table is mostly emptiness."[3] He refers to the scientific table as table no. 2. Of course, "There is a familiar table parallel to the scientific table." The familiar table is his table no. 1. Table no. 1 is solid and substantial. It supports my writing paper. This reliability is explicable, Eddington tells us, by the at least statistically predictable behavior of the fundamental particles that constitute table no. 2. The raw materials to which the modern physicist has recourse in reporting the laws of this "foreign territory" are electrons, quanta, potentials, Hamiltonian functions, etc., "and he is nowadays scrupulously careful to guard these from contamination by conceptions borrowed from the other world!" Yet Eddington says that it is not only table no. 1 that supports his writing paper. Table no. 2 does so also, and it does so because of the electrons that "keep on hitting the underside." "But," asks Susan Stebbing, "if electrons, belonging to world no. 2, are to be scrupulously guarded from contamination by world no. 1, how can it make sense to say that they 'keep on hitting the underside' of a sheet of paper that, indubitably, is part of the familiar furniture of the earth?"[4] As she goes on to remark, it is Eddington himself who is introducing contamination. This is a little hard on Eddington in that it is of the younger physicists that he is speaking when he mentions conceptual purism, and he concedes that he himself has difficulty disinfecting his thought. Still, he is confident that for the physicist this separation of the concepts of physics from everyday concepts can be achieved. Although scientific research begins with the familiar world and returns to it, the physicist as physicist is a traveler in foreign parts. It is for the philosopher to deal with the question of how the concepts of the familiar and those of the unfamiliar territories are related. It is presumably as a philosopher therefore that Eddington is speaking when he says of the scientific table that it is a duplicate of the familiar one, speaking not as do Newton's "vulgar People" who indulge in table talk without realizing that they are talking nonsense, but talking nonsense knowingly, because only nonsense will make sense to the uninitiated. Thus Newton begs our indulgence when he speaks "grossly" and "not properly" of light and rays as though they were colored and of the sound of a bell as anything other than "a trembling Motion."[5] Likewise Eddington:

> When I think of an electron there rises to my mind a hard, red, tiny ball; the proton similarly is neutral grey. Of course the colour is absurd— perhaps not more absurd than the rest of the conception—but I am incorrigible. I can well understand that the younger minds are finding these pictures too concrete and are striving to construct the world out of Hamiltonian functions and symbols so far removed from human preconception that they do not even obey the laws of orthodox arithmetic.

This amounts to the concession that he is talking figuratively when he says that a table is part of the subject matter of modern physics. Nor therefore must he be taken literally, as Stebbing takes him, when, on her reading, he employs the word "man" to describe what is left supposing "we eliminated all the unfilled space in a man's body and collected his protons and electrons into one mass," whether the residue be a mere speck or whether we are as generous as is the speaker in Valéry's *L'idée fixe* who says, "It appears that if one eliminates the inter- and intra-atomic voids, the entire substance of a man can be contained in a matchbox" (O II, p. 243). That the noun in Eddington's phrase "scientific plank" is not intended literally is evident from his acknowledgment that the picture conjured up by the familiar sense of the word "plank" is too concrete for strictly scientific purposes. So long as this is acknowledged, it is more than a little harsh to say, as Stebbing does, that "Nothing but confusion can result if, in one and the same sentence, we mix up language used appropriately for the furniture of earth and our daily dealings with it with language used for the purposes of philosophical and scientific discussion." Not only does this comment assume that the terms she is willing to accept as part of the scientific language—aether, electron, quantum, potential, etc.—are uncontaminated, an assumption Eddington also makes, it is false that nothing but confusion can result. Something else that can result is an advance to a new scientific hypothesis. However, what has been said so far is not a preface to another discussion of the function of the figurative in conceptual revision. The aim of this first section is to recall a paradigm case of appeal to a paradigm case purporting to fix the distinction between the literal, real, and proper, on the one hand, and the figurative, the imitation, and the improper, on the other. Here again is Stebbing's classic statement:

> The plank appears *solid* in that sense of the word "solid" in which the plank is, in fact solid. It is of the utmost importance to press the question: If the plank appears to be *solid*, but is really *non-solid*, what does "solid" mean? The pairs of words, "solid"–"empty," "solid"–"hollow," "solid"–"porous," belong to the vocabulary of common-sense language; in the case of each pair, if one of the two is without sense, so is the other.

Similarly, "The opposition between a *real* object and an *imitation* of a real object is clear," and "there could not be a *misuse*, nor a *figurative* use, unless there were some correct and literal usages." In what follows, certain texts of Derrida's, and texts that he cites, will be cited which suggest not that these oppositions are not for normal non-philosophical purposes clear and fixed, but that a traditional philosophical understanding of that clarity calls for questioning: that the fixedness of the oppositions may, in an extended sense of the word, be "fixed," and that philosophers at least may be prone to accept a far too simple understanding of understanding, of the opposition between the normal and the extended sense of a word, and of the opposition between philosophy and the non-philosophical. Other writers have challenged this traditional philosophical conception of clarity and distinctness, and Derrida has challenged it in more than one way. There is room here to treat of only one of those ways.

IMPLEX

In *Qual Quelle* Derrida cites passages from Valéry to show that the latter resists what he takes to be the Freudian theory of the interpretation of dreams because it is a theory of interpretation: a hermeneutic and a semantic theory. "My theories of the dream are completely opposed to those of the day. They are completely 'formal,' while the latter are completely significative" (C 17, p. 766). But it is possible to take a low view of a semantic theory of dreams without taking a low view of a semantic theory of waking consciousness. And there are passages in the *Cahiers* where Valéry contrasts the fluidity of dreams with the solidity of the world of our waking life. This poses a problem for anyone who wishes to recount dreams or to theorize about them. "One is seeking to apply the mechanics of solids to a world *in which things do not endure*" (C 8, pp. 504–505). So, as Valéry notes, there is something paradoxical about any attempt to put dreams into words. There is something paradoxical also, however, in the fact that although this first paradox arises because we are trying to apply words fitted for what endures to something that is transitive, words themselves are wanting in the kind of solidity that is attributed to them by many philosophers, indeed by "every philosophy" according to the entry in the *Cahiers* referred to in our opening section.

> The role of language is essential, but it is transitive—that is to say, one cannot dwell on it.
>
> That is why so many philosophical propositions and pseudo-definitions continue to be disputed.
>
> Only mathematics can allow itself to remain in language, having the audacity to render language *creative—by convention.*
>
> If philosophers consented to accept this condition and *to regard as mere products of conventions* the verbal abuses or verbal inventions they take advantage of, we could accept their metaphysics. Which amounts to treating their trade as an art or poetic fiction—which concocts abstractions. Every philosophy passes from the clear to the obscure, from the univocal to the equivocal by separating words from *real needs* and expedient and *instantaneous* applications. One should never linger on a word; fulfilling perfectly a real role, it has no other function to perform and yields nothing other than what is conferred upon it by immediate and transitive use. (C 29, pp. 58–59)

More specifically, the utility of a word does not depend on the existence of a meaning posited beneath or behind it like a source from which could flow more than one thinks when the word is before one's mind (C 2, p. 91, C 4, p. 926). Here is a very Nietzschean entry that merits quotation at length not only because it identifies unmistakably the philosophy of meaning and truth that Valéry rejects, but also because it reintroduces the question of the relation between sense and sensibility that was mentioned in our first section and is taken up by Derrida, as we shall find in our last.

> The ancient Philosophers came in various ways to treat everything sensible as appearance; but in general they posited behind such apparitions a certain hidden reality—*Ideas* or *Laws* or *Being*—which was protected from the relativity of sensible knowledge. But the necessity for these verbal objects (if there is any) is only formal. And they have this failing: they borrow from the ordinary reality of appearances the reality they deny that they have. That is to say then that the following odd substitution is made: the force or the feeling of power and compellingness of sensations is borrowed from the sensible, transferred to essences and entities and given independence, while that which provides and entails it is repudiated as illusion. (C 12, p. 47)

It is not the semantic theories only of ancient philosophers and modern psychoanalysts that Valéry rejects. He rejects any "Fido"/Fido account on the grounds that words do not have meaning in isolation. He replaces this kind of account with one that takes as its model the game of chess (C 23, p. 686). The meaning of a word is analogous to a *move* in a game of chess. "The meaning of a word obtains only in each particular employment of it" (C 2, p. 261). Just as Wittgenstein hopes that the expression "language game" may help us not to forget that games are *played,* so Valéry emphasizes that a word has meaning only in the context of an actual "transitive" operation. When he calls his theory of meaning formalist this is what he means. It is functionalist in the sense that, as for Wittgenstein, the meaning of a word is ultimately the jobs it performs on the particular occasion on which it is employed. So Valéry's account, like Wittgenstein's, differs from that of Saussure in an important respect, although all three draw the analogy with the game of chess in order to counter the notion that words have meaning in isolation. Saussure is mainly interested in launching a science of *langue* seen as a system in abstraction from particular acts of *parole.* Valéry and Wittgenstein consider it vital to retain contact with actual or imagined cases of use.

But performance is an exercise of competence. Competence is an aspect of what Valéry calls "implex." Implex covers the subjunctivity implicit in one's ability to indicate something, the depresence inseparable from presence, the distant in the instant, the resource that prevents the source from being an origin, the unpunctuality of the point of philosophy, preventing philosophy both in going ahead of it and in forestalling its arrival at itself. It is the *variété* that is Valéry's rewriting of *Vérité* and explains why he writes in the piece from volume III of *Variété* entitled *Léonard et les philosophes:* "Intellectual effort can no longer be regarded as converging upon a spiritual limit, upon *Truth*" (O I, p. 1240). It assembles a bewildering diversity of functions for which "memory" is as good a word as Valéry can find in common parlance, provided this be understood not as a repository of historical facts, but as disposition and the capacity to vary our response according to variations in circumstances (C 22, p. 109; 5, pp. 55–56). Skill and "schema of all possible movements" (C 3, p. 265), implex is Valéry's retrieval of Kant's *Urteilskraft* and Aristotle's *phronêsis* and *dynamis.* As contingency and counterfactual possibility, implex is the retention-protention of the Now whose implications for Husserlian phenomenology Derrida unravels in *La voix et le phénomène* and whose complications in the texts of Valéry he announces in describing implex, so far as it can be described, as "mathematical exponentiality of the value of presence, of everything the value of presence supports, that is of everything—that *is*" (M 360, M tr. 303). Implex is the eventuality of the event, the *Enteignis* of *Ereignis.* "This value of contingency, eventuality, describes what is at stake in the concept. The implex, a nonpresence, nonconsciousness, an alterity folded over in the *sourdre* of the source." Here Derrida, ventriloquist and mimic at the same time, is glossing Valéry's observation that "One must go back to the *source —*

which is not the *origin*. The *origin*, in all, is *imaginary*. The *source* is the fact within which the imaginary is proposed: water wells up there. Beneath, I do not know what takes place" (C 23, p. 592). I do not know what takes place there because I am made deaf (*sourd*) to what takes place there, supposing there is something that takes place there, supposing there is a place there, supposing there is a there supposed—made deaf to it by the noise of the surging (*sourdre*) of the water, unable to hear (*entendre*) or understand (*entendre*). No simple location. Instead, a *da* as complex as the implex. Indeed the implex and the source are co-implicates. This is why the source is not a simple origin. Implex is capacity incapable of being present to itself and oneself. "'Thinking' (in the sense of *mental work*) *is* therefore *re-thinking*" (C 26, p. 173). "*Recurrence*, repetition—an essential fact. Property of the *present*" (C 15, p. 134). The RE of representation is essential to presentation, externally constitutive of it, Derrida would say. At least where consciousness is consciousness of meaning or ideas, where there is ideality. As soon as there is *eidos*, whether this be understood as Form or Idea or concept or schema or image or impression or sense. Whether it be understood as form or content. As soon as there is presence. The presentation of the *eidos* is a Representation. For the *eidos* is intrinsically extrinsic not only because it is a universal and therefore imports the necessary possibility of another context, but because other contexts are not entirely predictable and because the context is constitutive of the text, constitutive of meaning.

Or, Derrida asks, do what Valéry calls timbre and style escape this law? On the face of it, this might seem to be so. For timbre, on Valéry's account, is what is unique to an author's voice, expressing his haecceity, as does the style of the writing the author leaves behind when he retires from the scene. His irrepeatable fingerprint. We shall discover in the final section of our discussion that Derrida distinguishes two repetitions in order to show that they cannot be separated. Our question here and his question there is how to mark this distinction, how to distinguish the timbre of Derrida's voice from that of Hegel, and how to distinguish their styles. If the repetition intrinsic to the ideality of form and content is liable to becoming interiorized and *aufgehoben* into infinite self-consciousness, what about timbre and style? If there are timbre and style as Valéry defines them—and Derrida warns us that he himself may have reasons for not granting the hypothesis—do they resist self-consciousness? The answer that Derrida extracts from Valéry is that they do. The timbre of my voice and the style of my writing cannot be present to me. They cannot then be present to themselves. They are unrecognizable by me. Their presence is a presence only for the other. Along this path there is no fulfillment of the desire for self-coincidence. The other is not one's own other, but an other that infects auto-affection with hetero-affection, spontaneity with passivity. Since, however, Derrida does not set out along this path, does not embrace the hypotheses of timbre and style as uniquely identifying *je ne sais quoi* and argues elsewhere that no mark is inimitable, he must find some other way to defeat the thought of an event uncontaminated by eventuality. He finds another way in Valéry.

Finds? This question is already the question of originality and the source. It arises everywhere in the texts of philosophy and non-philosophy and in Derrida's readings of them. It can be a relatively superficial question, as when similarities and dissimilarities between the writings of Valéry and Eddington, Valéry and Saussure, Valéry and Freud, Valéry and Nietzsche lead us to ask who read whom and when, the kind of question we ask on an author's birthday, as Derrida puts it (M 356, M tr. 300) Although Eddington's *Space, Time and Gravitation* was in Valéry's library, did he read *The Nature of the Physical World*? Since it was only late in his career that Valéry read Saussure, was the chess analogy suggested to him in his reading of Poincaré's *La valeur de la science*? These questions cause no more serious qualms than that of Shakespeare's indebtedness to Plutarch. They are put in place by Valéry's remark that "The desire for originality is the father of all borrowings/all imitations. Nothing more original, nothing more *oneself* than nourishing oneself on others—But they must be digested. The lion is made of assimilated sheep" (C 6, p. 137, to which is appended: "Originalité—Désirer être SOI. Désirer d'être neuf. Mais *soi* et *néant* font . . . Dix"). Less easily dealt with is that feeling we have of vertigo alternating with relief, when it seems that there is nothing new under the sun, the feeling we get when we begin to believe that Whitehead was right when he said that all philosophy goes back to Aristotle or Plato, but then go on to be struck by how much in Plato and Socrates goes back to the pre-Socratics and beyond them to the Orient. Is what Valéry capitalizes as the ORIENT DE L'ESPRIT the fountainhead of philosophy (O II, p. 1042)? And would that source be an origin?

One could not pursue these questions profitably unless one first distinguished the question of the origin from the question of the beginning. Derrida does not pursue the question of beginning insofar as that would be a question of etiology or etymology. He suspects our common notions of influence and cause, not to mention that of the common root. I suspect that he would not consider it entirely irrelevant to pause for thought, if not to linger, on the etymologies of "find" and "invent," and their common root in the concept of *invenire*. There are some indications that he would endorse the Valérian dictum that "One invents only what invents itself and wants to be invented" or at least the product issuing from a crossing of that with a similar dictum about finding. These indications include the above-mentioned reasons for his unwillingness to endorse the Valérian postulation of timbre and style, one of these reasons being a difficulty over a facile notion of authorship, authenticity, and event (*evenire, Ereignis*) which fails to recognize the complexity of the question as to who, in Derrida's monodialogue with Valéry, for example, is teacher and who is taught. In any reading and writing, do we have a proper idea as to who is master of what and of whom, of who is *seigneur*—or *Monseigneur* (M 353, M tr. 297), who *enseigneur*, who signer? In any dialogue, it is as though it is the ear that speaks, as though one needs to invoke Valéry's monstrous notion of a *Bouchoreille*, especially in the dialogue of the soul with itself; and when one's discourse draws its nourishment from oneself, this notion may call to be supplemented by the notion of otobiography (OA, 11–56).

As we were about to observe, Derrida credits Valéry with recognizing "the paradoxical law . . . that formality, far from simply being opposed to it, *simultaneously* produces and destroys the naturalist, 'originarist' illusion" (M 347, M tr. 292). The only approach to this law is by way of case histories and textual analysis. Before considering briefly two cases that Valéry and Derrida work through together, we should take note that the law in question *intervenes* between the poles of classical philosophical oppositions. It has to do with an essential complicity between the terms, a "structural" complicity, as Derrida sometimes says, leaving it for us to decide whether the inverted commas are scare quotes or not and whether quotation marks of some sort should be used when the paleonym (")essence(") is employed to identify the nature of the unnatural law according to which the classical binary contrasts self-deconstruct. The complicities whose construction and deconstruction this law dictates must be distinguished from confusions arising from an identifiable simple equivocation in one or both of the terms. In the latter case we should have on our hands a contingent complicity removable by disambiguation, a "verbal dispute" of the kind Hume dissolves in the third Appendix of the *Enquiry Concerning the Principles of Morals* by pointing out that justice or property can be both natural and artificial because "natural" may be opposed either to what is miraculous or to what involves social convention. The risk of mistaking a merely semantic confusion for an archi-syntactic complicity would be high if in the case of Valéry's promotion of formalism as opposed to semanticism we lost sight of the difference between his functionalist formalism and the Platonic theory of Forms. This risk is perhaps in Derrida's mind when he follows the statement reproduced at the beginning of this paragraph by saying: "Here we might elaborate the motif of a critique of formalist illusion which would complicate somewhat that which is often considered to be Valéry's formalism." We must also distinguish functionalist formalism, under which Valéry would subsume language quite generally, including everyday speech, and mathematical formalism, whose purity and precision is best exemplified, he suggests, by the graph. What he says of this recalls what Eddington says of the language of modern physics and its basic technical terms as contrasted with the terms of everyday speech:

> The *graph* has a continuity of movement that cannot be rendered in speech, and it is superior to speech in immediacy and precision. Doubtless it was speech that commanded the method to exist; doubtless it is now speech that assigns a meaning to it and interprets it; but it is no longer by speech that the act of mental possession is consummated. One sees taking shape little by little a kind of ideography of the represented (*figurées*) relations between qualities and quantities, a language that has for grammar a body of preliminary conventions (scales, axes, grids, etc.). (O I, pp. 1266–67)[6]

Now it may be that Valéry's *graphique* could be co-opted to introduce us to Derrida's *graphique,* the graphic that supplements logic and takes us beyond semiology to grammatology. Alan Bass thinks so, presumably, when he gives "graphic" as the translation for Valéry's *graphique.* Certainly, Derrida and Valéry are together at least in stressing script and spatiality, and the difference they introduce into the time of speech. But according to Derrida they thereby introduce discontinuity, *écart,* whereas Valéry's "conventional" graph is said to have a "continuity" and determinacy of which natural language is said to be incapable. Leaving aside the question whether the names for Valéry's conventions are as threatened by natural contamination as the vocabulary of Eddingtonian physics (for it is the marks on the graph paper that count), is Valéry's artificial language any purer of naturalism than the technical terms that philosophical writing hopes will furnish more solid planks to bridge the gaps that the words of natural and figurative (*figurée*) speech cannot always be relied on to do? Complicity between Valéry and Derrida there may well be, but that must extend far enough to entail that not only the philosophers whom Valéry attacks but also their assailant are subject to the paradoxical law that Derrida says Valéry recognizes. That this is so is perhaps what Derrida intends to communicate by citing Valéry's assertions that the lines of the graph are "traced by the things themselves" and succeed in "making the laws of science visible to the eyes." (We need have no qualms over attributing intentions to Derrida or anyone else. He has no such qualms himself. What he does have qualms over is a certain philosophical construal of what it is to intend.) If that is Derrida's intention, it is not intended as a criticism. If the unnatural law in question prescribes a structural necessity, one could hardly expect Valéry—or Derrida—to escape it. Valéry, on Derrida's account, is as anxious as any of the philosophers he judges to get back *zu den Sachen selbst,* while being acutely conscious of the ocular and auditory tropes whose employment to describe presence with the things themselves defers that very presence, deprivileges "the very element of our thought in so far as it is caught up in the language of metaphysics" (M 17, M tr. 16). Therefore "Presence is a determination and effect within a system which is no longer that of presence but that of difference." Philosophy appears to be subordinated to non-philosophy because metaphysics is postponed by metaphor. But the predicament is more complex than that, as we shall discover if we look more closely at the philosopher's employment of metaphor.

RESOURCE

Philosophy, says Novalis, has always been the desire to be at home everywhere. The philosopher, Derrida adds, has always tried to satisfy this nostalgia by hearing himself speak. Now Valéry, in Derrida's opinion, appreciated this "better than Husserl, and better than Hegel, who nevertheless had described phonic vibration as the element of temporality, of subjectivity, of interiorization, and of idealization in general, along with everything which thereby systematically lets itself be carried along in the circle of speculative dialectics" (M 341, M tr. 287). So we are in good hands with Valéry to lead us through this labyrinth, a labyrinth that is also a maze of speculative mirrors through which we are lured in the hope of seeing ourselves as we really are, at the source of the light by which we see ourselves.

But the source that would be a *point d'eau*, a point where water comes to light, is at the same time a *point d'eau*, a point where water is lacking. *Point d'eau* is an incalculable syntagm, unsublimatable in the circulation of speculative dialectics, impredicable in the predicate calculus and unpropoundable in propositional logic. Because in the *point d'eau* water's life-giving birth rhymes with water's absolute dearth. Its jet is a throw toward death, the death of the author. Furthermore, how can we understand this image of the source that returns again and again throughout Valéry's work unless we comprehend the literal meaning of origin, *origo*, orient? On the other hand, how do we understand this literal meaning of origin in general except via the relay of metaphor? The proper, literal meaning only pretends to be proper, "se donne comme sens propre."

> Proper meaning derives from derivation. The proper meaning or the primal meaning (of the word *source*, for example) is no longer simply the source, but the deported effect of a turn of speech, a return or detour. It is secondary in relation to that to which it seems to give birth, measuring a separation and a departure from it. The source itself is the effect of that (for) whose origin it passes. One no longer has the right to assimilate, as I have just pretended to do, the proper meaning and the primal meaning. That the proper is not the primal is what Valéry gives us to read. (M 333, M tr. 280)

That is to say, the only way we shall find the source itself will be by losing it. The things themselves to which philosophy dreams of getting back will turn out to be no more than tropes. "Philosophy is reduced to a logic and to a rhetoric or poetics" (C 8, p. 911). The philosopher "borrows metaphor from us [poets] and, by means of splendid images which we might well envy, he draws on all nature for the expression of his profoundest thought." "All nature" is *phusis*, emergence into light, the source "in all," as Derrida says, of whatever light the philosopher casts upon nature, including himself, the transcendental I which Kant distinguishes from the empirical I, the transcendental phenomenological consciousness that Husserl says is parallel to and covered by the purely psychological (VP 10, SP 11), the pure universal I that Valéry distinguishes from the person and has no relation with a face, "n'a pas de rapport avec un visage" (C 8, p. 104, O I, p. 1229). The pure I is neither the eye that sees nor what the eye sees. Yet Valéry is constrained to say that it is like a glance. The invisible I is figured through the visible eye of the face (*figure*), hidden by what shows it forth, doubly hidden when Narcissus sees himself mirrored in the water of the source. "Glance of the figure, figure of the glance, the source is always divided" (M 340, M tr. 285). Like the serpent's tongue.

The source itself cannot present itself to sight. Can it perhaps hear itself speak? Once again derivation is derived. The *causa sui* turns out to be a causeless effect. "In the return of the phonic circle, the source appears as such only at the moment, which is no longer a moment, the barely second second, of the instant emission in which the origin yields itself to receive what it produces" (M 342, M tr. 288). The phonic circuit is interrupted. In biting its own tail the serpent poisons itself. The pure I becomes impure as soon as its indestructible desire to hear itself speak is fulfilled and frustrated because it can hear itself speak only when its voice has become the voice of its ear. (The source has *become*. Another incalculable syntagm.) I find myself constitutionally incapable of finding myself. I wait for myself forever in my own queue. I am here, *da*, but I am simultaneously *fort*, elsewhere (C 10, p. 407, O II, p. 885, CP, 214, PC 199). Two moments of myself at one moment, a sending-receiving feedback. "What comes to 'mind'—to the lips—modifies you yourself in return. What you have just emitted, emits toward you, and what you have produced fecundates you. In saying something without having foreseen it, you see it like a foreign fact, an *origin*—something you had not known. You were delayed in relation to yourself" (C 12, p. 24, C 6, p. 195).

It is important to note that this description of the auto-hetero-affection that takes place in the monodialogue of the soul with itself is in principle indistinguishable from and inevitably modeled on the description of uttered communication with another. But the communication between the silent inner communication and the public communication is incommunicable. Like the identity of Eddington's table no. 1 and table no. 2, which are the same thing although we cannot answer literally the question, "Namely what?" Like the difference Husserl posits between transcendental and purely psychological consciousness, a difference for which "All names are lacking," there is here a "supplementary nothing" that gives us pause (Valéry delights in the etymological connection he supposes between *pausa* and *positum*), an unpresentable chiasmus that "passe donc l'entendement," exceeds hearing and understanding, perception and conception, exceeds the Concept. Exceeds philosophy, unless the philosopher, recognizing that non-philosophy is the constitutive outside of philosophy, recognizes that he must borrow metaphors, like the metaphors that Derrida borrows from Hegel, Husserl, Heidegger, and Valéry to track to its source the illusion that the sourcepoint (*Quellpunkt* writes Husserl in section 13 and Part II of the *Phenomenology of Internal Time Consciousness*) is primal, and to recite that the birth pangs (*Qual Quelle* writes Derrida, rewriting Hegel rewriting what Boehme writes in *Aurora*) of the unquenchable desire for the living present (ED 291, WD 194) are in undecidable complicity with the pain of passing beyond being to death: death, which is metaphor quite literally, if the literal may be no more than a metaphor that is dead, if that hypothesis makes sense.

PROTÊ PHILOSOPHIA

It is beginning to look as though the beginning of so-called first philosophy is philosophy's end, as though non-philosophy is, in Kant's words, "the death of all philosophy" (DTA 57, FH 463), a death than which nothing would be more natural: extrinsic, yet intrinsic; beyond philosophy's grave, yet at its center of gravity.

But there are two deaths in the case of "la mort de la philosophie" (M 323, M tr. 271), a double degeneration, de-generation, corresponding to the duplicity of the genitivity of "of," of *de:* a recto death no. 1 and a verso death no. 2. Since if we have seen reason to concede to Derrida that metaphor and non-philosophy lie beyond philosophy and are to metaphysics a metametaphysics—a metametataphysics, we might say, in memory of Aristotle, Eddington, and Anatole France (M 252, M tr. 212), we must now ask whether we should not also agree that philosophy, "simultaneously life and death" (ED 291–92, WD 194), incorporates non-philosophy insofar as by non-philosophy we understand the metaphorical. For what do we understand by the metaphorical, insofar as we understand it at all? In understanding the nature of the metaphorical we grasp an idea or form a concept, namely the idea or concept of an expression not used in its literal or proper sense. It therefore belongs to the same system as the literal and the proper. It remains a metaphysical concept (M 261, M tr. 219). As Susan Stebbing says, the opposition of the literal or proper that gives "metaphorical" what meaning it has assumes we understand the meaning of propriety, understand what propriety means literally and properly. But how can we understand properly what metaphor is, how can we have a philosophical understanding of metaphor, if the idea we are to grasp is "itself" not itself, because the very idea of idea—from *eidô,* to see—is metaphorical? "Philosophy, as a theory of metaphor, will first have been a metaphor of theory"—from *theôriô,* to look (M 303, M tr. 254)? Or can the distinctness of the opposition be salvaged by saying that the so-called primary metaphors on which philosophy depends—idea, concept, intuition, consciousness, etc.—are dead metaphors? Can we preserve philosophy by saying that the concept of idea and the idea of concept originally referred to concrete operations of states like grasping with the hands or seeing with the eye thanks to the natural light of the sun, then came to be employed metaphorically of intellectual functions and capacities, and finally came to lose even that metaphorical force, as Hegel, for example, says (M 268, M tr. 225)? Can we say with Nietzsche and Anatole France's Polyphilos that the basic terms of philosophy may be compared to coins whose relief has been so worn down that they have lost their cash value as coins of the realm, have "gone west," become the currency of the universe of philosophical discourse where they wear their nudity like the emperor wears his new clothes?

This contrast between living and worn-out metaphors might suffice to keep alive in daily use the opposition between what we call the literal and the metaphorical. It would not suffice to permit a purely philosophical account of that opposition, because that account would be dependent on the non-philosophical, on the metaphor of wear. We should still lack a meta-phorology. We should have in our hands no more than effects of literality and metaphor.

> This extra metaphor, remaining outside the field that it allows to be circumscribed, extracts or abstracts itself from this field, thus subtracting itself as a metaphor less. By virtue of what we might entitle, for reasons of economy, tropic supplementarity, since the extra turn of speech becomes the missing turn of speech, the taxonomy or history of philosophical metaphors will never make a profit. (M 261, M tr. 220)

The disappearance of metaphor (*plus de métaphore*) becomes the supple-mentary metaphor (*plus de métaphore*). The reduction of relief promises to compensate the bearer with relief, *Aufhebung*, into pure philosophy, thought thinking itself, but the pure philosophical thought is not forthcoming. *La métaphysique relève de la philosophie*. Philosophy sublates and interiorizes non-philosophy, but philosophy is "itself" non-philosophical. Its *for intérieur*, the source of its authority, is *fors*, transported outside itself: meta-phor; but, because accidentality is of its essence, the phor or vehicle is also in the *for*, the tenor or so-called theme. So the time of the thesis is unpunctual, deferred, out of joint. The position is de-posed, the locus displaced. The very instruments with which philosophy is to divide the chicken at its joints are divided against themselves. Hence, when Aristotle set up as the rule of philosophy absolute distinctness of sense (M 295, M tr. 248), he was inviting the charge that he was infringing that other rule of his, "to look for precision in each class of things just so far as the nature of the subject admits" (*Nic. Ethics* 1094b, 25). He was overlooking the possibility that philosophy and logic are no more than functions or effects of "an unheard of *graphic*" that is "an inscription of the relations between the philosophical and the non-philosophical," and that these relations are undecidable (ED 163, WD 110–11). Philosophy gets carried away by metaphor and metaphor "gets carried away with itself, cannot be what it is except in erasing itself, indefinitely constructing its destruction" (M 320, M tr. 268).

This suicide may be conceived, on the one hand, as the death suffered at their own hands by the philosophical figures of the *Phenomenology of Spirit* and the *Lectures on the History of Philosophy*, where their passing away is a passing upward into an anamnetic recollection of a truth that saves them for an ultimate atonement of thought infinitely thinking itself. Or, secondly, it may be the death in this alleged infinite self-presence, the death of the Concept, of Philosophy, "the death of a philosophy which does not see itself die and is no longer to be refound within philosophy"; the strewn ashes of truth: strewth.

Corresponding to these homonymous deaths are two homonymous rep-etitions and two *glas*. Repetition no. 1 is that of the sameness of the *eidos* and the Idea, of identity and resemblance. Even family resemblance belongs here with Platonic and Hegelian life-sustaining economic return surely, if we can say what Derrida, paraphrasing Du Marsais, says of the metaphor of the borrowed dwelling:

> it is a metaphor of metaphor; an expropriation, a being-outside-one's-own residence, but still in a dwelling, outside its own residence but still in a residence in which one comes back to oneself, recognizes oneself, reassembles oneself or resembles oneself, outside oneself in oneself. This is the philosophical metaphor as a detour within (or in sight of) reappropriation, parousia, the self-presence of the idea in its own light. The metaphorical trajectory from the Platonic *eidos* to the Hegelian Idea. (M 302, M tr. 353)

Repetition no. 1 is the repetition of typicality, essence, meaning, truth, consciousness, phenomenology, philosophy. Repetition no. 2 is the repetition of the typographical lapsus, of the accident when "the words come apart," when "bits and pieces of sentences are separated," when "the presence of what is gets lost" (D 195–96, D tr. 168–69); the repetition of unconsciousness, non-truth, and non-philosophy. It is the *glas* of the death knell's trembling motion, while repetition no. 1 is *glas* as living voice, *répétition vivante* (Gl 89 (107), Gl tr. 76). Derrida tells us that his title *La voix et le phénomène* becomes in Slovene *Glas in phenomen.* An audio-visual Anglo-Slovene scanning of this teaches the lesson that repetition no. 1 and repetition no. 2 are not parallels; they are related chiasmically, as are the two deaths and the two *glas. Glas* no. 1 as *viva voce* is in the phenomenon which according to post-Platonic phenomenology presents itself to consciousness as intimately as the voice that hears itself speak; so it already involves an intermixing of metaphors that Derrida marks with the image of the tympanum, which is, *entre autres,* the eardrum and the usually triangular panel above a doorway in which there is sometimes pierced a circular opening called an *oculus* (M XVII, M tr. xxii). *Glas* no. 2 is not heard by him for whom the bell tolls. (Did he overhear his death rattle, his final glottal full stop?) Where *glas* no. 1 is timbre, phone, and mnemic remembrance, *glas* no. 2 is style, graph, and the forgetfulness that requires the hypomnetic *aide-mémoire.* Yet *glas* no. 1 is where *glas* no. 2 "is," as repetition no. 2 is a repetition of repetition no. 1, the rehearsal of it that has differed and deferred the première from time immemorial.

The first is always second. First philosophy is non-philosophy or, since the "non" here should not be taken to imply a parallelist opposition, un- or in-philosophy, which is in philosophy, but indecidably (*indécidablement),* because philosophy is not simply in itself. Philosophy is exposed to the accidents of history no less than is the table on which it is written, whether this be the familiar solid and substantial piece of furniture of the earth on which Eddington composed the Gifford lectures he delivered at Edinburgh in a living tongue, the *pinax* and *tabula* of which his predecessors spoke in languages now dead, or the unearthly Paradigmatic Table Itself that is supposed never to become a paradigm case and is unutterable in any language, living, dead, or not yet born. And if philosophy is exposed to the accidents of history, so too is history. History is a history of accidents. Of necessity. Cruel necessity, Artaud would say (ED 291, WD 194). Beneath the syntactico-semantic law that is a principle of composition and classification, as its unoriginary and unprimal source, is an anasyntactic law of decomposition, like an inky-fingered *malin génie*, a printer's devil that deconstructs the typographical forms behind the compositor's back. This law of the law of genre, genus, generation, gender, family resemblance, kith, kin, kind, nature, essence, class, figure, form, and type makes distinct sense possible as theatrical function, staged performance, effect of a so-called "primal" scene, but impossible and impositable except as *mise en scène;* because "Beneath, I do not know what takes place." I am stone-deaf to it. The table of the law of the law of genre is "mostly emptiness." This metalaw "manages to do no more than transgress the figure of all possible representation. Which is difficult to conceive, as it is difficult to conceive anything at all beyond representation, but commits us perhaps to thinking altogether differently" (Ps 143, E 326, S 326). To thinking altogether differently the distinction between philosophy and non-philosophy.

4

IN THE NAME OF PHILOSOPHY

that anagram of "name," "Amen"

—JOHN LLEWELYN (in this work)

IN THE NAME OF GOD

In the discussion which followed Levinas's presentation at Louvain of the paper entitled "The Name of God in Certain Talmudic Texts," Antoine Vergote points out that Levinas had said that the revelation of the name of God is a relation which is irreducible to knowledge but had denied that ethical responsibility before another human being is a relation. Was Levinas not therefore inconsistent when he maintained that the divine revelation can be equated with (*se ramène à*) human responsibility (II 232)? Levinas replies by distinguishing two senses of "relation." As ordinarily understood a relation is a compresence of at least two terms (II 256). But God is not present as a term. Each of God's names is a proper name subsumed under the common name Name. His proper names—namely, *El* or *Eloha* or *Elohim* (God), *Shaddai* (Almighty), *Dayyan* (Judge), *Rachum* (Merciful), *Hannun* (Gracious), *Tzaddik* (Righteous), *Adonai* (My Lord), etc.—name modes of God's presence, but that presence is not a presence of a term. It is a proximity (*shekhinah*) in an absence and separation denoted by the words "holy," "*saint,*" "*kadosh.*" Hence the revelation of the name of God and ethical responsibility before the other is no ordinary relation. It is not a relation to a term, so it is not a knowledge. It is an extraordinary and absolute Relation, but not absolute knowledge.

Any difficulties that arise from Levinas's word "Relation" taken in this sense will arise too once we ask, as it is the chief purpose of the present chapter to ask, about the relation between the conception of philosophy expounded in, for example, *Otherwise than Being or Beyond Essence* and the conception of philosophy which this book says is traditionally associated with that name. In this book Levinas epitomizes his conception of philosophy as "the wisdom of love at the service of love" (AE 207, OB 162). On his understanding of the traditional acceptance of the word "philosophy" the wisdom (*sophia*) of which the name of philosophy says that it is the love or desire is a virtue ultimately grounded in a theoretical or practical knowledge of the highest kinds of being: sameness and difference, one and many, etc.

For at least three reasons it would be injudicious to yield to the temptation to epigrammatize Levinas's philosophy of philosophy by saying that in it the priority ascribed traditionally to the kind is shifted to kindness. First, because what Levinas understands by absolute responsibility and goodness beyond being is not benevolence or any other natural disposition. Secondly, because the "-ness" of kindness and goodness means that they too are each a kind, whether a lower kind or the highest, like that of which the common name is "the Name" and under which are assembled the different modalities or attributes of which the proper names are *El, Elohim, Adonai, Shaddai,* etc. Thirdly, because the virtue of wisdom as understood in traditional philosophy is concerned not only with being, the kinds into which it is divided and how the highest of these are related to each other; it is concerned not only with such objects of theoretical knowledge; it is concerned also with objectives of action such as the Platonic Good beyond being and the Neo-Platonic One. Anyone reading Levinas's writings with a view to determining how his conception of philosophy as the wisdom of love in the service of love relates to traditional philosophy as ontology will be struck by the frequency with which he draws upon philosophers of Platonic and Neo-Platonic lineage. This lineage includes Kant, for instance, as made manifest in the use Levinas makes of Husserl's phrase "Ideas in a Kantian sense." The Ideas here referred to are said by Kant himself to be derivatives of Ideas in a Platonic sense. The Ideas in both of these senses admit of a teleological interpretation, with Plato's Good yielding in Kant the notion of a Highest Good consisting in happiness in proportion to virtue. That is to say, there are elements in the philosophies of Plato and Kant which permit assimilation to the philosophy of Aristotle. It is not in such assimilation that Levinas perceives glimpses of philosophy as wisdom of love. Such eschatological interpretation of Ideas is typical of philosophy understood as love of wisdom. Even so, if the latter understanding of philosophy is represented by Aristotle, it should not be overlooked that he entertains the thought of *nous* entering the soul from outside.[1] That is a thought which Levinas would welcome as a hint toward the philosophy of philosophy as wisdom of love which the philosophy of philosophy as love of wisdom tends to hide. For this coming in from outside broaches the thought of a non-negative "reversal" of the direction of the intentionality which according to Husserl defines all so-called "mental acts" where this phrase refers not only to conceiving but also to the intuiting which for Kant is a mental passivity. When this last word is employed in contrast with activity or spontaneity by Levinas and in commentaries upon or translations of the writings of Kant, it should be noted that in those places where Kant's own word is not *Rezeptivität*, it is usually replaceable by this word. A reception party is not taken by surprise when the guest of honor arrives. Preparations have been made for the guest's arrival. In the philosophy of Kant those preparations have been made by the forms of intuition or receptivity, namely, space and time. Remembering this helps us to remember how the non-negative "reversal" of intentionality is a revision of the theories of space and time of Kant. For related reasons it is a revision too of the theories of space and time of Newton, of Leibniz and, more poignantly, of Heidegger, whose first accounts of space and time perceive Kant's doctrine of time through a lens provided by Husserl. In none of these ancient and modern predecessors does Levinas perceive more than glimpses of the accounts of temporality and spatiality which he outlines. If this is in any way a criticism of those predecessors, it is one that is accompanied by an admission of mitigating circumstances. Philosophy as the love of or desire for wisdom may not allow more than glimpses of what Levinas wishes his readers to see—or echoes of what he wishes us to hear. So it will in turn be no criticism of Levinas himself if after reading and rereading his work we feel that no more than glimpses or echoes have been vouchsafed. Pertinent to this is his acknowledgment of the importance for his own thinking of Vladimir Jankélévitch's philosophy of the glimpse (*entrevision*), as set out particularly in the latter's *La philosophie première*.[2]

TWO FIRST PHILOSOPHIES. LEVINAS AND JANKÉLÉVITCH

Jankélévitch's title translates the phrase *protê philosophia*, which for Levinas names the ethical, *l'éthique,* as distinguished from an ethics or a morality, *une éthique.* First philosophy has an ethical resonance also for Jankélévitch who, like Levinas, equates the ethical or proto-moral with metaphysics: "once it ceases to be a pure cognitive and synonymic deduction of duties, morality is no longer distinguishable from metaphysics."[3] Both authors contrast the ethical with the continuity upon which Bergson's doctrine of creative evolution is based. Jankélévitch had published a critical study of Bergson in 1931, and Levinas's project may be seen as an attempt, in the wake of what he considers to be Bergson's abortive one, to indicate a place or quasi-place for the radically new. These two readers of Bergson give an extra twist to Bergson's criticism of the theories of time and space expounded in Kant's first *Critique*, where it is maintained that time is the form of inner sense. Bergson maintains that the Kantian form of inner sense mimics space, the form of outer sense. Levinas goes back to this Bergsonian Kant and contends that there is indeed a certain spatiality to time. However, this spatiality—the Exteriority which the subtitle of *Totality and Infinity* proclaims to be the subject of that book—is no longer the homogeneous continuum in which physical objects are located, but an ethical externality which interrupts the consciousness of internal time whose continuity is assured according to Kant by memory and anticipation in the transcendental unity of apperception and according to Husserl by the retentions, recollections, protentions, and expectations investigated in his lectures on *The Phenomenology of Internal Time Consciousness*. Levinas glimpses the possibility of what might be provisionally named a phenomenology of the non-consciousness of external space in the references made in the fifth of the *Cartesian Meditations* (the one he himself translated) to the "awakening" (*Sich-wecken*) of one human being to consciousness of another. This denomination is provisional insofar as phenomenology is taken to be a way of studying consciousness and insofar as consciousness is taken to be noetic-noematic. Those criteria imply that Levinas goes on to practice ultra-phenomenology when he interprets the ethical as the exteriority to itself of temporality, the invasion of dia-chrony into the unity of retentive and protentive time. If that *outré* phenomenology can be said to be still a study of consciousness, consciousness can no longer be held to be always straight-forwardly intentional.

Levinas argues that awakening to co-consciousness is secondary to an awakeness of conscience which is not to be compared with an awakening into consciousness from sleep, but is rather a modification of an insomnia, a sleeplessness, a waking or a vigilance which falls outside the opposition of consciousness and unconsciousness. It interrupts continuous duration as conceived both by Husserl and Bergson. Although according to Bergson duration augments being with something absolutely new, according to Levinas this "newness of springtimes that flower in the instant (which, in good logic, is like the prior one) is already heavy with all the springtimes lived through" (TeI 260, TaI 283). Against this, he objects,

> The work of time goes beyond the suspension of the definitive which the continuity of duration makes possible. There must be a rupture of continuity, and continuation across this rupture. The essential in time consists in being a drama, a multiplicity of acts where the later act is the dénouement of the first. (Ibid.)

It is Nietzsche whom Levinas cites in clarifying the sense of "drama" intended here, drama not simply as deed but as religious event, occurrence, or enactment or ritual performance (*Ereignis*). In the pages of *Totality and Infinity* where the sentence just cited is found, the particular enactment in question is forgiving, a ceremony through which is conducted both a connection between a forgiving son and a father and the beginning of a new time. This time of triumph and triumph of time, Levinas ironically implies, brings about the death of Father Parmenides. In subverting the dense duration of Bergsonism, Levinas and Jankélévitch are letting air into the changeless being of the Eleatics. In his approach to this task Jankélévitch too invokes cognates of the verb *draô*. He writes of drastic positing or thesis. This corresponds in some respects to one of the senses in which Levinas writes of the hypostasis of the ego as identity turning into the hypostasis of the self as ipseity responsible for the other human being. Responsibility is the passivity to which reference has already been made, the passivity which Levinas says is more passive than the passivity of receptivity traditionally opposed to activity. This spontaneous activity traditionally opposed to passivity is not the dramatic performance to which allusion has just been made. In Levinas's conception of first philosophy the latter is prior to the traditional philosophical distinction between the active and the passive, as in the conception of first philosophy held by Jankélévitch it precedes both the level of the empirical datum with which the passivity of intuition is usually associated and the level of the logical which is traditionally taken to be the exercise of an "active intellect." What Jankélévitch calls drastic positing is both meta-empirical and metalogical. It is original decision or fiat. As such it is prior to predicative judgment, prior to form and content. Decisive of the *that* of existence in abstraction from the *what* of essence, it is, Jankélévitch says, the excluded third between being and non-being. Now although for Jankélé-vitch, as we shall go on to confirm, this excluded third is creation and for Levinas it is ethical responsibility, we shall go on to confirm too that for Jankélévitch creation has an ethical dimension.

If Jankélévitch claims that creative fiat is the excluded third between being and non-being, how can he also make the claim that the sheer and mere *that* of bringing into existence—*existentia*—has an ethical dimension? Does not the ethical imply law and therefore form or/and content—*essentiâ* and *quid*? Not if we make for Jankélévitch the distinction between the ethical and an ethics or ethic on which Levinas insists. *La philosophie première* leaves us in no doubt that it is to a metanomic ethical or moral force that the author of that book is referring when he writes of metalogical existence and decision. If we deny him the right to speak of the ethical in this way we have to deny the corresponding right to Levinas. To do that would be to take away the pivot on which Levinas's entire philosophy turns. Recall too that Levinas's account of the ethical appeals to what he calls illeity, and the ending -ty would normally be understood to have the same force as -ness, as for example in "goodness" and "kindness," both of which words are translatable by Levinas's "*bonté*," the word used by him to mark what according to Plato himself underlies and exceeds a Greekly philosophical concept of kind even though the meaning of the second syllable of Levinas's word is itself patently supported by that very concept. Even though? Precisely because. For the unGreek unconcept which enables the concept to breathe must run the risk of being submerged by the latter. Like the Israelites passing between the momentarily parted waves of the Red Sea, philosophy, as Levinas frequently says, echoing Plato again, must run the fine risk (AE 24, OB 20).[4]

If one consequence of taking the *beau risque* is the danger of enveloping in the concept what is prior to the concept, another is the danger of the confusion of postconceptual *illeité* with the preconceptual *il y a*. Like Levinas (and Blanchot), Jankélévitch uses the latter phrase of sheer impersonal existence devoid of existents: *quod* without *quid* or *quis,* devoid and hyphen-atedly de-void, that is to say empty even of complete emptiness and of the nothingness that is opposed to being. For the *ti esti* and the *hoti esti* are both *esti,* and the idea of existence implies that of something that might exist. Sheer or mere existence is not itself something, nor is it nothing. It is an almost nothing, a *presque rien.* The *nescioquid* or *on ne sait quoi* of Jankélé-vitch's *il y a* is haunted. It even carries the hint of malevolence and menace of the *il y a* as described by Levinas. Its *il* is an *il* that advenes, *advient.*[5] It is an almost nothing that approaches. And it provokes the kind of intellectual discomfiture, bad conscience, and malaise that is associated with aporia by

Plato, with the threat of the *malin génie* by Descartes and with a *mal d'amour* in *The Song of Songs* (AE 181, OB 142, 198). *The Song of Songs* admits of being read or sung as at once a poem of erotic nostalgia and a hymn to God. It can be taken as a symbol for the boundary in the work of Levinas between two ways of being bound: being bound to the enjoyment of being and the binding of ethical *religio*. This double bind to both the enjoyment of the fruits of the earth and to the other human being in a manner other than that of enjoyment is temporarily resolved only when, via the experience of the threat to the security and permanence of that enjoyment—for to enjoy something is to court the fine risk of its loss—the *il* of the *il y a* is converted into the *il* of an illeity which is still third personal, but not impersonal like the *il* of the *il y a*. This temporary resolution is far from being an elimination of a threat to my security. Rather is it an exposure to persecution by the thought of the fact that I can commit the crime of Cain, by the thought that as an occupant of a certain place in the sun I am already the usurper, though through no fault of my own—so on *ontological* grounds?—of a place in the sun that another might have occupied and therefore as such I already owe others something like a debt of reparation. I am persecuted further by the very thought that if my debt is one of reparation it is one that I owe as a term in a system of exchange which supports me and my egologicality. I am still further persecuted by the thought that as a *thought* of my debt my indebtedness is made easier to live with because the wounding edge of the accusation is blunted through being accommodated in a network of concepts. Although "The call to infinite responsibility confirms the subjectivity in its apologetic position" (TeI 223, TaI 245), more than an intellectual *apologia pro vita mea* is called for. The goods of the earth which I took to be given to me call to be given to the orphan, the widow, or the stranger who are or who represent everyone other than me. It is in this sense that is to be interpreted the absolute relation referred to in the opening paragraphs of this chapter. Relation is to be understood concretely as *rapport* and as *rapporter,* that is to say as giving, to the point of giving the gift of my life. Less dramatically, it also means giving the means of sustaining life, hence the giving of hard cash. *Rapport* is revenue, product and yield. The ethical on Levinas's account of it has an "economic base"—or an indispensable economic superstructure, for the ethical is an-archic, but it must employ the economic, the technological, and the political in responding to the call not to endanger the other's life. "This is the great paradox of human existence: we must use the ontological *for love of the other.*"[6] The ontological is what Jankélévitch and Bergson would call an *organe-obstacle.* It is both a limitation of and an instrument of the ethical. We use therefore not only the means-and-ends mechanism of commercial exchange but also that of linguistic communication and the conceptuality of the third-personal He and It intermediate between the preconceptual and prepredicative *il* of the *il y a* and the postconceptual *il* of *illéité.* Of postconceptual *illéité,* one would need to say here if one followed Derrida's practice in *Adieu,* as in this chapter I do not, of using the word

71

illéité not only of the tertiality Levinas introduces into his gloss on the word "God," but also of the tertiality of the third human being.[7] Note too, however, that it is also Derrida's practice in *Adieu* to supplement some of his readings of Levinas with concessions to the effect that "no doubt Levinas does not say that in this form," "even if Levinas never says this in this way," "in terms that are not literally Levinas's," "although Levinas does not call it this," "whether or not he spoke of this directly," etc.[8] Whether or not Levinas does call both the conceptual and the postconceptual tertiality *illéité*—and in at least one place in *Otherwise than Being* he refuses a golden opportunity to apply this word to what I am calling conceptual tertiality (AE 193, OB 151)—there is a kind of structural analogy between these two tertialities which calling them both *illéité* would mark. Or rather, there is a quasi-kind of quasi-structural quasi-analogy here. For what I have called postconceptual tertiality, in order to distinguish it from the tertiality of the third human person with whom conceptuality appears on the scene, is also preconceptual and therefore prior to kind, structure, and analogy. Having asserted that the tertiality of *illéité* is not the same as the tertiality of the third human being, Levinas goes on to remind his reader that he elsewhere equates *illéité* with the *trace* as unthematizable allegiance before any contractual oath, obedience to an order which comes not from any place where may be sought an authority like an idol or assumed like a principle, but which comes from my own "imprudent" signing over of myself when I say, before anything conceptual and informative is understood or heard or said, "I am here." These words precede the apriority of Greek *logos* and their "here" displaces the "there" of Dasein's maintenance of the structures of readiness and presence to hand in its now. The *maintenant* of that present moment is outstripped by the *main-tenant* of one who responds to the command not to let another die alone. That command, "Thou shalt not kill," and all that it implies, is one I hear only in the utterance of my response. It is a command which Levinas describes as *august*. We could also describe it as Augustinian. For among the texts where Levinas suspects that what he means by the ethical can be glimpsed is the paragraph of the tenth chapter of the *Confessions* which distinguishes the truth which may be open to proof, *veritas lucens,* truth which makes things visible to our regard, from the truth which opens us to reproof, *veritas redarguens,* the invisible *vérité regardante* which Levinas calls sincerity.

Because the illeity which is postconceptual in the expository order of *Time and the Other* and *Totality and Infinity* is a tertiality, it is liable to be confused with the tertiality of the *tertius quis.* This risk is enhanced by the fact that both of these tertialities are protective. The latter protects against the violence of what would otherwise be a pure duality in the face-to-face encounter. The former protects against a too-chummy relationship with the Infinite, very much as love of the Torah prevents a too-intimate love of God.[9] Because illeity is discovered to be preconceptual, older than anything that can be remembered, it is liable to be confused with preconceptual and prepredicative ilyaity.

The *Kehre* from the prepredicative *il* of ilyaity to the postpredicative *il* of illeity with which Levinas says the former could be mistakenly confused is a turn from It to He. Between these two, in the order of emergence of propositions in his genealogy of ethics, Levinas conjugates a discrete, intimate, and feminine Thou and an indiscrete masculine You. Via aesthetic sensibility and critical conceptuality, the impersonal It, resonant with the menace of *tohu-bohu*, impersonates the You and the He whose accusative and persecutory call to me is the ultra-essence of the ethical. What risk do we run if we ask whether there might be an etymological connection in Greek between *to kalon*, the fine, the beautiful, or the fair, and *kaleô*, to call or to summon, bearing in mind that the fair denotes both the good-looking and the just, both *apparaître* as visible appearance and *comparaître* as appearance before a court of law. What risk do we run if we ask whether there might be an etymological connection in Hebrew between the *eeytay* (אִ יְתַי), there is or *il y a*, and *eetay*, also written *eeytay* (יְתַ אִ), for which Gesenius's Lexicon suggests "neighboring," and which suggests *eteey*, ethical. If all these words are neighboring, there will be a precedent for the liability of the It of ilyaity to be confused with the ethical He of illeity, a liability which increases the liability of this ethical He to be confused in its turn with a religious He. If the ethical He can be distinguished from the confessionally religious He, would it be a mistake to confuse it with what Jankélévitch calls the *Lui-même*, a pronoun which, like the *il* of *illéité*, preserves an ambiguity between Itself and Himself? In turning from the impersonal It via aesthetic poiesis to the personal and ethical He, Levinas is turning from the sacred to the holy in the senses which the *sacré* and the *saint* have in those contexts where Levinas counts it necessary to contrast these two words with each other. This is a turning away from Jankélévitch.

At the defense at the Sorbonne of the doctoral dissertation which Levinas was to publish under the title *Totalité et Infini* in 1961, Jankélévitch was a member of the jury. There was only one other member, Jean Wahl. The third was to have been Merleau-Ponty, but he had died before the defense took place. Both Wahl and Jankélévitch were very impressed by the candidate and Jankélévitch remarked "it's you who should be sitting where I am."[10] Then, having expressed regret at the absence from the dissertation of a detailed discussion of the work of Bergson, he went on to provide that himself. The references made above to themes in the work of Jankélévitch may have given the impression that Levinas did go on to occupy the philosophical position to which the former subscribed. That he had no intention of going that far became evident during those proceedings at the Sorbonne when the candidate interrupted his examiner's variations on a Bergsonian theme, saying "Listen, Monsieur Jankélévitch, what you do is poetry, what I do is prose." One may still wonder whether that statement marks a clear philosophical break between the two men. Jankélévitch does indeed hold that the topic of philosophy should not be what he calls the prosaic. Philosophy should regard the prosaic rather as spatiality and chronology are regarded in the philosophy of Bergson, namely, as extinguished cinder. Works of authentic philosophy are fireworks. The true philosopher should be where the sparks fly up. But the scintilla can only be glimpsed, half-seen, *entrevue*. Neither plainly visible nor totally invisible, the scintilla's instantaneity permits only the fleeting access of an intuitive intervision. The object of philosophy is not an object. In philosophy "there is for sure only the indiscernible nuance of an Almost (*un Presque*): but this Almost is the whole of philosophy." As Levinas says of meditation on Shakespeare, the whole of philosophy might be meditation on the almost of the moment of decision between the to be and not to be, meditation on death (TA 60, TO 72). And nearer to the whole of philosophy than the system as described by Hegel might be Derrida's "almost absolute proximity to Hegel" (P 60, P tr. 44), or the ab-solute proximity, the separation in nearness, between Jankélévitch and Levinas with regard to what calls to be said and done in the name of philosophy.

If close behind Hegel stands Aristotle, behind Hegel stands too Plotinus. Plotinus is an advocate for the defense of Plato against the case for the prosecution conducted by Aristotle. It has been said of Plotinus that he "uses Plato in the way the mystics use *The Song of Songs*."[11] Now the *Enneads* are among the works most frequently cited by Jankélévitch, and one of the passages to which he refers is the one from *Enneads* V, 5, 5, cited by Levinas several times, in which a philosophical monotheism is affirmed:

> When it is a question of the principle prior to entities, the One, this reposes in itself; but even though it remains intact it is not a thing different from it that produces entities in conformity with it; it suffices to engender them . . . here, the trace of the One brings about the birth of essence, and the entity is only the trace of the One.

Among other sentences of the *Enneads* to which Jankélévitch refers are those which Derrida adopts as an exergue for his "note on the phenomenology of language" entitled "La forme et le vouloir-dire": "form is the trace of the formless" (M 187, M tr. 157). But there are two kinds of formlessness, or rather two formlessnesses neither of which is a kind. These are liable to be confused with each other, as Levinas observes of *illéité* and the *il y a*, and as Jankélévitch observes of the unspeakable alpha-unthingness of God and the unspeakable omega-unthingness of matter. "Plotinus sometimes characterizes matter almost in the same terms as the One: amorphous, unqualifiable . . ."—uncharacterizable, the difference being a difference of direction between, on the one hand, the point of departure of procession and the terminus at which conversion aims, and, on the other hand, the point from which conversion begins and the terminus of emanation. But there is all the world of difference between the deathly nothingness of the latter and the "fecund productivity" of the former. Jankélévitch emphasizes that for Plotinus there is more at stake than the difference between being and nothingness, therefore more than is sometimes supposed to be at stake in the question why there is anything at all and why things have the forms that they do. The principle which answers these questions cannot have any form. If it did we should have in consistency to ask those questions over again. Yet if the principle which explains everything has no form, how can it escape being anything other than nothing? But the origin of any thing cannot be nothing. It must be a something. Of this something we can say only that it is an almost nothing, something I know not what. It is because it is an amorphous almost nothing that it is a something I know not what. The producer or the creator or first positor, Himself, *Lui-même,* cannot be known.

Parmenides would deny that there is room sensibly to posit a first positor, for he would deny that it makes sense to posit a beginning of sheer being. But the motive for asking what first generates things and their kinds is a motive for asking what keeps in existence a continuity that had no beginning. In the second case we invoke a notion of eternity which we think of on analogy with infinite time. In the first case we picture an event that took place in "an infinite immemorial past that has never been present."[12] These words extracted from Jankélévitch's reflections on first philosophy could have been taken from Levinas's reflections on the same subject, but in the latter context they would mean something quite different. Even when Jankélévitch links them to the notion of a commandment, the commandment is the cosmogonical Fiat of creation following which every *quod* is the referent of a passive past participle of the *to ti ên einai.* Philosophy as practiced by Jankélévitch endeavors to recreate the unformed act of creation. It is a drastic decision which cannot be fully predetermined by the articulation of the joints of the world. It is a disruption of the order of the world. Like Levinas, Jankélévitch cites more than once the "To be or not to be" of Hamlet. He does so in the course of suggesting that the topic of philosophy is the unconceptual middle between being and non-being. First philosophy is not ontology or meontology. It is metalogy and therefore metontology. Its topic is the passing instant of creative production beyond and anterior to being, the instant which is

> the fine adamantine apex of intuition, of courage or joy, which is, to denote all three of these summits with one name, in the sharp point (*pointe*) of pure love that is the point at which the soul and the absolute touch; for it is one instant, now gnostic, now drastic, now pathic, that is embraced by intuitive intervision, faced in the courageous decision, felt in the joyful event, but, in their turn, the gnosis, drama and the pathos coincide in the punctuality of pure loving disinterestedness.[13]

Disinterestedness, often invoked by Levinas to mark the otherwise than being or non-being of the ethical, confirms, especially when qualified as loving disinterestedness, that there is an ethical dimension to the creative instant with which first philosophy according to Jankélévitch is preoccupied. What precedes these words in this extract shows that their force extends across the entire range of human faculties traditionally summed up in the triad of cognition, conation, and affectivity. The productive "one instant, now gnostic, now drastic, now pathic," inevitably recalls the productive imagination which Kant posited as possibly the common root of sensibility and intellection, a thought which might have led him, as for some distance it led Heidegger, to elaborate an account of the imagination as the common root of all three *Critiques.* This is not the place to develop those thoughts.[14] Nor can an examination of Jankélévitch's thoughts on first philosophy be taken any further here. Let us leave suspended the question whether what we could call the hypocritical imagination would offer a more generous or a less generous notion of the ethical than Levinas offers. And let us move to the account of the common root which Levinas considers to be deeper than the instant of creation as interpreted within the context of art.

THE LOVE OF WISDOM AND THE WISDOM OF LOVE

In an interview to which reference has already been made, in response to the question how he reconciles the phenomenological and the religious dimensions of his thinking, Levinas grants that although he makes a clear distinction between his philosophical and his confessional texts, they may have a common source of inspiration. A little later in the same interview, replying to the question how the ethical can be invoked to undermine the Greek and Heideggerian ontologies of presence, he speaks of two sources of inspiration. The *Deux sources* here referred to are religion and philosophy, two sources of inspiration inspired by the ethical common source. Here is a triangulation of spirit which alters the order of priority proposed for ethics, religion, and philosophy in the *Phenomenology of Spirit* and disrupts the Hegelian conception of the history of philosophy and the philosophy of history when it is multiplied by the chiasmus of philosophy to which the first section of this chapter referred and which must now be unpacked. I shall begin doing this "in terms that are not literally Levinas's."

Philosophy as love of wisdom is already multiplied by the doubling of its genitive. Not only is wisdom the object of love; wisdom has love intrinsic to it. And the love intrinsic to wisdom, wisdom's love, is different from philosophy as wisdom of love. Furthermore, the double genitivity of philosophy understood as wisdom of love is either wisdom which has love as its object or love which has wisdom intrinsic to it, love's wisdom. Again, this last is not merely a redescription of the first, of philosophy as love which has wisdom as its object. In both cases an intentional "of" and a constitutive "of" are to be distinguished. This does not mean that in both cases the former is separable from the latter. Philosophy as love which has wisdom as its object or objective may find itself unavoidably affected by the love which is intrinsic to its object wisdom, and philosophy as wisdom which has love as its intentional object may find itself unavoidably affected by the wisdom intrinsic to its object love.

On the one hand, the wisdom intended by love is less than wisdom unless it is love of wisdom's objects or objectives, and the latter may and ultimately may have to include love itself. On the other hand, the love which is the object or objective intended by wisdom will be defective if it is unwise, and if the object of wisdom's love does not include wisdom itself. Are we interpreting Levinas accurately if we now go on to say that the first hand is Greek and the second hand is Hebrew or Biblical? This obviously depends on what in each case we mean by wisdom and love.

Consider first wisdom, and first in the context of what in the already twice-mentioned interview Levinas calls "our history," the context of our "interhuman relation" and "being in the world."[15]

The Hebrew prophet, *nabi*, was a visionary, a seer, but he was concerned not with clarifying and explaining what he saw, bringing the truth of the matter into the light. Allowing the details of what he saw to remain in darkness, his attention was directed to hearing the overall ethico-religious meaning of what he saw. So since the prophet did not focus on the semantic contents of assertions and was speaking for others in advance of such factual understanding of what may have been said, one should not be surprised to find Levinas describing the words "I am here" (*hineni*), as pro-phetic, for they are speaking for the other in obedience to a command before any conceptual understanding. Furthermore, since the prophet's eye was the listening eye, it is not surprising to find that in explaining what he means by the prophetic, Levinas alludes to Claudel's doctrine that one should try to hear what is *sous-entendu* in the work of art (AE 38, 48, 49, OB 30, 37, 38).[16] Levinas himself concedes that as an inspired witness to the overall meaning of what he sees, the ancient prophet was akin to the poet. In a broad sense of the word, poetry "overflows with prophetic meanings" (SMB 79, PN 185). But what is a sage or wise man, *kham*? Can he be called a philosopher? And how should one translate into Greek the statement that Solomon was the wisest of men (I Kings 4:30–31)? The difficulty of these questions is increased by the fact that when Solomon is said to be the wisest of men he is being compared not with men from Greece, but with men from Egypt, Babylon, and Mesopotamia. And in what does his wisdom consist? "And he spake three thousand proverbs: and his songs were a thousand and five" (Prov. 4:32). So far he sounds like a poet. "And he spake of trees, from the cedar tree that is in Lebanon even unto the hyssop that springeth out of the wall: he spake also of beasts, and of fowl, and of creeping things, and of fishes" (Prov. 4:33). He was a botanist and zoologist? Perhaps. But the key to the meaning of his wisdom is that, whatever his scientific knowledge and skills with words may have been, they were to be used in the exercise of the gift for which he had asked God: not riches or honor, though these were added unto him, but "an understanding heart to judge thy people, that I may discern between good and bad" (Prov. 3: 9–13).

Although the wisdom of Solomon is a gift from God, the discernment and judgment he acquires is the sort of thing ordinary mortals might learn from experience of interhuman relations and being in the world. Worldly wisdom, *phronêsis, prudentia:* the meanings of these expressions at least

77

overlap those of *hochmah*. And when the know-how they refer to is codified or regarded as expressions of innate or transcendent principles and Ideas we are in the vicinity of a kind of knowledge for which the Greek expression is *sophia*. Wisdom which was practical has become theoretical instead or as well.

Whether practical or theoretical, wisdom proverbially begins with what the Bible calls the fear of God (Prov. 1:7, 2:5, 9:10). It is of critical significance for the topic of this chapter that what the Bible calls the fear of God is what Levinas calls the love of man. The so-called fear of God is "Fear and responsibility for the death of the other man, even if the ultimate meaning of this responsibility for the death of the other was responsibility before the inexorable and, in the last extremity, the obligation not to leave the other man alone in face of death."[17] The albeit anarchic source of at least Biblical wisdom and the source of the religious meaning of the name of God—that "extraordinary word," Levinas writes—is, in the words of Jankélévitch, the "loving disinterestedness" of obligation toward another ordinary mortal. The allegiance that binds me in an ethical obligation to another human being is the meaning of the religious bond to God. But because in being face to face with another facing his death I am faced by a third mortal human being, I am faced by the obligations of comparative justice which are posed in the abstract universals of a discourse that is paradigmatically Greek. So given the face-to-face intrigue with the other human being, I am *bound* to speak "Greek." Only the intrigue with the third party and therefore the Hellenic universality which makes it possible effect the dramatic dénouement of what would otherwise be a violently exclusive one-for-the-singular-other. As *Otherwise than Being* says, "Saying or responsibility call for (*réclament*) justice" (AE 58, OB 45). Conversely—and here we encounter the non-philosophical source of the internal genitivity remarked on in our analysis of the relation between the love of wisdom and the wisdom of love—justice calls for saying or responsibility. As *Totality and Infinity* remarkably says,

> justice summons me to go beyond the straight line of justice, and henceforth nothing can mark the end of this march; behind the straight line of the law the land of goodness extends infinite and unexplored, necessitating all the resources of a singular presence. I am therefore necessary for justice, as responsible beyond every limit fixed by an objective law. (TeI 223, TaI 245)

Only the prophetic and non-correlational saying of the one-for-the-other can forestall what would otherwise be the violence of human beings regarded as but particular cases of universal humanity, the uniqueness of their ethical responsibility obliterated by their being turned into the finite referents of a common name about which things are said, no room being left for the infinitivity of to-say. Only by sustaining these in Contra-Diction, as Derrida writes the word, pitting one violence against the other, can one hope to escape the language of war. Only through an alternation or *clignotement* of the saying and the said in the instant or the *clin d'œil*, as Jankélévitch and Levinas himself write,[18] can responsible use be maintained for a notion of messianism and the word "God." How can one justify these claims philosophically? How can one justify the claim that the phenomenological-ontological reduction operated upon traditional metaphysics to either the field of pure consciousness or to the question of the meaning of being calls to be in its turn reduced to the ethical which is metaphysics in a new sense, a sense which makes newness possible? A chance for these claims to be met can be kept open only if kept open too is the Contra-Diction in diachrony which Levinas refers to in *Otherwise than Being* and comes close to naming in his essay on and for Derrida in *Proper Names* (NP 85–86, PN 58–59),[19] only if there is no reconciliation of separation in proximity or proximity in separation among human beings and the intrigue of justice and responsibility in which—whether or not Levinas would express it thus—they are doubly bound (Ad 67), only thanks to the unfinishing chialogue between the love of wisdom and the wisdom of love spoken in the name of philosophy.

Philosophy, Plato, Aristotle, and Husserl say, begins in astonishment, *thaumazein*. It begins, Husserl says, over and over again. It begins over and over again, Levinas and Jankélévitch say, in scintillation (AE 206, OB 161). This infinite rebeginning, Levinas says, is the repetition of the moment of ambiguity between the visible and the invisible or, as he also says more accurately, the moment of ambiguity between the visible or invisible and what transcends that alternative (AE 201, cf. 202, 204, OB 158, cf. 159, 160). The *thaumazein* in which philosophy begins is the traumatism of astonishment (TeI 46, TaI 73, AE 228, OB 181) at the glory of responsibility for the other which puts philosophy itself under the responsibility to say anew the only real newness, that of the non-indifference of the one for the other which inspires the difference between the one and the other. Affected non-intentionally or counter-intentionally by the objective of its intentionality, philosophy as the wisdom of Desire at the service of Desire is called to thought by the tertiality of justice, but it is called to signify in that tertiality the tertiality of illeity which, without allowing "divinity" to be said, allows the name of God to be said in the name of philosophy.

5

WHAT IS ORIENTATION IN THINKING? FACING THE FACTS

> To orient one's self in the strict sense of the word means to find, from one's given direction in the world (one of the four into which we divide the horizon), the others, especially the east.
>
> —IMMANUEL KANT[1]

> Justice itself is born of love. They can seem to be strangers to each other when they are presented as successive stages, but they are in fact inseparable and simultaneous, save when one is on a desert island, without humanity, without a third party.
>
> —EMMANUEL LEVINAS[2]

REASON AND SENTIMENT

If the eighteenth century in Europe is the Age of Enlightenment, this is not because it is the Age of Reason in the way that the seventeenth century had been. If any philosophers are typical of the eighteenth century, they are not those who follow Descartes and Spinoza in taking as paradigms of reason rational intuition of clear and distinct ideas or deductive proof. If that is how *ratio* is defined, the eighteenth century is not the Age of Rationalism.

A case could be made for saying that the eighteenth century is the Age of Sentiment. The strength of this case will depend on which part of the century and which part of Europe one picks. If one picks, say, Rousseau's France or Geneva and the Scotland of David Hume and Adam Smith in the second half of the century—though the Ulster Scot Frances Hutcheson had produced his theory of moral feeling already in the century's first half—the title "Age of Sentiment" is by no means inept. Its aptness explains why the second half of that century may so readily be seen as announcing the one that follows, except that where the nineteenth century is typically the age of the *expression* of feelings, it is preceded by the age of feelings *impressed*. It is preceded by the Age of Affect or the Age of Empiricism, the Age of Empiricism being the age of double affect insofar as experience is affect as an impression or sensation and affect as a feeling that is provoked by sensation. The Enlightenment of this age is no longer primarily that of the derivation from intuitively necessary axioms of further necessary truths by the application of rules of logical inference. It is no longer Euclidean, Pythagorean, or Platonistic. Mathematics, mechanism, and calculability are no longer its covert or explicit ideals. Its ideals revert to a certain Aristotelianism, an Aristotelianism from which the intervening Age of Rationalism has purged some of the features that Scholasticism retained. Eighteenth-century Enlightenment is primarily the endeavor to bring to light, to collect, and to order matters of natural scientific fact: to seek to make order out of disorder, but to do so less by subsuming them within a purely *a priori* system than by embracing the totality of facts and of things within an organon or encyclopaedia, whether this be a compendium of synthetic *a posteriori* information, like the *Encyclopaedia* of Voltaire, Diderot, and D'Alembert, or a synthetic *a priori* system which is also a logic and biologic of history, like the *Encyclopaedia* of Hegel. Although it is not until the beginning of the nineteenth century that Hegel's *Encyclopaedia* is published, and although this is critical of Kantian *Critique*, it enlarges upon Kant's middle way between, on the one hand, the kinds of rationalism represented by Descartes, Spinoza, Leibniz, and Wolff, and, on the other hand, the kinds of empiricism represented by Hume and Condillac.

Both the Kantian and the Hegelian ways of transcending the opposition between epistemological rationalism and epistemological empiricism are transcended in the twentieth century by the Husserlian science of phenomenology, which suspends questions of empirical and metaphysical fact—hence supersedes also the opposition between metaphysical realism and metaphysical idealism—by restricting itself to questions of meaning. Expanding the horizons of meaning of Husserlian phenomenology, Levinas maintains that the ultimate meaning of meaning is "ethical" in an emphatic or hyperbolic sense of this word. The meaning of science is con-science. Levinas does not use the word "conscience" very often, and when he does so it is in order to give it again an emphatic or hyperbolic sense which blurs a number of classical philosophical distinctions, including those between the analytic *a priori*, the synthetic *a priori* and the synthetic *a posteriori*. The call of hyperbolic conscience is both *a priori* and *a posteriori*. On the one hand it is "logically" anterior to empirical experience. On the other hand it is an "experience" of sorts. It is an affect. It is even a "fact," one could say, as Kant says of the call of reason expressed in the moral law that it is a fact or, more cautiously, a fact "as it were."[3]

The preceding paragraphs present an unavoidably rapid and therefore unavoidably caricaturizing characterization of some of the directions taken by modern philosophical thinking. That in the preliminary indication of Levinas's redirection of it so many words have had to be written in inverted commas is a mark of the violence of the reorientation in philosophical thinking that his teaching would effect, in particular with regard to typically eighteenth-century patterns of thought. The violence extends to the very idea of pattern. Levinas would reintroduce disorder into that order which we said it is the aim of so much eighteenth-century thinking to impose: that order, for example, which Defoe's Crusoe seeks to impose.

INDIVIDUALISM

In a passage in which I italicize words that will help us get a sense of the new direction in which Levinas's teaching moves, Virginia Woolf writes of Crusoe:

> *He is incapable of enthusiasm.* [. . .] *Everything is capable of explanation,* he is sure, if only he had time to attend to it. [. . .] anything that this sturdy middle-class man notices can be taken for a *fact.* He is for ever counting his barrels, and making sensible provisions for his water supply; [. . .] A man must have an eye to everything; it is no time for *raptures* about Nature when the lightning may explode one's gunpowder—it is imperative to seek a *safer* lodging for it. [. . .] "Let the naturalists," he says, "*explain* these things, and the reason and the manner of them: all I can say to them is, to *describe the fact.* . . ." If you are Defoe, certainly to describe the fact is enough; for the fact is *the right fact.* [. . .] Thus Defoe, by reiterating that nothing but a plain earthenware pot stands in the foreground, persuades us to see the remote islands and the solitudes of the human soul. By believing fixedly in the solidity of the pot and its earthiness, *he has subdued every other element to his design; or he has roped the whole universe into harmony.* And is there any reason, we ask as we shut the book, why the perspective that a plain earthenware pot exacts should not *satisfy* us as completely, once we grasp it, as *man himself in all his sublimity* standing against a background of broken mountains and tumbling oceans with *stars flaming in the sky?*[4]

What is the right fact that is being described by this plain man when he reiterates that nothing but a plain earthenware pot stands in the foreground? Pre-eminently for Crusoe it is the fact that will enable him to survive, the useful fact. Crusoe is preoccupied with making what Virginia Woolf calls "sensible provisions." This self-styled Prodigal Son, having left his father's house because he "would be satisfied with nothing but going to Sea,"[5] finds himself cast up on an island near the mouth of the Orinoco off the east coast of South America. Yet there he finds himself returned to the state of *homo domesticus.* He finds himself under "the imperative to seek a safer lodging" wherein to keep not only his powder dry, but also to secure his other possessions, his own body and indeed his "human soul." As for the body, Crusoe's colligation of facts is a discovery of rules of thumb conducive to self-preservation. This is why the one book which Rousseau insists must be in Emile's library is not Aristotle, not Pliny, not Buffon, but *Robinson Crusoe,* though perhaps with the Friday episode left out.[6] That book is a manual in which regard for keeping body and soul together determines what its hero notices and what he overlooks. Everything he sees on his island world is seen as *Zeug,* that is to say under the category of what Heidegger calls *Zuhandenheit,* handiness, as distinct from that of being *vorhanden,* objectively present

82

at hand. "Let the naturalists explain these things, and the reason and the manner of them: all I can say to them is, to describe the fact," where the fact to be described is an economic fact. Domestic man is economic man.

Since Crusoe leaves theoretical explanation to others, he cannot be an economic individualist if to be that is to be the advocate of a theory. For the same reason, Crusoe cannot be an individualist if to be that is to propound "the selfish hypothesis" of Hobbes according to which the primary human motive is self-interest. This does not mean however that Crusoe's behavior cannot be explained by either of these theories, or that these theories could not be held by Defoe. In *The Rise of the Novel*, Ian Watt argues that Defoe depicts Crusoe as "an embodiment of economic individualism."[7] On the other hand, presumably with Watt's thesis in mind, Maximillian Novak argues that "By reminding his audience of Crusoe's failure to follow his calling, Defoe was directly attacking the economic mores of a society that was abandoning the trade ideals of mercantilism for those of *laissez faire* and economic individualism."[8] Novak goes on to mention that the idea of economic isolation occurred to Defoe some months after the return to England of a mariner who had lived alone for more than four years on the island of San Fernandez. This mariner is Alexander Selkirk, widely regarded as one of Crusoe's real life antecedents. Selkirk was a native of Largo, just twelve miles along the east coast of Scotland from Kirkaldy, the birthplace of the author of the bible of believers in *laissez faire*. Novak denies that this indirect proximity of birthplace linking Defoe via Crusoe and Selkirk to Adam Smith is matched by an ideological proximity resulting from Defoe's being influenced by Smith. When he cites from Defoe's *General History of Trade*— published in 1713, two years after Selkirk's return to Britain—the sentence "every Man should have been his own Labourer, or his own Manufacturer," Novak does so as evidence that the idea of economic individualism was in the air well before the publication of *Robinson Crusoe* in 1719 and the publication of *The Wealth of Nations* in 1776. It was already inherent, Novak maintains, in the "economic mores" of the age, and *Robinson Crusoe* is the medium through which Defoe laments this fact.

According to Bram Dijkstra, Novak's thesis is "that since Defoe could not be regarded as in sympathy with economic individualism, but in fact specifically opposed it, he must have designed his narratives as a moralistic refutation of the actions of his main characters"?[9] This seems to imply that according to Novak, Defoe has Crusoe behave like an economic individualist. That he does so behave is not borne out, Dijkstra says, by Novak's own statement regarding the extremely profitable plantation Crusoe had developed in Brazil that his decision to leave it "is an indication of his restlessness, but it is hardly the restlessness of the enterprising businessman."[10] The tenor of Novak's account of Crusoe is that he is driven by *Wanderlust*, and only incidentally by lust for gold: his troubles have their source in his incapacity to stay quietly in one room, the incapacity from which Pascal tells us humankind's unhappiness arises. And this nomadism is indeed what

Crusoe refers to as his Original Sin. Therefore on Novak's account, Crusoe could not be an embodiment of economic individualism in the sense of being a practical illustration of a theory that had either already been formulated or that was yet to be formulated by Adam Smith or someone else.

Whether this last inference is valid will depend on whether it is what Novak calls "the restlessness of the enterprising businessman" that is built into individualism when Watt defines individualism as a disposition "whose aim is never to maintain the *status quo,* but to transform itself incessantly. Leaving home, improving on the lot one was born to, is a vital feature of the individualist pattern of life."[11] Does not the reference here to leaving home in order to improve the lot to which one was born show that the restlessness of the capitalist entrepreneur is built into Watt's concept of individualism by his definition, hence that the inference in question is invalid? We shall have something to say about a different kind of restlessness and incessance at the end of this chapter. What is required to be noted here is that the Watt-Novak controversy—a controversy which the recent reprint of Watt's book may, for good or ill, lead some of Defoe's commentators to reopen—assumes agreement between the two commentators that *Robinson Crusoe* is a novel of ideas. This assumption is endorsed by J. Paul Hunter when in *The Reluctant Pilgrim* he supports Novak's statement that "Defoe created his fiction from ideas rather than from incidents."[12] A fiction of incidents, for Hunter, would be a fiction of facts, in this context such facts as a travelogue recounts. It would be a fiction of facts like the desert-island experience of Alexander Selkirk. Hence Hunter plays down the relevance of the accounts of Selkirk and of other historical castaways because they foster what he regards as the misguided tendency to believe that in *Robinson Crusoe* "Defoe's art is fact-centered rather than idea-centered."[13] However, his contrary belief does not rule out that the idea at the center of Defoe's art in this book is the idea of fact-centeredness. This is the idea expressed by Virginia Woolf in the sentences cited above, the idea that "the perspective that a plain earthenware pot exacts should . . . satisfy us as completely, once we grasp it, as man himself in all his sublimity standing against a background of broken mountains and tumbling oceans with stars flaming in the sky." Neither Defoe's Crusoe nor Crusoe's Defoe is struck by the sublimity of those broken mountains and tumbling oceans. Neither of them is impressed by the starry sky above which according to the Conclusion of Kant's *Critique of Practical Reason* is one of "the two things that fill the mind with ever new and increasing admiration and awe." The stars in the sky, like the sun, are means by which to navigate the tumbling oceans. Nor is either of these unimaginative men moved, it would seem, by the second of the two things Kant mentions, the highest principle of practical reason, the moral law from which man himself derives his sublimity. The highest principle of Crusoe's practice appears to be the Hobbesian principle of self-love that is echoed in Defoe's *Jure Divino* by the lines: "Self-Love's the Ground of all the things we do,/ Which they that talk on't least do most pursue . . ." and that Defoe is wont to cite in the form in which it is affirmed by the Earl of Rochester: "In my dear self I centre everything."[14] The first fact at the center of Crusoe's fact-centered story is Crusoe's dear self. And the "right fact" that it is enough to describe, according to Virginia Woolf's reading of that story, is the fact of the plain earthenware pot in the foreground of which the sight satisfies us as completely as it satisfies Crusoe—indeed, satisfies us and him, she says, "as completely, once we grasp it, as man himself in all his sublimity."

SALVAGE AND SALVATION

This is a moment at which Levinas would intervene to say that satisfaction is not enough. To speak of being satisfied by man in his sublimity, completely satisfied, is to fail to grasp that that sublimity cannot be grasped like an earthenware pot—or like anything else. The sublimity of the other human being is incomparable. It cannot be compared even with the starry sky above. Levinas would ask: Is the "right fact" one that could be described? Is it the fact of the nothing of the death Crusoe will encounter when he re-enters the elements of the earth or the water from which the pot and he himself were made? Is it a symbol of the pot in which, if he fails to elude the cannibals who visit his island, he himself will be *cuit*. Maybe the pot in the foreground is a very literal metaphor both of that by which he may die and of that by which he lives. Maybe it is a metaphor of the metaphor of the fact ("It happen'd one Day about Noon"[15]—"around the hour of noon, when the sun stood straight over Zarathustra's head"[16] and no shadow was yet cast upon Crusoe's place in the sun) that in the sand "there was exactly the very Print of a Foot" of which Crusoe says "how it came thither, I knew not, nor could in the least imagine." This last fact, that he could not imagine how it came there, is all that is needed to make the reader of his journal try to imagine how. How could it come there if there is only one? The fact that there is the print of only one foot is even odder than the two odd shoes he observes in the flotsam amongst which he is washed ashore. Odd too are the two occurrences of the word "one" in his remark "I went up the shore and down the shore, but it was all one, I could see no other impression but that one." He is so much the subject of an "affrighted imagination" (perhaps, *pace* Virginia Woolf, he has too much imagination, not too little) that when it comes to reporting the discovery he is still quite at a loss for words, still literally and somewhat illiterately spellbound. How strange too that the Print had survived the ebb and flow of many tides. Could it have been the trace of his own foot, he wonders. But it was larger than his own foot. True, the single print of his own foot would have been enlarged through having to bear all of his weight when Friday placed the other upon his own head in a gesture of subservience. But Friday does not appear on the scene until eight years later. Could it be a trick worked by the Devil? Although Crusoe rules out this explanation, it sows in the reader's mind doubt as to whether the Print is natural or supernatural. Is there any reason why in Crusoe's mind, and in Defoe's, it should not be both? Is it the print of a left foot or is it one of the right? They do not tell us. Maybe this is because Crusoe is so "perfectly confused" that the dexterous and the sinister are confused. It is as though we have not got the rightness of the right fact right unless we acknowledge that the oppositional relation between the right and the wrong derives from an ultrafactual absolute right or good and an absolute wrong or bad beyond being without which the specific rights and wrongs pertaining to my station in the world are in default of ethicality.

So "affrighted" is Crusoe, so "out of my self," that "I came Home to my Fortification, not feeling, as we say, the Ground I went on." "Out of himself," observes Michael Seidel, "he is like the apparition he thinks he has just seen, but his supposed apparition has a very tangible quality—it makes a real impression or, at least, a footprint—whereas Crusoe is so scared his feet barely touch the ground."[17] Out of himself, Levinas might observe, frightened out of himself by the fear of God or by an alterity whose divinity cannot be severed from humanity and from the *humanisme de l'autre homme,* the humanism of the other man, Man Friday or another other.[18] Out of himself, so that it is only the foot of another that leaves an ambiguous trace.

It soon becomes plain that God has a foot in Crusoe's life, notwithstanding Crusoe's wish to persuade himself that the footprint is his own, as much his own as the words with which his parrot rouses him when he lies "dead asleep," exhausted by having to save himself from being swept out to sea: "Robin, Robin, Robin Crusoe, poor Robin Crusoe, where are you, Robin Crusoe? Where are you? Where have you been?"[19] To save himself? "When I was on shore I fell on my knees and gave God thanks for my Deliverance, resolving to lay aside all thoughts of my Deliverance by my boat. . . ." The foot that God has in Crusoe's life is the foot of Him "that publisheth salvation" (Isaiah 52:7). Whatever interpretation may be put upon this last word in its Biblical context, it can hardly be doubted that although Crusoe discovers that he can respond to the call to "Call upon me in the Day of Trouble"[20] and although he learns that "Deliverance from Sin [is] a much greater Blessing than Deliverance from Affliction,"[21] the deliverance to be hoped for as interpreted by Crusoe is the deliverance *of* Crusoe's dear self, not deliverance *from* it.

Nevertheless, Crusoe's conversion, however limited, shows that we cannot without qualification say of him, as does Virginia Woolf, that "He is incapable of enthusiasm." This literal man is capable of enthusiasm in the literal sense of the word. He is capable of becoming possessed by God. Sure, Crusoe's dominating passion is fear, not awe, and when his life is in no immediate danger, he is generally an exemplar of prudent sobriety. The last phrase that would occur to anyone wanting to describe him is "God-intoxicated." He is as wary of *Schwärmerei* as Kant is of the mystical tendencies of some forms of Pietism and as Levinas is of the transports of the Hasidim (the Pious). He, like Levinas and Kant, is a rationalist, but he is a practical rationalist of the kind most common in the eighteenth century until the appearance of the Critical philosophy of Kant. For Crusoe reason is primarily instrumental. And, for the most part, one may say as much of his God. Above all, the Almighty is a means to the castaway's salvation, where the idea of salvation is that of being rescued "From lightning and tempest; from plague, pestilence, and famine; from battle and murder, and sudden death." Even when his island has acquired a human population, it shows no signs of becoming a kingdom of ends. It is a kingdom in which, although "I allow'd Liberty of Conscience throughout my dominions,"—in the roll call of whose subjects he lists Friday, now converted to Protestantism, Friday's father, still a pagan and a cannibal, and the Spaniard, a Papist—"I was absolute Lord and Lawgiver."[22] Jocularly spoken though these words are, they may be taken as evidence of how remote from Crusoe's thoughts is the idea of reason itself as the giver of a law to which the lord is no less subject than any other human being.

This idea of humanity held together not by a balance of dynamic forces but by an equality of respect is an idea which Levinas takes over from Kant. However, upon that idea Levinas puts a bias, and a bias which paradoxically returns to the dear self a certain priority: not the priority allocated to it by the Hobbesian selfish hypothesis and the Enlightenment concept of enlightened self-interest, but the priority which has the oddness of being derived, because it is the priority of a response and a responsibility. What precisely is this difference between Levinas and Kant? What is the re-orientation he gives to the orientation of Kant's thinking? Does the Copernican Revolution in ethics undergo a Ptolemaic Counter-revolution at his hands?

SOCIETY

Levinas says, on the one hand, "Justice supposes this original equality," meaning the equality of respect (EN 94), and, on the other hand, "Reciprocity is a structure founded on an original inequality" (DL 39, DF 22). The second of these assertions is what marks off his doctrine of ethicality from that of Kant. The difference is explained further by his claim that I have rights only thanks to others or to God and that my responsibility toward others is greater than anyone else's (AE 201–202, OB 158). The difference is one between the ways Levinas and Kant understand the pronouns "we" and "us." According to Kant these pronouns are simply the plural of "I." Humanity is the totality of egos related to one another symmetrically. This permits Kant to formulate the categorical imperative as the injunction to "Act in such a way that you always treat humanity, whether in your own person or in the person of any other, never simply as a means, but always at the same time as an end."[23] This is a command from a third-personal point of view which eliminates the difference between the first and second person pronouns. That is the view of what Smith calls the impartial spectator and others call God. In the same lineage is what Levinas calls *illéité* or He-ness, except that the third-person pronominality of this illeity is not to be divorced from the concreteness of a singular you face to face with me. In

Levinas's non-Newtonian optics of ethics justice defined in abstraction from the face invites an idolatry of the law. This idolatry can be avoided only if the focus of moral respect is neither oneself nor the abstract law nor even the person to whom one acts justly, but the person one justly acts *with*. However, this "with" is not the "with" of Humian or Smithian or Schelerian sym-pathy, or of the intersubjective reciprocity of Heideggerian *Mit-sein* or, at least on Levinas's reading of it, Buber's "I-Thou." The "with" of the "we" of Levinas's notion of proximity in separation is the asymmetric crossing of my being commanded to perform a work which supports the economy of the other and my commanding the other to command. Hence the "we" made up of humanity is not a totality of "I"s but a detotalitized totality of "me"s in the accusative commanded by "you"s. Since no "you" is equal in responsibility to the "me" which it commands—although my obedience to your command is already in my commanding you to command—Levinas can say that human-ity is a multiplicity of unequal singularities (TeI 230, TaI 251). In saying this he may seem to be giving us license to sum up the difference between him and Kant by saying that whereas for Kant humanity as the kingdom of ends is a multiplicity of symmetrically related particulars, for Levinas it is a dissymmetry understood as a symmetry of asymmetrically related singulars each of whom is a "me" that breaks up totality (AHN 182, ITN 157). But even this dissymmetrical universalization cannot be enjoined without offense. Only of myself can I say that I am more responsible than anyone else. Not only can I not say without the absurdity of self-contradiction that everyone is more responsible than everyone else and that everyone must substitute himself for the other; I cannot say this either, according to Levinas, without the ethical violence of advocating human sacrifice (AE 162, OB 126). Indeed, this violence would derive as much as does that absurdity from the principle of universalizability. For violence would result only if Levinas and each one of us could not advocate his own self-sacrifice without advocating their self-sacrifice to others. I cannot advocate to others their self-sacrifice without sacrificing the pre-eminence of my responsibility over theirs.

To put a finer point on this question of the difference between Levinas's rationalism and the rationalism of his great Enlightenment predecessor, one could say of Levinas that he refuses to accept without qualification the Kantian command to treat humanity in one's own person as an end in itself. In my own person I am ethically neither *en soi* nor *pour soi*, but *pour autrui*. This entails that ethically I am primarily a means. I am a means not in the way of a physical tool, for a physical tool is not, Levinas holds, capable of respect. Nor am I a means in the manner of a slave. That too, according to Levinas, would be an abasement inconsistent with my being a subject of respect in either the objective or the subjective interpretation of the genitive. I am a means in the manner of a servant, but as a servant who commands the master to command, welcoming the other, where "The term welcome of the Other expresses a simultaneity of activity and passivity which places the relation with the other outside of the dichotomies valid for things: the a priori and the a posteriori, activity and passivity" (TeI 62, TaI 89).

These dichotomies are the ones which the eighteenth century inherits from Hobbes's mechanistic or, to use Levinas's word, "allergic" dynamics of social relations. They still orient Adam Smith's account of sympathy as that by which we come to regard ourselves as others see us and achieve the idea of the impartial spectator, a doctrine in which self-regard as seeing oneself reflected in the mirror provided by other people in general—not a general will, but a general speculative eye—is the route to the moderating of self-regard as *amour de soi*, concern for oneself, or as *amour propre*, vanity. Such moderating may be a means to a longer term satisfaction of one's own interests, but this moral theory presented in Smith's *The Theory of Moral Sentiments* is supplemented in *The Wealth of Nations* by the economic theory of economic individualism and the doctrine of the invisible hand which cannily induces the chaotic multiplicity of acts motivated by self-interest to result in the harmony of a general good—somewhat as in the *Timaeus* the wandering elements are prevailed upon to settle down by the persuasion of reason.

Smith's doctrine of the invisible hand is a secular version of the doctrine of the hand of Providence to which from time to time Defoe's mariner refers. Defoe's pelagian is no Pelagian. He believes that God helps those who help themselves. Both he and his creator believe that the divine law is expressed through natural law, so that Crusoe's "sensible provisions" and the "Chequer Work of Providence" are cooperative.[24] Defoe criticizes the Deism embraced by Shaftesbury and his like.[25] God's hand in things is visible. So Defoe stands firm against the tide of proto-Unitarianism Socinianism which flows so strongly throughout the eighteenth century. However, his and Crusoe's monotheism is faith in a Fact. So it is crucial to distinguish the way in which in their monotheism the voice of nature, as Defoe says, expresses the will of God from the way in which in Levinas's monotheism the human face speaks the divine.

When in one of his essays on Judaism Levinas writes that "Ethics is not the corollary of the vision of God, it is that very vision," he gives us leave to read also in the reverse direction the statement he makes on the next page that "The way that leads to God therefore leads *ipso facto*—and not in addition— to man" (DL 35, DF 18). But the vision of God is the vision in which God and the other human being look at us—at me. It is not the vision of a fact or a Fact, since, as implied in what was said earlier in the discussion of the difference between Levinas and Kant, the face of the other human being and so the invisible face of God speak not in the indicative but in the imperative mood (ibid.).

That earlier discussion is more readily followed if one remembers Levinas's use of the phrase "simultaneity of activity and passivity," extremely rare in his writings in comparison with his use of the phrase "passivity more passive than passivity." Otherwise, one will wonder how the imperative that comes to me from the other can be commanded by me without this committing Levinas to positing the primacy of my activity over my passivity and thus to the primacy of the will to survive, which he challenges.[26] Affirmation of that primacy is common to the empiricist and sentimentalist writers of the eighteenth century whom we have taken Adam Smith to represent and to the rationalist approach manifested in Kant. In his essay asking "What is Enlightenment?" Kant answers his question by saying that it is "man's release from his self-contracted tutelage," where *selbst verschuldeten Unmündigkeit* is "man's inability to make use of his understanding without direction from another." He goes on to put another question: "Do we now live in an enlightened age?" He answers: "No, but we do live in an age of enlightenment."[27] In the *Critique of Pure Reason* he writes: "Our age is, in especial degree, the age of criticism, and to criticism everything must submit."[28] The call to criticism resounds in Levinas's re-orientation of our thinking about ethics,[29] but, while agreeing with Kant that everything must submit to criticism, he would say that this can take place only if to criticism every *one* must submit, and that means first of all *me*, for my facing the other is the condition of my facing things, of my facing the facts, such things as are taken for facts and obsessively inventoried by sturdy middle-class Crusoe, who is inclined to believe that the world is all that is the case.[30]

Criticism in Levinas's sense is the primary frankness that orients the world (TeI 72, TaI 98, AE 24–25, 116–17, OB 20, 91–92). It is speech, *Mündigkeit* (*Mund* is mouth), exit from infancy (*fans* is speaking), entrance into the economy of the free exchange of words which demands the generous exchange of wealth, an exchange that is ultimately one way: from me to the other by whom my freedom is invested (TeI 229, 75, TaI 101, 251). In the *sens unique* of this "new orientation of the inner life" (TeI 224, TaI 246) and of economy, property is not what is given to me either as a present or an instrument for my use; not merely object or merely *Zeug*, it is that which I am called to give to the other in testification, *Zeugnis*, of my "holy imprudence" (EN 234). The moral good is not the public result of an interaction of private unholy prudences as maintained by so many writers of the eighteenth century culminating in Bentham. And economic individualism—the mast to which so many of those writers nail their colors, the compass-bearing which Crusoe unreflectively follows—undergoes a sea-change at the delicate moment when the principle that individuates the individual turns out to be responsibility for the other human being (EN 126–27).[31]

THE DELIMITATION OF REASON ALONE

Crusoe's thoughts occasionally move beyond those directed toward his welfare on his island or elsewhere on land or sea to his welfare in heaven. Indeed, with Defoe's puritan contemporaries, he is inclined to regard his welfare and wealth as evidence of divine election to a condition of salvation likened to surviving a storm at sea to enjoy the security and comfort of a well-provisioned cave, a home back in England or a flourishing estate in Brazil. But when Crusoe begins "to consider seriously my condition" his inventory of what he calls its evils contains the fact that "I am divided from mankind, a solitaire, one banish'd from human society." Perhaps this is evidence that even before his "conversion" he is on the way to glimpsing what leads Levinas to say that the orientation given to phenomena by ethics of the other human being (TeI 71, TaI 98), although written large in the square letters which proclaim the vocation of Israel, is not dependent on an appeal to some Oriental theological wisdom (TeI 194, TaI 218), whether that be Judaic, Christian, or Islamic, let alone Buddhist, Jainist, or Hindu. So when in an essay included in a section entitled "The Bible and the Greeks" he writes that Moses Mendelssohn (to whom Kant's essay "What Is Orientation in Thinking?" is addressed), "without referring wholly to the philosophical coordinates of the Eighteenth Century," describes a new dimension of the Jewish mentality which opens up a new epoch of Jewish History that animates Judaism today (AHN 167, ITN 144), it is far from Levinas's intention to deny that the "universalist singularity" proclaimed so magnificently already by the ancient Hebrews is incompatible with the universalist universality claimed for the categorial coordinates of the Augustan Age, their Latin predecessors, and the language of the ancient Greeks. It is precisely in the *koinê*, the catholic "Greek" language of the others, that Levinas questions the teleological ethics of Eudaemonism to which so many of those who spoke that language subscribed. It is when you have been saved from captivity in Egypt or from your desert island (for "the Island was certainly a Prison to me")[32] that the ethical life begins, and to that life there is no "happy ending" to which I approach asymptotically. Rather does such an ending withdraw further and further away from me. For, according to Levinas's notion of the ethical, not only am I more responsible for the other than anyone else, my responsibility increases without end, since every exercise of, say, economic justice to one neighbor is an exercise of injustice to other neighbors, be they in faraway places of which I know little. "The more I am just—the more I am culpable" (AE 143, OB 112).[33] The culpability in question here is not that of a bad deed committed or a good deed omitted. It is the incessantly increasing culpability—innocent of crime and sin, albeit original—which puts me in question solely on the ground of, one is tempted to say, the *fact* that I occupy a place in the sun or a shelter from the rain that, except on an absolutely desert island, will always exclude someone else. My deliverance from my exile is my deliverance to my capacity to cause death. Furthermore, as Heidegger already recognizes in *Being and Time*, Dasein is always owing, always in debt. He says that this is a debt Dasein owes to itself, one contained within a cyclic economy.[34] Heidegger's existentiell-ontological Here, a *Da* which is encyclopedically egological without for that reason being naturally egoistic, gives place in Levinas's thinking to a metaphysical-ethical Here I Am, Send Me, *hineni, ici, ecce hic* which is alterological without for that reason being any of the various forms of sympathy, natural or naturalized benevolence or "humanity" so important in the moral theories of Hutcheson, Butler, Smith, and Hume.[35]

It could be said that the unsurveyable pre-worldy cosmogonic place (*chôra*) and receptacle (*hypodochê*) of Plato's *Timaeus* which "we behold as in a dream" and "cannot arouse ourselves truly to describe or determine,"[36] is hypoCritical. That is to say, it escapes the categories of measured property and propositionality.[37] It escapes them thanks to the *démesure* of the other man himself in all his sublimity who places his Print (*ichnos*) on the sands of the world to mark "the fact, as it were" that "my place in the sun" is inescapably more than a factual location from the standpoint of which one ropes the whole universe into harmony, subduing its elements to the design of one's own usurpative use. The Print reminds us that, before memory, and before the creation of the physical world, creation is anarchically ethical. Before being a merely geographical position to which I am swept by the tumbling oceans or guided, with sextant or telescope in my hand, by the stars flaming in the sky, my island is the point of cynosure of a spiritual optics in which the fact of being in a place is already being beheld by and beholden to a face. Even what Kant calls the fact or the "fact as it were" of the moral law calls to be turned to a face.

The individualism of Kantian Enlightenment defined by the light of the sun, of the starry sky above, and the moral law within is turned into the individuality which is the solitude of my soul commanding to be commanded before anyone else to pay a debt which with every payment grows ever greater. In this individualist economy I am always errant and always in arrears. As Levinas more or less says of the idea which God's infinity overflows, my solid earthenware pot is a receptacle that can never contain enough silver or soup to save from starvation those people there whose needs I have *ipso facto* neglected in exercising my autonomous choice to heed the needs of these people here. This may not mean that all hope for a happiness and salvation that includes mine has to be abandoned.[38] It does mean that happiness and salvation conceived in the manner of many eighteenth-century thinkers as the satisfaction of your and my desires will be conceivable by me, the Survivor, only on the assumption that my peace of mind is not perpetually disquieted by the heteronomous Desire of which satisfaction is not the end. Heteronomous Desire has no end.[39]

The unendingness of Desire as construed in Levinas's re-orientation of the thinking of ethics would end the reign of the idea of the happy ending as the ultimate source of ethical sense. This re-orientation is not a repetition in the twentieth century of the responses made by Johnson's *Rasselas* and Voltaire's *Candide* to the theodicial optimism expressed by Leibniz earlier in the eighteenth century and in the seventeenth. With reference to the idea of happiness shared by these optimists and pessimists, and to the ease with which this idea and the idea of salvation become confused with each other, as they do in the mind of Robinson Crusoe, it is relevant to note that salvation or happiness or welfare (where to fare is to go or to travel, whether on land, across the sea, or in the sky) can imply good fortune or help (Hebrew *'ezrah*). Now my call for someone to help me from being swallowed by the sea can be an acknowledgment of my weakness. It can thus be a swallowing of my pride. But to acknowledge my weakness is not to disown my responsibility. Indeed, my ultimate responsibility as understood by Levinas is itself my very impower. The responsibility of which Levinas speaks is not the responsibility of the power of free will, whether of the prudential will to survive or of the will that Kant equates with acknowledgment of the moral law.

But relevant here too is Levinas's assertion, commenting on Sanhedrin 36b–37a, that "personal perfection and personal salvation are, despite their nobility, still egoism, and that the purity of man which the hedge of roses protects is not an end in itself" (QLT 185, NTL 69). It is questionable whether a morality based on the idea of personal salvation would be nobler than what, in a section of *Time and the Other* under the words "Salvation through the World," Levinas describes as a first morality of earthly nourishments. For this first morality of secular nourishments seems more likely to be a salvation where the self is saved by being *forgotten* (TA 45–46, TO 62–64).

Without theodicy, without theology, and without soteriology—"within the limits of reason alone," but of a reason which breaks the limits of reason as understood in Kant's title[40]—Levinas's redirection of the rationalism of Kant in the spirit of Kant's contemporary Moses Mendelssohn[41] is a salutary subordination not only of election as choosing the means to one's own or to general happiness on earth, but also of being elected as being chosen for blissful salvation ever after, to a having been elected for assistance to others here and now, world with or without end, amen.

6

AMEN

I can no other, God help me!
Amen.

—NIETZSCHE (*Thus Spoke Zarathustra*)

ROSENZWEIG

At the beginning of the first chapter of *Otherwise than Being*, Levinas refers to "strange rumors about the death of God or the emptiness of the heavens" (AE 5, OB 5). That his book purports to say Amen to that rumor is evident from his making precise in the very next paragraph and in the very last paragraph of the book that the death here rumored, the death rumored by Nietzsche's Zarathustra, is the death of a certain God inhabiting a world behind the scenes. But what is it to say Amen?

In *The Star of Redemption,* the work of which Levinas says in the preface of *Totality and Infinity* that it is too often present in its text to be cited there, Franz Rosenzweig writes that God is neither dead nor living. "To say the one or the other of him, with the old [philosopher] that 'God is life,' or with the new one that 'God is dead,' reveals the same pagan bias. The only thing which does not resist verbal designation is that neither/nor of dead and alive."[1] The resistance to designation of what is other than this neither/nor referred to in the last book of the *Star* mirrors a similar resistance to designation referred to in the first book of the *Star,* where Rosenzweig writes of a word that is often considered to be the last word but is in fact the first, or rather is before the fact and before the law, before the distinction between the *de facto* and the *de jure*. This word is Amen, the first tremendous and unlimited Yes of a "positive theology." In the light of Levinas's acknowledgment of Rosenzweig as his guide, I propose to consider a few paragraphs in which Rosenzweig treats of the words Yes and God, in the hope that this may help to articulate together two allusions in Levinas's two main philosophical writings: first, his allusion in *Totality and Infinity* to the plane on which Yes is opposed to No, neither of these opposed words being that which institutes language (TeI 11–12, TaI 41–42) and second, his allusion in *Otherwise than Being* to an unconditioned and critical Yes (AE 156, OB 122). Because Rosenzweig's "grammatical thinking" of the word Yes is at the same time a grammatical thinking of the word "God," in pursuing my exegetical aim it is my hope also that we may make some progress toward either

94

allaying or deepening what for some of Levinas's readers may be more a disquietude than a question of exegesis.

Having endorsed Nietzsche's proclamation of the death of the God of ontotheology, why is Levinas either unable or unwilling to eliminate the word "God" from the lexicon in which he expounds what he himself describes as a humanism of the other man? Would the appropriateness of that description of Levinas's account of ethics not be increased if the description could be conducted without that word, at least once it had, for the reasons Levinas gives in the first section of *Totality and Infinity,* said good-bye, as Dante bade farewell to Virgil, to the gods of paganism? In other words, although Levinas is seeking to show in *Otherwise than Being* that, as he writes there, "the problem of transcendence and of God and the problem of subjectivity irreducible to essence—irreducible to essential immanence—go together" (AE 20; OB 17), could he show that the problem of transcendence and the problem of subjectivity go together without showing that these two problems go together with the problem of God? Is it possible that in this sentence of *Otherwise than Being* and in other sentences of that book the name of God is traced only with a view to its own effacement?

Bearing in mind these questions as well as their place within what, remembering Levinas's reference to the need to get away from the climate of Heidegger's philosophy (DE 19, EE 19), might be called the wider question of philosophical meteorology as to whether it is possible to breathe freely both in the atmosphere of Levinas's thinking and in that of Nietzsche's, let us now read a few paragraphs of Rosenzweig's "grammar of assent."

Having called Amen the first word of a "positive theology," Rosenzweig writes that the point of departure of negative theology is a Something from which by the negation of predicates it moves to a Nothing or a Naught, a *Nicht,* where, he says, mysticism and atheism shake hands. Rosenzweig's method is the reverse. Putting the Nothing behind it, even before the Yes and the No, it aims at a Something or at an Aught, as the English translation renders the *Icht* Rosenzweig prefers to *Etwas* in order to keep at arms length the Hegelian definition of the latter as a definitely qualified existing being whose moments are being-in-itself and being-for-another reflected into each other through the negation of negation. The *Nicht* that Rosenzweig here distinguishes from this *Icht,* although not defined, is yet not the uncircumscribed universal (*allgemein*) Nothing of Nothing at all. It is the Nothing of God. That alone is presupposed, the Nothing of a fragmentary all, not the Nothing of the one and universal totality. Rosenzweig, who is readier to write of methodology than Levinas is, contrasts his method with the method of decomposition, destruction, or deconstruction of essence, *Verwesung,* which is the method of atheism, and the method or way of *Entwesung,* which is the mystic way and which takes essence away. The dissolution or deportation of the essence of something leads to a formless night of nothing, a *Nacht des Nichts* that, notwithstanding Rosenzweig's concern to distance himself from Hegel, is a close relation of the night in which all cows

are black of Hegel's innuendo concerning Schelling. The method of annihilation, *Vernichtung,* the method of Mephistopheles, the method in which
atheism and mysticism shake hands, affirms the Nothing. As against these
methods, Rosenzweig's method is to ask hypothetico-positively: if God exists, what can be truly affirmed of his Nothing? This is not an affirmation
either of Nothing in general or of the Nothing of God. Nor is it a negation
of Nothing. Distinguishing the beginning from the point of departure,
which is at most the beginning of our knowledge, as Descartes does in the
Third Meditation and as Levinas will do in his meditation on that Meditation, Rosenzweig argues that No cannot be the beginning because it would
have to be the negation of a presupposed positive Yes. But both Yes and No
presuppose a Nothing that is no more than a positionless posit for the
posing of a problem. "It is no 'dark ground' or anything else that can be
named with the words of Eckhart, Boehme, or Schelling. It does not exist in
the beginning. *Es ist nicht im Anfang.*" In the beginning is the Yes. But, as
already explained, this Yes is not the Yes opposed to the No but the Yes
presupposed by the No. Before the neither/nor, it is before the either/or,
before the *enten . . . eller: Ent-Scheidung* before *Entscheidung, avant toute
décision,* prior to *every* decision (AE 153, OB 120).

It might reasonably be objected that this archetypal Yes presupposes an
archetypal No, the No of the presupposed Nothing. And Rosenzweig himself
admits an archetypal and, as he describes it, tremendous (*gewaltiges*) No. He
even says that the No is as original as the Yes and does not presuppose it. A
derived No may presuppose the archetypal No, but the original archetypal No
presupposes nothing but the Nothing. However, although it does not presuppose a Yes, a *Ja,* it does presuppose an affirmation, a *Bejahung:* in Nietzsche's
words, the "highest form of affirmation that can ever be reached."[2] For the
Nothing it presupposes is, as we have seen, not the utter Nothing of Meph-
istophelian meontological annihilation, of the "dark ground" or of the "abyss
of divinity," but the Nothing only of the cloud of unknowing as a problematic
point of departure from which affirmation concerning the divine essence
would come. On the basis of this fine distinction Rosenzweig asserts that the
archetypal word No is younger than the archetypal word Yes.

GOD'S YESSENCE

God's essence is infinite yessence. Here Rosenzweig's notion of the
infinite appears to be derived from the sense in which a judgment is defined
as infinite, for example by Kant, when it affirms that S is non-P. So although,
following Rosenzweig's method, only the Nothing of God is given, and since
the Yes cannot refer to the Nothing because that would be to exceed the
merely heuristic positing of the Nothing as a point of departure for knowledge, the Yes must relate to the non-Nothing: "Therefore the affirmation of
the non-Nothing circumscribes as inner limit the infinity of all that is not
Nothing. An infinity is affirmed: God's infinite essence, his infinite actuality,
his *phusis.*"[3]

That Rosenzweig is aware how difficult these sentences will be found by his reader is indicated by his warning that they state only purely formal preliminaries. An obvious source of difficulty for the reader following the *Star* as a guide to the interpretation of the words "God" and "Infinity" as understood by Levinas is Rosenzweig's reference to God's infinite essence. How can that be anything but a hindrance to interpreting the "beyond essence" referred to in the title of Levinas's book? This would be one reason for agreeing with the statement made by Robert Gibbs in his admirable *Correlations in Rosenzweig and Levinas* that in the sense intended in this title Levinas and Rosenzweig are not in correlation. It can be added that in Levinas's sense of that word no two human beings are ultimately in correlation. Rather, "Levinas creates a *drash*," Gibbs says, and the verb here is carefully chosen; "he makes an adaptation of Rosenzweig,"[4] However, it can be added also perhaps that Levinas creates a *drash*—a Hebrew-Greek chiasmic *drash*, perhaps one could say—of essence, as at least in *Totality and Infinity* he creates a *drash* of being. He exalts, emphasizes, creatively exaggerates these words beyond their ontological sense, or discovers that they exaggerate and produce themselves, as with scores of others, not least the word "ontological" and, to return to our immediate worry, the words Amen or Yes and God.

Yes, Rosenzweig writes,

> is the arche-word of language, one of those which first make possible, not sentences, but any kind of sentence-forming words at all, words as parts of a sentence. Yes is not a part of a sentence, but neither is it a shorthand symbol for a sentence, although it can be employed as such. Rather it is the silent accompaniment of all parts of a sentence, the confirmation, the "*sic!*," the "Amen" behind every word. It gives every word in the sentence its right to exist, it supplies the seat on which it may take its place, it "posits." The first Yes in God establishes the divine essence for all infinity. And this first Yes "is in the beginning."[5]

Why does Yes make words but not sentences possible? Rosenzweig's answer to this question both anticipates and qualifies the Saussurian structuralist doctrine that the meaning of a word is more negative than positive. While recognizing the reason for saying this, Rosenzweig says almost the opposite. Having associated position with the position of a word, he goes on to grant that what is posited depends not only on the other words in a given sentence but on words in other sentences in which that word might figure. The meaning of a word is the class of its sentence frames. But this relation of a word in one sentence to words in the same and other sentences is expressed by the arche-word No. This No expresses opposition rather than position. However, since the identity of what is posited is a function of the alterity of what is opposed and vice versa, a third original word has to be posited, the word And. This primordial And expresses the systematicity of language as *langue* on which every speech act of language as *langage* or *parole* depends. The question of the relative priority between Yes and No thus raises the question of the relative priority between system and act of speech, and this question raises the question or pseudo-question of the relative priority between historical and logical priority.

Saussure says that while the linguistic system and some mastery of it are logically presupposed by the performance of acts of speech, the latter are historically prior.[6] There are problems with this claim that can only be mentioned here in passing. For example, can even locutory acts (using words), let alone illocutory acts (saying something in using words) be performed without presupposing competence in finding one's way about a system of grammar? Are not *langue* and *parole* conditions of each other? Are they not equiprimordial? The same answer would seem to be called for when the analogous question is raised with regard to systematicity and sincerity as treated by Levinas. Yet Levinas sometimes says that the giving of my word to the Other is not equiprimordial with the grasp of a grammatical or conceptual system, but prior to it. In what sense can it be prior? In the sense of a priority that is presumably prior both to the priority of the formally logical system and to that of historical events. So the priority of neither, a priority that is constitutive and at the same time deconstitutive of the continuum of time and of the order of logical implication and presupposition: the priority of a certain primary "position," of a *Setzen* before *Gesetz*.

In trying to sort out Rosenzweig's answer to these questions concerning the order of priority of Yes and No and of the historical and logical, his distinction between originality and age must be recalled. When he says that the original *Non* is not *propter sic* but *post sic*, that is, not on account of but after the Thus affirmed by Yes, it sounds as though he is saying that although Yes and No, and we now conjoin And, are all original, Yes is in some sense historically older. But when he says that No is not on account of Yes, can he be denying that it is logically dependent on it? And has his quasi-Saussurian and quasi-Hegelian argument not shown that the reverse holds equally? It would seem that he is arguing both for systematicity and for its delimitation. If No is more immediately connected with the infinity of non-Ps affirmed of the Nothing of God from which Rosenzweig's argument departs, and if No is more directly connected, as he also maintains, with God's freedom, God's essence is, as we put it, his Yessence, because No itself is a word that must be affirmed. We must distinguish, on the one hand, the rhetorical opposition between the Yes and No of affirmation and denial, as well as the nonparallel semantic opposition of True and False, from, on the other hand, the affirmation that appends a speaker's signature, *firma*, or mark to what he says, whether what he says, the word that is marked by it, is positive or negative, and whether what he says is true or false.

We must distinguish truth from truthfulness or, as Levinas variously writes, from veracity or sincerity, meaning not the veracity that is opposed to the deceit or insincerity with which I may address myself to another or to myself but the veracity in the name of which even such deceitfulness must be practiced. A No may masquerade as a Yes. One may be suspicious whether what appears to be a Yes is a No, but one's suspicion is always backed by a Yes.

However far back one retreats, what one moves toward is not a No behind a Yes but a Yes behind a Yes or a No. Even the double denial, Nay Nay, of Nietzsche's ass is doubled by an Amen Amen posited in the beginning, however remotely the beginning is postponed, however immemorial its past, the past quasi-performative Thereby to which every Hereby owes its force. [7]

The difficult phrase "past quasi-performative Thereby" marks the difficult time and place of the tacit contract that any explicit contract presupposes. Rosenzweig's primal Amen is also tacit. He says, you will recall, that it is the silent accompaniment or companion (*der stille Begleiter*) of all parts of a sentence. This absolute reticence is required also by Levinas when he says that the Saying of witness without words, but not with empty hands ("Dire sans paroles, mais non pas les mains vides"), precedes the Said (DVI 121–22, GCM 74, CPP 170). In saying this he runs the risk, fine or otherwise, of implying a primal speechless scene behind the scenes, a post-ontotheological version of the theological transcendentalism with which he and Nietzsche try to break. It is all too easy to slip into thinking of the unrememberable past on analogy with the myth of an age before the ages of the world. Perhaps this idea is fostered by reading Levinas through an oversimple reading of Rosenzweig and of a book that is too often present to be cited in the text of *The Star of Redemption,* Schelling's *Ages of the World.* Such a reading of Levinas cannot be correct for it makes use of a naive continuist notion of time that would be at best appropriate only to the Said. Nor are matters much improved when Levinas's many references to the unrepresentable past are taken together with his less frequent references to the unrepresentable future and that future is pictured as a messianic promised land on which we have not yet set foot. The chances of interpreting in this way Levinas's assertion of the precedence of Saying to the Said are dashed and drashed by his apparently contradictory assertion that something must be said, *dit,* about how things are before saying only pure saying, *dire* (AE 183–84 n. 7, OB 198 n. 7). This appearance of contradiction is the pivot of Levinas's appeal to the return of skepticism despite skepticism's apparent self-refutation. Rather than repeat here what he says about that, let us note the apparent carelessness with which, in *Otherwise than Being* at least, Levinas employs the expressions "on this side" (*en deçà*) and "on the other side" (*au-delà*). There seems to be no consistent pattern in his uses of these expressions. To mention only a few of these uses: "on this side of" is prefixed to references to nature and its states (AE 106, OB 83), to being, to the said, to the free and unfree (AE 94, OB 75), to ontology (AE 59, OB 46); the Self is said to be on this side of coincidence with itself (AE 143 n. 17, OB 195 n. 17); responsibility is said to be on this side of memorable time. "On the other side" or "beyond" is prefixed to essence, but in one and the same paragraph, when writing of the reduction of the said to the saying, Levinas says that this is a reduction to what is on the other side of Logos, and when explaining that it is not to an entity that the reduction of being leads, he writes disjunctively of what is "on this side or on that side of being" (AE 57, cf. 121, OB 45, cf. 95). It is as though his title could just as well have been *Autrement qu'être ou en deçà de l'essence* or *Autrement qu'être ou au-delà ou en deçà de l'essence*. Either prepositional phrase is correct, depending on your point of view, and there are two points of view. However, to speak of points of view is to speak representationally and so to misrepresent the saying as a said. One moment of discourse is translated, but the other moment of discourse is betrayed (AE 31, 88, OB 24, 70). Betrayed, however, in both senses of the word. The point is made early in *Otherwise than Being* when Levinas distinguishes the verbal infinite to-be from nominalized essence but notes that the verbality of the propositional to-be "makes essence resound without entirely deadening the echo of the to-say that bears it and brings it to light" (AE 60, cp. ix; OB 47, cp. xli). Perhaps there is a reecho of this echo in John Austin's discovery that his original attempt to distinguish constative from performative speech acts ends in defeat, because on the hither and thither side of what is stated there resounds the "hereby," the "hear hear," or Amen of ratification performing constatation, perforating the message.[8] But the defeat of the moment of pure constatation is not the triumph of the moment of the pure to-say. The to-say must suffer the defeat of the attempt to constate it. Only thus, through struggle and the pain of mourning (*lutte et douleur*), is confirmed the "thus," the *sic* of the saying that confirms or ratifies; only by contestation does it receive attestation (AE 148 n., OB 195–96 n. 19). Only if the not entirely deadened echo of the to-say is an absolutely passive suffering in the activity of speech. Only if in this not entirely deadened echo resounds the death knell of a certain God, as Levinas says.

THE EXTRAORDINARY WORD

But, to return to our point of departure, why does his ethics within the bounds of ratification alone not also say Amen, Finis, End of History, to the word "God"? Why does his critique of pure religion say only *A-Dieu*, Goodbye, God-be-with-you, notwithstanding that the extraordinary word "God" will be a scandal to many potential readers of *Otherwise than Being*? One reason perhaps is that the God you don't know is better than the God you think you do. If "God" is a word in the life of those to whom one is addressing in "Greek" the claim that ethics is *protê philosophia*, then it is a word from which it would be dangerous to avert one's eyes. Ignored, it could hardly fail to be a stumbling block. This is a lesson Levinas teaches more insistently than do Heidegger and Derrida, the lesson that the old words cannot simply be abandoned in creating the new, that one cannot take leave without ceremony, the lesson, embalmed in the phrase *faire son deuil*, that to take one's leave may be to take on the difficulty of mourning. If, with some risk of oversimplification, it can be said that *Totality and Infinity* rises beyond being and fundamental ontology by demonstrating how being and ontology rise emphatically above their selves to what is "more ontological than ontology" (DVI 143, GCM 90), it can perhaps be said that *Otherwise than Being* performs a similar feat for the word "God." "I pronounce the word God," Levinas writes in that book, "without suppressing the intermediaries that lead me to this word, and, if I may say so, the anarchy of its entry into discourse, just as phenomenology states concepts without ever destroying the scaffoldings that permit one to climb up to them" (AE 165, OB 128). Indeed, maybe this hyperbolization of the word "God" leans on the hyperbolization of "being" and of another word whose power *Totality and Infinity* would interrupt: the word "power" itself, or *pouvoir,* to be able. For the de- and re-construal without destruction of the word "God" that *Otherwise than Being* would effect is modified by the adverb *peut-être,* "could-be." The essay entitled "The Name of God according to Certain Talmudic Texts" is collected in the volume entitled *Au-delà du verset.* Although the subtitle of this volume is *Lectures et discours talmudiques,* that does not make them purely confessional texts. For when Levinas seeks to get beyond the verse it is in order to teach a philosophical lesson, and to do so in "Greek" (TrI 47). The essay in question is grouped with other readings Levinas calls "Theologies" in the plural, meaning by this not that any dogmatic theology is propounded in them but that they seek to speak in a rational way about God. And it is in a subsection entitled "Philosophy" of the essay on the name of God that he writes: "But the language of thematization that we are using at this very same moment has maybe been rendered only possible (*a peut-être été rendu seulement possible*) by this Relation and is only ancillary" (ADV 157, BV 178). The Relation here referred to is that of the animating responsibility of which Levinas has said a moment before that "before discourse bearing on the said," it is "probably the essence of language." Here, meeting the difficulty for our "correlation" of Rosenzweig and Levinas presented by the fact that the latter wishes to pronounce the word "God" without letting divinity be said (AE 206, OB 162), the word "essence" wears the invisible shudder quotes with which Rosenzweig might have invested the word in the sentence I cited earlier which declares that "The first Yes in God establishes the divine essence for all infinity." Maybe the same should be said about the "maybe" in the sentence just cited from Levinas, even though he says in it that at that very same moment he is using the language of thematization. Does not the very same word in the moment of its thematization resound with the diachronically re- , pro- but not in-tended moment of the echoing Amen? And must not the same be said of those other modal words here encountered, "possible," "probably," and of the "maybe" as it is said once again in Levinas's statement that the word "illeity," a nominalized pronoun, marking the excluded third beyond being and non-being, beyond the modalities that are *Seinsweisen, manières d'être,* beyond skepticism and its self-refutation, marks maybe what is said also by the name or pronoun "God"?

This "maybe" is said, but still very unstraightforwardly, when Levinas refers to "the Revelation of the beyond being which is certainly maybe only a word (*qui certes n'est peut-être qu'un mot*)," adding: "but this 'maybe' belongs to an ambiguity where the anarchy of the Infinite resists the univocity of an origin or principle; to an ambiguity or ambivalence and an inversion that is enunciated precisely in the word God" (AE 199, OB 156). This "maybe" does not belong to Heideggerian belonging. It is not from the meaning of being that the meaning of maybeing is drawn. Its *peut-être* draws its breath in a climate other than that of *Seinkönnen*. However, Levinas's claim that ethics is protophilosophy is not a simple inversion of the claim Heidegger made at Zurich in 1951 that "the experience of God and his revelation (so far as this comes man's way) takes place in the dimension of being."[9] If we were to have tried to get to the bottom of the worry which has motivated the present chapter, it would have been necessary to speak of the shudder-producing things "the 'experience' of God" means for Levinas—*schauderhaft* things, we might say, following his citation from Goethe's *Faust* by way of epigraph to the final chapter of *Otherwise than Being*, where the last thing which that citation invokes is sacramental fear and trembling. That motivating worry is a disquietude in the sense of the *Besorgnis* which Heidegger distinguishes from and subordinates to *Sorge*, to existential care or concern and its existential modes.[10] It is the worry over what *more* might be said except "illeity" and that anagram of "name," "Amen," by the exceptional name or pro-name "God." It would have been necessary to try to speak of the tests, trials, or ordeals, *épreuves*, Levinas is remembering when he says that phenomenology must be concrete. Among these would be the events that took place between 1933 and 1945, of which he says that they contributed to his break with the later phenomenology of Husserl (EN 142). These events overflowed any idea of concrete experience Rosenzweig and Schelling could have invoked to explain what they meant when they described their philosophy or theology as "positive."[11] If Levinas is not caricaturing his teaching when he writes in *Entre nous* that human being is not only being-in-the-world, so not only being toward one's own death, but being toward the Book, *zum-Buch-sein* (EN 127), it may well be that the lay reader of that Book will have to make an effort to learn the ancient languages in which it was written, for "one cannot reject the Scriptures without knowing how to read them" (DL 77, DF 53). That is a responsibility and risk to which he may be called. However, if the *cri de coeur* of that reader after the death of God is to receive a response—and how, consistently with Levinas's doctrine, could the responsibility to give a response be denied?—it is important that that Book should be able to untie one's tongue from a shibboleth. It is important to see therefore that notwithstanding the oblique references on so many of Levinas's pages to the unpronounceable Name of God, notwithstanding his reference to the word "God" as a *hapax legomenon* (AE 199, OB 156), he insists that the relation to God is presented non-metaphorically in the relation to the transcendence of the face of the other human being.

It so happens that the transcendence of the face is traced through the transcendence of a word in an exegesis recorded by Levinas of an incident commented on in *Sôta* 53b. According to Numbers 5 a woman suspected by her husband of adultery must be taken to the Temple where the pontiff exclaims, "If a man had intercourse with you, may you be cursed by the Eternal [written as Tetragram]." And the woman responds, "Amen, amen."[12] The pontiff's words containing the Tetragram are then written in ink on a parchment from which they are effaced by being immersed in the bitter water. In this way, Levinas notes, the ancient prohibition against the effacement of the Name is superseded for the sake of the reconciliation of human beings (ADV 152–53, BV 123–24).

Another, though inevitably still not unenigmatic clue to the way an entry into the Book may be an entry into a humanism that is neither specifically Jewish nor specifically Christian is provided by Levinas's citation of the New Testament in support of his claim that although the Other is not to be identified with God, the Word of God is heard in the Other's face (*visage*), that is to say, in his or her looking to me (EN 128). According to Matthew 25:40, when those on the Lord's right hand and on his left protest that they have neither given nor refused food, drink, or shelter to Him, they are told, "Inasmuch as ye have done it unto one of the least of these my brethren ye have done it unto me."

So in this humanism of the other human being in which atheism is defined as the restriction of thinking to intentional representation where the thinking and what is represented may in principle be mutually adequate (EN 145, 246) and, precisely by being so defined, allows of subversion by the nonintentionality of ethical "experience" that accompanies every intentional experience (EN 146) as the pre-original *responsio* Amen accompanies (*begleitet*) every word, maybe that experience, although expressed by the word God, is not dependent on that word for its expression; maybe that word does not have to be said when one says Amen. "'Me voici, au nom de Dieu'. . . . 'Me voici' tout court!" (AE 190, OB 149).

Or, reminding ourselves that hidden stumbling blocks are more dangerous than unhidden ones, lest the silent return of the God of a reality behind the scenes be facilitated by the obliteration of his name, should perhaps the iterated effacement of that name be effaced in turn by the eternal return of the name, forever coming and forever going, enigmatically on the hither side and on the thither side of the opposition between Yes and No, like the winking of a star? If so, although we may begin by reminding ourselves, as Léon Brunschvicg reminds us, of the danger of worshipping the shadow of concepts we believe we have slain (DL 71, DF 48), and by realizing that a concept cannot be redefined without keeping the concept's old name, readers of Levinas must keep on reminding themselves that he is seeking neither to reinstate an old concept nor to introduce a new one in the manner of an astronomer scanning the heavens until his telescope comes to rest on a heavenly body so far overlooked. His writing is disastrous, a patient *écriture du dés-astre*. The frequentative trace in it of Rosenzweig's *Star* means precisely that the thinking beyond thinking which endures in it, its consideration beyond consideration, is not the tracking of a star, not *auf einen Stern zugehen*, even when that star is not a being but being, uniquely this, *nur dieses*

(DMT 164).[13] On the hither and thither side of any star fixed in the firmament, susception before and after perception and conception, is the Amen, the pre-original Yes in which experience originates, affirmed by the Other in me (TeI 66, TaI 93), thanks to whom this me is never a me and no more, never a me *tout court*. If You, *Autrui,* the pronoun of the pronoun Me, has as its pronoun He, and He is the pronoun of God, otherwise other than *Autrui,* then, Yes, Amen, like Jonah, I cannot escape from God. But if (hereby to repeat Levinas's constatation of contestation) voicing, the *en gage* of *langage,* is the fact (*sic: fait*) that "God" is the only word which always proffers itself as *Opfer* and is the very word which verily paroles transcendence, thereby suffering from an equivocity of which one moment is the contestation voiced by "It is maybe only a word" (AE 199, OB 156, NP 137, PN 93), then it is maybe the only word that voices the worry with that word from which I cannot escape.

7

THE IMPOSSIBILITY OF LEVINAS'S DEATH

For I have but the power to kill,
Without—the power to die—

—EMILY DICKINSON

BEING DEAD

Emmanuel Levinas died in Paris on the morning of Monday, 25 December 1995. It is a fact that he died there and then. It is a consequential fact that he is now dead. The event has taken place. And, since it is valid to argue from being to possibility, it was possible that that event should take place. From at least as early as the date of his birth, his death was a possibility. As was the death of Heidegger. But this empirical possibility of Heidegger's death is not to be confused with the phenomenological possibility of Dasein's death which in *Being and Time* Heidegger called a *Seinkönnen* and *Seinsmöglichkeit*.[1] Both empirical possibility and logical possibility, he maintains there, are derived from the possibility which is Dasein's way of transitively existing its world. The verbality of the verb-noun *Sein* means that the power or possibility of the way in which Dasein exists its being in the world, Dasein's worlding, is not to be construed in the manner of Aristotle and Scholasticism, where possibility or potentiality is conceived on analogy with a reservoir from which activity might spring. The possibility of being here referred to is being's possibility, where the possibility is constitutive of being's verbality and where what Heidegger wishes to convey is a notion in which the classical contrast between activity and passivity is exceeded. It could be said that that notion is a "condition of possibility" of that contrast, provided that this condition is not construed in the manner of Kantian transcendentalism as an analytic or synthetic *a priori* principle of judgment. The existentials into which *Being and Time* analyzes the possibility of being in the world are not *Grund-sätze* understood as principles, judgments, or contents of assertions. Contents of assertions have the status of what can be presented to a mind, whereas it is one of the aims of *Being and Time* to show that such presentedness to mind, like the presentedness to hand of material objects—their being on display—is secondary to an engagement or an involvement which is the point of pointing to, referring to, and intending any kind of object. It is therefore viciously circular to construe this involvement as ultimately a correlation of *noêsis* and *noêma* or *doxa* in the style of Husserl, who describes even axiological and practical mindsets as such correlations.

This objection to Husserl is underlined in Levinas's book on that philosopher.[2] In making this objection Levinas is in agreement with Heidegger. It is an objection concerning the scope of intentionality considered in abstraction from temporality. But neither for Husserl nor for Heidegger nor for Levinas can intentionality be separated from the temporality of consciousness. Heidegger writes in his foreword to *The Phenomenology of Internal Time Consciousness* that the book is "an exposition of the intentional character of time consciousness and the developing fundamental elucidation of intentionality in general."[3] And Levinas takes intentionality to imply protentionality and retentionality. He refers to protentionality and retentionality in a clause placed in apposition to a reference to intentionality in a sentence that proposes a reason for thinking that "the structure of time is not intentional, is not made up of protentions and retentions" (DMT 19). The reason he suggests is that maybe my relation with death exceeds the possibility of experience and the experience of possibility. Maybe it exceeds even the possibility of impossibility of my being toward my death that according to Heidegger is architectonic of all other possibilities of mine and of my very own mineness—of the *Eigentlichkeit* of which each individual I is capable. Maybe there is evidence of this, Levinas further suggests, in the excessive weeping of Apollodorus and Xanthippe and the other women at the scene of the death of Socrates described in the *Phaedo*. This may well be an indication that there is more than measure to the humanity of a life that appears to be limited and measured by death. And maybe this indicates not only something about what the death of another means for me as opposed to what my own death means for me. After endorsing Heidegger's warning against confusing the latter with the former, Levinas goes on to warn his readers against endorsing what he takes to be Heidegger's view that the death of the other is ontologically secondary compared with my concern for being, in that the latter embraces both concern for the other's death and concern for my own.

WHY ME?

Heidegger observes that for Dasein its death is certain. He says that it is *gewiss,* and in saying this he prepares the ground for his statement that Dasein's being toward its death underlies the ordinary concept of conscience, *Gewissen.* Heidegger does not take over without revision Husserl's conception of intentionality. Indeed, he seizes the opportunity of the above-mentioned foreword to *The Phenomenology of Internal Time Consciousness* to remark that "Even today, this term 'intentionality' is no all-explanatory word but one which designates a central problem." A year or so before writing this he had been attempting to cast light on that problem by substituting for Husserl's triad of retention, presence, and protention a triad of temporal ecstases not based, as Husserl's is, on representation: being already there in the world, being alongside things in the world and being ahead of oneself . Now this non-representational structure, considered by Heidegger to be fundamental to Dasein's everyday way of being in the world, is considered by Levinas to be an exercise of *conatus*. It is worth noting therefore that although involvement with things in their readiness or un-readiness to hand is plausibly described as one in which Dasein is trying to do something, and that the term *conatus* is derived from the Latin verb *conari*, to try, the philosophical and psychological notion of conation tradi-tionally contrasted with cognition and emotion is associated with the notion of willing. But Heidegger sees willing as the fundamental concept of Ger-man Idealism and sees his own thinking as an endeavor (so in that sense a *conatus*) to bring to attention a way of being that is more fundamental than willing and is a kind of freedom which is prior to freedom of will. One of his words for this is *Seinlassen,* and it is arguable that this letting-be belongs to a modality or voice which it is also Levinas's aim to bring to his reader's attention as prior to *conatus* as will, as power, and as will to power. For Levinas in turn sees his own thinking as an attempt to show that room must be found for a freedom which is older than freedom of will. Aided by Heidegger's explication of *Seinlassen* as a kind of listening and obedience, notions to which Levinas too appeals, the latter sometimes goes as far as to adapt Heidegger's expression *Seinlassen* to his own purpose.

Nevertheless, their purposes do differ. It is being that calls to be let be according to Heidegger, and this is a calling from and to the being of Dasein in its being toward its own death. According to Levinas it is from the other human being in his or her mortality that the call comes. It is a call to not leave the other to die alone, a call to non-indifference to the other's suffer-ing and isolation, a summons summed up in the commandment "Thou shalt not kill." The difference that this non-indifference introduces is other than the ontological difference between being and beings. It is therefore different from the meontological difference, the difference between being and non-being. Intervening into the realm of light and darkness, of conceal-ing and unconcealing, to which Dasein's being toward its own nothingness is confined, responsibility for the other human being is a response which defines mortality as the impossibility of possibility rather than, as in Hei-degger's definition, the possibility of impossibility. That is to say, prior to power is impower or unpower; prior according to a temporality which is not that of recollection, but of *accueil au-delà du recueil,* of welcome beyond recall: of acollection or adcollection, one might say, in recollection of the tie between *cueillir* and *colligere,* to tie together, where the sense of ligature is that which stirs, as Heidegger is fond of reminding his readers, in the word *legein,* to read, and in *logos,* a saying or a word. This word of welcome would be the first always already spoken word of allegiance which makes the stranger a neighbor—and *accolere* is to dwell near or be a neighbor to.

This confirms what was hinted at earlier, that a false dichotomy is made when it is asked whether it is my death or the death of the other that Levinas calls the impossibility of possibility. My being toward my death is my being

107

toward the death of the other in me and under my skin, as Levinas writes, the other who is a source of irritation. I am ab-aboriginally, from a time always already beyond the beginning of memory—like the silent first letter in the alephbet which precedes the first letter of the first word of the first book of the Hebrew Bible, *Bereshit*—infected and affected by the other whose coming (*venir*) is not within memory (*souvenir*). The mortal other intervenes and advenes, but this event (*événement*) is not the *Ereignis* of being or of the non-being that heralds being as such in the temporality described in *Being and Time*. *Ereignis* is another Heideggerian word that Levinas recruits, by no means put off by the sense of appropriation and possession that the German word bears. Translating this word as *événement* and with caution as "event," we can say that Levinas writes of an event of this event where sameness is broken into and broken up by otherness, an event even other than the nominalized abstractness of the -ness of otherness (DMT 131, 134). The event in question, in the question of the question that Levinas raises, is not the taking possession of myself when I become possessed by the question of the meaning and the truth of being. It is that dateless, always-already-happened happening of my having become possessed of myself through being possessed by the other: psychosis. My being possessed by the other is my being self-possessed by a self (*soi*) which is more than only my ego (*moi*) interested in its own survival. That selfhood is a singularity and uniqueness more complicated than the each-for-itselfness of what Heidegger calls *Jemeinigkeit*. In the *conatus essendi* of each for-itself, for whom the question of its own being and death is what is of primary interest, the disinterestedness, *dés-intér-esse-ment*, of the for-the-other is implicated. As the *posse* is superseded by the *imposse*, the *esse* is put in service to the otherwise than *esse* and beyond essence. Alterity is diachronically anteriorly ulterior to egological sameness—which does not mean that the latter cannot be naturally altruistic or benevolent.

These are not simple reversals. If intentionality is *conatus*, what subverts intentionality is not a simple counter-*conatus*. To suppose that it is would be to overlook Levinas's frequently repeated denials that the relation of all relations of responsibility for the other is a relation of power or force. It is not a relation of *energeia*. Primary sociality is not allergy, as it is said to be by philosophers as diverse as Hobbes and Hegel and Sartre. If it were, systematicity would be paramount, an interrelationship of terms affecting each other like Hegel's master and slave. Yet, as the above-mentioned notion of being irritated by the other under my skin leads us to expect, Levinas's conception of my primary dyadic rapport to *autrui* is no more comfortable than is the relation of the slave or bondsman to the master.

In the *Philosophy of Right* Hegel says: "Just as life as such is immediate, so death is its immediate negation and hence must come from without, either by natural causes or else, in the service of the Idea, by the hand of a foreigner (*von fremder Hand*)."[4] Some key differences between Hegel and Levinas can be brought out by reflection on this statement. Death, which

Hegel elsewhere calls the absolute master, is not according to Levinas a simple negation of life. And when it is threatened by the hand of someone who comes from without, it is not just a condition necessary to mutual recognition. Before being the foreigner who seeks to master me and the one with whom I would want to see eye to eye and be on equal terms, the other is the one by whom I am already seen, *déjà vu, eräugnet,* before he becomes *visé* or *vu* by me. Before I comprehend him in my gaze, *il me regarde:* his eyes are the source of my ethical concern, my *souci,* where *souci* is the word which Levinas also uses to translate *Sorge,* the word used by Heidegger that is usually translated as "care" or "concern." But Levinas agrees with Hegel and Heidegger in emphasizing that whether death approaches by the hand of another or as accident or disease and aging, it comes as a threat. It comes, according to Levinas, as an accusation. The other's look is an accusing look. This means not only that I am *accusé* by the other in the sense of made by the other's look to stand out like a figure on a ground. In Levinas's destructuring ethical revision of this figure-ground structure of Gestalt or Form Psychology, my physiognomical and phenomenological appearance as *apparaître* is dis-figured by my appearance as *comparaître* before the face of another who pursues and prosecutes me as though in a court of law.

PEACE AND QUIET

The face of the other expresses the command "Thou shalt not kill." It also commands me to command others likewise. This command is expressed also in the words of Leviticus 19:18, "Love thy neighbor as thyself." But it should not be overlooked that at the very moment of the utterance of those words (*en ce moment même*), after and before and again and again in the pages in which Leviticus records the words addressed to Moses, come the words "I am the Lord." The other human being is the Lord. Not, however, the Lord of the relation of lordship and bondage or master and slave analyzed in the *Phenomenology of Spirit.* The other human being is the master as *magister,* teacher. And although he teaches the laws and the statutes—"You shall keep my statutes" says the Lord to Moses—the other human being teaches that the statutes are not kept if they are applied to every human being in the way that laws of nature apply. The moment of their application must be a moment of response to the singularity of the other, just as in addressing Moses and addressing the law to him and through him to the people gathered at the foot of the mountain, Moses is one and unique because he is chosen.

But surely justice demands not only that Moses be chosen, and not only that those waiting at the foot of the mountain be chosen, but that every human being be chosen. And if he is to avoid the injustice of elitism must not Levinas say this of every human being? He does say this, and he cannot avoid saying this in expounding his doctrine philosophically in the "Greek" concepts of philosophy as love of wisdom. But he says that philosophy thus

109

understood must be understood at the same time as the wisdom of love or Desire. What that means can be partly explained by reference to Kant's statement that the person of good will is one who lives not only according to the law, but out of respect for the law. What Levinas underlines is that systematic respect for the law in the realm of ends in themselves is not enough. The good unwill calls too for respect for the singular other human being with whom I am face to face, notwithstanding that a second other and a third and a fourth speak through that first other's eyes. It is of this that the philosopher must repeatedly remind his or her readers and listeners. Philosophy must speak with an equivocal voice—Critically and hypoCritically.[5] It must by an abuse of language indicate the immediate responsibility I am under as a philosopher and a human being to not be content with the indifference implied by treating universalizability as what is primordially ethical. Universalizability may be the foundation of the ethical, but prior to the foundation and the bedrock of law is unfoundational, pre-principial, anarchic responsibility which for me is a responsibility entailing the sacrifice of my egological, though not therefore necessarily egoistic, persistence in being, and which substitutes for substance substitution for the other.

Dasein is such persistence in being toward its own death, whether or not the everydayness which it mostly is is also in ownmost possession of itself. Dasein has to be the possibility of its impossibility. That is what Levinas's philosophy would relegate to a second place. Levinas's philosophy is first of all phenomenological in its method, even if it employs that method in order to show that it deconstrues itself. In its first steps it is also ontological. Its point of departure is phenomeno-ontological, Husserlian and Heideggerian up to a certain point, to the point where certainty is sacrificed, and to the point where Levinas deems it necessary to increase notch by notch the shockingness of his descriptions, moving from saying that the self is subjectivity to saying that it is sub-jection, from saying that it is host to saying that it is hostage, from saying that it is for the other to saying that it is persecuted by the other. This acceleration in the torrential hemorrhage of Levinas's tropes can be compared to the unceasing refusal of Heidegger and Derrida to work with a settled lexicon. Their lexicon of paleonyms, neonyms, and anonyms must be worked *through* open-endedly and unendingly if through it are to be performed what Heidegger, Derrida, and Levinas philosophically constate.

This rhetoric of increasingly exasperating hyperbole suggests another comparison between Levinas and Heidegger. This rhetoric seeks to work against the rhetoric invoked by the irresistible inclination to construe the secret ethical moment as a public display, if not of intention, at least of intentionality, that is to say of meaning and giving of sense. But it is Levinas's claim that such giving of noetico-noematic sense ultimately depends for its sense upon the non-sense of traumatizing affectivity in which signification is reduced ultimately to my being a signifier that says "Hear me, call me, send me" (*hineni*). And that saying speaks for itself prior to and more

110

pluperfectly than any conative activity and more passively than the passivity to which activity is traditionally opposed. Does this mean that Levinas may be charged with quietism, as Heidegger often is? Or, rather than charging him with this, should we congratulate him on it? Has he not opened up a way to a language which speaks peace, a language which says, from its heart, *shalom*? Is not his incessant insistence on the absolute past-participiality of sacrifice to be welcomed? Whether it is or is not, the feeling that Levinas's account of non-indifference makes no difference may derive from misplaced expectations. In reading him, misled by his practice of supplementing what he calls formal or dialectical description with what he calls concrete application (a new ethical schematism beyond the schematism of the theory of application outlined in the *Critique of Pure Reason*) we can easily forget—and a similar forgetting threatens in reading Heidegger—that, like Heidegger and like Husserl, Levinas is regressing beyond transcendentally rational conceptual analyses or "expositions" such as are conducted by Kant, to an exposition which he sees as their phenomenological and more than phenomenological ethical quasi-condition. The universe of discourse of his philosophical texts is quasi-transcendental. "Metaphysical" is the word he himself uses, pouring new wine into the old bottle of metaphysics as this has been classically understood. This means that no claims are made for the validity or invalidity of specific moral maxims, any more than claims are made for the truth of any particular empirical laws in the *Critique of Pure Reason* (whatever we may think of Kant's attitude to some of the maxims cited in the second *Critique,* the *Groundwork,* "On a Supposed Right to Tell Lies from Benevolent Motives" and elsewhere). Hence, whether the disquietude into which the other throws me is to express itself as quietism in my moral relations with members of my family and in the marketplace is not a question for which we should expect Levinas's philosophy to provide an answer.

THE STING

Levinas underscores his denial that his philosophy of death aims to make death inoffensive, to justify it, or to preach eternal life. Its aim is to show how death confers meaning on "the human adventure, that is to say, on the ess*a*nce of being or on the beyond of ess*a*nce," where, as Levinas elsewhere explains, the spelling of this word with an *a* marks the verbal sense of being via a "suffix *ance* derived from *antia* or *entia* which gave birth [*naissance!*] to abstract nouns of action" (DMT 130, cf. 16n, AE ix, OB xli, DVI 78n). Despite this denial, does he not take the sting out of death by saying that what dies is not this man or this woman or this child, but, let us say, using his word, the "virility" of the man (and of the woman and of the child?)? It may seem that this reading blunts the acuity of death, sublimes its sharpness away. For it seems to require only that the ego's will to survive must succumb, allowing the responsible self to outlive that partial demise. This partialness of death is only an appearance, however, arising from the partialness of our account. The account can be taken a step further by putting into context Levinas's statement "Suicide is a contradictory concept" (TA 60, TO 72). In *Time and the Other* Levinas isolates the moment when Macbeth learns from Macduff that the latter was not born of woman. Macbeth learns thereby that he cannot count on the protection he believed was assured by the witches' prediction that no man born of woman could hurt him. Referring to the announcement Macbeth thereupon makes to Macduff, "I'll not fight with thee," Levinas comments: "Here is that passivity when there is an end to hope. Here is what I have called the end of virility. But straight away hope is reborn, and here are his last words: 'Though Burnam wood be come to Dunsinane, And though oppos'd, being of no woman born, Yet I will try the last.'" That is to say, trying, *conatus,* and the hope which the "I can" of the will to activity implies, implies in its turn the absolute passivity of death. That passivity is, so to speak, the principle of hope, *das Prinzip Hoffnung,* hope's *Urprinzip* or, more precisely, its *Unprinzip.*[6] How so? "To be or not to be," Levinas says, is an expression of Hamlet's realization of the impossibility of annihilating oneself. Hamlet grasps that he cannot grasp death. Because Levinas—notwithstanding what Heidegger calls the other thinking, *das andere Denken*—takes all thinking to be noetic-noematic, that is to say direct-edness at an object or objective, he maintains that death cannot be thought. But if death cannot be thought, neither can the nothingness to the thought of which Heidegger maintains the thought of death gives access; nor can being be thought if the way to the thought of being is the way to the thought of nothingness, as is maintained in *Being and Time.* Hence, Levinas concludes, that book's aim to be a fundamental ontology is not achieved. By pursuing it Heidegger cannot reach a description of the meaning of being. If the meaning of being is claimed to be temporality, if that meaning can be reached only through the thinking of nothingness, if the thinking of nothingness can be reached only through the thinking of death, and if the thinking of death is not a possibility, then perhaps instead of attempting to make sense of temporality via the nothingess indicated by mortality, we should attempt to make sense of mortality by first making sense of temporality. And that is Levinas's project.

Death is not nothingness. Ever to come, *à venir, avenir,* future, death is imminence which menaces the immanence of Dasein's being toward its death. *Minari,* meaning to menace and be imminent, is a deponent verb, and what the deferment intrinsic to death deposes is the persistent imperialist ego positing itself in its place in the sun, *Da,* there, ready to usurp the world. It is as though this Pascalian *pensée* leads to that other Pascalian *pensée* on the terror inspired by the silence of the infinite outer spaces occupied by the sun and the starry skies above, and as though the starry skies above were symbolic of the sublimity of the moral law and of the still higher height of the face of the other human being. But the face, although glorious, is not entirely benign. As observed earlier, it prosecutes me. It even persecutes me.

Again like the sublimity of the moral law, it is inimical to my monadic endeavor to survive. It haunts the phenomenological threat of death. That threat is phenomenologically social. This is the meaning Levinas takes from the statement "The Eternal brings death and brings life" (TeI 210, TaI 234). The Eternal is he over whom I can have no power, Levinas goes on to explain, and his explanation seems to entitle his reader to infer that what the Eternal stands for here is what also Satan stands for, for Levinas brackets the enemy and the accuser with God. What he is talking about is evil, as his essay "Transcendence and Evil" confirms (CPP 176–86). The evil or badness to which that essay points is not the evil which is opposed to the good. It is the primordial malevolence beyond the errance which according to Heidegger is the primordial partner of primordial truth. It is the menace beyond the opposition of evil and good and in virtue of which we may say that the good beyond being is also the ultra-ontological bad. We have already said that according to Levinas goodness pursues and persecutes me from the face of the other. We may say too, recalling that the French *mal* is either evil or illness, bad health, malady, that the evil of my death's imminence is an occasion for vigilance. Even in the approach my death makes to me in my growing old, vigilance is prescribed as indelibly as in the word *vieillissement* is inscribed the word *veille*. For the approach of death is not my approach toward it, not *Sein zum Tod,* but its approach toward me, and its approach to me is passive synthesis.

DUST AND ASHES

The phrase "passive synthesis" is Husserl's. Having cast Husserl as one of the sources of the misleading proposition that all consciousness is noetico-noematically intentional, Levinas acknowledges that Husserl's doctrine of temporality as operatively intentional non-representational passive synthesis is a source of his own correction of that error. "The room made in Husserlian phenomenology for non-representative phenomenology promised a significance (*signifiance*) not proceeding from knowledge, but the promise was not kept" (DMT 82). The promise is kept only where room is kept open for what Levinas here refers to as non-representative intentional consciousness and elsewhere refers to as non-intentional consciousness and inverse intentionality or intentionality *à rebours.* This last phrase has the sense of being against the grain or upstream, as when Levinas writes that the time of death flows upstream (TeI 213, TaI 235). Its literal meaning is against the lie of the hair. Against the lie, against the direction, against the *sens,* against *Sinn,* against straightforward sense. Remembering, as Heidegger does, that being healthy is being *sanus,* and remembering, as Nietzsche does, that *sanus* is cognate with *salvus, salve, salut,* salvation, Levinas maintains that it is thanks to the counter-sensicality, nonsensicality, and insanity announced in bad health and the death it announces that sense is saved for the life of the egological self. The bad health or insanitariness which announces death also announces the good

113

health of sanctity, the *Heiligkeit* which falls short of wholeness because it is the height of madness, of *folie*, of *Unheiligkeit*. Other than the *Angst* of being toward the indeterminacy of non-being which according to Heidegger is incorporated in the certainty of death, other than intension and intentionality, *meinen* and *jemeinen*, the affectively alterological fear of death is the apology for life egological.

It may seem that another step, a *pas encore*, has to be taken before we can understand why the meaning of egological *jemeiniges meinen*, meaning which is mine (Hegel) is rescued by the danger—the *Gefahr* (Heidegger, Hölderlin), the *beau risque* (Levinas, Plato)—of what we might call the *deinen*, the "thining," the being for the other whom the for-itself is to serve. It may seem that Levinas has still not told us how he gets from the fear *of* the other of which he writes in one paragraph of *Totality and Infinity* to the fear *for* the other of which he writes two paragraphs later (ibid.). But how this step is to be taken is implicit in what has already been said. This *pas encore* has already been taken there. If my death approaches as though inflicted on me by a hostile other, and if the one thus menaced is the ego persisting in its being, it is already a murderous being. The other's hostility is already accusation. I am the culpable survivor of the murderer I have always been from before my birth, before any commitment of myself to a contract that I could break and before the commission of any other particular offense. So Levinas is able to write: "My death is my part in the death of the other and in my death I die this death which is my fault. The death of the other is not simply a moment of the mineness of my ontological status" (DMT 50).

My part in the death of the other is my participation in the death of the other. We can glimpse how Levinas gets from the fear *of* the other to the fear *for* the other only if the menace of my mortality is not construed as the menace of an encounterable force. If my death is conceived as a force approaching me like a vehicle with which I am about to have a head-on collision, it will continue to be a puzzle to us how my involvement with such a physical *Anstoss* resisting my progress along the highway of life can carry any accusatory charge. Why should I not simply resent it? Levinas's lecture course on time and death gives the last word to Abraham: "The relation with the Infinite is the responsibility of one mortal for another. As in the passage in the Bible (Genesis 18:23 f.) where Abraham intercedes for Sodom. Abraham fears for the death of others and takes upon himself the responsibility of interceding. That is the moment when he says 'I am myself but ashes and dust.'" It would be quite wrong to suppose that Levinas takes Abraham's words as tantamount to the statement that he knows what it is to be mortal and can therefore experience sympathy with the Sodomites. Prior to feeling with that can be symmetrically returned—an unconditional condition of the sympathy that is primary according to moral theories like Hume's—is my being immediately and asymmetrically affected by the other in me and in the ever-present menace of my ever-future death. But it is not this latter feeling either which Levinas takes Abraham's words to express. Abraham's feeling is expressed rather in his taking upon himself the responsibility to intercede. What is expressed in his exclamation "I am myself but ashes and dust" is the absurdity of his death and the consequent gratuity of his taking upon himself that responsibility to intercede. He does it for nothing. That is how the nothingness of my death afflicts me: not as that which turns me back to the question of my own being, but as that which turns me, the culpable survivor, forward toward those who survive me in a time that is not an extension of my time, but is a time for the other without me, a time which would not be without me if it were imagined as some sort of afterlife; for the imagination of an afterlife would lend itself all too readily to becoming a consolatory way of once more being toward my death, another possibility of impossibility instead of the impossibility of possibility which alone secures the absolute gratuity without which responsibility toward the other might be recompensed if only by the self-congratulatory thought of my self-sacrifice (HAH 42–45, LBPW 49–51).

Abraham and the narrative of Genesis supply Levinas with the clues for the familial categories whose crossing with those drawn from Greek thinking and mythology *Totality and Infinity* describes. Abraham is the one who, in contrast with Ulysses, does not return to his home. The primacy of separateness and the irreducibility of alterity to sameness are already implicit in Levinas's analysis of femininity. Femininity according to this analysis is more than biological and sexual femaleness. Femininity, paternity, maternity, fecundity, filiation, and fraternity are "categories," "conditions of the possibility" of the empirical biological concepts they commonly denote. They are not genetic concepts, so they can apply where there is no woman in the house and where there is no biological son or daughter; they can apply, for example, to the relation of teacher and student (EeI 73–75, EaI 70–72). They are not generic concepts in the sense of the classificatory "catholic" universals of Plato and Aristotle. They are not abstract modes of representation, nor concrete universals in the manner of Hegel. They are concrete ways in which human being is accomplished, realized, and produced. Not being essences, genera, or species, they are not strictly conditions of possibility in the sense of formal or Kantian transcendental logic. Nor are they possibilities in the sense of Heidegger. Already beyond description in terms of "I can" is the innocent youthful enjoyment of oneself not yet disturbed by bad conscience and not yet amounting to straightforward intentional consciousness of noematic objects, but rather living from them. This "from" anticipates the inversely intentional affect of the erotic enjoyment of another human being, of feminine alterity. Erotic love is beyond concupiscent need; it does not seek satisfaction through possession. Yet, being a relation with an intimate thou, neither is it fully ethical desire of a You. Rather is it transcendence beyond the face of the other toward an ever more remote future of generations more future than my possibilities, incomprehensible in terms of the opposition of being and nothingness. For filiation is also disaffiliation. The temporality of filiation is a temporality of ethical filiation which severs ontological filiation, severs the head of Father Parmenides. Timeless being is killed by the commandment "Thou shalt not kill." All time is the time of death, but instead of being a time of which the length is defined as the persistence in being of a being running up toward its own death, it is a time of which the length is that of an infinite patience in the face of and beyond the face of another.

The deponence of the verb *patior* marks a time in which imminence puts off, defers, deposes the ontological persistence of a finite being's perdurance in favor of a persistence which is *infinite ethical endurance:*

Endurance, because a burden is carried.

Ethical, because the burden is not the burden of biological aging but the burden of responsibility arising from no contract or act performed in the time of biography or memoir, but going back to an absolutely and immemorably lapsed past of an aging that gives sense and direction to biological senescence by commanding vigilance on behalf of the other human being.

Infinite, because the responsibility (like the God of Descartes's *Meditations*) exceeds definition and comprehension within the frame of an idea and breaks up the flow of time finishing in death, whether this time be conceived as time measured by the position of the sun or the hands of a clock (Newton, Kant), as accumulative lived duration (Bergson), as ecstasis toward death (Heidegger) or as history totalizing itself in the end of history (Hegel). Into and cutting across temporal continuity there intervenes an interval which Levinas refers to as dead time. This is the between time of the separation between me and the other human being, whether the other human being is the one who is excluded from and threatens my egological enjoyment, the one who faces me and is welcomed into my home, or the son beyond the face (TeI 29, 260, TaI 58, 284).

Biological aging is produced, accomplished, and emphasized in an aging where the always already elapsedness of a past that was never present is my always already having lapsed in being overdue in taking up my responsibility. As aging is accomplished in the ethical absolute past, so filiation is emphasized as the ethical absolute future, the absolute youth of the son and his ability to give absolute forgiveness. As absolute culpability is not defined by empirical fault, neither is it for an empirical fault committed earlier in time that it receives absolute pardon. Pardon, understood absolutely, as the quasi-condition of the experience of the happiness of reconciliation (*felix culpa*) is constitutive of time (TeI 259, TaI 283). Across the space of dead time in which I do not go up to death but death comes to me, I am resurrected in the son, the uniquely chosen son who is nevertheless also the brother face to face with a brother, one among a plurality of brothers, each of whom is unique. Pardon as the judgment of human beings of future generations is ab-solution, that is to say, disaffiliation in filiation, the undoing of the judgment passed by history. Judgment is thereby delivered from anonymity, truth is kept in touch with the truthfulness of a person, freedom is invested in responsibility for the other. When the other's death becomes the key to the concept of death, when death is described as the impossibility of possibility and is emptied of the pathos that comes to it from the fact of its being mine, the concept of death is modified, Levinas says (TeI 217, TaI 239). So too is the concept of concept. For when the concept is conceived across conception, femininity, paternity, and the dead time of transubstantiative filiation—where these expressions stand for the metaphysical and ethical meaning of what is meant by their biological and theological homonyms—Desire is Desire for a being that Desires, so that the concept of concept transcends the egological finitude of *Sein zum Tod* and the impersonal infinitude of *Sein zur Totalität*. Levinas's modification of the concept of death is at the same time a modification of the concept of concept, because, in locating the center of gravity of life in the death of the other human being, it dislocates the limit of limit. Limit gets de-fined as *limen,* the threshold across which strangers are invited to enter, and across which they and the child and the widow may call me to exit for good.

117

8

THE POSSIBILITY OF HEIDEGGER'S DEATH

CLASSICAL MODALITIES

Martin Heidegger died at Freiburg-im-Breisgau on the morning of Wednesday, 26 May 1976. It is a fact that he died there and then. It is a consequential fact that he is now dead. So, since *ab esse ad posse valet consequentia,* it was possible that he would die and would be dead. His death was a possibility. Admittedly, knowing, as we do, that Heidegger is dead, it goes against the conventions of conversational implicature to say only that his death was or his being dead is a possibility. And for Heidegger to have said just that his death was a possibility would have implied that he was not certain that he would die. But because he knew he would die, he must have known that his death was a possibility. And it would have been in order for him or any other philosopher to say this. He did indeed say that his death and that of every other Dasein was a possibility. Why then does Professor Paul Edwards believe that in saying this Heidegger was guilty of a "fantastic misuse of the word 'possibility'"?[1] If Heidegger was, so are all those logicians who infer possibility from actuality. What misuse there might be seems no more serious than that of someone who says he believes something when in fact he knows it. Suppose therefore that Heidegger had only believed he and others would die. It would have been quite in order for him to say that death was a possibility.

Hence in saying that death is a possibility, Heidegger does not appear to be "Carrying the misuse of language to the ultimate degree."[2] But it may be that Heidegger's reasons for saying that death is a possibility are not good ones. And it must be stated without further ado that the good reason I have given for saying that death is a possibility is not a reason that Heidegger gives. My reason is couched in the terms of classical modal logic, but according to Heidegger, these are, although invaluable when employed in their proper logical space, inadequate for the existential ontology in which he claims logic has its foundation.

Edwards considers that there may be an argument in the logic of modalities behind some of the things Heidegger says, namely the argument that since death is not an *actuality* (and not an *im*possibility) it must be a possibility. Edwards does not mean that Heidegger denies that we die, but that he denies that being dead is a "state," i.e., either an action like singing or a passion like resting or sleeping. I do not myself count sleeping among the

118

passions. This makes no difference however to Edwards's point that Heidegger wrongly takes possibility and actuality to be exhaustive and exclusive alternatives relative to each other and to impossibility, whereas they are not, because another disjunct is sheer absence of state.

There would be something to say for Edwards's assertion that a false disjunction hovers in the background of Heidegger's discussion if he could persuade us that Heidegger overlooks this last disjunct. But he allows that Heidegger does not overlook it. Furthermore, Heidegger's affirmation of it is one of the few of his conclusions he endorses, though he laments the "hocus pocus" Heidegger indulges in on the way to it. "Bertrand Russell reached the same result with less effort and without fear of being misunderstood in his essay 'What I Believe' in which he wrote, quite simply, 'I believe that when I die I shall rot, and nothing of my ego will survive.'"

THE ONTOLOGICAL DIFFERENCE

Edwards is sure that in describing death as a possibility Heidegger is not intending possibility as opposed to certainty or probability, as when I say it is possible I shall die five years from now. For, Edwards writes, "Heidegger repeatedly insists—quite rightly, though not very originally—that death is a *certainty* and not just a possibility in *this* sense." What is *this* sense?

One must beware of being misled by Edwards's example. My death must be distinguished from the time of my death. Heidegger is not of course saying that we are certain of the time at which we shall die. On the contrary, "what is peculiar in death's certainty is that it is possible at any moment."[3] So it would appear that if we are looking for a way of making sense of Heidegger's phrase "the possibility of death" we may have found one in this possibility of death's coming at any time, "the indefiniteness (*Unbestimmtheit*) of its 'when.'" This interpretation could be supported by appealing to the fact that the genitive in the English phrase and in its German equivalent permits of being read either as an objective or a subjective genitive: what is meant could be either the possibility that death is or the possibility that death *has*. Death's indefiniteness, the possibility of its coming at any time, is a possibility that death has. As we have seen, Heidegger does say explicitly that death has this property. A signal warning the reader of what he does not mean when he says this is his use of the noun "das Eigentümliche" in referring to "what is peculiar in death's certainty." This is the word he employs for what is proper to something, "das Eigentum," "property," being the word reserved in Heidegger's fundamental phenomenological ontology for property or belonging in an authentic (*eigentlich*) sense which according to him founds and makes possible the inauthentic sense of "property" (*Eigenschaft*) met with in logic, epistemology—e.g., primary and secondary qualities—and non-fundamental ontology. The latter sense tends to distract us from the sense of the former, which is therefore out of the ordinary, peculiar, *eigentümlich*.

If it is only the factual possibility of its striking at any time that Heidegger has in mind when he speaks of the possibility of death, we should have to agree with Edwards that when Heidegger comes to the topic of death halfway through the published portion of *Being and Time* he in this connection and without warning begins using the word "possibility" in a different way from that indicated earlier in the book. But on my reading, although when Heidegger comes to the topic of death he introduces the idea of the possibility which death *has* of taking us by surprise, he continues to write of the possibility which death *is*. These two uses of "possibility" are made, for example, when he writes of "death's ownmost (or most peculiar) character as a possibility . . . a possibility which is certain and at the same time indefinite, that is to say, possible at any moment."[4] "Possible" in this last phrase refers to a feature of the time of death. "Possibility" refers in its two occurrences to a modality of death itself.

It is possibility as a modality of death which is said to be certain. There is no sign of any desire on Heidegger's part to argue from this certainty of death to death's possibility by appealing to rules of modal inference as discussed above in the first section.

There is hardly a page of *Being and Time* where Heidegger is not occupied with the ordinary employment of words. And many pages are occupied with the terms and status of formal logic and artificial languages. This is inevitable in a book which glosses the basic categorial lexicon of everyday language and of Western metaphysics and sciences with a lexicon which purports to uncover the still more basic "conditions of the possibility" of the traditionally recognized categories these latter are prone to conceal. The superstructural founded level, including that of Kant's categories of the understanding, is what Heidegger calls the "ontic" level, where the questions are about "beings" broadly understood to cover entities, events, processes, states of affairs, qualities, and relations, whether empirical or not. At the substructural founding level the questions at stake are "ontological," concerned with the structures of "being," whether being in general or being-there, Da-sein. He often has a different word in the ontological lexicon for the term which answers to it in the ontic lexicon, though there is frequently a shared etymological root, as with the already cited pair "Eigentum" and "Eigenschaft." This is to be expected if he is correct in his view that the ontic terms are declensions of the ontological words or connote deficient modes of the latter. Sometimes the difference, which he calls "the ontological difference," is marked merely by a hyphen. For example, he occasionally writes "Ent-schlossenheit" for resolvedness or un-closedness, an authentic way of being, to contrast with "Entschlossenheit" in its more usual meaning of resoluteness, this being more like a condition of being closed than un-closed.[5] Another example of hyphenation put to the same use is the pair "ent-fernend," removing the distance, and "entfernend," removing, placing at a distance. More cryptically, he at times makes a dual use of one word. This is the case with "Möglichkeit," "possibility." However, this word is sometimes used in compounds like "Seinsmöglichkeit" where the ontological interpretation is intended. It is sometimes written with inverted commas where the ontic, i.e., everyday or scientific or traditional logical or metaphysical interpretation is intended. It may seem paradoxical that the inverted commas should flank a word when it is being employed in its everyday or philosophically familiar way. But this practice is not unreasonable given Heidegger's idea that the empirical and other "normal" ontic meanings of these terms are founded upon ontological meanings.

Readers of Husserl will know how extravagant he is with inverted commas. Irritating though this indulgence can be, readers of Heidegger, his one-time assistant, may wish that his use of this device had been less sparing. This might have saved some of us, at least Paul Edwards and myself, the difficulty we experience in deciding what he means by "the possibility of death." For not only is "possibility" a dual-purpose word for Heidegger. So too is "death." A more liberal employment of inverted commas would have helped us determine when these words are being put to their ontic purpose and when to their ontological. For instance, it might have prevented Edwards from supposing that one of the main theses in Heidegger's discussion of death is that when we are dead we really are dead in the sense that there is a total absence of any conscious (or unconscious) state. How can that be a burden of Heidegger's discussion, how can he be agreeing with Russell and Edwards about the finality of death, given the following declaration, parts of which Edwards himself cites: "If death is defined as the 'end' of Dasein, that is to say, of Being-in-the-world, this does not imply any ontical decision whether 'after death' still another Being is possible, either higher or lower, or whether Dasein 'lives on' or even 'outlasts' itself and is 'immortal'."[6]

In the light of Heidegger's adoption of some of Kierkegaard's terminology and adaptation of some of his thinking, it is tempting to suppose that in this sentence he is endorsing what the Dane says about the question of immortality when he writes:

> the question of immortality is essentially not a learned question, rather is it a question of inwardness, which the subject by becoming subjective must put to himself. Objectively the question cannot be answered, because objectively it cannot be put, since immortality precisely is the potentiation and highest development of the developed subjectivity. Only by really willing to become subjective can the question properly emerge, therefore how could it be answered objectively? The question cannot be answered in social terms, for in social terms it cannot be expressed, inasmuch as only the subject who wills to become subjective can conceive the question and ask rightly, "Do *I* become immortal, or am *I* immortal?" . . . If one were systematically to hang up immortality on the wall, like Gessler's hat, before which we take off our hats as we pass by, that would not be equivalent to being immortal or to being conscious of one's immortality . . . to want to answer systematically a question which possesses the remarkable trait that systematically it cannot be put . . . is like wanting to paint Mars in the armour which rendered him invisible.[7]

There is no denying that this passage anticipates the part played in Heidegger's thinking by the idea that we are commonly too inclined to prate on questions whereof one should be silent. Although discourse (*Rede, logos*) is a fundamental ontological structure of Dasein, an "existential" as opposed to a category which is a structure of what does not ex-sist understandingly ahead of itself, and although in un-self-possessed or inauthentic Dasein that existential expresses itself with garrulity (*Gerede*) and keeps on saying "I" ("I think . . . ," "Cogito . . ."),[8] the mode of discourse of self-possessed, authentic, *ent-schlossen*, un-shut-in, free Dasein is silence. So too is the discourse of what Heidegger calls conscience, a topic to be returned to briefly below.

Notwithstanding this and other respects in which there is a kinship between the two thinkers, Heidegger considers that Kierkegaard, in spite of or because of his criticism of Hegel, has not liberated himself from the ontology of the Greeks as seen and developed by Hegel. Heidegger would have agreed with Kierkegaard in saying that in wondering about mortality and immortality a different mode of discourse is called for from that which treats death as an objective present-at-hand event which presently happens to each one of us. This is what Tolstoy's Ivan Ilych realized when it came home to him that death can be a more live issue than it is represented to be in the thought that since all men are mortal and Caius is a man, Caius is mortal. Yet neither Ivan Ilych nor Kierkegaard would dispute that death is an objective fact. Nor does Heidegger dispute this. The commentators on Heidegger whom Edwards cites are mistaken when they say or imply that, in the words of one of them, death is not according to Heidegger "a public fact out there in the world." Edwards must therefore be mistaken if he believes Heidegger purports to refute the "external" view of death for which his illustration is the statement of Epicurus that "when I am, death is not and when I am not, death is." As already observed, Heidegger does not set out to refute ontic assertions, whether made by laymen or by specialists. Nor does he set out directly to refute what other philosophers say. To do that would be to remain enclosed in their general ontology, as even Kierkegaard, in Heidegger's opinion, remains trapped in the general ontology of the philosophers he criticizes. That general ontology, Heidegger maintains, is not a fundamental ontology, because it asks about the being of beings without asking about the meaning of being. It is, as Heidegger uses the word, "ontic." This is why he counts Kierkegaard's edifying writings to be more important philosophically than those writings of his which have philosophical pretensions,[9] though the reader of *Being and Time* is advised not to expect edification from that work. Even the words "authentic" and "inauthentic" as used there are not meant to have a moral or other valuative force. They belong to the lexicon of fundamental ontology, whereas the imperatives of morality and inwardness are for him no less ontic than the laws of science.

Edwards should therefore not have agreed with those commentators who argue that because Heidegger supposedly denies the "external" view of death he follows Kierkegaard's teaching on subjectivity and inwardness, recommending an "interiorizing" of death. When Heidegger describes his account of death as this-worldly (*diesseitig*), there is no implication that it is not still *worldly,* or that it is inner-worldly as opposed to outer-worldly. The so-called inner world, i.e., the world of mental attitudes and psychological states, is an ontic region. More basic than it and the ontic outer world of sensory perception and science is ontological being-in-the-world. Death, Heidegger aims to show, is not only ontic deadness, the external or internal phenomenon of death, or the cause of that phenomenon. It is also, and more basically, an existential-ontological possibility of being-in-the-world.

This is not, as Edwards holds, arbitrarily to redefine the word "death" or to slur over and obscure two different senses.[10] It is to keep the everyday sense, but to keep it in its place. One of the themes developed throughout the entire length of *Being and Time* is that ordinary language obscures what is meant by words, e.g., the words "death" and "possibility." The way we ordinarily think about death obscures from us that besides the everyday ontic and inauthentic way of conceiving death (and presupposed by it) there is another ontological possibility, that of being toward death in an authentic way. Until we can demonstrate that Heidegger's philosophy of language is wrong in this regard, we cannot charge him with achieving his conclusions uninterestingly by simply stipulating new definitions of "death" and "possibility." We must be prepared to allow that he may indeed be clarifying and interpreting what we are committed to in our ordinary talk about death. We must be prepared to allow that he is doing phenomenological ontology as characterized in the introduction to *Being and Time,* i.e., describing not just what shows itself, but what hides itself thanks to a kind of transcendental illusion, a propensity to lapse (*Verfallen*) grounded in the ontological-existential deep structures of Dasein's discursiveness (*Rede*), which distracts us from those very structures. One may well ask how in that case Heidegger can manage to fill so many pages describing these structures which are so shy about showing themselves—many more pages even than Carlyle devotes to describing the geography of the great Empire of Silence. Analogous questions arise in connection with Freud and Marx. I shall limit myself here to a general and a related particular comment on this question as it arises in the Heideggerian context.

One of Heidegger's theses is that Dasein, hence human existence, is ontological. This thesis is also expressed by saying that Dasein is distinguished by being an entity for whom, in its very being, being is an issue or in question. This last phrase translates a phrase constructed with the verb "umgehen." I do not recall Heidegger or any of his commentators having the nerve to point out that "umgehen" also means "to evade." I should not put it past Heidegger to intend this duplicity, whether or not it places the syntax of the German sentence under some strain. It fits well his contention that fleeing in fear in the face of my ontic death, as exemplified in the attempt to remove its sting by affirming that of course death comes to us all, is itself evidence of the possibility that I could be more open with myself concerning the mortality, the being toward death, which is an ontological structure of my Dasein, i.e., a way of being toward my being, a way of manifesting my unavoidable regard for what it is to be.

> The falling everydayness of Dasein is acquainted with Dasein's certainty, and yet evades (*weicht aus*) being certain. But in the light of what it evades, this very evasion attests phenomenally that death must be conceived as one's ownmost possibility. . . . [11]

I DIE THEREFORE I AM

The positive outcome of the second section of this discussion is that since the average man is prone to treat death as an empirical fact of life, if a different way of approaching death is open to us it is not unnatural to describe this as a possibility. In this third section something is required to be said about a difficulty I share with Edwards which makes me wonder whether this interpretation gives the substance of the possibility involved in Heidegger's analysis of death.

Following Edwards I earlier distinguished factual deadness, the occurrence of death and the cause of that occurrence. The cause may be described in various ways, depending on whether one is or is not a physician, a coroner, or some other kind of specialist. The non-specialist at least would say that the cause of a particular death was, for example, being shot or cancer. Some deaths are sudden. Some are lingering. In the latter case there will be a more or less long period in which the patient will be dying. All these senses or aspects of death are factual and empirical and therefore ontic. Heidegger maintains that a full account of death cannot be given in ontic terms. An existential analysis is called for in which death, end, and possibility are understood not ontically as objective events, processes, conditions, or facts (*Tatsachen*), but as factical (*faktisch*), ontological ways of Dasein's being with regard to being. In the course of his analysis Heidegger asserts that "The 'ending' ('enden') which we have in view when we speak of death does not signify Dasein's being-at-an-end (*Zu-Ende-sein*), but a being-toward-the-end (*Sein zum Ende*) of this entity. Death is a way to be (*eine Weise zu Sein*) which Dasein takes over as soon as it is."[12] Of the word "dying" he says that it is to designate "that way of being (*Seinsweise*) in which Dasein is toward its death."[13] Dasein exists endingly.[14]

These elucidations immediately give rise to the problem that if the "ending" and "dying" of Heidegger's existential analysis are being toward the end and being toward death, there still seems to be wanting an account of what it is toward which we are.

One solution to this problem would be to say that the object or end toward which this way of being toward is directed is the ontic event which terminates life and which Heidegger calls demise (*Ableben*)—though strictly, perhaps, he should speak only of the demise of man, not of Dasein, since "Ableben" is an anthropological term belonging to the ontic lexicon, while "Dasein" belongs to the ontological lexicon. "Dasein's demise" commits a category mistake or, as we had better say in talking about Heidegger, a category-existential mistake because it loses sight of the "ontological difference" between categories, which are ontic, and existentials, which are ontological.

This solution is vulnerable to the objection that it makes existential being toward death contingent upon empirical beliefs, and Heidegger rules out this contingency.[15] Although a story or a death in the family may be the occasion of a child's first learning about the fact of death, "Dasein is a way to be which Dasein takes over as soon as it is." And a Dasein would be toward death in Heidegger's existential sense even if it believed itself immortal and, presumably, even if that belief were true.

The rejection of this solution allows that the intentional "object" of being toward death might be non-empirical and non-ontic. A solution along these lines would be in difficulty however if we felt that Heidegger could not distinguish the intentional object from the intending. We cited his elucidations of the words "ending" and "dying." We must also note that he says "*Death is,* as *Dasein's* end, in the being of this entity *toward* its end."[16] Does this mean that since death and Dasein's end have been swallowed up in dying, we are faced again with the problem of having no intentional object for Dasein to be toward? This would follow if Heidegger were saying that death, as Dasein's end, is being toward its end. What he in fact says is that death *is* (his italics), as Dasein's end, *in* (my italics) the being of Dasein toward its end. He is not here identifying death as end with dying as being toward its end. Although superficially the logic of what Heidegger is saying resembles that of the implication between "X is dead" and "X died," this resemblance is only superficial. For Heidegger's being toward death is, so to speak, a lifelong dying, and although the empirical statement "X is dead" entails the empirical statement "X died," it does not entail "X is dying." If X was the victim of an extremely sudden death there was no period over which he was dying.

However, if it is empirically true that someone is dying, then it is empirically true that he will be dead. It is the entailment in this direction which is not immediately relevant to the problem of interpretation we are presently occupied with, the problem of finding what I provisionally called an intentional object for the intentionality of "being toward." The problem can be solved, I believe, only if we pay heed to the "*in*" which I italicize in Heidegger's sentence "*Death is,* as *Dasein's* end, *in* the being of this entity *toward* its end." It should be noted that Heidegger himself italicizes the fourth word in this sentence. He is talking about the ec-sisting of Dasein. Dasein's way of being is different from that of hammers, jugs, and bridges (*Zeug* in the sense of tool or utensil or device), all of which fall initially and for the most part within the category of readiness to hand, and from pieces of wood or steel, dollops of clay, and heaps of stone which, unless we are seeking raw material out of which, for example, to make a hammer or build a bridge (*Zeug* in the sense of useful stuff), fall within the category of presence at hand. And Dasein's way of being is different by being at least pre-theoretically alive to this difference. This pre-theoretical way of being caught up with the question of being (of being, as Heidegger puts it, pre-ontologically ontological) has a parallel in the idea that, according to Kant, we do not have to read his first or second *Critique* in order to see the necessity of the principle of the second analogy and the moral law. We have already found ourselves asking "Why did this happen?" and "What if everyone did that?"

Heidegger claims that his existential analytic penetrates to a deeper stratum than Kant's transcendental analytic and analytic of pure practical reason. Kant exposes the deep structure of what it is to be a theoretician and a rational agent. Heidegger exposes the deep structure of what it is to be. Whereas Western philosophy has been dominated by questions about human nature posed in terms of rational animality and life, Heidegger aims to dismantle this framework of philosophical enquiry concerning the human understanding and the principles of morals, and to raise questions posed in terms of Dasein, being there, and death.

Being toward death is Dasein's most distinctive way of being there. Being toward death, not rationality or self-consciousness, is what enables Dasein to be all there, to be wholly itself, a finite whole because it exists endingly. When of the two possible ways of being toward its death, the authentic and the inauthentic, Dasein adopts the latter, the intentional object of its concern is the ontic eventuality which it expects. When Dasein adopts an authentic way of being toward death, the intentional object it cares about is a non-object, a non-thing. It is only by contrast with being toward its no-thingness that it can be toward, and take in, its own being there. Fear (or courage, or resignation) in the face of its expected demise is replaced by anxiety before the indefinite no-thingness which limits its own being, defines it. Anxiety detaches Dasein from its public, average, and impersonal self, enabling it to achieve a resolved and focused view of what it is to be totally itself. *Morior ergo sum.* The Cartesian *cogito* and the Kantian transcendental unity of apperception, i.e., the possibility of prefixing to any thought the thought that I think it, do not reach past the conception of the self as substance or logical subject. *Complete* self-consciousness is an awareness not only that I am thinking, but of other ways of being, above all and most distinctively, of my being toward being. This is not possible without my being toward no-thingness. Heidegger agrees with Hegel that pure being and pure nothing are the same, though not for the same reason; "not because the two . . . are one in their indefiniteness and immediacy, but because being itself is finite in essence and is only revealed in the transcendence of Dasein as held out into the nothing."[17] He tries to show that the self-subsistence (*Selbständigkeit*) of the subject and object as portrayed in the ontic epistemological metaphysics exemplified by Descartes and Kant is supplemented and founded by the ontological self-constancy (*Selbst-ständigkeit*) of Dasein.

Heidegger also attempts to show that ontic notions in the practical sphere presuppose ontological ones. For example, he insinuates that conscience as this is commonly conceived is the objective correlative of a non-objective and non-ontic conscience (*Gewissen*) which witnesses to Dasein's being toward death. Hearing the call of conscience in this ontological sense is an openness to the certainty (*Gewissheit*) of death. Understanding its call is wanting to have a conscience. Heidegger would no doubt claim that this *Gewissenhabenwollen* is the ontological foundation of the ontic Kantian will. He might also say that somewhat as the natural world unified by laws of nature is for Kant a "typic" or model of the intelligible world unified by the moral law, so death and the existential facticity of Dasein's being born to die is a memento or memorial of the possibility of Dasein's being face to face with its being and nothingness, as it is when it finds itself wondering why there is any thing at all and not rather no thing. There being no created thing was at least a logical possibility which Leibniz's God had to face. It is the ontological possibility of there being nothing which Heidegger's Dasein faces when it exists authentically toward its death.

SUMMARY

I have distinguished three senses in which death may be described as a possibility.

(1) Death understood as the fact of deadness, the event of becoming dead, and the process of dying are possibilities, logical and empirical, because they can be actualities. This is not a sense in which Heidegger is interested in describing death as a possibility. However, he would not deny that death is a possibility in this sense. Nor would he deny that being toward death in the ontological sense that does interest him is a logical and empirical possibility. For he emphasizes that the existential-ontological ways of being he analyzes are existentiell possibilities, by which he means that they must be capable of ontic instantiation in an individual Dasein.

(2) Death understood not as an ontic empirical event in the manner of (1) but as the ontological "advent" (*Ereignis*) of my non-being can come at any moment. It is indefinite, i.e., it is at any moment possible. Here the possibility is a possibility of the time of death, not, as in (1), of death itself.[18]

(3) Death as *authentic* being toward death is a possibility in the sense of being an alternative to being toward death inauthentically.

A problem may be thought to arise in connection with this third sense. This was touched on when I said that Heidegger's ontological analysis of death is consistent with the fact that a bereavement may be the occasion on which a child learns of ontic death. What are we to say of the child *before* it learns of ontic death? It is unlikely that Heidegger would want to say such a child is authentically toward death, and it seems that it cannot be inauthentically toward death because on our hypothesis it does not have the concept of death as an ontic event. It may be suggested that a solution to this problem can be found by going back to what Heidegger writes earlier in *Being and Time* about our dealings with objects and other people, what he calls, respectively, *Besorgen* (concern or preoccupation) and *Fürsorge* (solicitude). These terms designate not only positive modes. Solicitude, for instance, covers not just attentiveness toward others, but also the deficient mode of neglect and the neutral mode of indifference, rather as "man" is not (yet) restricted to the male of the species of humanity. Given that *Besorgen* and *Fürsorge* are modes of *Sorge,* care, and that this is Heidegger's name for the whole structure of Dasein whose wholeness is realized in authentic being toward death, it appears reasonable to assume that as well as the authentic and inauthentic modes of being toward death Heidegger would admit a third and neutral mode. If so, and if we are unable to see how the child who has not reached the age of consenting to its death could be toward death either authentically or inauthentically, this could be the mode in which it would be. This way out of the problem is indicated by Heidegger's statement as early as p. 53 of *Being and Time* that Dasein exists either authentically or inauthentically or in a way which is undifferentiated with respect to these modes. However, the adoption of this way out of the problem opens the door to questions like "Is there Dasein in dreamless sleep?" "What are the structures of so-called primitive Dasein?" "How subnormal can a person be before he is no longer Dasein?" and, by extrapolation, to the idea, rejected by Heidegger, that beasts may be Dasein. We should perhaps say therefore that Heidegger's position is similar to that of all those philosophers who have felt that the existence of children and idiots does not prevent one offering an analysis of rationality. So maybe the problem imagined in this paragraph does not arise. To ask whether a child is Dasein and so exists ontologically toward death may be a category-cum-existential mistake like the one previously mentioned of talking of Dasein's demise.

Finally, there is a further sense, not so far isolated, in which death may be described as a possibility:

(4) The distinction between a possibility which something *has* and a possibility which something *is* compels us to take notice that Heidegger writes not only of death as a possibility of being, a *Seinsmöglichkeit,* but also of death as a *Seinkönnen.* A *Können* is a capacity, power, or potentiality. Ontic potentialities are abilities which things have and may develop, as a child may have and develop its potentiality to reason. But being toward death is an ontological potentiality, a potentiality of and for being. Dasein *is* its death itself.[19] Of course, shouting a word does not help to clarify its meaning. But it does help to bear in mind that Heidegger suggests that the first person singular "ich bin" is the key to an understanding of the verb "to be" when this applies to Dasein, for, he contends, appealing to the authority of Jakob Grimm, this part of the verb is connected with words meaning to cultivate, build, and inhabit.[20] It helps also to remember his transitive use of "exist." This permits him to say that Dasein exists its death, which is another way of

saying that it is ahead of itself toward it. Unlike beings that are not strictly speaking mortal, according to Heidegger, but perish (*verenden*), Dasein makes it possible for death to be existed as death. "We now call mortals mortals—not because their earthly life comes to an end, but because they are capable of death as death. (Die Sterblichen nennen wir jetzt die Sterblichen—nicht weil ihr irdisches Leben endet, sondern weil sie den Tod als Tod vermögen)."[21] This is not, Heidegger maintains, a possibility for beasts. It is distinctive of Dasein. Furthermore, while according to Kierkegaard "immortality precisely is the potentiation and highest development of the developed subjectivity," according to Heidegger Dasein is most wholly itself when it fulfills the potentiality for being which embraces all its other potentialities, by realizing the possibility of being authentically toward its mortality.

9

sELection

> At the time the children were burned on big
> piles of wood. The crematoria could not work at
> the time, and therefore the people were just
> burned in open fields with those grills, and also
> children were burned among them. Children
> were crying helplessly, and that is why the camp
> administration ordered that an orchestra be
> assembled of a hundred inmates and should
> play. They played very loud all the time. They
> played the Blue Danube or Rosamunde; so that
> even the people in the city of Auschwitz could
> not hear the screams. Without the orchestra they
> would have heard the screams of horror; they
> would have been terrible screams. The people
> two kilometres from there could even hear the
> screams, namely, the ones that came from the
> transports of children. . . . When one of the SS
> people sort of had pity with the children, he
> would take a child and beat the head against a
> stone before putting it on the pile of fire and
> wood, so the child lost consciousness. However,
> the regular way they did it was just throwing the
> children on the pile. . . . They used to put a sheet
> of wood, then the whole thing was sprinkled with
> petrol, then wood again, and petrol—and then
> people were placed there. Then the whole thing
> was lighted.[1]

The above epigraph or epitaph is not an exergue in relation to what follows.
Much of what follows will be an exergue in relation to it. Some of what
follows will also be a kind of blasphemy, depending upon how one answers
the question "Where is God?" Here is one answer to that question, the
answer of A-7713, where "A" is for Auschwitz and the number is that given
Elie Wiesel as a young boy:

> Roll call. SS all round us, machine guns trained: the traditional ceremony.
> Three victims in chains—and one of them, the little servant, the sad-eyed
> angel.
>
> The SS seemed more preoccupied, more disturbed than usual. To hang
> a young boy in front of thousands of spectators was no light matter. The
> head of the camp read the verdict. All eyes were on the child. He was lividly
> pale, almost calm, biting his lips. The gallows threw its shadow over him.

130

This time the Lagerkapo refused to act as executioner. Three SS re-placed him.

The three victims mounted together on to the chairs.

The three necks were placed at the same moment within nooses.

"Long live liberty!" cried the two adults.

But the child was silent.

"Where is God? Where is He?" someone behind me asked.

At a sign from the head of the camp, the three chairs tipped over.

Total silence throughout the camp. On the horizon the sun was setting.

[. . .]

Then the march past began. The two adults were no longer alive. Their tongues hung swollen, blue-tinged. But the third rope was still moving; being so light, the child was still alive. . . .

For more than half an hour he stayed there, struggling between life and death, dying in slow agony under our eyes. And we had to look him full in the face. He was still alive when I passed in front of him. His tongue was still red, his eyes were not yet glazed.

Behind me, I heard the same man asking:

"Where is God now?"

And I heard a voice within me answer him:

"Where is He? Here He is—He is hanging here on this gallows."[2]

If that is so, and if, as has been said, Auschwitz is the face of a child, then what follows may be blasphemy. Like so many of the people we meet through the writings of Elie Wiesel, the sad-eyed child with whom he was face to face as the sun was setting on that terrible day bit his lip. He was silent. But that silence commands us to speak. In his foreword to a book asking *How Can We Commit the Unthinkable?* Wiesel himself writes that "Be-cause we have seen the triumph of the night, we must tell of the suffering and the resistance of its victims. Because we have seen evil at work, we must denounce it."[3]

However, what I have agreed to tell of is, in the words of the letter in which the editors of this volume invite me to contribute to it, "the relationship of post-modernism and the Holocaust."[4] How much less inappropriate after Auschwitz to write a poem. At least a poem can cause a reader to bite his or her lip, and then perhaps to rage. But post-modern philosophy? Post-Holocaust philosophy?[5] How can they not be blasphemous unless they remember that suffering and that evil? Unless they remember and remind, if only by being written with the shadow of the gallows thrown across the page or by the light of those flames. Or by being written by someone other than me, a victim or a survivor, as most of this contribution so far has been. A collage of quotations, that would be post-modern. It would have been post-modern, and post-modern because post-Holocaust, to alternate words of my own with the words of someone else, not as a dialogue, but as contrapuntal interruption. One could write post-modern philosophy after the manner of the prayer with which another survivor, André Schwarz-Bart, refused to bring *The Last of the Just* to an end: "And praised. Auschwitz. Be.

Majdanek. The Eternal. Treblinka. And praised. Buchenwald. Be. Maut-
hausen. The Eternal. Belzec. And praised. Sobibor. Be. Chelmno. The
Eternal. Ponary. And praised. Theresienstadt. Be. Warsaw. The Eternal.
Vilno. And praised . . ."[6] This way of remembering, employing a mnemo-
graphic technique adapted also in David Krell's *Of Memory, Reminiscence, and
Writing*, where the verticality of the columns of Derrida's *Glas* is spun
through ninety degrees,[7] slows down comprehension even more than the
layered layout of a page of the Talmud.

On the other side of the page on which *The Last of the Just* says its prayer
in memory of Ernie Levy, "six million times dead," Ernie Levy himself,
drawing his last breath of Cyclon B, remembers the story his father once told
him of Rabbi Chanina ben Teradion who, from the fire into which the
Romans had thrown him wrapped in the scroll of the Torah for teaching the
Law thereon inscribed, when asked by his pupils "Master, what do you see?"
replied with his last breath "I see the the parchment burning, but the letters
are taking wing . . ." And Ernie Levy repeats, "Yes, surely, the letters are
taking wing."

How are we to comprehend this repetition? After Auschwitz, in the era
after the Final Solution, AFS, from out of the millions of words—diaries,
chronicles, annals, poems, novels, and now theological and philosophical
papers—written upon the six million names so that in the Holocaust those
names are not entirely burned, has been put together a question that
appears to be comparable with the philosophico-theological question raised
by the ancient unfinished prayer that takes wing from the lips of those
crushed into the gas chamber with Ernie Levy: "Hear, O Israel, the Lord our
God is one Lord . . . Who is like unto Thee, O merciful Father, and who with
Thee can be compared? . . ."

Incomparability. Let. Skarzysko. us. Bergen-Belsen. steal. Janow. time.
Dora. to. Neuengamme. think. Pustkow. about. Kovno. the. Gorazde. unthinkable. Rwanda. . . . praying that our theft is not the "subtle larceny" of
which George Steiner accuses those who, without having themselves been
involved in the event or having family or friends who were, "invoke the
echoes and trappings of Auschwitz and appropriate an enormity of ready
emotion in their own private design."[8] Steiner goes on to wonder whether in
her last poems Sylvia Plath is innocent of this charge, and whether they do
not embody "a dim resentment at not having been there." After Auschwitz
it is as if Being-there, *Dasein* and *Daseyn* as described by Heidegger, demands
to be inscribed by a Being-*There* in which *There* means a place in Poland,
Hungary, Czechoslovakia, or Germany where musicians wearing pajamas
were ordered to play Rosamunde and the Blue Danube to accompany the
saying of the *Shema'* or to camouflage the children's screams. As though
when Karl Löwith met Martin Heidegger in Rome in 1936, the latter should
have been wearing on his arm not the swastika as if consenting to horror, but
the six-pointed star of David (the star on Heidegger's tombstone has eight).[9]
Is it not conceivable that one of the forces behind National Socialism was

and is a dim resentment and a "fearful envy" of the chosenness of the Jews, driving it to put the Aryans in the Jews' place to the point of willing even the total annihilation of the Reich when the Nazis realized that their hopes of completing the *Endlösung* were coming to an end with the approaching end of the war?

Despite or because of Sylvia Plath's subconscious wish, her poem after Auschwitz "Daddy," Steiner says, is "the 'Guernica' of modern poetry" and, like Picasso's masterpiece, "achieves the classic act of generalization, translating a private, obviously intolerable hurt into a code of plain statement, of instantaneously public images which concern us all." So it escapes the snare of self-serving particularism of ideology, the

> barb wire snare.
> Ich, ich, ich, ich,
> . . . . [10]

It may not have escaped a sort of blasphemy if her "Ach, du" Da-Du "Daddy, I have had to kill you" apostrophizes among others the God of a post-Holocaust atheology, a God who was not there at Pustkow, Neuengamme . . . Treblinka, Majdanek or, to name the name of all those places, Auschwitz, for "the name of the town is common."

The commonness of a proper name or pro-name is what Auschwitz may seem to have led philosophers and theologians to think anew, again but otherwise, under the rubric that "A purely theoretical or academic theodicy is a form of idolatry and even blasphemy, because it takes the name of God and subjects it to the imaginings of the human mind and the ideological self-deifications of the human spirit."[11] Under that rubric reflection upon the commonness and incomparability of a proper name by those of us who remember Auschwitz solely, in Steiner's phrase, "by fiat of imagination," may escape idolatry and blasphemy only if "God" and "Auschwitz" are pro-names, and pro-names not for the Being Nietzsche's Zarathustra proclaimed we had killed by making the metaphysical declaration that he exists, but pro-names for the other human being, the *du* of whom Celan says in the words cited by Levinas as an epigraph to the chapter entitled "Substitution" in *Otherwise than Being*, "Ich bin du, wenn ich ich bin" (AE 125, OB 99). Therefore it would also be a form of blasphemy for Job's brother to latch on to Auschwitz to justify his saying "I told you so" under the rubric of atheism.[12]

The *Shema'* makes no metaphysical declaration that God exists or that he is one. It is an affirmation of witness and trust. Indeed the last letters of the Hebrew *Shema'*, "Hear," and *ehad*, "one," spell a word meaning "witness." These letters are traditionally written very large to obviate confusion with letters that would yield words for "perhaps" and "another." Perversely and, in the words of the title of one of Levinas's books, beyond the verse, *Au-delà du verset*, these are two words that play pivotal roles in his thinking.

Peut-être, "perhaps" or preferably "maybe," is a word whose role in late writings of Levinas can easily pass unnoticed. It is hardly a word one would expect to play any positive role in the exposition of his teaching given that his teaching purports to probe beyond the fundamental ontology of Heidegger where *pouvoir* (*können*) and *être* (*sein*) do play leading parts. No doubt the fact that these latter words are architectonic in *Being and Time* is one reason why Levinas employs the composite term in his criticism of Heidegger. However, in his employment these components are "emphasized" beyond their classical metaphysical senses and beyond the senses they bear in Heidegger's phenomenological ontology. The adumbration of these extended senses would require attention to Levinas's distinction between, on the one hand, a sign as the correlate of something signified either as meaning or reference with which one could in principle be presented and, on the other hand, a trace as beyond the difference between being and beings and thus beyond the capacity to be present. Beyond being, beyond truth, beyond verification and falsification, trace or tracing is an enigma. It is that of which one can speak only allusively (*ainissomai*) in that the attempt to make it the object of an assertion—as I am unsuccessfully attempting not to do in this assertion—is to suppose that it can be categorized. Whereas it is the enigma that categorizes us. Before it we stand accused. It is the Good beyond Being, so beyond the "is" and the "it," which yet finds itself inevitably in the guise of the "is" and the "it," predicate or subject or matter of fact. The incomparable measure of all measure, value beyond valuation, we yet fix upon it a price. And by a sort of transcendental illusion and false consciousness we understand the "can" either as Dasein's capacity to know or as Dasein's capacity to be, so that the "perhaps" gets limited to human limitation, finitude, and doubt. It is precisely in the excessive doubt of skepticism and the maybe-but-maybe-not of Pyrrhonism that Levinas traces a "maybe" which is the anarchic condition of the possibility and impossibility of the ethical in the classical meanings of these modal categories. For excessive universal skepticism exceeds itself by refuting itself, and yet it continually returns. Perhaps in this continual return lies the enigmatic "perhaps" of ethical reason beyond reason, that is, beyond reason measured by the principle of contradiction which embraces me and my interlocutor in one and the same logical space-time. Perhaps, as well as occupying one and the same space-time, the other, like the father in the son, is the one who constitutes my identity as the other for whom I go bail, the other for whom I am substantially one by substituting myself for him or her in response to a call that is diachronic in the sense that it has no location in the memorable, synchronizable time of the unity of apperception or in the ecstatic temporality of being and the phenomenon. These dark sayings about the enigma and the perhaps of the ethical fine risk are all we have room for here.[13] They will be put to use below. Now for some remarks about the second of the terms mentioned above, which we have found ourselves unable to avoid in our comments upon the first.

Another or the other is manifestly invoked in reference to the other human being, the You or the *du*. The other human being, *Autrui,* is singularly plural in the sense that there is more than one other facing me. Each other is a You related to me dissymmetrically because I am more responsible than each and every other to the point of being responsible even for their responsibilities. This is why my relationship with them is not merely that of an individual to other individuals of the same genus. And this is why instead of relying upon Aristotelian, Linnaean or Darwinian modes of classification, Levinas appeals to the model of monotheism in order to prevent the ethics of the singular other being lost without trace in the arithmetic of totalization and the universality of the case. Ethically I am my brother's and my sister's keeper. *Kol Israèl arévim zé lazé* (*Shebuot* 39a). I go surety for everyone else. In referring directly or indirectly to monotheism and relatedness to one Father, Levinas would have us not overlook that as human son I am responsible for my human father, a notion to which a route is prepared by the fact that the son is not the property of the father any more than that my being my brother's and sister's keeper means that they belong to me. Each and every other is separate from me, every neighbor is a stranger in his or her proximity. In particular, fatherhood understood not causally but ethically means to be sub-stantially in one's son without this in any way diminishing the exteriority of the son to the father (TeI 256, TaI 278–79). This kills again Father Parmenides and his monism without killing the monotheistic father. However, although monotheism was described as a model for the ethical a moment ago, it must be said now that the theological idea of one God as well as the word God as invoked in religion can be approached according to Levinas only through the humanism of the other human being, hence through paternity ethically understood. If according to Father Parmenides and Martin Heidegger, Being calls for the assistance of man, according to Emmanuel Levinas and a strong Judaic tradition transmitted in, for example, the partly Kabbalistic writings of Rabbi Hayyim of Volozhin and Rabbi Elijah ben Solomon Zalmon, Gaon of Vilna, man's assistance is called for by God.[14] As though God was not at liberty not to create man, and yet already on the very morning of his creation man was God's help in ages perhaps immemorially past.

In defense of monotheism Kabbalists go as far as to argue that God is the root of all evil in that it was only by an original contraction that God gave Himself room to expand into the world. Rabbi Hayyim cites from *Zohar* III, 31b, "There is no good or evil, holy or impure, that does not have its root and origin in the superior world."[15] In Levinas's philosophy of ethics as first philosophy the parallel to this cosmogonic principle of the metaphysical unity of good and evil is the idea of the Good beyond being as the Good which is beyond the opposition of moral good and evil. So that the *il y a*, the there-is, described by Levinas as the malign menace of impersonal indifference and lassitude that might be called "the banality of evil," is the counterpart of illeity, by which Levinas means the trace of pre-original, pre-principial anarchic infinity, the excluded third beyond being and non-being that "maybe is said by the word God," identified by theology with the Father of all humankind

(ADV 157, BV 128). But, older than the God of theology, illeity announces the Him who is addressing me in each and every You commanding my responsibility, a responsibility that I cannot decline and which I acknowledge even when I am willingly doing wrong.[16] Illeity, despite the nominalization in the -ness betrayed by its final syllable ("ty," from the *té* of *illéité* and the *tas* of *illeitas*), is the moment of addressing. But addressing is always betrayed. Its vertical to-say sinks into a horizonal said. Its moment of diachrony, as the final syllable of Levinas's word "illeity" itself displays, is absorbed into a moment synthesizable with other moments of uninterrupted time. But time was interrupted. There was a knock at the door, even if though "I opened to my beloved, but my beloved had turned and gone. My soul failed me when he spoke, I sought him and found him not: I called him but he gave no answer."[17] My answerability remains nevertheless. And if Levinas is to be taken at his word when he says that I am always more responsible than anyone else, then if God is foremost the other human being, I am responsible for Him and more responsible than He is Himself.

Is that a blasphemy because a diminution of the power of the absolutely other? It can be this only if the responsibility in question is mistaken for the grounding responsibility of a sovereignly active free will. Whereas this agency responsible for initiating alteration in the world is free only if it serves responsibility that is outside the opposition of activity and passivity. It is outside the interplay of forces from which that opposition gets its sense, absolutely passive responsibility not for alteration or for the maintenance of the *status quo* in the world, but for alterity, for the other human being. If selfhood is defined as primarily active or passive power, then the relation of one self to another will be fundamentally one of war. Peace will be a secondary result of the negotiation of explicit or tacit contract. Levinas's description of the identity of the self postulates the primacy of peace through the self's identity being one in which the identity of an ego intent on its own survival is interrupted by the demand of the other formulable as "Thou shalt not kill," where what is *said* in this formula puts in words the infinite infinitive *to-say* of every address, the trace of the response of obedience always already given to the *Shema'*, to "Hear!"

Levinas is therefore speaking of a *Shema'* that, however much inspired by the "Hear, O Israel," equates Israel with every me and makes each me the one that responds "Hear, send me," *Hineni*. My oneness is a oneness beyond number. It is the uniqueness of being elect. This does not mean that others are not unique too; "each son of the father is the unique son, the chosen son" (TeI 256, TaI 279). Therefore plurality, generality, and universality can be described in a way that safeguards against the loss of uniqueness when one moves beyond the face to face and beyond the face into the sphere of justice involving third parties unknown to me and into the realm of history where the consequences of my actions and interactions with others cannot be foreseen. Beyond the alternatives of society as the interaction of discrete atoms and as holism in which the terms are exhaustively defined by their interrelations, it would be a mistake to suppose that Levinas's "new ethic" of absolute passivity—which in fact is both very young and very old—is an ethic of absolute pacificism. Such a mistake rests on the failure to see that the absolute passivity, the absolute pastness, and the absolute withdrawal from the world said by Levinas to be demanded if any ethic is to escape totalitarian violence, in turn command me to intervene in the world of others with incarnate egos that suffer and cause others to suffer too. What may at first look like transcendentalism that keeps its hands clean demands concretization, just as there is no to-say or saying without something that is said.

The figure in the Hegelian phenomenology of spirit from which Levinas distinguishes his position most frequently is that of "the beautiful soul." He also takes care to point out that the goodness beyond good will to which the ethical goes back is more than the goodness of good intentions and of the feeling of respect. One does not go to the other with empty hands. Whether with them I give bread from my mouth or cash from my pocket, it may be that I should have given them to somebody else. Indeed absolute passivity is not inconsistent with actual war. Absolute passivity may or may not coincide with passive resistance. What is called for is something one can only discover or fail to discover by hard experience and by taking advice. Gillian Rose rightly says that "my immediate experience of 'the Other' leaves me with no way to understand my mistakes by attempting to recover the interference of meaning or mediation."[18] However, it is precisely in order to mediate such immediacy and to keep the feet of ethics firmly planted on the ground, thereby forestalling "unhappy consciousness," that the teaching and assignment (*enseignement*) addressed to me by the other has to be spelled out by such precepts as those of the Torah as interpreted and reinterpreted endlessly by the rabbis. This is why, blasphemy or not, "I love him, but even more I love the Torah," because the Torah is "protection against the madness of direct contact with the Sacred without mediation of reasons" (DL 192, DF 144).

Levinas's prolegomenon for an ancient and new ethic is not then an apologia for powerlessness. It subordinates the power of the "I can" to an absolute passivity which is therefore more powerful than it, which as power raised to a higher power gives the "I can" its sense. This *pouvoir* of his ethical *peut-être* that is not the "maybe" of incertitude is conjoined with a to-be that is beyond the being of which the sense is the time of recuperable memory and an ecstatically projected to-come. It empowers a to-be of which the sense is the to-say of the approach to the other who is never present in herself or himself or representable by a sign, but whose to-be is "to leave a trace, to pass, to go away, to become absolved" (EDE 200, HAH 60, CPP 105, LBPW 62).[19] This does not propose a theodicy for God's absence at Auschwitz on the grounds that His only way of being present is going away. It cannot be this if every question regarding God gets its meaning from my responsibility which is always greater than that of anyone else including Him—including Him because He is "included" in every You. And since every You, the other (*Autrui*) under my skin, is interruptively constitutive of my self, deconstructively constructive and creative of my identity, then these things have to be said no less of Him. He is the pre-original source of the call I have always already obeyed—of the call of and to conscience that hails both from without me and from within. Pre-original because before the law, *Vor dem Gesetz,* or the law of what will have been law: my having been chosen to choose.

So God's question to Job, "Where wast thou when I laid the foundations of the earth?" may be heard as a reminder of my continuing excessive ethical responsibility for the creation of the world to the point of being responsible even for the commands of those who command me. For that creation continues. Creation is not an event after which all that remains is to sustain what has been created. From this it seems to follow that everyone is my contemporary in the diachronic time of responsibility, that there is a sense in which I was at Auschwitz, and that that is something which also Sylvia Plath could have said of herself. I am *there* in the sense that my being there only "by fiat of imagination" of the unimaginable event implicates my responsibility to actively remember my anti-Semitism where anti-Semitism is

> not simply the hostility felt by a majority toward a minority, nor only xenophobia, nor any ordinary racism, even if it were the ultimate rationale of these phenomena that are derived from it. . . . It is a repugnance felt for the unknown within the psyche of the Other, for the mystery of its interiority or, beyond any agglomeration within an ensemble or any organization within an organism, a repugnance for the pure proximity of the other man, that is to say, for sociality itself. (ADV 223, BV 190, HLR 279)

That is to say, I am *there* at Auschwitz in the diachronic time of ethical responsibility because Auschwitz puts me on the spot, demanding that I be not a bystander when atrocities contemporary with me in the synchronic time of history are perpetrated in Lebanon, Somalia, Timor, Bosnia, Rwanda. . . . The underground organizations in Denmark who sought to save Jewish citizens and refugees from Theresienstadt and Auschwitz wished to have it understood that they did so not because those people were Jews but because they were human beings. Levinas's way of approving of this attitude is to say that, as well as being all anti-Semites, all human beings are Jews. Human beings simply as human beings, "independently of any religious consideration deriving from a confession or set of beliefs," are, in Manès Sperber's phrase, "victims of chosenness."[20] "Is it for the Jew to say?" Levinas asks two years after the Six-Day War, and answers:

> But *every survivor of the Hitlerian massacres—whether or not a Jew—is Other in relation to martyrs*. He is consequently responsible and unable to remain silent. He is obligated to Israel for the reasons that obligate every man. These reasons are therefore common to Jew and Arab and ought to help them talk to each other. (DL 39, DF 132)

Although the words Israel and Jew are employed here in a non-universal sense, Levinas goes on to say that the religion in terms of which that non-universal sense is defined requires the Jew to appeal to reasons that bind human beings universally. For him to "preach for his saint" is to preach for the Other. Jewish universalism is consistent with Israel having been chosen historically to preach universalism and to be an example to light the way for the Gentiles, but the lesson it teaches on Levinas's interpretation is that this historical particularism reflects the ethical particularism of each and every Jew's or Gentile's being in a relation of inequality with each and every other because I demand more of myself than of others. Indeed, "Rabbi Meir—one of the chief teachers of the Law—has gone as far as to say that a pagan who knows the Torah is the equal of the High Priest" (DL 39, DF 22). Ethical "monotheism" is therefore compatible with religious polytheism. And with secularism. In *Long Night's Journey into Day* the Eckardts write with reference to "those Jews who choose not to be 'religious'":

> After the Holocaust, the sanctifying of the divine Name (*kiddush haShem*) is carried forward and accomplished in new ways through the sanctifying of human life as such (*kiddush hahayyim*). This unfolding of the covenant destroys any invidious judgements against the secular human being in contrast to the religious person. The flesh and the spirit are equals.[21]

On Levinas's ethical definition of the Jew this holds not only for the historical Jew who ceases to profess a confessional faith. It holds for each and every secular person in his or her particular universality. But why do the Eckardts say "After the Holocaust"? Why does what they refer to as "the final and sublime logic in the avowal of total liberation" come into play only after the launching of the plan for the Final Solution? Why could that sublime logic not have held sway BFS, Before the Final Solution? In explaining what they mean by liberation they refer to the Talmudic saying that when God and man laugh together both achieve a triumphal state of grace announcing the coming of the Messiah. "When this mutual laughter is able to replace accusation or recrimination, joy can be unfettered rather than conditional." How can laughter after the Holocaust be anything other than hollow? It is worth noting that Levinas applauds Nietzsche's recognition of the place played by laughter in the revaluation of all values following upon the death of God, that is to say in his bringing of the gods down to earth. Laughter is an interruption of the logic of comprehension no less than are tears, curses, apostrophe, forgiveness, or refusal to forgive. Hence by way of further explanation of what the Eckardts mean by liberation from mutual recrimination they cite another teacher of the Talmud who observes that a strict interpretation of the Hebrew reveals that God *asks* Abraham to offer up Isaac. Abraham is not bound by a command to bind his son. This reading of the *Akedah*, Eliezer Berkovits observes, amounts to

> a recognition that the sacrificial way of the innocent through history is not to be vindicated or justified! It remains unforgivable. God Himself has to ask an Abraham to favor Him by accepting the imposition of such a sacrifice. The divine request accompanies all those through history who

139

suffer for the only reason that God created man, whom God Himself has to endure. Within time and history God remains indebted to His people. He may be long-suffering only at their expense. It was hardly ever as true as in our own days, after the Holocaust.[22]

To say that within time and history it was hardly ever as true as after the Holocaust that theodicy was impossible is to imply that there is some truth in the idea that theodicy may have been impossible at other times in that history, if not at the destruction of the temple, then at the expulsion from Spain or the Chmielnicki massacres. In his foreword to *How Can We Commit the Unthinkable?*, published in 1982, Elie Wiesel refers to the atrocities then being committed in Paraguay and Cambodia. When he writes that they should not be compared to the Holocaust he must already have made some sort of comparison in order to have a reason to refrain. There are likenesses and unlikenesses which it might be irresponsible not to record, as it would be irresponsible not to compare and contrast the Holocaust of the 1940s with the possible repetition implicit in the cry "Never again," and with the still live possibility of a nuclear holocaust to come. It has been said that the uniqueness of the Holocaust metonymically called Auschwitz is the fact that in it Jews are slaughtered just because they are Jews; there is no difference between the means and the end.[23] The same must be said about the Nazis' treatment of gypsies, Jesuits, Slavs, homosexuals, Communists, and others who fell foul of the National Socialist plan. So it cannot be said that the term Aryan had for the Nazis no other meaning than non-Jew, as maintained by Emil Fackenheim, who writes: "The term 'Aryan' had no clear connotation, other than 'non-Jew,' and the Nazis were not anti-Semites because they were racists, but rather racists because they were anti-Semites. The exaltation of the 'Aryan' had no positive significance."[24] On the other hand, since not even Eichmann set out to destroy all mankind, one has to look closely at what can be intended when the "modern radical evil" which Hannah Arendt is said to have found in him is defined as the desire to make men superfluous *qua* men.[25] This definition of evil would cover the special horror of the fact that most of the victims of the Holocaust were denied even the dignity of martyrs, if a martyr is someone who has the opportunity wittingly to sacrifice his or her life. This consolation was certainly denied to most of the million and a quarter children represented by the silent sad-eyed angel of *Night,* a fact that would lead Elie Wiesel to challenge Jürgen Moltmann's invocation of that episode in *Night* as another exemplification of the theology of double binding and double delivering up (*paradidonai*) allegedly represented by the *akedot* of Abraham and Isaac and the sacrifice of Christ on the Cross.[26]

Arendt's definition of radical evil is better understood when interpreted in the light of Levinas's doctrine of incomparability. Given the centrality of suffering, patience, and passion to his thinking, this may seem a surprising suggestion, for central to her thinking of the Holocaust is the wish to break with the history of the Jews as the people destined to suffer. She says Hear, hear, O Israel, when another Jew, Rosa Luxemburg, protests "Why do you come with your special Jewish sorrows? I feel just as sorry for the wretched Indian victims in Putamayo, for the Negroes in Africa."[27] But what is central in Levinas's humanism of the other human being is not simply suffering and feeling sorrow for the sufferers. To stress that would be to concur with a more christianizing conception of the suffering servant of Isaiah 53 where the man of sorrows "is brought as a lamb to the slaughter, and as a sheep before her shearers is dumb, so he openeth not his mouth." After Auschwitz, the Redeemer the Holy One (*Ha-Kadosh*) of Israel is revealed as the One whose Holiness means an apartness so apart (*kadosh*) that it reveals itself as departedness, the One who does not reveal Himself, the One who is long-suffering only at the expense of his people, the One whom they may find it impossible to forgive. In a contribution to a symposium on the scandal of evil, Levinas cites from the treatise *Avot*, which as he remarks long predates Auschwitz, the call to serve without expectation of recompense. To this call is appended the sentence "And may the fear of God be upon you."[28] Can we not say therefore, he wonders, that Sacred History is maybe not after all interrupted? In the same paragraph as his citation from the text that long predates Auschwitz he writes that Auschwitz names "the radical rupture between evil and mercy, between evil and meaning." Twenty years later he writes that what the Jews suffered under Hitler was

> an ordeal without name, and cannot be placed within any sociological category. It is a lie to locate it within a series of natural causes and effects or to defer to "the human sciences" and seek to explain it by examining the thoughts and "readings" of an Eichmann, the "inner crises" of a Goebbels or the "structures" of European society between the wars. (DL 173, DF 129)

Such diagnoses and explanations, incorporating phenomena under universal hypotheses and models in order to make them make sense, fail to recognize that there is more than the phenomenal to be witnessed in such phenomenal events as took place at Auschwitz, more than meets the eye, more than can be indicated by a symptom or marked by a sign. When Levinas wonders if at Auschwitz Sacred History is maybe not after all interrupted, the thought that maybe it is not must be accompanied by the acknowledgment that this could be so only because Sacred History, which we have learned from him to equate with the proto-history of the ethical, is itself none other than interruption, interruption by the other.

At Auschwitz that interruption of phenomenality and sense was the interruption by the excess that is not more than a less, but absolute, whether we call it evil or good. For both of the alternatives of evil and good that face us daily with problems of choice trace their genealogy to a Good or God beyond being and before choice, to an excess so utterly excessive, yet conditioning problems and questions answerable by Yes, No, or Perhaps, that it could be called the Evil or the Devil beyond being too. As though the Holocaust was the contraction of *En Sof*.

141

A vacancy was left by that laborious contraction of what went by the name or pro-name God of which Edmond Jabès writes that it "was, or was no more than the only word for suffering sufficiently vast, sufficiently empty that all sufferings may be contained within it."[29] That emptiness is filled by the suffering of human beings. But that suffering is more, Levinas insists, than any and every pain. It is not only the suffering from which I naturally desire to be saved. First and foremost it is the pain of the care that is latent in the caress, a care older than the care for being, a metaphysical because ethical care that is explicit in apostrophe and address. Not suffering from the privation of something I need or lack, but suffering from the suffering of others from which it is my Desire to save them, counting myself responsible for them before any covenant or contract with them in the emptiness left by the contraction of God. It is this counting that is unaccountable. Whether with the Eckardts, Wiesel, and Arthur A. Cohen I say that in the consecutive time of narrated history the Holocaust was a uniquely unique *sui generis* rupture,[30] whether I say with Richard Rubinstein that it was the climax of a trend and explicable by the human sciences,[31] whether with Emil Fackenheim I hover between or combine these extremes, any comparison within the temporality that retains or restrains memory will be a comparison in the universal dimension of politics and sociology of what are incomparables in the dimension of ethical particularity by which that dimension is interrupted. I may choose to say that the Holocaust was the interruption of God in the objectively genitive sense or in the subjectively genitive sense of the preposition. Because of the Holocaust or independently of the Holocaust I may choose to reject altogether the idea of divine or demoniacal powers that by their presence or absence could interrupt or make whatever sense human existence may seem to have. In any case, that sense makes sense, beyond the time that is said to be the sense of being, only through the time in which my will to survive for myself is interrupted by a summons to responsibility beyond choice for the other human being whom I face. It is the facing of ethical regard that makes sense in this diachronic time. And this time is diachronic because the face of the other human being is a trace of a responsibility that I cannot forget only because it exceeds any conscious remembrance. Of that immemorially instituted responsibility the Holocaust was and, provided I respond to that responsibility, will remain, a traumatic historic memorial.[32]

10

JEWGREEK OR GREEKJEW

Das Sein selber das Strittige ist.

—Martin Heidegger

WRITING WITH BOTH HANDS

On the one hand and on the other hand. This is a pattern one finds in and among the writings of Derrida. It is a pattern one used to find in leading articles of *The Times* of London. In *The Times* the outcome was either a neutral, middle of the road compromise or a dissolution of an apparent conflict through the exposure of an equivocation in the terms in which the views of the parties to the dispute were expressed. This chapter will come round to considering whether it is a meeting of extremes of this latter sort that we find in the essay by Derrida which is entitled "Violence and Metaphysics" and which ends with the citation of the words "Extremes meet" from "perhaps the most Hegelian of modern novelists" (ED 228, WD 153). We can assert at the start that if Derrida subscribes to the idea that extremes meet, he certainly does not subscribe to the idea that they meet in some neutral middle ground, for example a higher or deeper synthesis such as is posited by the aforementioned Hegelianism.

It is not only in Hegelian phenomenology and ontology that Derrida encounters difficulties. He encounters them in Husserlian phenomenology and Heideggerian ontology also, as, to mention only three of his publications, *Speech and Phenomena,* "Ousia and Grammê," and "The Ends of Man" demonstrate. Now Hegel, Husserl, and Heidegger are arraigned too by Levinas, and declared guilty of advocating philosophies of neutrality. How then is it possible for Derrida in "Violence and Metaphysics" to question the coherence of what Levinas writes in *Totality and Infinity* and before?

In seeking an answer to this question via Derrida's comments on Levinas's comments on Hegel, Husserl, and Heidegger, we shall not be able to avoid "the prosaic disembodiment into conceptual frameworks that is the first violence of all commentary" (ED 124, WD 312). This violence will be all the starker in our treatment of Hegel because, although he is, as Derrida says, the philosopher most on trial in *Totality and Infinity,* the bearing of the comments on him will be for the most part only implicit in those made on Husserl and Heidegger. In Levinas's own writings, explicit references to Husserl and Heidegger are more numerous than references to Hegel, so it is not surprising that this should hold for "Violence and Metaphysics" and in turn for our exposition.

From the explicit references that are made to Hegel in "Violence and Metaphysics," we soon learn that Derrida is perhaps by no means the least Hegelian of modern philosophers. The extent to which Levinas qualifies as a candidate for that description may be gauged from his reaction to the doctrine of self-consciousness put forward in *The Phenomenology of Spirit*. There Hegel writes:

> I distinguish myself from myself, and in so doing I am directly aware that what is distinguished from myself is not different. I, the selfsame being, repel myself from myself; but what is posited as distinct from me, or as unlike me, is immediately, in being so distinguished from me, not a distinction for me.[1]

Levinas has two things to say about this. First, the identity of the I (*moi*) and the self (*soi*), my selfsameness, is not a provisional condition destined to be revealed as merely provisional in the light of a dialectical transition to its truth. Second, this unrendable (*indéchirable*) identity of the I and the self is not the "I am I" that Kant had already classified as a purely formal tautology. It is the concrete identity of an I at home in its world, *chez soi*. The world is over against me, hence other, but it is a world in which I am more or less free to exercise my power to make things, to take things into my possession . . . and to give them to others.

> The identification of the same is not the void of a tautology nor a dialectical opposition to the other, but the concreteness of egoism. This is important for the possibility of metaphysics. If the same would establish its identity by simple *opposition to the other*, it would already be a part of a totality encompassing the same and the other. (TeI 8, TaI 38)

By metaphysics Levinas means Desire for what is beyond *phusis*, beyond nature and need: my relationship, which is not a surveyable relation, to the ab-solutely other, the Other (*Autrui*) who commands me, the Stranger who disrupts from over there the being at home with myself in a world where what I lack is nevertheless something that might satisfy a need. The Other is incapable of satisfying Desire. He commands me, and the more I respond to him the greater becomes my responsibility, the more I am called upon to sacrifice. The metaphysical is ethical Desire that supervenes upon happy atheism as the unhappiness of a religion that is supererogatory as regards enjoyment and need, *un besoin luxueux*, a "need" surplus to need.

The Other is not the subject matter of theology or theory. He surpasses all understanding. I cannot represent him. I cannot represent him even as another I. "He and I do not form a number. The collectivity in which I say 'you' (*tu*) or 'we' is not a plural of the 'I.' I, you—these are not individuals of a common concept" (TeI 9, TaI 39). For Levinas, subjectivity is my being subject to the Other, my being his servant, which is not to say his slave. Hence, while I cannot represent him, neither can he stand in for me. No one can be my substitute. Only in the universe of need is that possible, in the system in which I am the center. In the asymmetrical system of metaphysical ethics I am accused, subjective as absolutely accusative.

The Littré dictionary states that *Autrui* never occurs in the subject place of a sentence, but is always governed by a preposition. But the Littré and older grammar books are not reliable guides to the metaphysics of the Levinasian *Autrui*. *Autrui* is governed by nothing. *Autrui* is the Governor. He is the Master and Teacher. As is Emmanuel Levinas presumably vis-à-vis his reader. And the reader of *Totalité et Infini* will not read far before he discovers "*Autrui*" in sentences of which it occupies the subject or the object place. The Grévisse grammar notices that this practice is not so rare as some grammarians maintain. It quotes examples from half a dozen modern authors, including Proust. One French grammarian permits himself the philosophical observation, "In fact, the world is made up of *soi* and *autrui.*" Levinas would beg to differ on the grounds that this leaves out of account the goods on which we live, but he would agree with the implication, assuming that the *autrui* with a lower case *a* here is intended to be equivalent to *les autres,* that *Autrui* is *not* of this world. *Autrui* is exorbitant. *Autrui* is absolutely unenglobable, unencompassable (EDE 199, CPP 104, LBPW 61). He is no more among that of which the world is "made up" than is the Cartesian Maker of the world. Descartes's Creator is a safer guide to the unique status of the *Autrui* whose denomination with an upper case Alpha is not the name of a case and not a proper name. *Autrui* is absolutely other as is according to Descartes the Infinity of God which overflows our idea of it, and that idea is not one we can generate by negation of the idea of our own finiteness.

Yet the singularity of the Other demands the plural pronoun *Vous*. Perhaps Levinas exaggerates the distance between Buber and himself, as Derrida and Buber maintain (ED 156, WD 314).[2] But Levinas's preference for the respectful *Vous* makes it plain that the Other is not inferior to me and I am not equal with him, implications that could be carried by speaking of the relationship as that of a *je* and a *tu,* and were evidently carried by Buber's *Ich* and *Du*. Despite the clarifications of the postscript which Buber added to *I and Thou,* its final paragraph still adheres to the idea of mutuality between God and man. There is no mutuality between the I and the Other. That is the force of Levinas's assertion that the Other is Highness. I have to look up to him in his Humility that commands.

To him. As well as being Majuscule and Majesty, the Other is masculine, like Bossuet's *Autrui* (see Littré again). But this masculinity is for Levinas metaphysical, not biological. It is metaphysically and ethically speaking that the Other is Father. Not biologically or theologically.

Levinas's perception of his departure from Buber can be put in Heideggerian language by saying that I and the Other are not participants in *Mitdasein*. To say that the Other is Dasein is already to say that he is indeterminately *da,* here or there. According to Levinas, the Other is always only over there and up there. He is *Illic*.

And he is Illeity. This illeity is not the itness or the thatness of an object in my world which Buber and Marcel, followed by Levinas, distinguish from the Thou. Nor is illeity the Thou of familiarity. The illeity of the face of the Other is not of my world. It is absolved from it. It is the extra-mundane origin of the Other's absolute alterity (EDE 197–202, CPP 102–107, LBPW 59–64).

Levinas would have us understand that this absolute alterity is other than the alterity of Hegelian dialectic. It does not admit of totalization. Not my recognition of the Other, but my recognition of his irrecuperability is the condition of my showing him respect. I fail to show him respect if I regard him as another I. Derrida asks whether this is so. Is not my treating another as another I a condition of my treating him with respect? Are not Hegel and Husserl and Kant closer to the truth of this matter than Levinas? Unless I treat another as another I, how can one make the distinction Levinas wants to make, no less than these other philosophers, between persons and things like stones, the distinction he contends Buber blurs when he allows that it is not only with persons that I can have an I-Thou rapport? Has Levinas been led perhaps to question the Kantian, Hegelian, and Husserlian standpoints here, Derrida wonders, because he has given insufficient attention to the distinction between the transcendental and the empirical? Cannot a *Phenomenology of Spirit* and a *Logic* permit a *conceptual* assimilation of the other and the I in a social whole that transcends them without this destroying the *factual* alterity of the other? And is not this factual alterity of the other compatible with his being another I *factically* within the *epochê* of transcendental phenomenology that suspends questions of empirical and metaphysical fact? Levinas may be forgetting Husserl's warning against confusing creation and constitution, a warning Levinas himself repeats in *The Theory of Intuition in the Phenomenology of Husserl* where he emphasizes the distinction between Husserl's transcendental idealism of noematic meanings and the metaphysical sensualism of Berkeley, the distinction that §89 of *Ideas* captures in the dictum that meanings do not burn. The constitution of the other with which the fifth of the *Cartesian Meditations* is preoccupied does not make the other a part of my world, even if phenomenological constitution is an operation of the meditating philosopher's own consciousness. Within the *epochê* that abstracts all but the ego's sphere of ownness, Husserl writes in §44 of the *Cartesian Meditations,* "I, the reduced 'human Ego' ('psychophysical' Ego) am constituted, accordingly, as a member of the 'world' with a multiplicity of 'objects outside me.' But I myself constitute all this in my 'psyche' and bear it intentionally within me." However, nothing in this "world," any more than the phenomenological consciousness of the ego whose noetic "psyche"—or "psychism," as Levinas would say—has this world as its noematic object, "is worldly in the natural sense (hence all the quotation marks)."

Is there not room for Levinas to say about the ethical something parallel to what Husserl says about the psychological: that it is parallel to the phenomenological? Derrida does not have recourse to this notion of parallelism in framing his questions for Levinas in "Violence and Metaphysics." If we think that he might have cast his questions in this form, we shall be committed to acknowledging that to read the paragraphs in "Violence and Metaphysics" on Husserl as a defense of Husserl would be shortsighted. It would be to neglect the "difficulties" he raises for and from Husserl in the paragraphs Derrida devotes to this parallelist doctrine elsewhere. On the one hand and on the other hand. Derrida writes with both hands. But the hands do not write parallel texts. He is ambidextrous all right. He is also ambisinistrous. Sometimes the right hand plays the left-hand part while the right-hand part is played by the left. In "Violence and Metaphysics" this double crossing of hands is practiced in the opening paragraphs that tentatively pose the question of the question, and in the pages at the end that recapitulate some of the historical and structural or, rather, historico-structural reasons why this question remains open. Still, if we leave out of account these outer movements and the wider context of the essay that Derrida's other compositions supply, we could be forgiven for believing that Derrida's chief aim is to demonstrate that Levinas does violence to the dialectical phenomenology of Hegel, to the transcendental phenomenology of Husserl, and to the fundamental ontology and essential thinking of Heidegger.

Not only does Levinas appear to misread Husserl on constitution; he compounds this error by paying too little heed to Husserl's insistence that there is no constitution of horizons, only horizons of constitution (ED 177, WD 120). This insistence is a mark of phenomenology's respect for the physical object and the other self. This respect is the spirit of Husserl's teaching that there can be apodicticity without adequacy. That is to say, for example, that the physical object has profiles with which neither I nor even God can be confronted. And the horizon that lies beyond that which confronts me in my living present is an analogue of the other's experience, an experience that I can never enjoy. "If," observes Derrida, "a consciousness of infinite inadequation to the infinite (and even to the finite) distinguishes a body of thought careful to respect exteriority, it is difficult to see how Levinas can depart from Husserl, on this point at least. Is not intentionality respect itself?" (ED 177–78, WD 121).

SOUCIANCE

Turning to Levinas's polemic with Heidegger, Derrida asks, What about *Fürsorge, Seinlassen*, and *Sein*? Do not these Heideggerian notions accommodate the respect for the Other that Levinas believes Heidegger's thinking fails to show? Care (*Sorge*) on Levinas's interpretation of Heidegger, is Dasein's envelopment of its world in an initially practical project. It regards the Other as a co-inhabitant of the world that I comprehend. To do this, Levinas says, is to do violence to the Other by ignoring the ethical alterity that resists the embrace of a neutral being-with as much as it resists the power of the "I can" of transcendental phenomenology and the categories of Hegelian dialectic.

147

However, what Heidegger means by care is not, as Levinas usually assumes, a structure of practice as opposed to theory. Since it is an existential-ontological structure, it is prior to the distinction between the theoretical and the practical, therefore prior to the ethical.[3] Further, the manifestation of *Sorge* that Heidegger calls *Fürsorge,* solicitude, does not have to be a taking over of the Other. Authentic being-with "helps the Other to become transparent to himself *in* his care and to become *free for* it." It "frees the Other in his freedom for himself."[4] How can this be a violation? Does not this letting be of the Other which is neither interference nor indifference leave room for everything that Kant means by moral respect?

There's the rub. For Kant moral respect is the essence of freedom. For Levinas freedom is anchored in the satisfaction of the ego's need. For him egoity is autonomy and heteronomy is ethical Desire for the Other. The Kantian order is inverted. And with it the Heideggerian. In *Kant and the Problem of Metaphysics,* Heidegger ties in his thinking of *Seinlassen* with Kant's analysis of the notion of respect.

There are other aspects of Kant's metaphysics of morals that Levinas cannot endorse, despite the indebtedness he avows. Thus, although Levinas's Other who commands me to command has something in common with Kant's categorical imperative, it is difficult to see how Levinas could accept Kant's idea that what commands my respect in another person is the rationality that that person embodies. For that rationality is embodied also in me as a citizen with equal rights and duties in the kingdom of ends. In that kingdom God too is a citizen subject to the same moral law as we are. In Levinas's face to face the Other and I are not equals. If this is a reservation Levinas would make regarding Kant, it is one that would carry over to Heidegger. Levinas could agree with Derrida that Kant, Hegel, Husserl, and Heidegger provide for respect for persons. He could continue to object that they do not provide for sufficient respect or for respect of the right kind rightly directed. But we should continue to require assurance that this objection does not stem from a failure to perceive that a transcendental or ontological symmetry is compatible with a factual or factical or ontic asymmetry.

Is Derrida's suspicion that Levinas does fail to perceive this compatible with the former's assertion that the latter is not claiming to outline *a* morality? If we take Kant's metaphysics of morals as a specimen of what is not *a* morality, but a purely formal structure that would yield *a* morality only when applied in concrete historical circumstances, there is nothing to prevent his citing specific injunctions—do not break promises, do not commit suicide, and so on—as examples of maxims that the moral law would require or allow in certain or indeed in all historical circumstances. Levinas says, however, that "Thou shalt not commit murder" is the first word (*le premier mot*) that I read in the Other's eyes (TeI 199, TaI 173). This sounds like the basis of a morality, even if to describe the basis as a principle or maxim would be to risk lapsing into the tradition questioned by Levinas which substitutes "ideas for persons, the theme for the interlocutor and the interiority of the logical relation for the exteriority of interpellation" (TeI 60, TaI 88). We can agree at least that "Thou shalt not commit murder" would be only the beginning of a moral code. And because conspicuously absent from *Totality and Infinity* is any serious attempt to draw up a table of commandments (though a second commandment might be "Give to the other the bread from thy mouth"), maybe we should understand Derrida's denial that Levinas is purporting to give us a morality as a denial that "Thou shalt not commit murder" is even a rudimentary morality. Maybe we should after all read this commandment as the Levinasian version of Kant's formu-lation of the categorical imperative calling upon us to "Act in such a way that you always use humanity, whether in your own person or in the person of another, never simply as a means, but always at the same time as an end." That is to say, "Thou shalt not commit murder" would be the command to abstain from doing violence to the other by treating the other as though the other were subsumable within a causal nexus, conceptual system, or a referential totality (*Verweisungsganzheit*) of the sort Heidegger describes in §§15–17 of *Being and Time*. Levinas's "Thou shalt not commit murder" would be a "version" only because it is doubtful whether he would be in favor of our using (*brauchen*) humanity as an end, and because, as noted above, Kant's scheme is symmetrical, whereas his is initially hierarchical. Initially and ultimately. For it is by way of the face of the second person (you), of the Master, of the Other (*Autrui*) that I have access to the third person, Others (*les Autres*), to humanity, to justice, and to language or discourse (*le langage*). Alphonso Lingis often gives "conversation" where Levinas has *langage*. With good reason, even if it can sometimes seem that there is little conversation in the face to face, but instead the Master addressing me and me in my turn as Master responding by addressing third parties. This impression is not dispelled by the following passage which shows Levinas outlining an ac-count of humanity that he hopes will preserve precedence for plurality over totality while escaping both the neutrality of Anyone (*das Man*) on which Heidegger's analysis of Dasein is based and the kind of subjectivity on which Husserl grounds his analysis of society.

> The third party looks at me in the eyes of the Other—language is justice. It is not that there first would be the face, and then the being it manifests or expresses would concern himself with justice; the epiphany of the face qua face opens humanity. The face in its nakedness as a face presents to me the destitution of the poor one and the stranger; but this poverty and exile which appeal to my powers, address me, do not deliver themselves over to these powers as givens, remain the expression of the face. The poor one, the stranger, presents himself as an equal. His equality within this essential poverty consists in referring to the *third party*, thus present at the encoun-ter, whom in the midst of his destitution the Other already serves. He comes to join me. But he joins me to himself for service; he commands me as a Master. This command can concern me only inasmuch as I am master myself; consequently this command commands me to command. The *thou*

is posited in front of a *we*. To be we is not to "jostle" one another or get together around a common task. The presence of the face, the infinity of the other, is a destituteness, a presence of the third party (that is, of the whole of humanity which looks at us), and a command that commands commanding. (TeI 188, TaI 213)

Conversation as an intimate exchange between an I and a thou who love and forgive each other takes place against a background of a we of justice and service in which I am joined not only by the You who is the Other, *Autrui*, but also with Others, *les Autres*, who are his equals, but not mine, for the third party that looks at me in the eyes of the Other is also my Master, another Other, and I have a greater responsibility than anyone else. "We are all guilty of everything and before each other, but I more than anyone," as Dostoyevsky writes in *The Brothers Karamazov*. And, as Levinas writes in *Totality and Infinity*, brotherhood presupposes fatherhood, a fatherhood that is a key to an ethical monotheism presupposed by the ontological atheism of the free self cultivating its own garden.

In "Le mot je, le mot tu, le mot Dieu," an article published by *Le Monde* in 1978, continuing the dialogue with Buber and Marcel, Levinas writes:

that above the neighbour's gravity in being or nothingness, without ontology, fraternity should be capable of being invested with an excessive importance, through which meaning is taken on immediately by the God who "*opens my lips*" (Psalm 51:15), therein lies the great originality of a mode of thinking in which the word God ceases to orientate life in stating the unconditioned ground of the world and cosmology, to reveal, in the face of the other man, the secret of its semantics.[5]

Transcending atheistic egoity, fraternity depends on monotheistic but atheological paternity.

Human fraternity has then two aspects: it involves individualities whose logical status is not reducible to the status of ultimate differences in a genus, for their singularity consists in each referring to itself. (An individual having a common genus with another individual would not be removed enough from it.) On the other hand, it involves the commonness of father, as though the commonness of race would not bring together enough. Society must be a fraternal community to be commensurate with the straightforwardness, the primary proximity, in which the face presents itself to my welcome. Monotheism signifies this human kinship, this idea of a human race that refers back to the approach of the Other in the face, in a dimension of height, in responsibility for oneself and for the Other. (TeI 189–90, TaI 214)

The God here appealed to is not a first cause, but an Infinite Goodness that interpellates me from beyond Being, *epekeina tês ousias*, and therefore beyond the possibility of mystical union: conscience that cannot be incorporated by my freedom or encompassed by the conceptualizing of my consciousness; "in conscience I have an experience that is not commensurate with any a priori framework—a conceptless experience." (TeI 74, TaI 101)

"Conceptless experience"? That would not be a bad translation of the *Erfahrung* which for Heidegger is the experience of the sense (*Sinn*) of Being, the experience which is certainly not Dasein's consciousness of an object, but Dasein's experience that is a *Seinlassen* and therefore at the same time the *Fahren,* the passage—in Levinasian language, *la passe* (EDE 20I, CPP 106, LBPW 63)—that is Being's history and history's Being. History that is a differing, as Derrida observes when he says that Levinas appears not to have taken to heart Heidegger's statement in the "Letter on 'Humanism,'" "Identity and Difference," and elsewhere that Being is not a concept or category and that the Same is not the concept of identity or equality. "The Same shuns all haste to resolve differences in the Equal" (ED 206, 214, WD 3I7 n. 67 and n. 68, 318 n. 80). Levinas equates or at least assimilates Heidegger's Being to his own *il y a,* the neutral presence of the absence of every determinate thing, "essential anonymity" (DE 95, EE 58). A more fitting assimilation would be one to the word of the *Sophist* that "teaches us to think that Being—which is other than the other and other than the same, is the same as itself, and is implied by all genres to the extent that they are— far from closing difference, on the contrary liberates it, and itself is what it is only by this liberation" (ED 205–206, WD 317 n. 66). As Derrida also says, Being is foreign to the finite totality without being an infinite totality or a higher existent. If it is neither a concept or essence nor an existent, but what makes the distinction between essence and existence possible, how can Levinas attribute to it an oppressive domination in contrast to the non-totalitarian domination by the Other? The thinking of Being is no more onto-theology than is ethical Desire. And since the thinking of Being which is Being's thinking is the truth which is the unconcealing, *a-lêtheia,* of Being that is inseparable from concealment and primordial erring, "how can one accuse this thinking of interminable wandering of being a new paganism of the Site, a complacent cult of the Sedentary?" (ED 213, WD I45). This thinking is always under way from one ontic epoch to another, being diverted from the light of Being by each of its ontic determinations. "The unconcealment of beings, the brightness granted them, obscures the light of Being." "As it reveals itself in beings, Being withdraws." That withdrawal is itself Being's *epochê.*[6] Being is always historically disclosed-undisclosed in existents. So there is no cause for complaint that Heidegger makes beings factually secondary to Being. Could it even make sense to state the entailment of this thesis, to state that Being is factually, ontically, prior to beings?

VIOLENCE AND VIOLENCE

Although Derrida adduces ample evidence that Levinas is not attentive enough to the undomiciliary in Heidegger's thinking that invalidates the interpretation of it as a thinking of pure *chez soi,* there remains the difference that whereas it is Being that conceals itself according to Heidegger, what does not appear according to Levinas is the face of an existent. The face of the Other is a non-phenomenal trace not because it is a noumenal thing in itself, but because it is ethical command—the rumor of the Kantian *Critiques* that there remains the ghost of a chance that, unknown to us, the ethical has an ontological foundation, that rumor Levinas believes he has scotched (TeI 153, 156–57, TaI 178–79, 181). Also, once we have recognized the *unzuhause* aspect of Heidegger's thinking, must we not recognize also that it betrays a nostalgia for the *Behausung* of Dasein? And is it not Heidegger who tells us that language is the house of Being? Derrida reminds us in "The Ends of Man" that Heidegger's man seeks the overcoming of homelessness, *die Überwindung der Heimatlosigkeit* (M 154, M tr. 128). But he reminds us as well that the *Heimat* here in question is not a nation or three acres and a cow. Nor is it a community of nations. If there is nostalgia here it is for what is Greek, where by what is Greek is not meant, say, the Ithaca of Ulysses.

But is there nostalgia here? Or is there rather nomadism?[7] Both and neither. "When we are historical we are neither a great nor a small distance from what is Greek. Rather, we are in errancy toward it."[8] "The Site, therefore, is not an empirical Here but always an *Illic:* for Heidegger, as for the Jew and the Poet," the poet Hölderlin, in connection with whose poem *Heimkunft* Heidegger comments that the word "country" is "thought in an essential sense, not at all a patriotic sense, not a nationalist sense, but rather, from the point of view of the History of Being" (ED 214–15, WD 145, 319 n. 80).[9] What is near may also be far off, a notion that is as nonsensical (*Thörig* is Hölderlin's word) as that of a wandering Greek or a wandering Jew who senses that the proximity of home is inseparable from the separation of exile, that "if man is to find his way once again into the nearness of Being, he must first learn to exist in the nameless" (M 154, M tr. 128–9).[10]

Given that "In our way of speaking, 'Greek' does not designate a particular people or nation, not a cultural or anthropological group," and that "What is Greek is the dawn of that destiny in which Being illuminates itself in beings and so propounds a certain essence of man,"[11] we must return to the question: How can the Jew be true to his Jewishness? But what is the essence of Jewishness to which the Jew is to be true? The very question is Greek. For even if the answer we make is that it is of the essence of Jewishness to give priority to experiencing the existent over the thinking of essence, this is a Greek distinction that has as its condition the nonconceptual Being and Same that is the wonder with which Greek thinking, philosophy, begins, the very opening of the question and the openness of the naked face of the Other who commands and accuses me.

> Here it is a question of knowing whether the trace permits us to think presence in its system, or whether the reverse order is the true one. It is doubtless the *true order.* But it is indeed the *order of truth* which is in question. Levinas's thought is maintained between these two postulations. (ED 160, WD 108)

It is as philosopher that Levinas maintains that justice is presupposed by truth and that prophecy and proffering are above and beyond philosophy. There is no inconsistency in this, it might seem. But there is at least a "difficulty" if philosophy comes on the scene with the verb to be. If that is so, how could we escape the totalitarian violence which Levinas associates with predication? Only, Derrida suggests, by postulating a language without verbs; for predication implies the verb, in particular the unparticular verb to be. The language without which there could be no justice and no ethical command would have to be a language of pure invocation. "The Greeks, who have taught us what *Logos* means, would never have accepted this" (ED 219, WD 147). If we cannot accept this, must we accept silence? But pre-logical silence would surely be a greater violence than the "secondary war" against the silence of pre-historical night waged to win secondary peace by polemical Being articulating itself historically in the brightness of the concept.

In the polemic between the Jewgreek and the Greekjew, Derrida poses this dilemma:

> Like pure violence, pure nonviolence is a contradictory concept. Contradictory beyond what Levinas calls "formal logic." Pure violence, a relationship between beings without face, is not yet violence, is pure nonviolence. And inversely: pure nonviolence, the nonrelation of the same to the other (in the sense understood by Levinas) is pure violence. Only a face can arrest violence, but can do so, in the first place, only because a face can provoke it. Levinas says it well: "Violence can only aim at the face" ("La violence ne peut viser qu'un visage" (TeI 200, TaI 225)). Further, without the thought of Being which opens the face, there would be only pure violence or pure nonviolence. Therefore, the thought of Being, in its unveiling, is never foreign to a certain violence. (ED 218, WD 146–47)

Is this dilemma resolved as soon as Levinas acknowledges the distinction between the conceptual sense of Being and Heidegger's nonconceptual sense? We seem to be on the way to a resolution if we can agree with Derrida that "Levinas doubtless would not deny that every historical language carries within it an irreducible conceptual moment, and therefore a certain violence" (ED 219, WD 148). For the difference between Levinas and Heidegger to vanish altogether, would it be enough if Levinas admitted that he has been speaking of Being in only one of the senses Heidegger distinguishes? To put a finer point on the question, could Levinas say that nonconceptual Being is compatible with the respect that he holds is due to the Signifier, where the Signifier is not the acoustic image or the mark that along with the signified concept makes up the sign of Saussurean semiology, but is the Other who addresses me and to whom I say "Speak, Lord, for thy servant heareth"? Is the Signifier above nonconceptual Being? If we emphasize that nonconceptual Being determines itself historically in concepts, in order that the Signifier shall not be submerged we shall have to emphasize no less what for Heidegger is in excess of the concept. We must then ask whether the Signifier is excluded or shown disrespect by the way in which Heidegger thinks that excess. What answer are we to give to this question?

One answer, an answer we have found Derrida giving to this question, is that if my ethical relationship to the Signifier is a relationship within the ontic field, no disrespect to the Signifier is shown, because Heidegger's thinking of Being is thinking that thinks what in *Being and Time* he still calls the ontological, the thinking of nonconceptual Being as distinguished from beings. Since Heidegger distinguishes in the ontic field beings that are Dasein and beings that are not, beings whose being is comprehended through existentials and beings of which the being is comprehended through categories, has Heidegger not allowed for everything that Levinas demands? Levinas cannot complain that to talk of comprehension here is already to fall short, since he is himself attempting to enable us to comprehend the relationship of the Other to me, to grasp that that relationship is a nonrelation or a "relation of relations" and cannot be comprehended from the point of view of the so-called impartial spectator, the *uninteressierte Zuschauer,* as what is required is neither interest nor disinterest, but *dés-intér-esse-ment.*

In presenting his account, in revealing, for example, that the Signifier does not reveal himself, Levinas does not deny that he is giving an account of the essence of being. Exteriority, he says, is "the essence of being" (TeI 268, TaI 292). This does not mean that the being the essence of whose being is being described cannot be a being that surpasses being; it is precisely in the relation to exteriority that being, Levinas tells us, "produces" and surpasses itself (TeI 278, 281, TaI 302, 304): superlates. But this surpassing of being must show itself in the extension of the meaning of words, in the manifold senses of *on* and *logos,* of "being" and "description" or "account," in order to permit that what can be given one sort of description cannot be given a description of another sort; in order to permit that something may be coherently described as indescribable, metadescribed as resistant to, for example, phenomenal description.

The point may seem trivial, "merely semantic," as the saying goes. It begins to look less trivial as soon as we see that it leads to the question whether "something" (as it occurs, for instance, in the sentence two before this one) is descriptive, to the question whether "being" is a predicate, and to the problem of the analogy of being. The philosophers who have debated these questions for two thousand years have been fighting battles in what Derrida calls secondary war. And Levinas is waging this war when he says that it is of the essence of being to transcend being, to transcend essence, or, as the tidy-minded wish he would say, to transcend "essence" to essence, or essence to "essence." Where it is a question of transcending essence, being, knowledge, intentionality, phenomenology, etc. to their namesakes, Levinas employs inverted commas no more than Heidegger does when, on his account, phenomenology comes to include as its topic not only what appears but also the disappearing of being. Indeed, what in Heidegger and Levinas may appear to be a mere strategy of rhetorical style is itself a passage in the history of being, understood in the sense which most preoccupies Heidegger, the sense he says we so readily forget, the sense which Levinas forgets, thereby demonstrating a sameness once more in his difference with Heidegger. What Levinas forgets, Derrida says, is the *as such* of metaphor. He couples the human face and the hidden face of God, but in offering us this metaphor he forgets the metaphorization that is going on here, thus betraying his "etymological empiricism, the hidden root of all empiricism"

(ED 204, WD 139). "As Hegel says somewhere, empiricism always forgets, at very least, that it employs the words to be."

So is that the conclusion Derrida reaches in "Violence and Metaphysics," that Levinas is appropriated by the Greeks, by Heidegger if not also by Hegel? No such conclusion is reached. No conclusion is reached. The question and the question of the opening of the question is left open. The essay ends by asking:

> Are we Greek? Are we Jews? But who, we? Are we (not a chronological, but a pre-logical question) *first* Jews or *first* Greeks? And does the strange dialogue between the Jew and the Greek, peace itself, have the form of the absolute, speculative logic of Hegel, the living logic which *reconciles* formal tautology and empirical heterology after having *thought* prophetic discourse in the preface to the *Phenomenology of Spirit?* Or, on the contrary, does this peace have the form of infinite separation and of the unthinkable, unsayable transcendence of the other? To what horizon of peace does the language which asks this question belong? Whence does it draw the energy of its question? Can it account for the historical *coupling* of Judaism and Hellenism? And what is the legitimacy, what is the meaning of the copula in this proposition from perhaps the most Hegelian of modern novelists: "Jewgreek is Greekjew. Extremes meet"?

Do the extremes meet? If they do, it is the strange meeting Derrida describes as a "reciprocal surpassing," the kind of meeting Levinas describes at the end of the essay on Derrida, "Tout autrement":

> The ridiculous ambition to "improve" a true philosopher is certainly not part of our plan. To cross his path is already quite something and probably just what is to be expected of a philosophical encounter. In underlining the primordial importance of the questions Derrida poses we have wanted to express the pleasure of making contact at the heart of a chiasmus. (NP 89, PN 62)

For although it may have begun to seem from what we have said in this chapter on Derrida on Levinas that a philosophical encounter of a closer kind between Levinas on the one hand and on the other hand Heidegger could be expected if only Levinas accepted that nonconceptual ontology or thinking of Being is prior to the ontic, and that morality eventuates as an aspect of the ontic after first philosophy divides itself into morality, logic, theory of knowledge, and so on. Levinas is explicit that "Morality is not a branch of philosophy, but first philosophy" (TeI 281, TaI 304) and shows no sign of revising that thesis in the works he has written since having the opportunity to think about Heidegger again in the light of "Violence and Metaphysics." As he puts this thesis in *Totality and Infinity, logos* as vocation and invocation precedes *logos* as thesis. As he puts it in *Otherwise than Being or Beyond Essence, logos* as Saying, *Dire,* is prior to *logos* as the Said, *Dit.* But if, on pain of begging the question, priority must be prior to *logos* in both of these senses, prior to the Jew and prior to the Greek, how are we to understand, let alone answer, Derrida's question whether we are first Jews or first Greeks?

11

AT THIS VERY MOMENT . . .
A REPETITION THAT IS NOT ONE

Mastery therefore of femininity?

OPEN OPUS

In this very place, the library of the château of Cerisy-la-Salle, at the time of the *décade* of 1986 dedicated to the works of Emmanuel Levinas, Jacques Rolland relayed the apologies of his Italian colleague Silvano Petrosino, whom he and Jean Greisch had invited to participate, for having, throughout the presentation of his paper, regularly pronounced the word "oeuvre" as "ouvre."

Provided this overture were understood not as that of the disclosure of being but as that of exposition to the Other, could it not have been said by Levinas—for whom, as for Petrosino, French is not his mother tongue, and who, even more demanding than the Socrates of *Phaedrus* 276, took responsibility for the words pronounced by the other participants at the colloquium—that this passage from *operari* to *aperire* was not such a bad thing. Unless in accepting this faulty pronunciation he removes the fault that is necessary (*qu'il faut*) for a text for Emmanuel Levinas not to come back to him, E.L. In that case, Petrosino's text would have closed the circuit of an economical exchange within the hermeneutic circle of ontology. It is in order to escape this eventuality that Levinas demands that we be ungrateful for what these texts offer us. And it is in order to respond to this demand that, in another text for Emmanuel Levinas, the interlocutors of the polylogue signed "Jacques Derrida" and entitled "En ce moment même dans cet ouvrage me voici" devise a work in which ingratitude is translated by a dislocation of personal and other pronouns. A dislocation that traduces itself as dis-locution insofar as the interlocutors are distinguished as locutor, locutrix, lector, lextrix, speaking, or writing—and it is difficult to distinguish the polylogue from a polygraph, for example an exchange or nonexchange of letters like "the one I write you," "celle que je t'écris" (TEL 25, Ps 163, RRL 14). So the one who said of the other at the beginning that she heard him, that she heard him for example repeat the little phrase "he will have obligated," "il aura obligé," admits at the end "I no longer know if you are saying the contrary, or if you have already written something wholly other," adding immediately "I no longer hear your voice." He no longer hears the other's voice because, as he says: "I have difficulty distinguishing

156

it from mine, from any other. . . . " But he also says that he no longer hears the other's voice in default of not being able to read his fault. From a beginning, which is not a beginning, at which "something unheard of " is felt (TEL 21, Ps 159, RRL 11), one arrives, or does not arrive, at a shore where one no longer hears a voice on account of something illegible (TEL 59, Ps 201, RRL 46)—namely, and unnamably, a fault: namely, and unnamably, the more than typographical fault of the substitution of the pronoun "elle" for the pronoun "il." *Il* and *elle,* the interlocutor and the interlocutrix, have conspired—I do not say coupled—to produce a text purportedly for Emmanuel Levinas, a text, however, that passes him by, it appears, but more and more illegibly, insofar as the il-legibility turns out to be inscribed by a difference that preseals (présc*elle*) her and him, the feminine difference. *Elle,* the feminine difference, dictates that the phrase "il aura obligé" recalled at the outset by the masculine voice and repeated several times in the course of the dis-course, recalls the words *"elle aura obligé"* pronounced one single time by the feminine voice a little before the end.

OTHER PASSAGES

How does this passage come to pass? Aporetically? Not at all. *Pas du tout.* It is a matter of a step (*pas*) that is not (*pas*) a step beyond; of a *pas* which does not remain to be made; of a *pas* that is a *fait accompli*—or rather of a *pas* which is accomplished but which is not and never has been made. There has been no *factum,* no *actum,* so no speech act, no *fatum,* but pure passivity, passedness, patience, even passion, Levinas would say (like, if not with, Hume), there where the gap between "is" and "ought" ("Hume's gap") finds itself always already crossed, the frontier already passed over. In what way passed over? Not as with Heidegger because the interlacing of how one finds oneself, *Befindlichkeit,* and understanding, *Verstehen,* is before (*devance*) the opposition of what is described as the spontaneous act and what is described as the passive impression. According to Levinas, the absolute passivity of illeity as super-impression is before (*devance*) both this opposition and the interlacing of the existentials. And this super-impression comes to pass earlier than the Husserlian proto-impression. The ethical and metaphysical before-cum-owing (*devant*) of illeity finds itself prior to the *a priori* and to phenomeno-ontological *hylê.* And elleity? According to whom and how does it find itself anterior to the exteriority of the *Il*? Does not the *elle* belong to interiority according to E.L.? Although in *Totality and Infinity* the discrete presence of the Feminine is the first relation to the Other that precedes the height, *hauteur,* of the indiscrete face of the Master, this is not a precedence in what in "At this very moment . . . " is called the serial order, the order that is classically, for example in Descartes, the order of exposition, the peda-gogical order. According to Levinas, in the order of metaphysical giving of orders (*ordonnance*), the order which, he would say, is the only truly exposi-tory and pedagogical order, the order that introduces disorder into the order of the truth of the ontological opening, anteriority is given to the pronouns "il" and "Il." But with what right does the feminine voice of "At this very moment . . ." maintain that the pronouns "il" and "Il" are pronouns which refer to the proto-pronoun "Elle"?

The interlocutrix, but anticipated by her interlocutor, who is anticipated by pages 142–43 of *Otherwise than Being* (AE 181–82, OB 142–43), which are anticipated by the *Song of Songs,* interpELLates her interlocutor, interrupts him in mid-phrase, in mid-sentence one could say, speaking juridically, following up on p. 22 of "At this very moment . . ." in *Textes pour Emmanuel Levinas* (Ps 160, RRL 11), in order to re-recite the *Song of Songs,* and to pose the question "Il or elle?" concerning the supposition that it is a masculine Me who is accused and declined before all declining; therefore before all servility in the service of others, in the accusative absolute of "Here I am" ("See me here," "me voici"). She says that it is the woman of the *Song* who says this, granted that when the latter says "I am sick with love" the simple enunciation of the "I" says quasi- and proto-performatively "Here I am" (TEL 46, Ps 187, RRL 35). Quasi- and proto-performatively because it is a question of a performative where "by these presents" refers back to a past that was never present, a past anterior written in the feminine—"passée antérieure" (TEL 48, Ps 189, RRL 36)—by the interscriptor under the dictation of the interlocutrix who remains "lectrice obligée" (TEL 51, Ps 192, RRL 39), obligated, she also dictates, by the work, *oeuvre,* of E.L. (TEL 45, Ps 186, RRL 33). "You have dictated it to me," he writes, "and yet what I write at this very moment, 'the work of E.L. will have obligated,' articulating together those common nouns and proper names, you don't yet (*encore*) know what that means."

INTERRUPTION

Il faut, it is necessary to interrupt his discourse at this very moment to recall this in relation to this word "yet" ("encore"): we have already (*encore*) remarked, toward the end of the work entitled "At this very moment . . . ," toward the toward or on the hither side of the verse, *vers les vers ou en deçà du verset,* that, so to speak, it is the scriptor who says to the dictrix that he is without knowledge. And our remark does not interpret the work faultily. Except that the reason why he says "I no longer hear your voice" is more complicated. He no longer hears her voice not simply because her voice is difficult to distinguish from his own—which implies, *nota bene,* that there is no confusion of voices at all; another good, or bad, reason why he does not hear her voice is that it is not solely a matter of voice, but also of writing. There is, but at the heart of a vertiginous place that one no longer recognizes (TEL 21, Ps 159, RRL 11; NP 88, 95, PN 62, 65), this chiasmus of a dictrix-auditrix, who will have been maybe a scriptrix, and a scriptor-auditor who will be maybe a dictor. Although it may happen from one moment to another that she announces "I knew" (TEL 51, Ps 192, RRL 39) or "I knew it" (TEL 56, Ps 198, RRL 43), the one and the other are absolutely "without knowing it" (TEL 36, Ps 176, RRL 25) as to the question of the sex of the totally other, as soon as the reading of the self-styled philosophical work of E.L. is inspired by commentaries that one reads in his Talmudic lectures. According to this double reading, one comprehends that the work of E.L. comprehends a way of reading *otherwise otherwise* the "il" of "il aura obligé" and of "il faut." One begins to comprehend that it is necessary (*il faut*) to read "autrement" otherwise from the moment at which the obligated lectrix wonders if Emmanuel Levinas would accept her replacing this "il" with E.L. (TEL 45, Ps 185, RRL 33). If he accepted this, that would probably not be a fault, and his work would have put itself out of work by dint of its having been given back to him.

Pursuing maybe the trace of the enthymeme of ELoHiM in the ellipse of EL (the ellipse of an enthymeme of a trace of a plural that is as singular as *Autrui* is a singular plural), and dissimulating this syllable in square letters which no one in "At this very moment . . ." at any moment pronounces (unless EL is pronounced in the blink of the parenthesis which opens each time there is written the secret and secretarial *entr(el)acement* of a performative such as "(come)" with a constatation such as that she is coming), let us ask what would happen if the exemplary lectrix should come and ask whether she was comprehended by the work of E.L. (TEL 51, Ps 192, RRL 39).[1] She would then have begun to comprehend that one must comprehend *totally otherwisely otherwise* both the upper-case "Il" and the lower-case "il" that refers to the first of these two. Not that the first of these two is the only one that calls for the inscription of height. And not that it is decided that the first occupies the first place. This can be occupied maybe by a third, by her of whom *Totality and Infinity* says both that she occupies the Home and that she is the other, but not the absolutely other, who welcomes me there (TeI 145–46, TaI 170–71). However, is she not the absolutely other if she is the other of the masculine other, *Il*, and if she is not his symmetrical and dialectical other but the dissymmetrical and ethical other? In that case, as is said by her who dictates throughout "At this very moment . . . ," is not Illeity dictated by elleity? Let us accept that that appears to follow from what Levinas says as commentator upon certain Talmudic texts which, in his opinion, do not make *Elle* as such secondary vis-à-vis *Il*, but make secondary rather the sexual difference posited as the origin of femininity (TEL 55, Ps 197, RRL 43). The following would follow:

> The effect of secondarization allegedly demanded by the totally other (as *Il*), would become the cause, otherwise said the other of the totally other, the other of a totally other who is no longer sexually neutral but *posed* (outside the series in the seriasure), suddenly determined as *Il*. Then the Work apparently signed with the Pro-noun *Il* would be dictated, aspired by the desire to make *Elle* secondary, therefore by *Elle*.

Here is a consequence of which the logic appears to be Graeco-Hegelian, the logic of appearing, being, and truth inside which what should not

159

appear or be, the exterior totally other, *Il,* appears to be included, that is to say is in truth excluded as the one that masters without dominating and teaches without seigniory, *enseigne sans seigneurie.* Does there remain to *Il* the possibility of being in truth neither simply included nor simply excluded insofar as *Il* is let be by the truth of being which neither is master who teaches and Majusculy inspires metaphysico-ethical Desire nor (because only a being could dominate) is a dominating seigniory like that which finds itself at home in classical metaphysics (ED 200–201, WD 136–37)?

OPEN QUESTIONS

Neither including, nor excluding, nor concluding, but leaving the work (*oeuvre*) as opening (*ouverture, ouvrance, "ouevre"*) "open to the totally other," "ouverte au tout autre" (TEL 27, Ps 166, RRL 16), exposed, let us pose a few other questions, textual questions concerning the lectrix, then concerning the lector. But first it is necessary, *il faut,* to respond to a question concerning them both—without wishing to exclude the eventuality that from the beginning of the polylogue he and she share the same voice, the voice of the other (FC 11).

1. "I should have been a little more unfaithful to him still, more ungrateful . . . ," she says a little before the end, and he and she accept this apposition throughout the length of their colloquy. Are they not wrong to accept this? Can't one be unfaithful without feeling oneself ungrateful? A little after the beginning the lector cites from "At this very moment . . ." words in listening to which one would do well to recall the sense of "movement" that the word "moment" recalls: "The Work thought to the end requires a radical generosity of the movement in which the Same goes toward the Other. Consequently, it requires an *ingratitude* from the other." For E.L. here it is ingratitude that is at issue. From this citation, however, the lector derives a certain antinomy concerning infidelity. He says that if he is faithful he is unfaithful, faulty, and that if he does not faithfully make restitution of the text in giving beyond restitution, he risks fault (TEL 24, Ps 163, RRL 14). He allows the loophole of this "risk": he does not say "and if I am faithful I am not faithful" or "and if I am not at fault I am at fault," because the logic of the antinomy he appeals to is not simply formal and does not concern only what is said, *le dit.* Therefore there is no trap. In wanting to give to E.L. beyond restitution it is necessary to do it, *il faut,* in making restitution to him of what he has said or will have said about the Work. Nevertheless, the question remains open of knowing if there is a means of resolving the dilemma from the side of the saying, *dire.* We shall come back to this question of risk.

What is in question here is the passage made by the lectrix from infidelity to ingratitude and the passage made by the lector to infidelity from the ingratitude spoken of by the author E.L. Are not these two passages *faux pas,* two infidelities, two faults too many? In order that "At this very moment . . ."

160

do a Work, it is necessary, *il faut,* that it retain this minimum of fidelity to the work of E.L. To be unfaithful to it in not making restitution of it to itself, it is necessary, *il faut,* that it retains at least the faithful memory of it. And it is memory that gives the response to this question of passage. The absolute ingratitude that responds to the radical generosity of E.L., "the only homage possible to his work," is that of the ungrateful, unfaithful memory, that of the memory which is already at work in hearing or understanding E.L., therefore in already recognizing and making restitution to him what his work gives. Absolute ingratitude is not at all a psychological state. No more than is the absolute non-jealousy that conditions every relative jealousy and gratitude, as the absolute trace of the immemorial past conditions the traces of the memory of gratitude or ingratitude. The lector distinguishes this non-jealousy from the proprietary jealousy with which the author could keep "the sufficiency of self assured of its signature," *la suffisance du moi assuré de sa signature* (TEL 26, Ps 164, RRL 15), the jealousy against which the lectrix says that she plays ingratitude, "jealousy through which, seeing without seeing all and, above all, without being seen, before and beyond the phenomenon, the without-jealousy jealously guards itself, otherwise said loses itself, keeps-itself-loses-itself (TEL 58, Ps 201, RRL 46).

2. First question for her. When she writes that the Work would be inspired by the desire to make *Elle* secondary, does she mean that it is a question here of possessive or erotic minuscular, lower-case, desire? And is a valid consequence indicated by the "therefore" ("donc") of the passage "inspired, aspired by the desire to secondarize *Elle,* therefore (*donc*) by *Elle*"—which does not seem to be legitimated by the passage from the secondarization of sexual difference to the secondarization of the feminine about which the obligated lectrix asks, *mais pourquoi donc?*, "but why therefore?" (TEL 54, Ps 201, RRL 41). Let us leave this question here in what she would call its ellipse, in order to ask according to what syntax this "therefore" could indicate or trace a valid or faulty consequence. Would it be the syntax of the dominant implicative logic or would it be the complicative syntax of meta-physico-ethical Mastery?

The response and responsibility is heard maybe in the question that the obligated scriptrix poses in turn to the obligated lector, the question "Mastery therefore *of* femininity?" (her emphasis), which passes from the objective genitive to its subjective supplement and, maybe, from the minuscular and therefore dominative mastery to the Majuscular and majestically metaphysical Mastery. She underlines also that She, majuscular *Elle,* would under-sign or countersign the one that under-signs the Work of the work, though neither in the sense in which to appose one's under-signature would be equivalent to confirming nor in the sense in which countersigning would be equivalent to opposing, but *otherwise than signing.* Which means at the same time that the desire to secondarize *Elle* is the Desire that under-signs erotic desire and that the "therefore" in question cannot be simply that of the dominant logic of the said; it is necessary that it be that of a telegraphy which inscribes, subscribes,

161

and interrupts this logic of the said said to be contaminating, that it be the "therefore" of an alternative syntax of a saying which repeats throughout the entire length of the dis-cursive presentation: Amen, Amen, Hear Hear, So be it, So be it, *Soit, Soit* (TEL 51, Ps 192–93, RRL 39). . . .

3. Second question for her. If everything she suggests follows from what E.L. says in commenting upon the rabbis, and if, as she says, "what he comments on is consonant with a whole network of affirmations that are his, or those of him, '*il*'," the domestication of this last by *Elle*, the last or first hostage and the first hostess, the one who welcomes, is it not consonant with "the entire system of his saying of the other"? If she inflicts a "faulty violence," has this violence not already taken place in the body of his, E.L.'s, work, in spite of and even because of his position as man? Does not the body suffer the traumatism? Does not this offer itself, does it not open itself in his work since forever, a wound "fore-
(she writes with a hyphen across the passage from one line to another, uniting-disuniting them) closed"?

Whatever his response may be, according to the interdiction against effacing the names of God even when faultily recopied (TEL 56–57, Ps 199, RLL 44–45; ADV 146, BV 118, 212), it will have been necessary that the defunct infanta, still-born, issue by fil(l)iation from the maybe incestuous chiasmus of *Il* and *Elle*, be fore-closed, encrypted away in the closure of an aneconomic *oikos* so that *il-elle*, still-born, may be a non-neuter and non-androgynous text for E.L. that does not return to him.

4. Finally a question for the one who conducts the liturgy of mourning transcribed in square letters in the last moment of the text, a liturgy that both resembles a girl who, beyond the face, is and is not her father or mother, and resembles a song of the *Song of Songs* or a poem of the *Poem of Poems*, a work of art, from the body of which one will have been obligated by E.L. or by *Il* or by *Elle* to question *viva voce* every fissible anatomic atom, assisting (m)orally at one's word if this work is to make the passage from a merely ritual and rhythmical liturgy, "fine words" which say something of the song (TEL 28, Ps 167, RRL 17; FC 12), to the Liturgy which disenchants and gives food and drink, to the Work of prayer without request, without petition, but not without a repetition that is not one without letter, *sans lettre*.

Why is the repetition not one without letter? Because to the question "Why is she dead?" concerning the *infans*, her to whom words have not been given and who is on the point of being buried, the reply of him who pronounces edifying words from the mouth of the open crypt over which he leans, as Plato leaned over the *pharmakon*, is that it must be given to be read (D 195, D tr. 169). Although it expresses *viva voce* what the di(re)ctrix has just said to him, saying does not go without writing and writing does not go without the written, no less than the "Hebrew" without the "Greek" and the "Greek" without the "Hebrew": "Jerusalem" and "Yeroushalaïm" she sings, improvising on Chouraqui, in the repetitions of the *Song of Songs* in *Textes pour Emmanuel Levinas* and *Psychè* (TEL 30, Ps 168–69, RRL 19). How distinguish the *yod* from the self-styled *i grec?*

The scriptor cites *Totality and Infinity:* "The Other can dispossess me of my work. . . . The work is vowed to this foreign *Sinngebung.* . . . " (TEL 50, Ps 192, RRL 38; TeI 202–204, TaI 227–28). The foreign *Sinngebung* which is consonant with these words according to him does not entail that in absenting itself from its author the written word absents itself from responsibility, as one could have thought from the perspective of *Phaedrus* 276, so frequently cited by E. L. and J. D. It is just because the author, *auteur,* paternal according to Plato, does not assist at his work in order to come to my help, it is just because height, *hauteur,* is exposed to the risk that the trace of a "maybe" underwriting the power of being can always appear enigmatically as a sign, it is just because the one and the other are thus exposed to my instigation, that the responsibility which will have obligated without constraint devolves uniquely on me, on my self-identical subjectivity become since forever diachronic sub-jectilelleity for you and for you and for you . . . at this very moment.

12

LEVINAS AND LANGUAGE

And thine ears shall hear a word behind thee

—Isaiah 30:21

This chapter seeks to expound Levinas's philosophy of language by seeking to explain the reference made in the final crowded sentence of *Otherwise than Being* to "the trace—the unpronounceable writing—of what, always already past—always *'il,'* Pro-noun, does not enter into any present, to which names designating beings or verbs in which their *essence* resounds are no longer suited—but which marks with its seal everything that can be named" (AE 233, OB 185).[1] I begin by giving brief accounts of two of the philosophies of language that dominated the intellectual scene when his main works were being composed.

STRUCTURALISM

The cluster of ideas that goes under the name structuralism derives largely from Ferdinand de Saussure's *Course of General Linguistics,*[2] though, as Levinas reminds us, structuralism is anticipated by the philosophical ideal of a *mathesis universalis* proposed by Descartes and Leibniz (AE 122, OB 96). While nine-teenth-century theoreticians had focused mainly on the evolution of lan-guage, Saussure projects a science that subordinates the diachronic to the synchronic. Distinguishing acts of speech (*parole*) from language regarded as a system (*langue*), he aims to show how the units assembled in a linguistic system signify not "positively" by standing independently for objects signified, but "negatively" through the combinatorial differences among them. Accord-ing to Saussure, a sign comprises two distinguishable but inseparable compo-nents: a phonetic, graphic, or otherwise embodied signifier (*signifiant*) and a signified concept (*signifié*). He lays down a program for a general science of signs, a semiology of all systems of signs that extends to other special fields the lessons of the science of language. In this program, relatively simple signs are identified by the places they can and cannot fill, as in chess what matters is the moves that can be made with the pieces, not their shapes or the material of which they are made.

Levinas takes over from structuralism the word *signifiant.* However, priz-ing it away from the *signifié* understood as the conceptual aspect of signs, he applies it to the speaker, but to the speaker not regarded only third-person-ally or as one of a first-person plural *we.* For Levinas the *signifiant* is primarily the speaker in the first-person singular subjectivity of its *me*, in the accusative case—except that the word "case" is misleading. Before being a case, the speaker is a face, the face that speaks. And what the face primarily says, its *signifié*, is nothing but its saying. When I say something there will normally be some semantic signification of a message, but such sense-giving *Sinngebung* is already *signifiance*, where my saying is my saying of my saying. Hence, while on the structuralist theory the positivity of the signs we use depends upon negativity defined by differences among the constituents of the systematic interdependent totalities of *signifiants* and of *signifiés*, *signifiance* as what I shall call "deep" saying testifies to the positivity of my being accosted by another human being, an event that holds "the secret of the birth (*naissance*) of thought itself and of the verbal proposition by which it is conveyed" (EDE 235, CPP 125). Signifiance is without horizon or world. Although or because it is the expression of the face of my neighbor, it infinitely transcends the confines of culture; so its saying is prior to every historical language (EDE 231–32, CPP 122). Other than the countenance, the face has no features or properties or substance, no *ousia*. The signifiance of the face is abstract, but its abstractness is prior to the abstractness defined by the structuralist as the separability of the intersubstitutability of propositional signs from a given empirical embodiment.

Precisely because in structuralist semiotics the components or terms owe their meaning to their internal interrelations, it is arguable that there is only one unit, the system as a whole. This suggests an analogy with mathematical systems, where it is arguable that the mathematician reads off from the system as a whole the theorems he calculates or infers. One might say that it is the system that thinks through the mathematician. And something like this is what is said by some of the human scientists who apply Saussure's model to their own special fields. With some structuralists the idea that "it" (*es, ça*) thinks in me turns into the idea of "the death of man," so that it becomes questionable whether they can properly be called "human" scientists. Lacan in psychoanalysis, Althusser in political theory, Lévi-Strauss in anthropology, and Foucault in the genealogies of knowledge and power are among those Levinas would see as representatives of "modern antihumanism" (AE 164, OB 127). Although this is a description many structuralists embrace, they do so, Levinas maintains, only because they identify humanism with the idea that the human being is first and foremost the author of his acts, including his acts of speech. Kantianism is typical of humanism understood in this way. Spontaneity and freedom are stressed too by the existentialism against which structuralism reacts. One of Sartre's titles declares that existentialism is a humanism.[3] For him, as for Kant and for the tradition culminating in them, humanism is a humanism of the first person singular subject.

ONTOLOGISM

According to Levinas, much the same holds when one turns from the humanism of the subject to a humanism of a being whose way of being is not that of being placed, being somewhere, here or there: Da-sein. Dasein, Heidegger maintains in *Being and Time,* is in each case mine (*jemeinig*). Dasein is mine-ish. Dasein is a being that interprets itself and its place (Da) in its world. Its way of being is for its being to be in question. It is therefore with a questioning of questioning that the analysis of Dasein begins. Heidegger enumerates the elements of investigative questioning—*Untersuchung,* as in the German title of the *Logical Investigations* of Husserl, the dedicatee of *Being and Time.* These components include: the topic, which in the case of Heidegger's book is being; what we seek to discover about the topic, which in this case is the meaning of being; and that at which attention must be directed in order to discover this, here the beings in which being resides. The being pre-eminently to be addressed, Heidegger maintains, is precisely the being that is able to raise the question of the meaning of being, the so-called "human being" or Dasein. Heidegger also maintains that the question of the meaning of being is first and foremost the question each Dasein puts to itself about its own being. To state this in the terminology of *Being and Time,* ontological and existential questioning begins in questioning that is ontic and existentiell. It will turn out to be of importance for our understanding of Levinas's teaching that in Heidegger's analysis the being to whom is put the existentiell leading question is none other than the person by whom that question is put. For Heidegger questioning is first self-questioning: not initially *fragen,* but *sich fragen,* Dasein's ability to ask itself about its own way of being toward its own death.

LINGUISTIC POSSESSIONS

In the "Letter on 'Humanism'" Heidegger calls language the house of being.[4] Taking the liberty of reading *Being and Time* in the light of this later remark, but appealing also to Heidegger's demonstration in the earlier work itself that Dasein's being in the world is its being in language or discourse (*Rede*), could one say that while the point of entry into Heidegger's account of language in *Being and Time* is the question and questionability, the point of entry into Levinas's account of language is the response and responsibility? This would be to oversimplify. For a notion and sense of responsibility (*Antwortlichkeit*) is all-pervasive in *Being and Time.*

But the responsibility that figures in that book and in Heidegger's later works is finally the responsibility toward being, whereas the responsibility that is first and last in Levinas's treatment of language is responsibility to the other human being. And insofar as the target of his "humanism of the other man" is the "antihumanism" he sees in theories like structuralism, it cannot fail to have in its sights at the same time the accounts of language put forth by Heidegger in the course of which we are told both that Dasein has language and that Dasein is, as we might say, had by language.[5] Language is not merely a competence possessed by a subclass of animals, the rational ones, the *zôon logon echon* of Aristotle. Dasein is and has in its essence to be the place (the Da) where language speaks. There is then a mutual belonging of Dasein and language, as is indicated formally by the conjunction of the name Dasein with the statement that language is the house of being and with the idea that Dasein has to be (*zu sein hat*), to take on, to assume the responsibility for the that and the how of its being.[6] Language on this account is not ultimately to be compared, as Wittgenstein compares it, with a toolbox.[7] We speak English or German or French, but that is because we already belong to the linguisticality of which the speaking of natural languages is a manifestation. *Language* speaks, "die *Sprache* spricht."[8] Although it is not incorrect to say that we possess this or that language and the ability to speak it, prior to that is our being possessed by language.

Prior to my being possessed by language, Levinas maintains, is my possession by the human being who speaks to me. But, again, this formulation of the difference between Levinas's and Heidegger's doctrines of language is too simple unless we acknowledge the difference between what each of them means by possession and recognize that the difference between Heidegger's and Levinas's doctrines of language is not merely a difference between monologue and dialogue. Already in *Being and Time* Dasein's being possessed by language, understood as a basic structure of Dasein's occupying a place in the world, is a way of Dasein's being with others, *mit-da-sein*. Being in the world is being in dialogue. *Sprache* is *Gespräch*. He can say this despite his saying that language is monologue,[9] for what he means when he says that language is monologue is that although it is language al*one* (*all*ein) that speaks authentically and although this speaking is *lone*some (ein*sam*), lonesomeness is possible only if one is not alone, not solitary, not cut off from community. Lonesomeness is a way of not being alone; it is a privative way of being *with* others. Therefore our earlier reference to the self-reference of Dasein's questioning must not be taken to imply that the mine-ishness of each Dasein is incompatible with an original sociality.

However, there is more than one way of understanding this sociality. For both Heidegger and Levinas it is linguistic, and a way of being possessed by language. But, to repeat, whereas for Heidegger possession by language is a way of *being with others,* for Levinas it is also a *possession by others.* This latter possession disrupts my being possessed by language as this is understood by Heidegger. My possession by language is obsession at the same time—or rather from a time beyond recall of which the diachrony is anterior to the diachrony correlatively opposed to synchrony by the structuralist. The other's call to responsibility to her or to him and to the third party, that is to say, to the whole of humanity, is anterior to the call to responsibility to being. Its anteriority is announced in a pluperfect tense marking the diachrony of a time incommensurable with what a verb in the present tense might have reported. This ab-solute, separated past is contained neither by the structuralist's idea of language as a synchronous totality nor by the Heideggerian ontologist's description of a historical (*geschichtlich*) dispensation (*Geschick*) as a unitary whole in which Dasein's having-been, coming-toward, and making-present are co-implicated.

167

Combining Heidegger's turn of phrase with one of Levinas's, we can say that the human other breaks into the house of being like a thief (AE 16, OB 13). This possession by the other is a dispossession of my home and my belongings, a discomforting that is, to use Heidegger's word, *un-heimlich,* unhomely. I am disconcerted, discountenanced, and decentered. Prior to the subject's self-consciousness, prior to the mine-ishness of the self that says "I," and prior to all consciousness, the self is the me accused by some other human being whose place in the sun I have always already usurped simply by being here, simply as ego or Dasein. Levinas goes as far as to call this obsessive possession by the other psychosis, intending us to hear in this resonances both of Husserl's *Beseelung,* animation, and of madness or folly, the topic taken up from Freud in the work of Foucault and Lacan.

Another of Levinas's contemporaries who should be mentioned in this context is Ricoeur. No less critical of structuralism than is Levinas, holding, like him (and John Austin[10]), that the study of language as an object of science must be supplemented by reflection upon momentary acts of speech, he makes a special analysis of avowals. But this analysis, like psychoanalysis, is conducted within the framework of the symbols and primarily Greek myths where the notions of impurity and culpability arise in the West. So the concern with *parole* that Ricoeur shares with Levinas is of a sort that leads him to stress the importance of narrative even in his investigation of confessions of guilt. Typically, the confession of guilt isolates the person who confesses. In owning up I come to own myself, even if the guilt is shared.[11] On Ricoeur's account the isolation effected in the acknowledgment of culpability is not itself isolated from the context of a narrative or myth. It therefore serves well to bring out the boldness of Levinas's account. For, according to the latter, culpability is independent of such narrative or mythological contexts, notwithstanding that Levinas sometimes cites even in his more philosophical writings stories from the Hebrew Bible by way of illustration.

NOUNS, VERBS, AND VERBAL NOUNS

A narrative is a sequence of statements. Among the simplest statements, at least in Indo-European languages, are predicative ones in which something is said about something or somebody. The subject about which or whom the statement says something is represented in the sentence by a noun or noun-like term. What is said about it is expressed in a phrase involving either the verb "to be" explicitly or a short-form verb, e.g. "runs," paraphrasable by a long-form copulative expression, e.g. "is running." Taking the hint from languages like German, where "Das Himmel blaut" says "The sky is blue," some logicians, for instance Quine, have pointed out that long forms can generally be transposed into short forms, as in "The President of the United States bushizes," "The teacher of Plato socratizes," "Pegasus pegasizes."[12] Following what he takes to be Heidegger's teaching on the verb and verbal noun (AE 49, OB 189), Levinas gives as examples of identity statements "Socrates socratizes" and "Red reds." Another example given by him orally, but not to my knowledge in print, is "Le violoncelle violoncellise."[13] These express, he says, the *fashion* (*façon*) in which, for example, Socrates is (AE 53, OB 41). He italicizes this word in order to bring to our attention that it derives from the Latin *facere,* to do or to make, and in order to help us to hear in predication the time, tense, and verbality of being and the adverbiality of being's modalities, its *Seinsweisen.* But here Levinas's word for "being" is "essence." In a note at the outset of *Otherwise than Being* he explains that he does not use the word "essence" as it is traditionally used, for the nature or whatness of something. He uses it in the verbal sense in which *Sein* is used in German and in *Being and Time* in opposition to *Seiendes,* this latter standing for *a* being, an *étant.* Nevertheless, the second syllable of *étant* retains a trace of the suffix *ance* from which abstract nouns of action are formed through derivation from *antia* and *entia,* for example *naissance,* a word we earlier found him using in the course of explaining this point, and *signifiance,* a word to which we shall return below. Other examples are *tendance,* a word used in *Otherwise than Being* in conjunction with a family of words based on *tendere,* e.g. ostension, and *essance.* This last is a word he says he will not be so bold as to use there, notwithstanding that it would have represented well the verb-noun ambiguity of *Sein* and *Wesen* and the fact that *être* can be either a verb or a noun. The hidden difference at issue here is what Heidegger calls the ontological difference, the difference between being and a being present already in the ambiguity of the Greek word *on.* Levinas calls this difference an amphibology. Because there survives in the second syllable of *étant* a hint of the action and verbal-cum-adverbial *fashion* exemplifed in "Socrates socratizes," Levinas might have had no objection to translating this into "Socratizing socratizes," on analogy with Borges's Heraclitean verbalizing conversion of "The moon rose above the river" into "Upward behind the onstreaming it mooned." But note in this last example the pronominal "it" that insists on itself as stubbornly as it does in "It is raining," "It reds," "Es gibt Sein," and "Es gibt Zeit." These last two, meaning "There is being" and "There is time" (literally "It gives being" and "It gives time") pose what may seem to be a problem. In his essay "Time and Being" Heidegger says that the belonging together of these two statements, signaled by the "and" of his title, is expressed by the word *Ereignis.*[14] In colloquial German this word means a happening or event. Now just as one cannot say either of being or of time that it is or *gibt,* neither can this be said of *Ereignis.* To say any of these things would be to treat being as a being, time as in time, and happening as a happening. The best we can do, Heidegger concludes, is to say "Das Ereignis ereignet." Although Levinas may have this apparent tautology in mind when he writes "Socrates socratizes," it should be observed that the latter is a statement about *a* being in time. Heidegger's statement on the other hand purports to be about being and time, yet, as the definite article "Das" indicates, it puts being in the same logico-grammatical slot as is occupied by the proper name "Socrates." Heidegger's statement fails to mark the onto-logical difference. Of this he is quite aware. He goes as far as to argue that the history of philosophy is a history of the forgetting of this difference by philosophers and of their failure to become aware of this forgetting. Hence they fail to ask how one can speak of being without saying the opposite of what one means or wants to say.[15]

Frege raises the question how one can consistently say either "The concept horse is a concept" or "The concept horse is not a concept."[16] Appearances to the contrary, the first of these is not an analytical truth, and the second is not a contradiction. Both suffer from what he calls the unavoidable linguistic difficulty (*Härte*) that a concept is what the predicate of a statement connotes, whereas in both of these statements the form of words preceding the copula, the grammatical subject of the sentences, converts the alleged concept into an object. What we are calling Heidegger's problem is analogous, but it is more deep-seated than Frege's, because it is about being as such.

What we are calling Heidegger's problem is not Levinas's problem. But we have been obliged to outline it in order to go on to show now where the crucial difference lies. The relation between saying (*dire*) and the said (*dit*) treated in *Otherwise than Being* is a relation between a verb and a nominal part of speech. It may therefore seem to correspond at the linguistic level with the ontological difference between being and beings and to be a derivative of this. But Levinas is concerned less with the *dire* that is a speech act correlative with what is said than with a *Dire* that is somehow presupposed by that correlation. That deep *Dire* is therefore different both from the pair of correlative dictions and from the pair opposed in the ontological difference. So, if a problem is a question that can in principle be answered, it is not a problem that is raised by the relation between this *Dire* and the ontological difference or amphibology. Answerable questions arise as to being and beings (where among beings are included processes, events, and whatever else there is). The question as to how these questions and their answers and topics are related to the uncorre-lative saying is not then strictly a question. Deep saying is the expression of answerability prior to the expression of questions and answers. But it must now be acknowledged that Levinasian deep saying has a parallel in the Heideggerian deep being or *Ereignis* of the differentiation *between* being and a being. If no answerable question or problem can be posed about that, we shall have reached a deeper analogy between Levinas and Heidegger. Nev-ertheless, this leaves it open for Levinas to maintain that the verbality of the infinitive *dire*, to say—the verb of or for infinity and the unfinished (AE 16, OB 13)—expresses an excluded third infinitely deeper and older than the verbality of to-be-or-not-to-be.

PRONOUNS AND PRONUNCIATION

Like Heidegger and Frege and Wittgenstein, Levinas is confronted with the difficulty of saying or otherwise showing how the philosopher can avoid saying precisely the opposite of what he wants to say. He cites the sentence in which Hegel poses this difficulty (AE 105, OB 84),[17] and would have his readers remember the context in which Hegel's sentence occurs. It occurs in the context of the discussion of the theory of sensible certainty according to which the richest and truest knowledge is the allegedly immediate apprehension of a sensible datum denoted by the demonstrative pronoun "this." Hegel challenges the advocate of this theory to write that pronoun down. He does not have to wait long before he is in a position to point out that the unmediated datum the pronoun was supposed to denote earlier may now denote something else, and that the same can be said of "then" and "now" as well as of the first person pronoun "I," should the advocate defend himself by asserting "This richest and truest knowledge is the sensible apprehension I am experiencing here and now." For all these pronouns, along with "my," "your," and the other possessive adjectives cognate with them, shift from one referent to another. Therefore they do not register a purely immediate apprehension, but import the mediation of comprehension. They designate not pure sensible receptivity, but engage the conceptualizing activity of the understanding, albeit not in the same way as do common nouns.

The challenge "Write this down" is the part of Hegel's reply that is very relevant to the understanding of Levinas's teaching on language and pronominality. The written word is especially exposed to interpretation in ways different from what the author intended. The mortal author cannot be there always to forestall the misinterpretation of his intentions. And this holds for any work, whether set down in ink or produced in paint or in bronze or in tablets of stone.

Plato's *Phaedrus* is the work on which Levinas draws in making this distinction between a work (*oeuvre*) and the spoken word. Yet in the part of the dialogue that is most relevant here, sections 275–76, this distinction is blurred. Although Socrates is keen to get Phaedrus to agree that there is a kind of discourse that is preferable to writing, this preferable kind of discourse is said to be written in the human being's soul; and Levinas too notes how fitting this metaphor is for discourse that expresses knowledge of principles (AE 189, OB 148). We saw that in the final sentence of *Otherwise than Being* cited at the beginning of this chapter Levinas goes as far as to describe as "unpronounceable writing" what he wishes to contrast with a work. This is not writing in any ordinary sense. It is related to the archiwriting to which, discussing the same Platonic dialogue, Derrida appealed in 1968 to indicate what is somehow presupposed by both writing and speaking understood in their usual senses as correlatives.[18] Compare Levinas's special use of "Saying" to mark what is called for by both poles of the correlation of saying and what is said. This archi-saying, as we might call it—provided we remember that it is not a formal principle, but an-archic— is the trace of the absolutely third-personal pronoun "he," the *il* of *illéité* that perhaps, without letting divinity be said, is pronounced by the word "God."

This word is extra-ordinary. It does not belong to any order. Neither a proper name nor a common name, it names neither nothing nor anything that can be present or represented. It falls within no grammatical category, not even that of the vocative case, perhaps not even the vocative case of prayer (ADV 157, BV 128; AE 190, 206, OB 149, 162).

This "he" is pronounced or invoked as soon as there is language and as soon as there is justice or injustice. And there is justice or injustice as soon as there is a person facing me whom I address as "you"; for you—as indicated by the French *vous,* a grammatical plural used in polite address to a single person—are one among others, not the "thou" of the exclusive, intimate duality Levinas takes Buber's I-Thou relationship to be (HS 64–65, OS 43–44). The violent exclusiveness of preoccupation by a single other person is forestalled by the "he" implicit in your looking at me, as in an essay in *Difficult Freedom* on the danger of loving God more than the Torah the written and oral Law or Teaching is said to come between me and a devotion that runs the risk of becoming a private indulgence, a religious equivalent of the sensible certainty criticized by Hegel. Love of the Torah is practical love of all others. That is a way of saying that they are in the trace of *illéité* (HAH 63, CPP 107, LBPW 63). But *illéité* is the third-personality not simply of the third party who looks at me already in your eyes, but the third-personality both of the third party over against me and of myself as a third party over against and thanks to them and you or, as Levinas also writes, thanks to God, blessed be He, *béni-soit-Il* (ADV 147, 151, BV 119, 122). Further, if Levinas's neologism *illéité* is built on this upper-case *Il* or lower-case *il,* it is built also on the Latin pronoun *ille* denoting remoteness and disjunction from the speaker, separatedness or absolutely pluperfect past-ness (AE 15, OB 12): "always already past—always '*il*'," says the final sentence of *Otherwise than Being.* It denotes our *parenté,* where this is our being bound in a relationship of fraternity that is neither our being united under a Father in the way of a particular monotheistic religion, nor a biological common descendence, but our being bound ethically in a sociality. In this sociality not only has my responsibility to *you* been complicated by my responsibility to *him* and to *her;* more than this, the hitherto incomparably responsible *me* is now a member of society with comparable rights, one of a *we* that is not and is not founded upon being-with-others as described in *Being and Time* (AE 201–202, OB 158).

Fraternity means that the other commands me to command, but that the superiority of the other in this relationship consists in the other's face being the face of the poor, the stranger, the widow, and the orphan (TeI 229, TaI 251).[19] I am not commanded as a slave (TeI 188, TaI 213). I am commanded to serve, to serve the other and the other other. The other assigns me in my responsibility to the third party who looks at me already in the first other's eyes. Because the other's eyes speak, they speak justice, for "language is justice" (ibid.), where the word "language" translates *langage,* the intersection of *langue* and *parole.* "Signification signifies in justice" (AE 201, OB

158). Therefore the other's imperative both belongs to and exceeds a systematic *syntax* of tenses and aspects and cases. In Levinas's philosophy of language, speaking is primarily but non-foundationally speaking for the other. The *sich fragen* of self-addressed questioning that guides Heidegger's fundamental ontology is superseded. In Levinas's philosophy of first philosophy as ethics, the German pronoun *sich* (and the French pronoun *se* and the English pronoun "me") is an absolute accusative, not merely a declension from a nominative. Nomination or denomination as the appending of a noun or a name risks stifling the sound of the voice that calls me by name only in order to call me to respond by speaking for the other who addresses me and for the other other for whom that first other speaks. Levinas is thus able to write both that "language is justice," and that the face is (probably) "the very essence of language prior to language" without implying that the face is prior to justice (EDE 231–32, CPP 122; ADV 157, BV 128). "I am . . . necessary for justice, as responsible beyond every limit fixed by an objective law" (TeI 223, TaI 245). I am in a double bind: the face as saying and responsibility is the "essence" of language as what is said, of what is, of being, and of conceptual essence because the latter require the former if they are not to be a violence; at the same time the former require the latter in order to meet the demand for justice for every other (AE 58, 203, OB 45, 159).

This last requirement means that there is an ambiguity not only between the different tertialities marked by the two uses of the third-personal pronoun distinguished by Levinas in *Otherwise than Being* discussed in this section so far (AE 191, OB 150), but also between these and an impersonal use like that discussed in the preceding section. It is as though the *il* of the third party is attracted "upward" toward the *il* of *illéité* and "downward" to the *il* of what Levinas calls the *il y a,* the "there is," so that, independent of the fact that *il* can translate "it" as well as "he," there is a risk of the extremes being confused (DVI 115, GCM 69, LBPW 141). The impersonal pronoun *il* of the *il y a* is the anonymous *ça,* the anonymous It, one is tempted to say, that susurrates in the interstices of the essance that is sung in the poetic word and in the essence formulated prosaically in the linguistics of structuralism. Through their inevitable liability to lapse from responsibility into the half-sense either of a prejudiced privacy or of a neutral indifferent publicity, the language of the poet (the *Gedicht*) venerated by Heidegger and on the other hand the structures of language abstracted as a topic for science by Saussure (which Heidegger would have called framework, *Gestell*) expose one to suffocation by the utter and unutterable non-sense of what we cannot strictly call "Itness" on analogy with the translation of "illéité" as "He-ness." "It" already implies determinacy. So too does "ness," for it connotes whatness or essence. Determinacy of being, limitation, is a function of negation, whereas the nothingness of the "there is" is not a nothingness that limits being, but is indistinguishable from being. The "there is" is beyond contradiction (DEE, 105, EE 64). *Apeirôn,* unbounded, its unfinishedness is that of the "horrible eternity" into which the conceptual diction of essence always threatens to fall (AE 223, OB 176).

Responsibility is interpreted by Levinas, following the *Phaedrus,* as response, and response is interpreted as saying, whether or not out loud. But this speaking responsibility is not unlimited if it is limited to the diction of essence. If it were so limited it would belong to a symmetrical system in which the other and I would be from the start equals before the law. The other and I would be thought together, com-pensated, and there would be no reason why I should not think that a responsibility carried out by me on behalf of another earned for me the right to expect to be treated likewise. In such a case the expectation and the responsibility are supported by a law. *Before* the law, however, prior to the laws of syntax and semantics that regulate the intersubstitutability of pronouns, the responsibility of my unsubstitutability is groundless. And the responsibility grounded in my particular situation is ethical and unviolent only if it is a response to my groundless responsibility, my responsibility toward this other whom I call "you," and to that other whom I call "her" or "him," who is also a you not simply on account of case law and syntax, but because they all call me. I am called to support all of them and everything on their behalf *without reason.* My being called by them is my owing it to them not to require a demonstration of their right, not to require even that philosophy produce a logical refutation of the conclusion of some antihumanist sciences that ethical responsibility is a laughable delusion. What is without reason par excellence is the anarchic *il y a.* Only thanks to the meaninglessness of its sublinguistic, subliterary, and so subpoetic murmuring can meaning and rationality be regained through ethics. Therefore language is rational only in the face of the menace of the non-rationality of the "there is"—the non-rationality into which language risks slipping if construed in the manner of the doctrines of structuralism and ontologism, with their corollaries that the human being is possessed by language and that what speaks first and last is language in its totality. These doctrines turn out to be of positive assistance in enabling Levinas to describe the fine risk that language on his own ethical doctrine of it must inevitably run. I can only witness to the other in responsibility if, beyond knowing and doubt, there may be no more to illeity than ilyaity. The ambiguity or enigma of this incognitive maybe is necessary to the good beyond being.

SAYING, SAID, AND SILENCE

Signifiance is another of those words referred to earlier regarding which Levinas tells us that they preserve the *verbal* sense of "being" and give rise to abstract nouns of action. It would indeed be quite natural to say that signifiance names an action performed in a speech act understood as the saying that is correlated with something said. But this oppositional correlation is anarchically conditioned by archi-saying, rather as the ordinary opposition of saying and writing is conditioned by what we can just as well call archi-writing as archi-saying. Levinas describes speaking (*langage*) as "the first action over and above labor, action without action," a generous offering of one's labor and the world to another, "the first ethical gesture" (TeI 149, TeI 174). The generosity extends to the exposition of one's very speech intentions, so that "The act of speaking is the passivity of passivity" (AE 117, OB 92).

The correlation of saying and said is an instance of the correlation of mental intending and object intended that Husserl claims to be fundamental to all consciousness. In this noetic-noematic structure the hyphenation, like the bar between the signifier and the signified in Saussure's schema of the sign,[20] marks a distinction that is not a separation. It is, Husserl maintains, the structure of all meaning or intending. It holds where the speech act is one for which the standard syntactical form expressing it is an indicative sentence. It holds too, he says, where the standard syntactical form is not an indicative sentence. Speech acts standardly performed in syntactically interrogative and imperative sentences are based on the same noetic-noematic foundations as assertions. Levinas devotes several pages of *Otherwise than Being* and several paragraphs of the essay "Language and Proximity" to explaining why there is more than many commentators allow to the Husserlian doctrine of intentionality that "all consciousness is consciousness of an object." As applied, for example, to a predicative statement of one's experience of the sensible world, this formula fails to bring out Husserl's point, accepted and indeed insisted upon by Levinas, that no predication merely represents a sensation passively received. Predication, he says, glossing Husserl and up to a point Hegel, is kerygmatic. It proclaims. The intentionality is not only a directedness at an object, but an understanding of an object as such and such, a classification and identification where the intending is a meaning in the sense of the German *meinen* and of the French *vouloir dire:* it is an engagement of will or desire as wanting to say (EDE 221–22, CPP 112–13).

Note again the use here of words based on *tendere,* with the connotations of reaching, tension, and tense that are preserved in the stretching and ecstasis that Heidegger's analysis of tense develops from the notions of temporal retention and protention employed by Husserl in lectures edited by Heidegger.[21] But note too that *entendre* can mean either to understand or to hear. This ambiguity has consequences for the interpretation of Levinas's doctrine of deep saying, for it determines what we make of another doctrine he frequently illustrates by citing from Isaiah 65:24 the words "before they call I will answer" (AE 192, OB 150). This deep saying, we have seen, is a saying of myself as an unsituated and naked self face to face with another such self in abstraction from empirical paraphernalia behind which I might hide like Gyges concealing himself by twisting his ring (AE 185, OB 145).[22] My exposure of my self to another, whomsoever he or she may be, is an exposure of myself to another in a saying over and above the saying of something said, in the saying of my saying itself. Here the *signifié* is the *signifiant,* the signifying that exposes the sayer, me, as expressed in the Hebrew *hineni* and the French *me voici, envoie-moi,* "See me here, send me."

Connected with the indeterminacy of the Greek word *logos,* there is a philosophical tradition extending from Plato to Husserl and Frege according to which phonetic language (*logos*) is the phenomenal exteriorization of a language of thoughts (*logoi*). Levinas is attempting to direct the attention of philosophers to a doubling different from this traditional one in which the phonetic or graphic doubling of the unexpressed or only secretly expressed thought is an otiose extra. He wants to direct attention to a silent saying that is extra because extra-ordinary, but far from otiose (DVI 122, GCM 74, LBPW 145). The "good silence" of this saying is contrasted with the "bad silence" of Gyges' secrecy and with the "sygetic" resounding or ringing of silence, *das Geläut der Stille,* that Heidegger refers to in his essay "The Nature of Language."[23] The latter silent saying (*Sage*) is the silence of essence, essance, or essencing (*Wesen*) that resounds in the poetic word. The poetic word points to a verbal noun that assembles a world, bringing the things of its different regions into a so-called face-to-face proximity (*in die Nähe des Gegen-einander-über*). But this is the proximity of being in general, not the face-to-face proximity to another human being (AE 172, OB 135). Interpreting Stefan George's poem "Words," Heidegger says that when the beautiful (*formosus*) words of poetry break off, the formal conceptuality of propositions is disrupted, allowing the language of being to be heard. Levinas says that both that language and the conceptuality of propositions are disordered by the face-to-face language of one human being addressing another.

This brings us back to the methodological difficulty referred to above in connection with Hegel, Frege, Wittgenstein, and Heidegger, the difficulty Heidegger attempts to circumvent by turning away from the phenomenological and therefore descriptive mode of discourse of *Being and Time* to a more "poetic" mode of expression, the difficulty to which Levinas returns repeatedly in the final pages of *Otherwise than Being.*

THE LANGUAGE OF LEVINAS'S PHILOSOPHY OF LANGUAGE

Am I not, Levinas asks again and again, undermining what I am trying to express in the very act of trying to express it? Perhaps the response to this difficulty may be traced in this "again and again." This would be a response that refuses to remain only a theoretical answer which, as such, apparently says the very opposite of what one wants to say. To contradict oneself in this way would indeed be an abuse of language as flagrant as that of which the epistemological skeptic would be culpable if he claimed to know that we can know nothing. Yet it may be through just such an abuse of language that the force of what Levinas desires to say might get expressed. The more I iterate what present themselves unavoidably as constative affirmations of knowledge, opinion, or *doxa* with their idealizing identifications of this-as-the-same-as-that and their subsumption of particulars under universals, the more through these very affirmations is my responsibility performatively affirmed and confirmed as by the appending of a signature (Italian *firma*) that is both the sign and the trace of my always already having given my word to my interlocutor.

In the forgetting of what Heidegger calls the ontological difference, being again and again gets represented as *a* being, empirical or metaphysical, human or divine. In what Levinas might have called the dictive difference, a trace is what is absolutely forgotten in the sense that it bears witness to what is neither recollected nor forgotten in the epistemic sense of these terms when it is represented as a sign. Strictly speaking, it is incapable of representing any *what* whatsoever, so full is it of my "representing" my interlocutor in the sense of my standing for and substituting myself for my interlocutor in response to her or his "Hear me." The remembrance without recollection of what Levinas calls trace is nevertheless effected in "body language," in that (to re-echo Hegel) the directness of the trace calls for mediation by the body of a sign, a conventional verbal sign belonging to the context and structure of a syntactic system. This sign ultimately mediates the sign that is the speaker's body. The speaker's body regarded as the expression of a trace is what Levinas refers to quasi-metonymically as "face." Just as the face in his semio-ethical use of the word is distinguished but inextricable from the body, so the trace is different but inextricable from the sign. Hence, if we are to go on talking of a "deep" saying, we must take care not to think that this entails a level of deep saying below a level of surface saying to which belongs the saying that is correlative with what is said. Rather as the difference of what Heidegger calls the ontological difference does not belong simply either to being or beings regarded as opposed levels or sides, so too the dictive difference in Levinas's philosophy of language is irreducibly ambiguous and enigmatic. This is why the absolute forgetting and unrecollective remembrancing always already effected in the trace does not hark back (anymore than does what Heidegger calls *Ereignis*) to an event like some proto-ethical Big Bang in, at, or before the time of historiography. When, against the structuralist's stressing of synchrony, Levinas emphasizes diachrony, he means that every moment of the recollectable time of my going forward toward my own death is cut through (*dia*) by the interlocution of other mortal human beings (TeI 146, TaI 171).

Levinas's philosophy of language is a philosophy of philosophy according to which, like language quite generally, the language of philosophy is paradoxically prophetic. Prophecy is speaking for another, but in a way that cannot be comprehended by the concepts of philosophy. What they cannot comprehend is that while my speaking is a response to another's command, my perception of that command is my signifying of it in obeying it. The call is understood in the response (AE 190, OB 149). I am diachronically in command and commanded. My commanding is at the "same" dia-chronic moment an obedience, an *ob-audire* that is a *Dire*, a ventrilocution of the other's command; for my command gives voice to the allocution of the other who is like an irritating foreign body "under my skin" prior to my

177

being myself "in my skin," *dans ma peau,* comfortably at home. I am in my place, but, ethically speaking, the other has usurped that place before me (AE 146, OB 115). The meaning of my command is not then a straightforwardly intentional *meinen* or *vouloir dire.* Motivated by Desire carrying an ethical emphasis that, like the many other ethical emphases given to apparently ontological terms throughout Levinas's writings, postpones Hegelian conceptual elevation (*Aufhebung*), my command is at the same time obedience. This is why Levinas ascribes to it a passivity that is not the passivity of the passive voice or the passivity that is contrasted with activity in theories of knowledge based on a classical construal of subjectivity. In response to the command of an interlocutor, where the reception of the command is in the response, the identity of the constituting and constituted subject is deconstituted and displaced through the deposition of the egoity of its enjoyment of life. That deponent command expresses an incoming, in-ventive intentionality that alters the direction of the ecstatic intentionality which, without that alteration, would be, in the words of Pascal cited among the epigraphs of *Otherwise than Being,* the beginning of "the usurpation of the whole world." Not usurpation of the whole world, but responsibility for the whole world is what I am called to by the singular categorical imperative with which the other addresses me in an asymmetry without which the symmetry of communication would be the violence either of exclusive intimacy or of purely formal legal universality. The so-called origin of language is "originally" the non-ontological, non-cosmological, and non-theological creation of the world, of "everything that can be named." It is not only in the semiotic ways described by generative grammarians that language is infinitely regenerative and creative.[24] In the beginning was the semio-ethical word.

13

THRESHOLDS

I was coming to that.

—ROBERT GRAVES (*Welsh Incident*)

WHAT GOES ON BETWEEN THE AFFECT AND THE *SEING*?
(GL 51 (58), GL TR. 42)

Hegel's semiology is dialectical. The sense of the sign is a middle between the sensible and the intelligible, as the Kantian schema is a sensible concept in the imagination.[1] In the sign itself the internalized essence of external particulars is incorporated and re-externalized in objective thought in itself, that is to say, in the public memory of a spoken language.

The imagination (*Einbildungskraft*) is a threshold where a rite of passage is performed that confers a right of way between sensibility and sense. Its raw materials are the images of externally intuited particulars. These images are appropriated and stored in the subliminal pit or reservoir of private memory (*Erinnerung*). Images, which can be reproduced more or less at will, are a relatively concrete kind of representation. Their content or material, like that of any other intellectual representation, is given and found, as a matter of fact, to be. "The representation is the middle term in the syllogism of the elevation (*Erhebung*) of intelligence, the link between the two significations of self-relatedness, namely that of being and that of universality, which are distinguished in consciousness as object and subject" (Hegel, *Encyclopaedia* (Enc) §455). Images are "more universal" than intuitions (Enc §456). But they become general ideas only when they are associated by the spontaneous activity of the subject. This is not an association that produces a merely mechanical collocation of an external image and an internal general idea. The unity produced is not neuter, *ne-uter*, neither just the one nor just the other. The general idea is the subjection of the relatively external objecthood of the image which otherwise simply happens to be there. The general idea "makes itself into the image's soul." It inwardizes itself and in the image becomes for itself, since it becomes manifest in the image that has now taken on the form of a work of art in which, for example, the eagle stands for Jupiter's strength.

This pictorial product of the creative imagination (*Phantasie*) is prophetic, no more than an annunciation of language, an apocalypse. The internal essence of intuited external particulars assumes a new form of externality when it becomes objective thought in itself (*Denken*) as a sign in the public memory (*Gedächtnis, Mnemosyne*) of language. Signs, in comparison with symbols, are arbitrary and more original in that whereas the eagle is made to symbolize the strength of Jupiter because of what is thought to be a natural resemblance, no such resemblance is thought to hold between a cockade or a flag or a tombstone and what they severally signify. Hegel's sign corresponds to the body in Saussure's analogy for the signifier, where the signified meaning is the soul. The sign is "the pyramid into which a foreign soul has been conveyed, and where it is conserved" (Enc §458). The pyramid is the semaphore of the sign, Derrida observes, alluding to the connections made in the *Cratylus* between *sêma,* sign or tomb, and *sôma,* prison house or body. It is also worthy of note that in Homer *sôma* means corpse, *Körper,* and that only later, as in Plato, did it come to be used both of that and of the living body, the *Leib.* Hegel must have thought that this development in the history of Greek oiled the wheels of the semiological dialectic, the Janus logic of which Derrida parses as follows:

> The tomb is the life of the body as sign of death, the body as the other of the soul, of the animated psyche, of the living breath. But the tomb is also that which shelters life and keeps it reserved in its thesaurus marking its continuation elsewhere. Family vault: *oikêsis.* It consecrates the disappearance of life in testifying to its persistence. So it also shelters it from death. It averts (*avertit*) and adverts to (*avertit*) the possible death of the soul. (M 95, M tr. 82)

The sign, regarded as the composite of signifier and signified, the animated signifier, is a monument both of life in death and of death in life. It is the threshold between life and life after or, better, through death, facing in both directions, *à double sens.* Signification, sign making, has the dialecticality of any other *Aufhebung* of the phenomenology of spirit. The transition from the physical body to the spiritual body and from the private meaning stored in the dark underground reservoir of the unconscious to the public meaning manifest in the medium of discourse is a passing away that is also a passing on, a revocation that is also a reinvocation, a destruction and a reconstruction at the same time. We can look forward to witnessing the destruction of the fabric of this semiologic when Derrida teases out its threads and reconstrues them with yarns suspended on the tenterhooks of what he calls deconstruction.

The passage across a dialectical threshold is negation and affirmation. The sign is the deposition of the symbol and the preposition of its truth. It is the symbol internalized (*erinnert*) and surpassed. Whereas the pyramid is the sign of signification, the Sphinx is the symbol of symbolism. The animal form of the Sphinx mirrors the natural forms of hieroglyphics, which were polysemic and enigmatic even for the Egyptians. And the pyramid is the sign of only a degenerate form of signification, since as an object in space it is naturally taken to stand for the written sign. The written sign is less fully linguistic than the phonetic sign in, for instance, the alphabetic language with which the Greeks "deconstituted" (M 116, M tr. 99) the hieroglyphic

symbolism of the Egyptians. Hegel dramatizes this epoch-making translation in terms of Oedipus's deciphering the enigma of the Sphinx and
"destroying" the Sphinx in so doing. This promotion of the spoken word at
the expense of writing is, as Derrida reminds us in "La pharmacie de
Platon," a dominant theme in the *Phaedrus* and other dialogues of Plato. It
may strike one as odd that in spite of the phonologism that Plato and Hegel
share, the former appears to hold mathematics in much greater esteem
than does the latter. Think of the Pythagoreanism of the *Timaeus*. For Hegel
Pythagoreanism is a term of abuse for Chinese philosophy, which gives
priority to the abstract sensuousness of spatiality in taking as its paradigm
the mathematical calculus whose very name indicates kinship with glyp-
tography. The air of paradox is somewhat dissipated if we recall that in the
Republic and elsewhere the mathematicals are intermediate between sensible things and the intelligible ideas; as for Kant the schema of number is
a medium between sensible particulars and concepts; as for Hegel number
is the other of the concept and therefore facilitates its emergence because
it is the pure thought of thought's own extraneation: "sie ist der reine
Gedanke der eigenen Entäußerung des Gedankens" (*Wissenschaft der Logik*
(WL) I, I, II, 2, A, Anm. 2). The paradoxicality evaporates completely if we
think of Plato's Pythagoreanism as a theory of musical harmony, since for
Hegel music "makes the point of transition between the abstract spatial
sensuousness of painting and the abstract spirituality of poetry."[2]

Furthermore, sound is the "incipient ideality of matter which appears no
longer as spatial but as temporal ideality."[3] It is, in Derrida's words, the
becoming time of space (M 8, M tr. 8). Time is space *aufgehoben,* passed over,
displaced, surpassed, *gewesen*: the essence (*Wesen*) of space, its truth; in
Derrida's words again, what space will have meant (*aura voulu dire*). What
goes on between the affect and the *sein-g,* the entire process of consignment
from pit to pyramid, from sensible intuition via subconscious private image
and natural symbol to freely instituted sign, homes in on meaning, which
has put behind it the gap between itself and the symbol or sign by which it
is represented. Symbol and sign "must in their turn be thought (*aufgehoben,*
relevés, recuperated) by the living concept, by languageless language, language which has become the thing itself, the inner voice whispering in the
mind's ear the identity of the name (and) of being" (M 125, M 106). This is
the phenomenological voice of logocentrism. The center of logocentrism is
the idea or ideal of understanding (*entendement*) which hears itself speak
(*s'entend parler*) in closest proximity to itself and in the immediate presence
of its subject matter. The sign, the spirit incarnate, is the *Vor-stellung,* the
(p)re-presentation of absolute knowing as Christianity is the *Vor-stellung* of
philosophy (Gl 40 (44), Gl tr. 32).

WHAT IS THE ABSOLUTE DIFFERENCE?

Jean Hyppolite, whose seminars Derrida took part in and whose works he
frequently cites, asks of the language of philosophy "Qui parle?"

Who or what is speaking? The answer is neither "one" [or "das Man"] nor "it" [or "the id"], nor quite "the I" or "the we." This name *dialectic* which Hegel has revived and interpreted and which designates a dialectic of things themselves, not an instrument of knowledge, is itself at the heart of this problem. What is a philosophical presentation and what is its structure? It is remarkable that in trying to present the system of the articulations and determinations of thought Hegel saw both their objectivity—they are a universal consciousness of Being—and what opposes them to the thing itself, to Nature. The Logos says also the absolute difference since this difference belongs as well [still (*encore*)] to the Logos. Universal Knowledge therefore knows too its own limit. It measures the limits of signification or sense, the quota of *nonsense* that still invests signification, what Hegel saw as the rapport of Logos and Nature, the play of their identity and difference. For Hegel this was not a question of a negative theology, of a meaning so to speak beyond meaning, but of an irremediable finitude, a lost meaning (as one talks of a lost cause) which can never be completely recovered.[4]

Derrida knows the paper from which these sentences are extracted. He himself gave a paper at the Baltimore symposium of 1966 at which it was distributed. He knows too what Hegel says about absolute difference. What does Derrida say about what Hegel says about this? Are what Derrida says and what Hyppolite says about what Hegel says in any way different?

In the section of the *Science of Logic* entitled "Der absolute Unterschied" Hegel tells us that absolute difference is "the negativity which reflection has within it." It is "difference in and for itself, not difference resulting from anything external, but *self-related* (*sich auf sich beziehender*), therefore *simple* (*einfacher*) difference." He writes of "the simple *not*" and in the *Phenomenology of Spirit*, where it is more evident that his remarks have Kant and Fichte as their target, he refers to "the simple *category*" and "the simple *unity*," the essential unity of being and self-consciousness:

> in other words, the category means this, that self-consciousness and being are the same essence, the same, not through comparison, but in and for themselves. It is only one-sided, spurious idealism that lets this unity come on the scene again as consciousness, on the one hand, confronted by an *in-itself*, on the other. But now this category or *simple* unity of self-consciousness and being possesses difference *in itself*; for its essence is just this, to be immediately one and selfsame in *otherness*, or in absolute difference. (*Phänomenologie des Geistes* C [AA], V)

Hegel is distinguishing the opposition or otherness of absolute difference, which is a procedure of reflection and essence (*Wesen*), the been (*gewesen*), from the relative or comparative opposition of determinate beings. In the case of the latter the opposed beings are each opposed to the other and each has an immediately present being for itself. With absolute difference each other, since its otherness is reflected, is the other not only for itself but also in itself. As reflected difference it is posited as difference of itself from itself. This means that difference is both the whole in which it differentiates itself from its other, identity, and the moment, difference, which differentiates itself. In the section leading up to the one in which the *Science of Logic* spells out the logic of difference, complementary formulas are asserted of identity: for example, "it is the whole, but, as reflective, it posits itself as its own moment, as positedness, from which it is the return into itself. It is only as such moment of itself that it is identity as such, as *determination* of simple equality with itself in contrast to absolute difference."

The co-respondence between identity and difference is not a contradiction to be lamented. Although ordinary understanding abhors contradiction as nature abhors a vacuum, speculative thinking knows that contradiction is the principle that moves the world, *"Was überhaupt die Welt bewegt"* (*Enzyklopädie* §119). For when each of the opposed moments falls to the ground (*zugrunde geht*) speculative thinking realizes the truth of what difference and identity have turned out to be, namely Ground, the more realized concept in which identity and difference are united. However,

> we must be careful, when we say that the ground is the unity of identity and difference, not to understand by this unity an abstract identity. Otherwise we only change the name, while we still think the identity (of understanding) already seen to be false. To avoid this misconception we may say that the ground, besides being the unity, is also the difference of identity and difference. In that case in the ground, which promised at first to supersede the contradiction, a new contradiction seems to arise. It is, however, a contradiction which, so far from persisting quietly in itself, is rather the repulsion (*Abstossen*) of it from itself. (Enc §121)

If contradiction is the principle that moves the world, so is difference, in the two senses of *bewegt* Hegel plays on in the opening paragraphs of the Doctrine of Essence. There he announces that the truth of being is essence. Essence, *Wesen,* is timelessly past being, as suggested by *gewesen,* the past participle of *sein* (as in *sein-g*). This mediation of being by essence is the path (*Weg*) of knowing and the pathfinding motivation of being. This wordplay is compounded with one to the same effect on *Gang,* path, and *vergangenen,* past. And it is now timely to interpolate that while the Doctrine of Being treats of the timeless present of immediate being and the Doctrine of Essence treats of Being's mediated timeless past, these two doctrines constituting Objective Logic, the Subjective Logic of the Doctrine of the Concept treats of the sense in and into which Being was timelessly to come.

Derrida recognizes this way-making activity of absolute difference. He endorses Koyré's reading of passages in the *Jena Logic* in which Hegel departs from his usual practice of using the word *Unterschied* for difference and speaks of an *absolute differente Beziehung,* for which Koyré proposes the translation "absolutely differentiating relation," in which *differente* is given an active sense (M 14–15, M tr. 13–14). The activity in question in the pages Koyré cites is the activity of the simple present. The present is divided against itself, as is indicated by the German word for the present, *Gegen-wart.* Its presence is *dikhôs,* two-way, januarial. (That's Shell, that was.) It has its deaths and entrances. Its simplicity is a one-foldedness that is a once folded-ness, a duplicity that gives itself away.

> This simple, in this absolute negating, is the active, the infinite opposed to itself as an equal to itself; as negating it is as absolutely related to its opposite, and its activity, its simple negating, is a relation to its opposite, and the now is the immediately opposite of itself, its self-negating. While this limit sublates itself in its excluding or in its activity, what acts against and negates itself is rather the non-being of this limit. This immediate non-being in itself of the limit, this non-being opposed to itself as the active, or as that which rather is in itself and excludes its opposite, is the *future* which the now cannot resist; since it is the essence of the present which is in effect its own non-being. . . . The present is but the self-negating simple limit which, with its negative moments kept apart, is a relation between its excluding and that which does the excluding. This relation is presence [*Gegenwart*, without a definite article] as [adopting Koyré's translation of *eine differente Beziehung*] a differentiating relation.[5]

Although Derrida endorses Koyré's translation of *differente*, he denies that it does all the jobs so far envisaged for *la différance*. Three of these are specified in the paper which has these words for a title. First, *différance* is the nonidentity of differents. Second, it is the polemical productive activity of differends (M 8, M tr. 8). However, whereas the activity of Hegel's absolute difference is a kind of logical contradicting productive of meaning and truth, Derrida, although he often calls *différance* a contradiction, suggests we try to view *différance* as a conflict of forces or (*pace* Levinas!) an allergy (M 8, M tr. 8, P 60, P tr. 101). This is already a violent displacement of Hegel even if we accept Hyppolite's interpretation cited above, in which Hegel's abso-lute difference is, if we accept the English version published in the tran-script of the Baltimore symposium, "the measure of meaninglessness that invests all meaning." The risk run here is that of having the concept of meaninglessness get its meaning from its opposition to meaningfulness, thus binding it to the system of dialectical logic as firmly as a proposition that is false because self-contradictory is held within the analytic calculus of propositions. Hegel himself, Doctor Dialectic, would be the last to call this a risk. What is at risk is the plausibility of any attempt Hyppolite may be making to show that there is a something or a nothing that remains beyond the dialectic's pale, whether or not Hegel acknowledges this. The risk is reduced if we read his "non-sens" not as the contrary of the meaningful only, but as the metalinguistic excluder of both the meaningful and the meaning-less. Derrida's rereading of contradiction as a conflict of forces or of ener-gies, instead of a conflict of concepts or propositions, is one way in which he tries to loosen the grip that the conception of dialectical difference and the metaphysics of meaning have on the project of differance. A conflict of forces or energies cannot meaningfully be said to be either meaningful or meaningless. This grip is further loosened by the third dimension of *différance*.

The third dimension of *différance* is postponement, deferment, delay, reservation, or representation. Incidentally, if some of these words, the last two for instance, appear to be at odds with the others, it will help to remember that they are two-faced vehicles of conflicting forces. Reservation is not just keeping but also keeping back and holding off. And "representation" represents *Vor-stellung*. Surely, in the appeal to such crosswordings Hegel is Derrida's past master? But postponement, Derrida says, is not a power of the Greek *diapherein*. This loss in the most characteristically philosophical language is, however, compensated by *differre* in the less philosophical language of Latin. Despite Hegel's recourse in the *Jena Logic* to the Latinate *differente*, his thinking is too Greek for Derrida, as it is for Heidegger. It cannot, even with the help of Koyré's "differentiation," summon up the force to perform the third operation of *différance*, for which Derrida uses the nonterminal term "temporization."

Nonetheless, Hyppolite's Hegel is reminiscent or evocative of the appendix that difference supplies to Hegel's text. Was there feedback from Derrida to Hyppolite, as when Wittgenstein was *in statu pupillari* to Russell? Or are we exaggerating the unfamiliarity in Hyppolite's reading? His references to the *non-sens* in Hegel are references to his opposition of knowing to being and of logos to nature. The second term of each of these pairs limits the former, and absolute knowing knows this limit. Now there is a singular sentence in the paper as published in 1941: "Le Logos dit aussi la différance absolue, mais il n'est pas lui-même la différence absolue car cette différence appartient encore au Logos." Did he not intend to say, it might be asked, and perhaps in his original 1966 manuscript did say, that the difference belongs as well to *nature*? This would be in line with his answer to the question "Who or what speaks?" that it is the dialectic and that this is not an instrument of knowledge but a dialectic of things themselves. If the sentence as published does represent Hyppolite's original intentions, his point would seem to be that *logos* or language (philosophical language being the topic of the paper) cannot be identified with absolute difference, because the latter is a function of the former, somewhat as a property of a thing cannot be all there is to that thing. Thus understood, Hyppolite would be paraphrasing the statement reproduced above from the *Phenomenology of Spirit* that "this category or *simple* unity of self-consciousness and being possesses difference *in itself*." We may never know for sure what Hyppolite intended. We may have here a case of meaning lost beyond recovery. I am inclined to say, however, that we could in principle find out at least whether there had been a lapsus by getting someone to dig out Hyppolite's manuscript and compare it with the typescript and the proofs.[6]

Derrida is inclined to say that this would not show that there is not here and everywhere a loss of meaning that cannot be recovered by any amount of research. Successful searching for answers to empirical and in general "ontic" questions about lost manuscripts and mislaid umbrellas does not guarantee success when we seek answers to "ontological" questions like "what is meaning?" "what is being?" and, in the context of dialectical ontology, "what is *Aufhebung?*" In a style resembling Wittgenstein's reaction to the first and Heidegger's reaction to the second, Derrida remarks on the third of these questions:

> As soon as the ontological question (What's this? What is? What is the meaning of being? etc.) gets deployed according to the process and structure of *Aufhebung*, is con-founded with the absolute of *Aufhebung*, it can no longer be asked: What *is Aufhebung?* as one would ask: What is this or that? or What is the definition of such and such a particular concept? Being is *Aufhebung*. *Aufhebung* is being, not like a determinate state or like the determinable totality of what is, but as the "active" essence which produces being. It cannot therefore be the *object* of any determinate question. We are unendingly referred in that direction, but this reference refers to nothing determinable. (Gl 42–43 (47), Gl tr. 34)

Similarly with the questions Derrida puts in "La Différance" echoing these and Hyppolite's "Who or what is speaking?": Who or what de(dif)fers? What is differance?

WHAT IS TRANSGRESSION?

As Derrida would ask, what goes on in Bataille's "transgression" of Hegel, *qu'est-ce qui se passe* in this passage? Put baldly, what takes place is a move from a restricted to a general economy. What Bataille calls general economy connects with what Derrida, in "La Différance," *Positions, La dissémination*, and elsewhere, calls the general text, and with what, in a contribution to the colloquium provoked by his writings which was held at Cerisy in 1980, he calls generalized *Verstimmung* (off-tuning?). All three of these expressions, along with "writing," "dissemination," and many others on which Derrida rings the changes, are universal operators whose generality is so generous that it cannot be contained within a universal concept or the covers of a book, no matter how encyclopedic the book may be.

At the outset of Derrida's meditation on Bataille there is a hint that the treatment will neither cure nor kill. Recognizing the importance that dissemination has in Derrida's scheme, one might expect that if he entitles his essay on Bataille "From Restricted to General Economy" he will be for Bataille rather than against. This would be to take too naive a view of deconstruction and of his deconstruction of Bataille in particular, for Derrida's subtitle is "A Hegelianism without Reserve." Does that mean that Bataille follows Hegel up to a point but transgresses or dislocates him by moving from an anal economy of saving and thrift to an economy of prodigal spending? Or does it mean that Bataille's project for a general economy is unreservedly Hegelian? Which? Both? Neither? These questions are left undecided by Derrida's choosing as an exergue for this piece Bataille's statement "He [Hegel] did not know to what extent he was right," "Il ne sut pas dans quelle mesure il avait raison." Does he underestimate or overestimate the scope of reason? Was he, Hegel, less right about its limits than he thought, or more? Was Bataille?

Derrida says "Bataille is less Hegelian than he thinks" (ED 405, WD 275). He says this because Bataille himself says transgression is within the domain of the Hegelian dialectic. Bataille forgets he has been arguing that *Aufhebung* is an operation of a slavish mentality which takes as its point of departure the prohibitions of the master and invests them with a fuller meaning on the way to fulfillment in absolute knowing. On this account, one not obviously in keeping with Hyppolite's, *Aufhebung* is an economy of reproduction restricted to market values in which meanings are circulated without in the long run any profit or loss. Transgression, on the other hand, is a "sovereign operation" of a general economy which exceeds the opposition of master and slave. Bataille's sovereignty is not, therefore, to be confused with Hegel's mastery. For the semantic economy of the latter is overcome by the semantic economy of the victorious slave, but also preserved by it. The latter is the truth of the former and both function within the realm of knowledge and sense.

Sovereignty (f. OF soverain f. LL SUPER-(anus -AN);—g—by assoc. *reign*), as Bataille writes of it, is beyond the realm of sense, a procedure of *Ent-sinnung* or dis-semination that suspends all phenomenological suspension (ED 393, WD 268). A non-knowledge. A non-science. A non-sense. It is the outlawing of the law, the ruling out of rules, the interdiction (*interdire*: to disconcert, nonplus, bewilder, render speechless) of interdiction (interdict: authoritative prohibition). On Derrida's parsing of it, therefore, it cannot be an *Aufhebung* of Hegel's difference. It can only be the *différance of* difference. Its eye, to employ one of Bataille's metaphors, turns in toward the blind spot on the retina of knowledge. "Sovereignty is absolute when it absolves itself from every relation and remains in the night of the secret. The continuum of sovereign communication has as its element this night of secret difference" (ED 391, WD 266).

Yet although this transgressive operation of sovereignty is *différance*, not an *Aufhebung* of Hegelian difference, it is, Derrida adds, "powerless to transform the core (*noyau*) of predicates. Every attribute applied to sovereignty is borrowed from the (Hegelian) logic of mastery. We cannot, and Bataille could and should not resort to any other concept or any other sign, of any other union of word and meaning. In its opposition to servility the sign 'sovereign' has already issued from the same mold as that of mastery." On the scale of continuity-discontinuity, Bataille's transgression and Derrida's displacement are somewhere between a Hegelian transmissive *Aufhebung* and a Bachelardian or Kuhnian intermissive break (*coupure*).

But Bataille does not know to what degree he is right. He thinks he is more Hegelian than is in fact the case. Sometimes his thought follows extremely Hegelian lines, as Derrida brings out. "One could even abstract in Bataille's text an entire zone which encircles sovereignty within a classic philosophy of the *subject* and above all within that *voluntarism* Heidegger has shown to have been confounded by Hegel and Nietzsche with the essence of metaphysics." However, if we are to have Bataille's general text to read, the warp of this line of thought must be unpicked and rewoven with a very un-Hegelian weft. So Derrida puts out a sobering reminder that sovereignty comes from the same mold as mastery and that Bataille's so-called gnostic materialism, like any other attempt to displace the oppositions of classical philosophy, including Derrida's own ("differance remains a metaphysical name," M 28, M tr. 26), depends on that philosophy. Even so, he cites from Bataille some sentences in which transgression is transgressed to the brink of a Bachelardian break.

> And it is not enough to say that one cannot speak about the sovereign moment without altering it, without altering it in respect of its true sovereignty. No less contradictory than speaking of it is trying to track down its movements. The moment we search for something, whatever it may be, we do not live sovereignly; we subordinate the present moment to a future one which will succeed it. We shall perhaps achieve the sovereign moment following our effort and it is indeed possible that an effort is necessary, but between the time of the effort and the sovereign time there is inevitably a break (*coupure*), one could even say an abyss. (ED 392, WD 336)

How we see the relation between Bataille's transgression, Hegel's *Aufhebung,* Derrida's displacement, and Bachelard's break will depend in part, of course, on our reading of Hegel's doctrine of difference. We saw that Hyppolite's reading assimilates it toward the inklings we are coming to have of Derridean *différance* and displacement. Derrida gives two readings of Hegel, or perhaps we should say a double reading. Where he is describing Bataille's "Hegelianism without reserve" he notes that Bataille describes himself as a Hegelian. Derrida also notes how misleading this is. In explaining why this is so he gives a more conservative reading of Hegel's doctrine of difference than does Hyppolite, and he assimilates Bataille's transgression to Derridean *différance* and displacement. Elsewhere his reading is more unreservedly like that given by Hyppolite. There is a hint of such a reading in "Le puits et la pyramide," the first version of which was presented at Hyppolite's seminar at the Collège de France in January 1968. He cites some sentences from the end of a remark in the *Science of Logic* entitled "The Employment of Numerical Distinctions for Expressing Philosophical Concepts":

> Calculation being so much an external and therefore mechanical business, it has been possible to construct machines which perform mathematical operations with complete accuracy. A knowledge of just this one fact about the nature of calculation is sufficient for an appraisal of the idea of making calculation the principal means for educating the mind and stretching it on the rack in order to perfect it as a machine. (WL I, I, II, 2, A, Anm. 2)

Derrida comments on the irony of these sentences. It is with more irony that he suggests they may be made—though not without more stretching on the rack—to cough up that "secret difference" of the dead loss no name can name, no sign can signify, and no dialectical breath of life can remedy. Hegel would be the last to confess such an eldritch secret. But Derrida diagnoses symptoms of dis-ease in what he takes to be nondialectical contradictions, unresolvable inconsistencies, in certain of Hegel's pronouncements about mathematical abstraction, formalistic understanding, and the priority of speech over writing. For example, Hegel maintains that the Chinese epoch is one in which formalism and mathematics predominate. Since he says that these, as well as the degree of grammatical development and differentiatedness of a language, are functions of the understanding, one would expect the grammar of Chinese to be highly differentiated. But Hegel denies that it is. On the other hand, he does claim that Chinese lexicology is very rich. He says this too of German, which he therefore considers spiritually and philosophically advanced. Yet he deems the Chinese moment of cultural history, in spite of the abundance of its lexicology, spiritually and philosophically retarded.

Other sentences in which Hegel expresses his low opinion of Chinese hieroglyphism and of nonphonetic writing in general are quoted in the early part of *De la grammatologie,* which may be regarded, Derrida mentions, as a development of a paper published in December 1965 and January 1966, that is, six or seven months before Hyppolite's Baltimore paper was distributed. Despite the higher estimation of speaking compared with writing that is manifest passim by the author of the books we know as the *Encyclopaedia* and the Larger Logic, everything Hegel has thought within the horizon of the metaphysics of propriety, Derrida concedes, everything except the eschatology

> can be reread as a meditation on writing. Hegel is also the thinker of
> irreducible difference. He has rehabilitated thinking as memory *produc-*
> *tive* of signs. And he has reintroduced . . . the essential necessity of the
> written trace into a philosophical—i.e., Socratic—discourse which had
> always believed it could manage without it: the last philosopher of the
> book and the first thinker of writing. (DG 41, OG 26)

If Bataille and Derrida are on the threshold, Hegel is only slightly preliminary. Although he remains the *thinker* of writing, he is on the way to a deconstruction of the opposition between explication and the clean break, between smooth continuity and sudden discontinuity (Gl 123–24 (150–51), Gl tr. 107–108), a displacement of displacement. This shows that although Hegel is said to be the last philosopher of the book and the first thinker of writing, and although the chapter where this is said is entitled "The End of the Book and the beginning of writing," the book has no end and there is no beginning of writing (P 23, P tr. 14).

Hegel is only slightly preliminary only if exception is made for his eschatology. In the foursome with Bachelard and Bataille, Hegel and Derrida do not see eye to eye where what is in question is the teleology of absolute knowing. Here their vis-à-vis becomes a dos-à-dos. The teleology of absolute knowing is a doctrine of possible presence, *parousia.* Im-possible *para-parousia* is the threshold marked by the footprints of Derrida. And Levinas.

14

SEMIOETHICS

So that we are left wondering whence it came,
   from within or without;
and when it is gone, we say, "It was here. Yet no;
   it was beyond."

—Plotinus (*Enneads*, 5, 11, 8)

The now classical theory of systems of signs called semiotic, semiotics, or semiology includes pragmatics, the theory of the relation between signs and their users, semantics, the theory of the relation between signs and their meaning or truth, and syntactics, the theory of the relation of one sign to another. The point of departure of this chapter is a difficulty concerning the relation between pragmatics and semantics arising out of a difficulty in the syntactics of translation. This is a lexicographic difficulty in the treatment of which signification, hence the classical theory of signification called semiotics, is compelled to make a retreat. But this retreat is strategic and provisional. It is a withdrawal made with a view to a redrawing of the limits of signification and semiotics. One consequence of the redrawing is an advance beyond what some of the contributors to the collection *Approaches to Semiotics* might call proxemics toward what could be called proto-proxemics or a semioethics of approach: toward what could be called a semioethics of calling itself or calling as such were it not that it is the itself and the as such that proto-proxemics calls into question. On the approaches to this semioethics a difficulty concerning culture is met.[1] This *approche* is at once a *rapprochement* and an *Auseinandersetzung* in which some of the strands of Derrida's and Levinas's ichnographies come together and move apart as in a plait or *plethyn* or *tresse*.

SIGNIFICATION

The word "signifier" is ambiguous. Sometimes it is used synonymously with "sign," sometimes for one aspect of a sign, for what is called the *signifiant* or the acoustic image in the semiotics of Saussure. In this second sense the signifier is contrasted with concept, the signified, the *signifié*. But since it is natural to say that what a sign is used for on a particular occasion is what is signified on that occasion, it is not unnatural to refer to the complex sign as a signifier. Saussure warns his readers of the risk of confusion when he makes it explicit that on his definition of the linguistic sign,

"The linguistic sign unites not a thing and a name, but a concept and an acoustic image."[2] This is another way of saying that the subject matter of his *Course* is not acts of speech, *parole,* but *langue,* the system of signs to which recourse is made in performing acts of *parole*. This explains why he prefers not to call the sound-image a phoneme. To do so would imply that an act of speech is performed and that, as he puts it, the interior image is necessarily realized in discourse.

Saussure sometimes says that this interior image is material, but he asks his readers to take care not to be misled by this. The adjective "material" is employed only in contrast to the "generally more abstract" concept with which it is paired. This phrase implies that the so-called material is generally less abstract. But it is abstract. The sensory (sonal) image must be in principle applicable to more than one case of the concept with which it constitutes a sign.

Saussure observes further that although which signifier is associated with which signified is originally arbitrary, in the sign there is necessarily both a signifier and a signified. Derrida takes this to be the traditional understanding of the nature of the sign despite Saussure's arguments for replacing the substantivist *signum-signatum* account of signification given in Stoic semiotics by a diacritical account according to which signification is a function of the lateral interrelations among signifiers and the lateral interrelations among signifieds. Because of the traditional understanding, in Derrida's discussion of the theory of *Bedeutung* in the first of Husserl's *Logical Investigations,* he does not refer to this theory as a theory of signification. For "significant sign" is pleonastic, whereas *bedeutsame Zeichen* is not, and to say that a sign has no signification is a contradiction in terms, whereas Husserl argues that some signs, indicative ones (*Anzeichen*), are without *Bedeutungen* (VP 17–18, SP 17). Indicative signs belonging to a historical culture are necessary, Husserl maintains, only for communication (compare Saussure's acts of *parole*), but are in principle effaceable in his envisaged science of purely expressive meanings (compare Saussure's science of *langue*).

MEANINGS

Dorian Cairns and the French translation of Husserl's *Logische Untersuchungen* use the English or French "signification" where Husserl uses the word "Bedeutung." Derrida and J. N. Findlay's English translation of this book do not use the English or French "signification" for "Bedeutung" as employed by Husserl.[3] The reason Derrida gives is that to do so would run the risk of begging the question. Husserl wants to allow for *Bedeutungen* that can stand independently of verbal signs or signifiers, and this would appear to be disallowed the moment "Bedeutung" is translated as "signification" (VP 17–18, SP 17). In signification as classically understood a signifier stands for a signified, and the signifier is a physical or psychological entity or, in Saussurian semiotics, a relation between such entities. Real indicative signs (*Anzeichen*) belonging to a historical culture are necessary only for communication, Husserl maintains, but are in principle dispensable in his envisaged science of purely expressive meanings. Hence Derrida's decision to suspend employment of the term "signification" and to employ instead the locution "vouloir-dire." And hence the almost total abstinence from use of "signification" in this section of the present chapter. This section is a note on a note in *Autrement qu'être ou au-delà de l'essence*, in which occurs a sentence that may be partially translated as follows:

> A word has a "Meinung" which is not simply a *visée*. M. Derrida has felicitously and boldly translated this word as *vouloir dire*, uniting in its reference to (the) *vouloir* (which every intention remains) and to the exteriority of language (*langue*), the allegedly interior aspect of meaning (*sens*). See Derrida, *La voix et le phénomène*. (AE 46, OB, 189)

The reference to "exteriority of language" is made in Derrida's description of what Levinas calls "the allegedly interior aspect of meaning":

> When I speak, not only am I conscious of being present to what I think, but I am conscious also of keeping as close as possible to my thought, or to the "concept," a signifier that does not fall into the world, a signifier that I hear as soon as I emit it, that seems to depend upon my pure spontaneity, requiring the use of no instrument, no accessory, no force taken from the world. Not only do the signifier and signified seem to unite, but also, in this confusion, the signifier seems to erase itself or to become transparent, in order to allow the concept to present itself as what it is, referring to nothing other than its presence. The exteriority of the signifier seems reduced. (P 32–33, P tr. 22)

If Derrida is to question the possibility of this last-mentioned reduction, he must take care not to beg the question by assuming from the start the exteriority—or exteriorities—to which he and Levinas refer. His critique of Husserl must be "internal." His endeavor to avoid begging the question against Husserl is undermined immediately by his recourse to "dire" in the expression "vouloir-dire" unless he recognizes that the "saying" attributed to Husserl's account by this French translation of his intentions is the phenomenologically reduced expression which Husserl will distinguish from empirically audible speech. The exteriority Derrida and Levinas refer to must therefore be understood in the first place as the non-real exteriority of a systematic field of meanings relative to the *vouloir* of the subject intending meanings in that field. Only when understood in this way can saying be an exteriority within what Levinas refers to as the alleged interior aspect of meaning. For the time being, the exteriority—or exteriorities—too must be no more than "alleged."

Alphonso Lingis translates "vouloir" as "will" and "vouloir dire" as "meaning to say." A difficulty presented by using "will" for "vouloir" is that it appears to license the translation of "vouloir dire" as "will to say." Alan Bass, who also has "meaning to say" for Derrida's (hyphenated) "vouloir-dire,"[4] comments that the French "vouloir" is etymologically connected with the Latin "voluntas" and that "vouloir-dire" carries the connotation that meaning is "will to say" (P tr. 98). Whether this phrase is good, bad, or dubious English, it sounds more emphatically voluntaristic than the French. Yet, judging by Littré, the French word too has had a checkered career in its journey from Latin. Having cited Vaugel's remark that "vouloir" is no longer used, at least in prose, with the sense of "volonté" ("will") and Voltaire's doubtless ironic observation that the use of "vouloir" as in "le vouloir de Dieu" ("the will of God") is archaic, Littré goes on to say that usage has since proved them wrong. Nevertheless, Levinas implies that there is a reduction of this voluntaristic force of "vouloir" in the Husserlian phenomenological usage for which he says in his note that Derrida's "vouloir-dire" is so appropriate. This is implied in what he writes about "volonté" in his next note, where he says:

> The Mediaeval term intentionality, taken up by Brentano and Husserl, does indeed have in scholasticism and in phenomenology a neutralized meaning with respect to the will (*volonté*). It is the teleological movement animating thematization that justifies the recourse, however neutralized it may be, to voluntaristic language. (AE 47, OB 189)

It is precisely the voluntarist teleology of Husserl's theory of meaning or intending to say that provokes the attention of Derrida and Levinas, as the voluntarist teleology of German idealism provokes the attention of Heidegger; so that it becomes pertinent to consider together, as this chapter does, what Husserlian phenomenology and the phenomenology of spirit say about meaning to say.

When Levinas says that "vouloir dire" refers to "vouloir" ("au vouloir") he means to say, like Bass, that meaning and meaning to say allude to the will. This is what he wants to say about what in English we call wanting or wishing or desiring to say—although, presumably, wanting, wishing, and desiring do not have here the operative force of the testamentary "I will" or of "We desire you to approach" pronounced by a monarch whose wish is her command, like the *vouloir* of God.

However, if we translate "vouloir dire" as "wanting to say," we restrict "vouloir dire" to what a speaker wants to say, whereas "vouloir dire" is the phrase one might use to ask what a word, sign, or expression means, instead of using "signifier," a verb we are studiously avoiding here for Derrida's reason reported above and for another reason he gives that we shall come to below. Because in English we do not ordinarily ask what a word wants to say, "vouloir dire" invites translation by "want to say" or "mean to say" in order to cope with the difference between what a word means and what a speaker means. We could say simply "means," as I have just said. Then we should have to ask what "means" here means. We could begin to answer this question by asking how the word "means" would be translated into German, whether as "meinen" or as "bedeuten," either of which would be possible in appropriate contexts (as too would be "heissen," a term to which we shall return). We are already put under an obligation to ask this question anyway by what one is tempted to call Levinas's bold statement about Derrida's bold and felicitous translation, leaving open for the moment whether Levinas's statement also will turn out to be felicitous. Is Levinas's statement too bold, too bold because based on a mistake?

Levinas says that Derrida proposes "vouloir dire" as a translation of "Mein-ung." For confirmation he refers to *Speech and Phenomena*. However, when we turn to the page in that book where Derrida first proposes his translation or, rather, definition, we find that he is talking about Husserl's use of "bedeuten" and "Bedeutung." He writes: "Without forcing Husserl's intention we could perhaps define, if not translate, *bedeuten* as 'vouloir dire'" (VP 18, SP 18). Derrida's first illustration of the use of this phrase is one in which something is meant by a person rather than a word. This would not prevent his equating "vouloir dire" and "meinen." But that he intends to make this equation is rendered prima facie unlikely by the fact that his second illustration is of something meant by an expression. Although "meinen" feels comfortable in the first case, it pinches in the second if, as Derrida says Husserl says, "An expression is a purely linguistic sign." If an expression is a purely linguistic sign, we should be able to ask what the meaning of the expression is where Husserl says "Logical meaning (*Bedeutung*) is an expression." Although philosophers and others inquire into the meaning of meaning, and we all frequently ask about the meaning of an expression, it is unclear what it could mean to ask about the meaning of a meaning.

The solution to this difficulty lies in noting that the expression "expression" is, in Husserl's words, a remarkable form. If by "expression" is meant the verbal sound (*Wortlaut*) or the sign understood as signifier, we must not forget that it owes its expressiveness to the fact that the meaning it expresses (the *Wortbedeutung*) is already an expression, an expression of a *Sinn*. Hence "One may *not* say that an expressing act *expresses* a doxic act, if by expressing act one understands, as we do here at every point, the act of meaning (*Bedeuten*) itself." The expressing act *is* the doxic act. "If, however, the phrase 'expressing act' relates to the verbal sound, one could very well speak after the manner in question, but the sense (*Sinn*) would then be altered."[5]

No less worthy of remark is the fact that in successive paragraphs Husserl calls the meaning that the act of *Bedeuten* expresses a *Meinung* or *gemeint* and a *Sinn*. In the essay "La forme et le vouloir-dire," first published in the same year as was *La voix et le phénomène*, Derrida cites the following sentence in which Husserl distinguishes *Meinung* from *Bedeutung:* "Whatever is 'meant (visé, *gemeint*) as such,' every meaning (*Meinung*) in the noematic sense (*im noematischen Sinn*) (understanding by that the noematic nucleus), whatever the act may be, is *susceptible of receiving expression through 'meanings' ('Bedeutungen,' 'vouloir-dire')*" (M 196, M tr. 164, modifying Bass, who has "of the noematic sense").[6] Because Husserl reserves "Bedeutung" for conceptual sense, leaving "Sinn" to cover both conceptual and perceptual sense, it follows that his "Meinung" cannot be defined as "Bedeutung," though, precisely because "Sinn" covers conceptual as well as perceptual sense, *Meinung* can include *Bedeutung;* that is to say, some cases of the former will be cases of the latter. Hence, if "vouloir-dire" is what is meant by Husserl's "Bedeutung," it cannot define his "Meinung" and it can translate it only where the sense that is meant is conceptual. This is why in his translation of the passage just cited Derrida gives "vouloir-dire" for "Bedeutung." So it seems that in this particular context Derrida would have had no objection to allowing "vouloir-dire" to stand as a translation of "Meinung" if Husserl had written this instead of "Bedeutung" in that or another context where what is meant is conceptual. Restricted to translation in such contexts, therefore, what Levinas says about *translation* would to that extent be consistent with what Derrida writes about *definition.* The apparent divergence between them can be decreased by taking Levinas at his word when he writes "translate" and Derrida at his when he writes "define, if not translate."

But what if we take each at his word when we read that for "Meinung," noetic meaning or intending, and for "gemeint," what is meant or intended, Derrida has, respectively, "visée" and "visé" (which latter Elie, Kelkel, and Scherer have also for "vermeint"), whereas Levinas, also commenting on Husserl, decries the translation of "Meinung" as "visée"? In the note with which we began, Levinas denies that *Meinung* is simply *visée.* To think that it is, he adds in the next note, is to misconstrue the manner in which "Meinung" operates in identificatory statements. If this attribution of *Meinung* to a statement attributes *Meinung* to the statement as a whole, an escape is offered to the threat presented by the attribution of *Meinung* in the earlier note to a word: the threat of inconsistency with the common German usage according to which a word has *Bedeutung* or *Sinn* but not a *Meinung.* The complexity of a thought, proposition, or proponible is greater than that of a word. A thought or *Annahme* in this Fregean sense can be someone's *Meinung* in the sense of what someone thinks, means, or intends in saying what he or she says. However, this escape route is of little avail, for when Levinas speaks of the *Meinung* of identificatory statements, it is of the *Meinung* of identificatory expressions in them that he is speaking, words identifying that of which something is said. The word, "le mot," about which he writes in his note is not a lexicographical item of *langue,* so we can at least set aside as irrelevant the fact, if it is one, that although a dictionary definition gives a word's *Bedeutung,* it does not give its *Meinung.*[7] The word in question in Levinas's note is the word in discursive use, *langage.* So that if he and Derrida are not to be at cross purposes it had better be the case that Derrida's reference to definition is to a definition in use or an analysis, as it must be insofar as he, like Levinas, is writing about what Husserl writes about expressive intentions.

We still need to know why Derrida is apparently happy to translate or define "Meinung" in the noetic sense as "visée" while Levinas is not. Let us adopt the simplest explanation, namely that he sees no special need to depart here from Ricoeur's translation of *Ideen* because his chief concern in *Speech and Phenomena* is with what he has suggested we call "vouloir-dire." He is not here speaking on this topic *in propria persona*—or not very univocally, perhaps one should say, given the general difficulty of deciding when he is ventriloquizing, when he is being ventriloquized, and when he, or anyone else, is talking absolutely straight. This explanation brings with it the bonus that it also explains why Mohanty finds in *Speech and Phenomena* little if any explicit reference to reference, assuming that in his commentary on Husserl, Derrida would allow that "viser" and "meinen" have or can have the meaning of "refer."[8] Husserl's account of conceptual meaning provides Derrida with a sufficient basis for what he wants to say in that book.

This explanation could also explain why Levinas does not take Derrida to task over the translation of "Meinung" as "visée." When he comes across this in Derrida's text perhaps he reads it as only a citation. So that if anyone is being criticized by Levinas here it is Ricoeur. How "Meinung" and "meinen" are translated into French matters more to Levinas because, although reference is peripheral to Derrida's analyses in *Speech and Phenomena,* it is the topic of many pages in *Otherwise than Being or Beyond Essence* and in some of his essays, for instance "Language and Proximity" (EDE 217–36, CPP 109–26). Levinas would probably be happy with Suzanne Bachelard's word "opinion" in those places where Husserl uses "Meinung" in the noematic sense of view, belief, *avis* or, as English has it, opinion. For Husserl's "meinen" or "Meinung" with the noetic sense of "to intend," instead of the "visée" of the Ricoeur translation followed by Derrida, she has "vouloir dire"! Whether or not we were successful in our earlier attempt to show that using "vouloir-dire" for "Meinung" is consistent with Derrida's using it for "Bedeutung," Levinas's endorsement of "vouloir-dire" for "Meinung" is an endorsement of the Bachelard translation published twenty years before *Otherwise than Being.* And her translation certainly suits the argument he advances there about the intentionality of identification. For *opiner* is not simply to hold an opinion, view, or belief. It is to assent or consent, to pronounce oneself for or against something. Like *opiner, meinen* in identificatory statements has an operative force that is absent from the sighting, having in one's sights, and envisioning of *viser.* It is to hear and understand something, to *entendre* and intend it to be taken as such and such in the kerygmatic sense of naming and proclaiming. To be able to sight, *viser,* an object, the object must already be there to be sighted, but there is no object meant that is not first constituted and instituted *as* this or that. The "of" of consciousness of a thing is quite different from the "of" of a photograph of a thing.

Levinas's talk of institution, proclamation, even of consecration, may lead one to suppose that he is speaking of naming as baptism, giving a name for the first time. He, following Husserl, is indeed speaking of that. But he is also speaking of referring to something by its name or description, as are the sections of Husserl's *Experience and Judgment* which he mentions. On the one hand, a naming ceremony assumes that the object being named is already subsumed under a predicate which subsumes it within a cultural history and a historical culture of sedimented beliefs. On the other hand, the recognition of an object as belonging to a class, as falling under a certain predicate, is recognition in the ceremonial sense of the word, subscribing to and endorsing a practice. What Husserl, followed by Levinas, is here opposing is the simple opposition of activity and passivity reflected in the opposition of classical rationalism and psychologistic empiricism. The proclamation of meaning, *sens*, performed through an identifying statement is not an act as opposed to the passive sensible impressions or contents of classical empiricism. If a name is typically a stand-in for an inactive object given to sense and if a verb typically denotes agency, *energeia*, or its limiting case, the "kerygmatic word" is a verbal noun or an action of identifying nomination. As Derrida writes in *Glas*, "there are always after all, of the remain(s), two functions overlapping each other. *Le mot* [compare Levinas's *mot*] *bande double:* the word double binds: transitively and intransitively, nominally and verbally" (Gl 225 (280), Gl tr. 201).

In *Totality and Infinity*, the kerygmatic word is called a "first action over and above labor, an action without action" (TeI 149, TaI 174). Naming is generalization and generalization is universalization, "but universalization is not the entry of a sensible thing into a no man's land of the ideal." Nor is identification, the topic of the section of *Otherwise than Being* to which is appended the note about *Meinung* which served as our point of departure. Identification involves universalization because it is the understanding of a this *as* a this or of this *as* that. In understanding sighting, *viser,* becomes seeing as. It could perhaps be said that as soon as the philosopher sees this, he sees understanding as imagination. As Kant and Heidegger see imagination: as the common root of sensibility and understanding. As Husserl sees imagination: as the lifeblood of phenomenology and any other eidetic science.[9] So, contrary to the view Husserl seems to have held at the time of the *Logical Investigations*, an identifying expression is not a sign of a *Sinn*, but a predication in the etymological sense of *praedicatum,* from *praedicare,* to announce, publish or proclaim, rather than from *praedicere,* to say before, though predication does proclaim the identification of a this with a that or a this as that in the *praedictum,* the already said. "Identification is *understood* on the basis of a mysterious schematism, of the already said, an antecedent *doxa* which every relationship between the individual and the universal presupposes" (AE 45, OB 35). Here "is understood" translates "s'entend," which Levinas wants to be read also as "is heard." Identification is *ouï-dire,* hear-say, and *oui-dire,* yea-say, affirmation of a sedimented, understood, *sous-entendu déjà dit.* Subscription to a culture. Someone's meaning to say ("j'entends dire ceci ou cela") is an obedience at the heart of wanting ("obéissance au sein du vouloir"). This obedience (*obaudire*) is the listening and heeding to cultural norms assumed even where a norm is being challenged, judged, and disobeyed. However—and with this we arrive at his judgment of semiotics—Levinas proclaims that before this disobedience and the obedience it assumes, before the law, as Derrida and Kafka say, an older obedience is called for, the e-normity of which is more anarchic than the breaking of or departure from a law. For it is the breakup of legality as such, the departure from the *as such,* the undermining of the *as.*

THE DIVINE NATURE OF LANGUAGE

The undermining of the *as* and the *as such* of essence would be the undermining of *meinen* by a *deinen* (a making thine) and *dienen* (a serving) that per-form the formality of Husserl'*s Formal and Transcendental Logic.* It would ex-press, exteriorize, utter, force out of itself the expression of meaning as described in the the *Logical Investigations* and *Ideas,* whether "meaning" here be translated as "Bedeutung," "Meinung" or "vouloir-dire." Paradoxically, older than the most proto proto-doxa, this de-position of position and this pro-position before proposition undermine the meanings of cultural semiosis by being, before being, its quasi-transcendental condition. That is to say, it makes possible the signification of the said by supplementing it with a *signifiance* of a semioethical Saying or To-say without-and-with which the signification of the hear-said and the semiotic identificatory *Dire* cannot be complete. That is to say, the semioethical Saying beyond being and beyond the thinking and meaning of being is beyond the possible. It breaks up *pouvoir* and *vouloir.* It interrupts *Seinkönnen* and "I can." It prefaces, prefaces, and traces the bad infinite of "the other and other" (*autre*), the never fully fulfilled desiring to say (*vouloir dire*), with a To-say of Desire for the Other (*Autrui*) which is the Infinite of the Good.

For both Derrida and Levinas, but not obviously following the same route, the tracing of the so-called signifier is its resensibilization, its re-exteriorization, the quasi-transcendental reduction of Husserl's eidetic and transcendental reductions—a resensibilization, however, that is not only opposed to, but is the quasi-condition of, the ideality of sense and meaning. Derrida's strategy is to work through Husserl's texts to bring out that, despite their expressed intention—they themselves are a living proof that the allegedly pure *eidos* of expressive meaning is exposed to the historicality and materiality of the signifier, though here historicality is not opposed to spirit, mind, or life. The intrication of an allegedly pure signified with a historically material signifier is necessary, as Saussure already shows, even if for him the materiality is that of a sound-acoustic image. Saussure's sound-image, less abstract than the concept but abstract all the same, is an essence, a universal. However, if, as Derrida argues, the "essence" of essence and universality is iteration, the apparently enclosed interiority of semantic possibility is exposed to the intrusion of eventuality in new contexts. Does not even the father of transcendental phenomenology, in declining to answer or even put the question "What is the essence of the sign?" betray his suspicion that there is no such essence, no such "thing" as a sign (VP 26, SP 25)? Is he not rather—as the midwife (*Hebamme, SAge-femme*) of the phenomenology of spirit—pursuing the teleological ideal where writing is sub-sumed within the temporality of the voice, yet, in passing and in parentheses (those very parentheses that are the metaphor of transcendental phenom-enological reduction, the metaphor of the metaphor of empirical fact), conceding the irreducibility of punctuation, shape, and other marks of spati-ality when in the course of a commentary on Leibniz in §459 of the *Encyclopae-dia* (s)he writes "(and hieroglyphics are used even where there is alphabetic writing, as in the signs for numbers, the planets, chemical elements, etc.)" (M 112, M tr. 95–96)? I write "(s)he" in deference to the feminine pronoun by which the midwife of the phenomenology of spirit is named in my parenthe-sis, and because in Derrida's hieroglyphics that pronoun stands for "Savoir Absolu," Absolute Sapience. We shall see how it represents *as*, the *as* of predication and kerygma.

Derrida writes:

> This word [*Bedeutung*] is usually translated as "signification." Having at-tempted, in commenting elsewhere upon the *Logical Investigations,* to inter-pret it as the content of a *vouloir-dire*, I would like to demonstrate here that such an interpretation is also valid for the Hegelian text. (M 94, M tr. 82)

Lingering with the Hegelian text will therefore help us gauge the force of Derrida's and Levinas's reservations concerning Husserl, and at the same time advance our understanding of the puzzle presented by Levinas's read-ing of what precisely Derrida takes the expression "vouloir dire" to translate (or define).

But let us first give ourselves a brief reminder that what we will learn from going back to the phenomenological science of the experience of conscious-ness will tell us something too about the science of structural semiology or semiotics, the two so-called sciences, the Hegelian and the Saussurian, which are hybridized in the diachronic structuralism of Lévi-Strauss. In conceiving the signifier as an acoustic mental image, Saussure commits himself to the idea of a transcendental signified at the very same time as he advocates a differential, relational, non-substantive account of meaning at odds with that idea (P 49, P tr. 36). While applauding Saussure's affirmation that in the sign the signifier and the signified are interdependent, Derrida substitutes a crossing for the parallelism Saussure maintains between the sign's two components. One consequence of this is that semantic motivation is seen to be more and necessarily accident-prone through the corporeality of the sign than is allowed by Saussure, whose playing down of the relevance of ono-matopoeia to the science of signs is symptomatic of his inability, despite himself, to wake up from the dream of the transcendental signified. The so-to-speak vertical arbitrariness of the signifier vis-à-vis the signified, which Saussure rightly stressed without denying the limits imposed by socio-cul-tural motivation, is implicated with a so-to-speak horizontal arbitrariness of the signifier vis-à-vis other signifiers which is incompatible with the break between a predicate or concept and history insisted on by Frege and

Saussure. It calls into question the synchrony or achrony Saussure claims for the subject matter of his projected semiotic science and leads Lévi-Strauss to project a diachronic structuralism. The unpredicted risks and opportunities to which signs are exposed by this diachrony are for our purposes here conveniently illustrated in a note in *Limited Inc* where Derrida writes in connection with the limited liability company S.a.r.l., the *société à responsabilité limitée* incorporating John Searle, John Austin, and, among others, the underwriter of the note himself:

> My friends know that I have composed an entire book with *ça* (the sign of the Saussurian signifier, of Hegel's Absolute Knowing, in French *savoir absolu*, of Freud's Id [the *Ça*], the feminine possessive). I did not, however, think of the s.a. of speech acts, nor of the problems (formalizable?) of their relation to the signifier, absolute knowing, the Unconscious or even to the feminine possessive. If that [*ça*] didn't interest me, perhaps I'd not have had enough desire to respond. All this [*ça*] to pose the question: *ça*, is it *used* or *mentioned*? (G2S 81, G2 254, LI 109–10)

This *ça*, this this or that, interests also us because, as Hegel would have been pleased to reflect, it is also the *ça* of sensible certainty from which the phenomenology of spirit begins its return journey toward *Sa*. It is also a point of departure from which we can learn to appreciate the felicity and boldness of Levinas's translation of *Meinung* as *vouloir-dire* and to see the difficulty we had with it in our first section from another point of view.

Paul de Man appears to add his approval to the translation of *Meinung* as *vouloir dire* in his essay "Sign and Symbol in Hegel's *Aesthetics*."[10] He reports there part of Hegel's argument for the universality and mediacy of indexical expressions like "this," "now," "here," and "I," hence for the incoherence of the assertion that immediate sensory awareness is the fullest knowledge there is. The incoherence of this assertion, the split in it that makes it split on itself like the assertion of universal skepticism, arises from its purporting to say something about an object or subject allegedly presented immediately by pronouns and other lexical expressions that can stand for any other objects and subjects, allowance made for the differences of gender and number which some of the pronouns mark. There is a contradiction, he writes, between *sagen* and *meinen*, between to say and to mean, between *dire* and *vouloir dire*. That is, de Man takes *vouloir dire*, Hegel's *sagen-wollen*, to translate *meinen*. Does this not blur a distinction that has to be made if we are to get the full picture of Hegel's argument? Does it not mask a distinction that is almost but not quite touched upon by de Man when he writes, quoting Hegel first in translation then in the original: "'Since language states only what is general, I cannot say what is only my opinion (. . . *so kann ich nicht sagen was ich nur meine*).' The German version is indispensable here since the English word 'opinion,' as in public opinion (*öffentliche Meinung*), does not have the connotation of 'meaning' that is present, to some degree, in the verb *meinen*."

We have already endorsed the statement de Man makes in the second of these two sentences. Before one also endorses the Hegelian thesis he reports in the first it should be noted that he is talking about the *meinen* of what is asserted, commanded, asked, and so on, that is, of what Frege calls an *Annahme* or a thought and Husserl a *doxa*. So *meinen* in this sense is translatable or definable by *vouloir dire*. And Hegel himself uses *sagen wollen* interchangeably with *meinen* in this sense. He says that to affirm the philosophical thesis of sensible certainty, namely that the reality of the purely sensory has absolute truth for consciousness, is to say the opposite of what one wants to say, *das Gegenteil von dem sagt, was sie sagen will*. However, Hegel does not substitute *sagen wollen* for *meinen* where the accusative is not something someone wants to say but something referred to about which someone may want to say something.

This distinction is important if we are to understand how the Hegelian dissolution of sensible certainty illuminates and is illuminated by Levinas's curious note purporting to endorse the introduction of *vouloir-dire* into Derrida's interpretation of Husserl's semiotics. For Levinas denies that *Meinung* is just *visée* on the grounds that nothing can be meant or intended in the sense of *gemeint* without being intended as (*gemeint als*) an *instance*.[11] This denial amounts to an agreement with Hegel's denial of the thesis of sensible certainty. Neither Hegel nor Levinas is denying that there can be *visée*. Whether or not they are denying that there can be *Meinung* which is not *visée*, as the Ricoeur translation of *Ideen* used by Derrida implies that Husserl would, Levinas seems to agree with Hegel that at least in the context of identification there cannot be *visée* which is not also *Meinung*. In that context, Hegel writes, speaking of those who hold that one can mean an absolutely singular "this" bit of paper: "but what they mean is not what they say. If they actually wanted to *say* and *wanted to say* it, then this is impossible, because the sensuous This that is meant cannot be reached by language, which belongs to consciousness, i.e. to that which is inherently universal." What Hegel wants to say here is that because to say something is to use words that are *allgemein*, I cannot say something *gemeint* that is only and idiosyncratically mine, *mein*. He is not saying that something cannot be simply *gemeint*. *Meinung*, meaning here non-doxic *Meinung*, is not being ruled out. "They certainly mean, then, *this* bit of paper here on which I am writing—or rather have written—'this'." Nor, plainly, does Hegel rule out the doxic *Meinung* of the thesis of sensible certainty, for he writes that "those who put forward such an assertion also themselves say the direct opposite of what they mean (*meinen*)."[12]

What exactly is Hegel ruling out? Neither Baillie nor Miller stress in their translations a word that is stressed in the original. This can lead the reader not to notice that when Hegel says "this is impossible," the "this" (*dies*) could refer, other things being equal, either to *saying* what is meant (*gemeint*) or to *wanting to say* what is meant. The distinction is not trivial. It can be impossible to say something yet possible to want to say it, for instance when one has the false belief that one can say, in the sense of assert (the *aussagen* of

Encyclopaedia, §24), not only propositions but also a physical object. When Rilke writes "sagen: Haus, Brücke, Brunnen ..." and when Mallarmé writes "Je dis: une fleur" they are not asserting or assuming one can assert houses and flowers. Nor is anyone asserting houses and flowers even in asserting "I assert houses and flowers." So the piece of paper that someone may indeed mean is not something that one can say in the sense of assert. One could think one could assert it only if one were confusing logical categories. However, since such confusion is possible, this reason why one cannot assert a sensible "This like a flower or a house" is not a reason why one cannot want to assert it. And indeed Hegel allows that the proponent of sensible certainty may want to assert the sensible This that he means. However the reason Hegel gives to explain why this desire cannot be realized is not that what is assertorically said cannot, logically cannot, be a red flower but can be only *that* this flower is red. Since the proponent of sensible certainty would presumably agree that a flower instantiates a universal, Hegel's objection must concern more plausible claimants to pure sensory denotation like "this," "here," "now," and "I." His objection therefore is that the "divine nature of language" is such that universality extends even to these expressions and that one can mean and even point to a sensible This only *as* one among many.[13]

LESSONS

This exposition of Hegel's pages on sensible certainty brings us to a point where it can be rewarding to ask what lessons can be drawn from it for an interpretation of Levinas.

One lesson relates to the point of Hegel's exposition at which we have just arrived. It is not only Husserl's account of identification but also Hegel's objection to sensible certainty that Levinas is endorsing when he resists the translation of "Meinung" as "visée" in the notes of *Otherwise than Being* referring to Derrida which were our point of departure. If we still need confirmation that this is the case, and that Levinas is defining the limits of his agreement with Hegel in order then to call into question his method, this is unmistakably provided by his statement that "thought cannot reach the individual except by way of the detour through the universal. For philosophy as discourse, the universal precedes the individual and is, in every sense of the term, a priori" (EDE 222; CPP 113). So that Levinas's "endorsement" of the translation of "Meinung" as "vouloir-dire" attributed to Derrida has a double effect. It puts Levinas on common ground with Hegel on the topic of *Meinung*. It also puts us, Levinas's readers, on the alert as to how he will leave that ground shared with the philosopher of exteriorizing-interiorizing, *entäussernd-erinnernd*, totalizing spirit—of *Ent-äusserung*, we might say, playing on the privative force of the prefix—in order to move to a philosophy of Infinition where expression is not the *Äusserung*, the (o)uttering, of an interior meaning in the manner of what we shall later find Derrida calling the "congenital expressivism" of semantic signification, but the ex-closure and ex-plosure which calls philosophy to attest to meaning's always already having been inspired by an absolute exteriority.

Another lesson we have just learned is that if, first, "vouloir dire" is an acceptable translation of "sagen wollen," to deny which one would have to be very bold indeed, and if, secondly, by "dire" is meant "to assert," and if, thirdly, we have a clear view of the category mistake involved in wanting to assert a non-propositional entity propositionally (we are not concerned here with the assertion of, for example, one's strength), then we could be expected not to want to say, not to *vouloir dire,* something that can nonetheless be non-doxically *gemeint.* This diminishes the felicity of translating or defining "Mein-ung" ubiquitously as "vouloir-dire." However, we have seen that Hegel's rejection of the thesis of sensible certainty does not turn on this argument. It turns on an argument relating to saying in general, not saying understood specifically as assertion. Although his argument uses the word "aussagen," this can have the less special sense of other words used in the presentation of this argument in the *Phenomenology of Spirit* and the *Encyclopaedia,* namely "aus-sprechen" and "ausdrücken," to speak out, utter, or express.

We have seen further that purely expressive meaning according to Hus-serl is meaning from which allusion to the empirical and hence to indexical and otherwise indicative signification has been suppressed. Husserlian phe-nomenologically expressive meaning is suppressive meaning. And we have seen that Derrida questions the possibility of this suppression or repression of the sensibility and materiality of the signifier. The author of *Logical Investigations* and *Ideas* himself goes on to acknowledge in *The Crisis of European Sciences and Transcendental Phenomenology* that the experience of original evidence attains and sustains a tradition of objectivity only because, as we can put it, inquirers have obeyed the request the author of the *Phenomenology of Spirit* makes to the defender of sensible certainty: "Write this down." The critical dilemma is that writing is exposed to a "bad" infinity of misreadings in which the putative original evidence is betrayed. Culture is both a rescue and a risk, a risk to transcendental phenomenology itself which, even when it becomes a phenomenology of culture, is, as Husserl sometimes admits, a part of culture itself (HO, 44ff., HO tr. 56ff.). Derrida's intervention in this dilemma traces something like writing, archi-writing, in the alleged pure transcendentally signified evidence. No signified can es-cape the eventuality of becoming in its turn a signifier. That is to say, his intervention reinstates sensibility, though in a way that no longer regards it as the simple opposite of intelligibility. For sensibility is of the essence of the intelligibility of signification. Signification can now be reinscribed in the discourse of meaning and sense with the recognition that sense as meaning is inseparable from sense as sensibility. This reinstatement of sensibility, however, is not a restatement of sensible certainty. Nor is it that for Levinas. But both he and Derrida take the beginning of the phenomenology of spirit as a shared point of departure. Both move away from this in different ways from Hegel, different ways that are the same as each other insofar as they both insist on the irreducibility of sensibility.

We have briefly noted how in at least the earlier writings of Derrida, sensibility is salvaged by archi-writing. However, the introduction of the pseudo-concept or conceit of archi-writing seems at first sight not to lead on its own beyond a revision of our ideas of ideas, concepts, predicates, and what is said by the syntactico-semantic signs of which Saussure's semiotics was to be the science. When we turn once more to the semiotics of Levinas and ask how sensibility is salvaged there, we find that the sensibility emphasized there is not so much that of the lexical or graphic signifiers as that of the utterers of these and their bodies. And what these Signifiers signify is not abstract noematic Objectives which get fulfilled by what Husserl and Merleau-Ponty describe metaphorically as the "flesh and bone" of objects, *Gegenstände*. The Signifiers of the semiotics of Levinas are and signify other Signifiers who are made of non-metaphorical flesh and bone and sensitive, vulnerable skin. His semiotics is a somatics. And that is why it is a semioethics. More exactly, if ethics is conceived on analogy with a systematic legal code, it is a proto-ethical semiotics which precedes and transcends the proto-doxa of Husserl's transcendental phenomenology and the sensible certainty that remains over from and is left behind by the phenomenology of spirit. For the essence or *Wesen* of this an-archic proto-ethics is a past and a passed or *Gewesen* that was never a present and cannot ever be "retained" as Husserlian proto-doxa are when they are re-presented in a livingly present act or passion of consciousness. Nor can it be *aufgehoben* in a dialectic of determinate negation which cancels and kills it only to transmit and transfigure it into a new phase in the life of consciousness. Somatico-semio-proto-ethics is prior to consciousness. The phenomenology of spirit in which the voluntarism of German Idealism culminates remains teleological. Even the Austrian phenomenology that succeeds it retains in its memory the Idea in a Kantian sense and bolsters its teleologism with the doctrine that all consciousness is an active intending of something and all expressive meaning a wanting to say. Yet it is in the many pages Husserl writes about passive synthesis and sensory hyletic data that Levinas discovers pointers toward a phenomenology of sensibility that exceeds the epistemological and ontological polarities of certainty and uncertainty, subject and object, being and nothingness, passivity and activity, and exceeds phenomenology itself when it reaches a semiotics where meaning as erotic *conatus dicendi, désirer-dire*, finds itself harking back to a signifiance which is Desire to say and to answer for the other human being who addresses me, to stand and substitute for him or her with a patience whose passivity is greater than that of the passivity opposed to activity in the dynamics of the struggle for existence, the war of each against each, including the war of words. Before the war of words and the word of war, already before any initiation of hostilities and before any initiative at all, resounds the word of peace.

THE WORD OF PEACE

"Shalom," "Salaam," "Hullo," "Bonjour," or, at exits and entrances, "After you." However conventional and convenient these expressions of politeness may seem, perhaps they indexically signify an ex-position of oneself in which a dominant philosophy of one's self as dominant is exposed. This exposition is attempted by Levinas and Derrida, both of them departing from Heidegger's attempt, and each of them departing from the other. How they depart from and are traceable in each other is not at all easy to say, not easy, by his own admission, for Derrida himself (A 75).[14] Derrida declares in an interview published in 1986 that he is ready to subscribe to everything Levinas says on the subject of alterity and the alterity of the subject. The only difference between them, he suspects, is one of "signature," for example the difference between Levinas's readiness to use the word "ethics" and his own unreadiness because of the charge the word carries from its philosophical past. Even this recourse to that word would worry him less so long as we articulate how that word is being, as Levinas would say, "emphasized" or "produced"—where the force of the word "production" is also being pro-duced (TeI XIV, TaI 26, A 70–75). Levinas remotivates philosophical paleonyms, for after all it is metaphysics that his "metaphysical ethics" would "produce"; but he is not averse to introducing into this allegedly Western lexicon Biblical words associated with the East. Derrida prompts philosophical paleonyms to betray the play of forces that produce their apparently oppositional pairings; and to allude to that play neographisms are introduced.

RESPONSIBILITY AND PLAY

This word "play" may make us want to ask how Derrida can subscribe to what Levinas says about responsibility. Bearing in mind that primary significance in the semioethics of Levinas is self-substitutive responsibility for the other, we could begin answering this question by going back once more to the note we cited from *Limited Inc* in which Derrida refers to limited responsibility. How can the semiotics of Derrida, we might ask, allow room for even limited responsibility, let alone the infinite responsibility of which Levinas speaks?

In a preliminary note in *Otherwise than Being or Beyond Essence*, Levinas confesses that he was tempted to write the last word of that title with an "a," a temptation he resists also in the paper on which is based the chapter on Substitution in that book, but not in some of his later works (e.g., ADV 178, BV 214).[15] This spelling would have marked the etymological connection the suffix has with "antia" and "entia" from which abstract nouns of action are derived, and so with the mixed verbal-substantivity of "Sein" and "Wesen," which correspond to the "Being" and "Essence" of Levinas's title. That suffix with an "a" is retained in the word "signifiance" that both he and Derrida use, thereby signifying their recognition of the difficulty of giving meaning to the words "beyond being." When used in the interview with Julia Kristeva entitled "Semiology and Grammatology" that is included in *Positions*, the "ance" of "signifiance," as too of "mouvance," "restance," "revenance," "différance" et al, indicates the supplementary plus or minus of impower brought to the power of the subject through the subjection of the subject's sign-giving to the expository explication of the text and the in-terminable extension of its tissue in the way the structural semiotics of Saussure is stretched when it is educated out of its "congenital expressivism" by Peirce's redefinition of a sign as that of which the interpretant becomes in turn a sign and so on ad infinitum (P 46, P tr. 34, DG 70–73, OG 48–50). Grammatology would be semiology minus expressology and phonology. It would disestablish not only the personal transcendental subject but also would transcribe the impersonality of "die Sprache spricht" into "die Ur-schrift schreibt." This leaves us with an impersonality which might well seem, and has indeed seemed to some of Derrida's readers and non-readers, incompatible with responsibility.

This impersonality could seem to be incompatible, for example, with a person's *standing by* his or her word and with a *person's* standing by his or her own word, as described by Levinas and in the dialogue *Phaedrus* (276) to which both he and Derrida so frequently refer. For Levinas, "signifiance" is primarily a sign of my being assigned by the Other not to go back on my word, and of my always prior commitment to stand by the other even by standing for him or her. This sounds like a personalism, indeed a Personal-ism of the highest majuscule degree. Although I am less of—and more than—an I such as is posited in transcendental egology, I am accused as a me, made by the Other's call to stand out in relief, unrelievably, without possibility of being *aufgehoben,* without possibility of being, without *Sein-können,* and without anything to identify me, to say who or what I am, other than my saying without wanting to say, the *dire* without *voulour-dire.* I am accused not exactly as an accusative *case* but as a unique elected singular *one* unconfusable with the impersonal one of *das Man* and with another person who by the laws of traditional and dialectical logic could substitute for me. Although in semioethical signification I cannot not substitute for the other, no other can substitute for me. Here my singularity is not that of a subject persisting in its will to have its say, but of a self subjected to a categorical imperative that categorizes me in the quasi-legal sense of the Greek word, selecting and summoning me above all to go to the assistance of the other in whose place in the sun I find myself and who has always already called for my help. Me above all and below all, because the other is the Other in the majesty Descartes attributes to the Infinite—though, it must be added at once, this majesty is attributed by Levinas to the Other's being the hungry stranger, the orphan, and the widow. The service to which I am called is not slavery, for the asystemic semioethical "relation" before the systemic rela-tions of structural semiotics and the asymmetrical "communication" before the symmetrical intercommunication (*Mitteilung*) Husserl would exclude from phenomenological expression are not a being-with, not a *Mitsein* or communication between powers. *Ipse* rather than *idem,* no longer am I the single-minded ego anxious to mark its property by leaving its scent on the gateposts of its world. I am the host, a hostage ex-tradited to the other by a trad-ition that is betrayed by the tradition of culture—betrayed in the sense of represented, not only in the sense of misrepresented, if cultural gifts are no less things requiring to be given, *donanda,* than is bread. I am in exile in my own home, hospitable to the point at which possessions make sense only in being given gratuitously to the ungrateful, as the gift of bread from my mouth, on the point of becoming part of myself, is the sign of my self and my word already having been given. The *Sinngebung* of semantic signification, a signifier standing for a signified, is given its sense by the foolish signifiance of a human Signifier standing for the other human being, both of them both transcendent of being and possessed of the flesh and the bone without which no one can labor or have hands (with which) to give.

However, is not this humanism of the other human being phonological? So when the Signifier Emmanuel Levinas signifies to the Other, Jacques Derrida, "Me voici," "Hineni," "Here am I. Send me," will Derrida not have reason to fear, as he says of Husserl and Hegel and Saussure in the words of *Positions* reproduced above, that the signifier is heard by the speaker as soon as it is emitted? Not if we hear and understand *obaudire* as an obedience prior to hearing and to the doxic obedience Levinas, following Husserl and Hegel, ascribes to the understanding of intentional meaning, *meinen* or *vouloir-dire.* Not if, in the words of *Otherwise than Being,* "Obedience precedes any hearing of the command" (AE 189, OB 148). Not if we can accept "The possibility of finding, anachronously, the order in the obedience itself, and of receiving the order out of oneself...." Not if the semioethical is somehow prior to the semi*otic,* prior to what pertains to the ear and to hearing as phenomenal sensation, if not prior to the hearing of "Hear me." So, appearances notwithstanding, this is no return to a phenomenology of self-consciousness or of speech and phenomenon, for "the appeal is understood in the response" (AE 190, OB 149) and the response is not vocal words, but going to the other in what in Kant's universalistic ethics of free will is called autonomy or non-pathological, practical love and in Levinas's pre-principial semioethics of singular signification prior to the freedom of will is called hetero-affection, susceptibility, responsibility, or being called.

But is proto-semiotic heterography of the Derridian trace prior to the trace of Levinasian semioethics? Or does the latter come first? We have already cited a remark of Derrida's about Levinas which suggests that these words are mal-posed. The notion of a pre- or proto-ethical semioethics of being called, of *Geheiss* before *Meinung* and *vouloir-dire,* is a topic in Derrida's writings at least from the late 1970s. In the late 1960s he had already written of his concept of trace and with reference to "The Trace of the Other" of 1963: "I relate the concept of trace to what is at the center of the latest work of Emmanuel Levinas and his critique of ontology: relationship to illeity as to the alterity of a past that never was and can never be lived in the originary or modified form of presence" (DG 102–103, OG 70). But how does Derrida relate his concept of trace to relationship, to alterity?

Levinas's archi-trace looks or sounds less like archi-writing than like archi-speech, the "vocative absolute" that the Derridian archi-trace suspends (DG 164, OG 112). For Levinas the archi-trace is that which supplements with obliqueness the directness of the face to face with *Autrui.* In his earlier writings Derrida's topic seems to be less often *Autrui,* the other human being, than alterity in general, *l'autre.* Of course, like Levinas and many other readers of Husserl, he is provoked by what is said in the fifth meditation of the *Cartesian Meditations* about the other human being. But it often seems that what Derrida is provoked to write about can be said without the need, stressed by Levinas, to get further than thinking of the other human being as another ego. Thus the approach to the trace made in *Speech and Phenomena* hinges on the manner in which the subject's self-affection demands a predicative or pre-predicative alterity with respect to itself. The ideality of the living self-presence that is demanded by Husserl's account of expressive meaning is found to demand the possibility of the subject's mortality. The appearance to me of ideality, the infinite possibility of repetition, demands my finitude, the possibility of my disappearance. In Levinas's response to Husserl's Fifth Meditation, priority is given to the death of the other. For Levinas the primary relation is for-the-Other, *pour Autrui.* Derrida, moving to the *Cartesian Meditations* in order to treat questions about the alleged independence of expressive meaning from indicative signification posed in Husserl's *Logical Investigations* and *Ideas,* is understandably preoccupied with the more general question of something standing for something else, *für etwas.* So expressive meaning is shown to be dictated by indicative signification when it is shown that if "I am alive" is written down, its expressive meaning implies the fact of my being dead. It is not dependent on my being alive for its meaningfulness. If the phenomenological field of meanings would survive the destruction of the whole natural world, as Husserl claims in *Ideas I* (§§47, 49), then its survival of my death is implied. That is to say, and Derrida says it, the written "I" is anonymous, even when endorsed by the signature I append to my will. For my signature too is something of which, of necessity, I can be dispossessed. And when I am dispossessed of my life, the signatory of the death certificate is not I. This seems a long way still from the uniqueness of the *me* accused by and elected to responsibility for the Other, a responsibility that is expressed to the Other when I say "Here I am" and perhaps already in saying only "I" or "me" or "only me."

Yet Derrida claims to be interested in a certain uniqueness. He writes: "To think the unique *within* the system, to inscribe it there, such is the gesture of archi-writing: archi-violence, the loss of the proper, of absolute proximity . . ." (DG 164, OG 112). How is this uniqueness related to the illeity to which Levinas relates the concept of trace? We begin to answer this question when we begin to understand that the Derridian trace and Levinasian illeity are both ways by which something like the primacy of singularity (defeated by mediative universality in Hegel's treatment of sensible certainty) may be rediscovered within the *system* of semiotics, Hegel's, Husserl's, or Saussure's, because they are both ways of exposing a paradoxical unprincipial principle of uncertainty which allows or conditions or quasi-conditions non-causally and non-logically the metaphysical oppositions of sensibility and intelligibility, passivity and activity, particularity and universality, rendering these oppositions undecidable except as surfacial effects.

15

NO HAPPY ENDING

between Kant and Lévinas

—JACQUES DERRIDA (*Adieu à Emmanuel Lévinas*)

AFFIRMATION

Alongside or, rather, in chiasmus with Levinas's statement in *Otherwise than Being* that "Yes" is the first word of "spirit" that makes "negativity," "consciousness," and all the other words possible (AE 156, OB 121–22), can be apposed Derrida's reference in "Nombre de oui" ("The Name, the Number, and the Shadow of the Yes I hear")[1] to a Yes before the Yes one opposes to No, a first Yes, a tremendous unheard Yes, a *oui inouï*, by which this second Yes is pre-echoed, foreshadowed, ghostridden, ghostwritten (Ps 648–49). In several other publications, for example his dis-phenomenology and dis-ontology of spirit "Of Spirit," Derrida reworks Heidegger's reflections on the promissory affirmation (*Zusage*) that, like an excluded middle of responsibility, *Ent-scheidung* before *Entscheidung*, calls into question the primacy of the question to which the answer is either a Yes or a No. But the book first published by him, the introduction to Husserl's *The Origin of Geometry*, because it is concerned with Husserl, is inevitably concerned with responsibility, as is another book on Husserl written earlier, but published only in 1990. The last words of this latter book, Derrida's *Le problème de la genèse dans la phénoménologie de Husserl*,[2] report the conversation Husserl had with his sister during his last illness when he said "I did not know it was so hard to die. . . . at the very moment when I feel totally penetrated by the feeling of responsibility for a task . . . I have to interrupt that task and leave it unfinished. At the very moment when I reach the end and everything for me is finished, I know I have to take everything up again from the beginning" (PG 283).

Emmanuel Levinas and Jacques Derrida are among the writers who take everything up again from the beginning or still earlier on Edmund Husserl's behalf. Both of them readers of Franz Rosenzweig's *The Star of Redemption*, they both refer back to a passage in that book which suggests that maybe the first semioethical word, the foreword, is the one that usually comes at the end: "Amen."

Perhaps it can be said of "Amen" rather than of "to be" that it "is the first or the last word to withstand the deconstruction of a language of words" (VP

83, SP 74). This would not mean that it would succeed in withstanding deconstruction, at least if success is opposed to failure. The last word is only the latest, always too late and too early. Even "deconstruction" is exposed to the trace of penultimacy, antepenultimacy, and so on. And so is "trace." The pseudonyms for the shaking of foundations themselves shiver and shake. Where the identity of "trace" is sealed in promissory marks, what is to prevent Derridian trace, as we have been calling it, finding affiliated to itself the trace of Levinas, not being and being it in a non-Parmenidean way, the way Levinas tells us the father and son are related (TeI 255–56, TaI 278–79)? What is to prevent these traces from getting grafted onto Rosenzweig?

"Amen," Rosenzweig suggests, is the silent accompaniment to every word in a proposition, a "*sic*"—or, Derrida might suggest, a "sec," a proxy secretarial signature *p.p.* (not to be confused with primary process). Adding or prepending a sign of affirmation to Frege's sign of assertion, witnessing thereby with a *firma* to a truth older than the truth of propositional representation and even older than the truth of a-lethic presencing, the four-letter foreword "Amen" may be what makes the judgment of cultures possible. There is a twofold difficulty with the statement to this effect that Levinas makes in an essay in which he reverses the priority of meaning over signification claimed by Husserl. Levinas's statement appears to imply the possibility of a context-free universalism, that cultures can be judged from a neutral point of view independent of cultures, and that all cultures are not equivalent, but are required to be judged. Is this universalism not, paradoxically, a form of ethnocentrism? The context-free universalism to which it appeals seems to be an outdated ideal of Platonism that is difficult to sustain even in its updated Husserlian version, as has been shown by, among others, Derrida and Levinas himself.

UNIVERSALITY AND CULTURAL COLONIZATION

The dedication of *Otherwise than Being* is more than enough to show that Levinas is no less aware than others of the violence of ideological colonization, conducted in the name of emancipation and supraculturally objective truth, backed up perhaps by a conviction that one has heard that truth pronounced over the telephone by God.[3] How can this awareness be reconciled with his assertion that whereas the perceived and scientific world do not permit us to rejoin the norms of the absolute, "the norms of morality are not embarked in history and culture. They are not even islands that emerge from it—for they make all, even cultural, signification possible, and allow Cultures to be judged" (HAH 56, CPP 101-102, LBPW 59)?

Can Levinas be meaning moral principles when he refers here to the "the norms of morality"? Is it significant that he writes "morality" here rather than "ethics"? And can he be denying that the norms of morality depend for their content on culture? If he is denying this, he is exposing himself to the objections of modern cultural historians and ethnologists. If he replies that he means moral principles of a purely contentless kind like the Kantian moral law, he is exposing himself not only to the objection that such a principle is useless because vacuous—an objection that he could meet by saying, like Kant could, that it gets its content from the maxims to which it applies; he is exposing himself also to the objection that this very principle of universalizability is a product of the discredited universalism of Plato, a Western ideal, even if, through its being assumed and applied to the abstract idea of the human being as such, it prescribes respect for personality in whatever historical and ethnic context it manifests itself.

Levinas does not want to be committed to morality founded upon universalistic Kantism or Platonism, but he does see himself to be rejoining Platonism in a way different from the way of Kant and Husserl. When he writes that the norms of morality are not "embarked in" history and culture, he means that they are not founded in meaning either as what one wants to have said, the *dit* of a *vouloir-dire,* or as doxic or non-doxic intending, *Meinung.* Before culture, because before purporting to say, before the expounding of opinion, before meaning intentions, even before the alleged immediacy of pointing that Hegel and Wittgenstein and Levinas discredit, is the signifying of myself for the other in the immediacy of the separation in proximity of the dyadic face to face: the *vis-à-vis* before *avis* and *visée.* Before culture.

But before in a new way. For the priority of saying over the said is a priority that is "in" that which is posterior to it, "in" in a new way. The very historiality of history, the very acculturation of culture, its *Bildung,* even the nativity and nature of a nation is alter-nation. Culture is anarchy. As is so-called human nature. Levinas is no personalist if personalism presumes personal identity which allows alteration only as change. The ego maintaining itself ecstatically, ahead-of-itself up to its death, has its monadic existence expanded by human and other beings it is *with.* But the oneness—and, Levinas would say, wonderfulness—of the self is the uniqueness of my election to responsibility for the other who calls me in the voice of absolute conscience absolved from absolute knowing, heard in me yet as though coming from without, from above and from a never present past. Not expansion, but unevadable invasion of the identical ego, turning it inside out into a self that is not a self-possessed psyche, but the psychism of owing my self to the other, heteropossession, psychosis.

If the dyadic face to face, which is the society of the self, is what makes multiple society possible, then the latter and the cultural and historical meanings that go with it and which Husserl treats in the Fifth Cartesian Meditation and in the *Crisis,* are never out of crisis, ever under de-cisive judgment, *Ur-teil,* as is the judge himself. Thanks to semioethical signifying, the vanishing trace, always passed, of the non-appearing face that the mask of the persona betrays—and, Levinas would add, thanks to God, provided "God" is not heard as a theological or ontological name, but as the infinite illeity that is "pronounced without 'divinity' being said" (AE 206, OB 162),

211

without uniqueness being sacrificed in gaining universality and justice, as it is sacrificed in gaining universality and justice by "the divine nature of language"—there can be criticism and judgment of history understood as the narratable deposit of events, judgment of culture and civilizations understood as the systematic semiotic structures of institutions, criticism of those Values and world views so dear to the Neo-Kantian philosophy of which Heidegger's fundamental ontology was meant to be a criticism. For such criticism to be possible for philosophy, Levinas is saying, philosophy must somehow be beyond being, *epekeina tês ousias*. If this is so, and if philosophy is itself within history and culture, then although history and culture are self-contained like the chapters of a book, they also face out from themselves as in a book's preface the author addresses the reader. There is an oscillation between sedimentation and its interruption, between said and saying or unsaying, a chiasmus of *Einbildung* and *Abbildung*, forming and deforming, imaginative construction and deconstruction, at the difficult, hard place or non-place under the skin of *to on* where *to agathon* is neither idea nor value, not even the value of universality or respect for persons as such. Permitting real newness and creation, not just the make-believe and makeshift novelty of furniture being shifted around that is the metaphor of what Levinas and Blanchot call the *il y a*, Levinas's return to Platonism "in a new way" is not vacuously formal. For it is not formal. It is per-formative, and de-formative of Platonic Forms. Without a basis in universal reason, Levinas's Neo-Neoplatonism of newness and creation by the Good is an ultimately baseless and, by the norms of formal and dialectical logic, incoherent, unfundamental de-ontology of the uniquely signifying signature retracing the trace (*ichnos*) of the Plotinian One, as the trace that is said to be the form of the formless in the *Enneads* is retraced by the anarchi-writing of Derrida (*Enneads*, 5, 5, 5; 6, 7, 33; CP 205, PC 190; CPP 106, LBPW 63; M 187, M. tr.157).

To the extent that we *do* judge and criticize history and culture, a favorable judgment upon philosophy itself is due if Levinas's philosophy of the face to face can show, albeit not without enigma, that this critical practice escapes vicious circularity thanks to the re-facing of signification. By testifying to what is admittedly a certain pre-predicative folly and incoherence, philosophy would be demonstrating that my judgment of cultures or culture as such is not without coherence, provided I acknowledge that it is me above all who calls to be judged—and is responsible for the judgments made by others!

It remains to ask ourselves whether we *should* judge and criticize history and cultures, for instance our own or the Cultures of Fascism Levinas no doubt has indelibly in mind when in the French text of "Signification et sens" he spells the word with a capital "C." And how should we justly judge this "should" unless semiotics is, to speak the language of Husserl and Hegel, animated or enspirited, *beseelt* or *begeistert*, haunted, as Derrida and Levinas enigmatically indicate, by the semioethical foreword "Amen"?

TELEOLOGY AND DEONTOLOGY

Even so, if, in the wake of Rosenzweig and other more ancient writings, Amen or Yea (*nai,* Rev 1:7) is for Levinas a foreword for us all, to what, if anything, does it look forward? Can it look forward to anything without teleology? Is not teleology the quintessence of looking forward?

Kant's *Critique of Teleological Judgement* is a qualified endorsement of an idea that belongs to the cluster of ideas of which the open-textured notion of Romantic philosophy is fabricated. Much favored especially among the philosophers of at least German Romanticism is the notion of teleology. I use the word "notion" here generically, to cover both concept and Idea in the Kantian sense. Roughly speaking, one of the differences between the German Romantics and Kant is that for the former the notion of organic teleology is a constitutive and theoretical concept, whereas for Kant it is a regulative and practical Idea. For the Romantics, if I may use that label to cut a long story short, nature is a living organism. And that is also the model for their view of relations among human beings. Ethics and politics are painted with the same brush as nature. Physics and ethics and politics are aesthetics. Beauty is truth. The world as a whole is a work of art. Like a novel. For the Romantic the world is a *roman.* But not a fiction. For the world's romanesque form is for the Romantic the form of the factual world.

For Kant the factual world is still in broad terms Newtonian as to its form, except that the sensible and conceptual forms of empirical factuality are not independent of human mentality. This does not mean that these forms are fictive in the way that the plot of a novel might be. For according to Kant the forms of sensibility (space and time) and the forms of the understanding (the categories and principles) are necessary conditions of experience. Necessary too are even the forms of Reason (the Ideas) which Kant says are the conditions of the investigation of experience and empirical facts. But to say that they are conditions of investigation or research is to say that they are not constitutive but regulative, and regulative in a way different from that in which Kant says that the non-mathematical principles of the understanding are regulative. The Ideas of Reason are regulative of the empirical laws whose lawfulness as such is constituted by the principles and concepts of the understanding. Among these Ideas is the Idea of the world as an organic whole. That Idea is an extension to the totality of an Idea we cannot help applying to some parts of the totality, the vegetable and animal kingdom. Scientific knowledge of plants and animals would be mechanistic. Biological knowledge would be physics. But the study of organisms could not proceed without adopting as a heuristic principle the notion of a teleological order. To describe this principle as heuristic is to say that it is not a principle of knowledge, but a principle guiding the search for knowledge.

No human being can have theoretical knowledge of the world as a whole. This is the lesson of the various antinomies deduced in Kant's Critiques. If that holds of the natural world, it holds *a fortiori* of what Kant calls the

213

intelligible kingdom, the society of human beings and any divine being there may be, thought as ordered according to the moral law. It follows that no human being can have theoretical knowledge of the totality of these totalities, assuming that the sensible world and the world of pure practical reason may be treated as two worlds. Even if we treat them as aspects of one world, there is still a duality. And for the human being, according to Kant, this duality is expressed as the difference between happiness and virtue.

Because the Idea of a kingdom of ends is an Idea and is therefore not groundable in sensible schematizable experience, Kant holds that to make sense of it we use as an analogy or Type the Idea of a teleological system of nature, nature as organon. It is not unreasonable that this teleological structure should be postulated of the whole made up of the combination of happiness with virtue. For although it follows from the arguments of the Critiques that we can have no theoretical knowledge of any end imposed upon the natural and human world as a whole, and no theoretical knowledge of a being who might impose that end, the human being is a being who as a sensible being is directed toward an end, namely happiness. Toward the achievement of that end the human being follows rules of technical skill subordinated to counsels of prudence. These are expressions of what we might call impure practical reason—though their practicality is based ultimately on theoretical fact. Pure practical reason is expressed by the moral law which prescribes minimally that no rule of skill, counsel of prudence, or other maxim of behavior should be followed which either could not be or could not be willed or advocated as a law for all. For me to advocate that a maxim be a law for all is to advocate that others do likewise. The categorical imperative commands me to command them and commands them to command me.

Now Kant maintains that I am commanded to promote the happiness of others provided such promotion is not inconsistent with the principle of universalizability. Does this not mean that I am commanded to command them to promote my happiness, so long as in doing so they follow no non-universalizable maxim? Is this not making it my duty and a direct duty, to promote my happiness, even if I am doing so indirectly? But Kant denies that I have a duty to promote my own happiness.

It should be noted in passing that the apparent dilemma posed here is not resolved by distinguishing with Kant perfect and imperfect duties. My duty to further another's happiness leaves open the way, the when, the where, and the how much, but an imperfect duty is still a duty.

If the dilemma cannot be removed by making this distinction between perfect and imperfect duties, can it be removed by distinguishing means from ends? It is by making this distinction that Kant dismisses what he calls the plausible objection that I should make my physical happiness my end because my aches and pains tempt me not to do what I morally should. This is no real objection, Kant replies, since it leaves my happiness as no more than a means of getting rid of obstacles to my performing my duty. My duty, not my happiness, remains my end.

Kant cannot make this reply to resolve the contradiction that seems to be entailed by the joint endorsement of the claim that I have a duty to further the happiness of others and the principle of universalizability, which I take to entail the transitivity of command. That joint endorsement seems to prevent his saying that my duty, not my happiness, is my end. For the joint endorsement implies that my happiness is one of the ends I am duty-bound to seek.

Can the dilemma be resolved by distinguishing not means from ends, but ends from consequences? That is, should we say that although one of the ends commanded by the categorical imperative is the happiness of others, it does not follow that any consequence of adopting that end is an end. After all, my keeping a promise or refusing to tell a lie may have uncomfortable consequences for me, and I am not morally obliged to make these consequences an end by the fact that they follow from my being obliged to make it one of my moral ends to keep promises and not to lie. This, however, is not an appropriate comparison. For there may or may not be certain painful consequences of keeping a promise. The consequences are contingent and empirical. The consequences in the case it is meant to illustrate are necessary and logical. If I am obliged to further your happiness and my obligation falls under a universal law, then I am obliged to oblige you to further the happiness of others, and those others will include me. (I consider and dismiss a defense similar to this one in the next but one section of this chapter. Throughout I take willing, as invoked in the various formulations of the categorical imperative, to be equivalent to being willing to command.)

Note that this dilemma is one that concerns obligation, not that part of morality where what orders our thinking and action is not the categorical imperative, but the Idea of organic teleology. However, the dilemma does arise in the latter part of morality too, that is to say, the part of morality dealt with not just in the Analytic of Pure Practical Reason in the second *Critique,* but also in the Dialectic of Pure Practical Reason. There Kant allows that action determined by the categorical imperative is performed under the non-determining teleological Idea of the unconditioned totality which he calls the highest good. This *summum bonum* is the combination of what he calls the supreme good,[4] namely virtue, that is to say the disposition to act from respect for the moral law, and happiness. Here we are concerned not just with my good will and my happiness, but with the Idea of a totality of rational beings in which the happiness of each is commensurate with the virtue of each. Whereas it is within the scope of my will to act virtuously— ought implies can—it is not within my power alone to realize the highest good. And we cannot know that the highest good is realizable. Kant nevertheless claims to show in the Dialectic that the arguments against the realizability of the highest good are invalid, because they confuse knowledge with belief or faith. The realizability of the highest good is not an impossibility. Indeed, the Idea of it is necessary as an article of faith. Although no single human being and no totality of human beings has the power to bring it about, it is an offense to reason to suppose that the wicked should prosper and the innocent should suffer, as all too frequently seems to be the case. Hence Kant's theodicy. Although there can be no speculative basis for belief in a God who measures out happiness in proportion to desert, there can be no theoretical or speculative objection to this belief. And this belief is necessary for practice. Practically necessary too is the belief in the possibility of an afterlife. For the highest good has as its condition the fullest realization of virtue. As no one achieves that in this life, it must be possible reasonably to hope for an afterlife in which a progress toward moral perfection, that is to say, holiness, may be continued. Whether or not it must be possible to continue this *in finitum,* as Kant says, is another question, which I shall not pursue. Instead, I shall take the mention of infinity and holiness as a cue for turning now back to Levinas.

INFINITY AND TOTALITY

Infinity as invoked in the title *Totality and Infinity* is not a part of a whole as it is in the case of that totality which Kant calls the highest good. It is what interrupts such an Idea of totality because it interrupts every Idea, idea or concept. Ethical binding is unbounded. It interrupts even the moral law conceived as a principle of practical universality. And because for Kant the moral law is the law of a free will, infinity as Levinas construes it disturbs the free will because in a manner of speaking it contravenes the law. Speaking contradicts the moral law. It is inconsistent with the principle of universalization. However, this is not a contradiction in the space of logical form. It is a ContraDiction between that space defined by the principle of non-contradiction and another space, ethical exteriority, a ContraDiction between two dictions: diction as what is said and diction as saying. Not saying as the utterance of a speech act, which is correlative with what is said, that is, with the proposition affirmed, the question asked, or the command commanded. Rather, a saying which is anterior to that correlation, a saying that is the condition of that correlation. Not a condition in the way that a principle of the understanding or of reason would be a condition. For such principles are things said. Rather, an anarchic condition. Ethical infinity according to Levinas's teaching is not archaeological. Nor is it teleological. If its infinity means that it is unbounded, without limit, it also means that it is without finality. Kantian ethics does at least have an end toward which the agent is required to strive, even if that striving does not cease. The incessance of Levinas's ethics beyond essence is an unfinishedness that is not measured by distance from the realization of any totality. It differs then from Kantianism in this respect, if we take Kantianism along with Fichteanism as philosophies for which what is primary is duty. And in this respect it differs from German philosophical Romanticism, if we take that as a philosophy for which what is primary is beauty. Needless to say, it differs from Hegelianism, where both the Kantian-Fichtean end and the Schellingian and generally

German Idealist end are embraced and taken up via revealed religion into the end of absolute knowledge or wisdom.

WOE IS ME

Yet it might be said—and it has been said—that Levinas's doctrine of the ethical is an exemplification of what Hegel calls Unhappy Consciousness. In refusing the happy ending, apparently excluding from the ethical all talk of the beautiful and refusing to appeal to the analogy of a work of art, for instance a novel where everyone lives happily ever after, Levinas disqualifies himself from being counted a philosophical Romantic defined as a philosopher who posits teleology tending toward organic totality. But in so doing, does he not qualify to be described as a Romantic in the sense of one who is, as Carlyle says of Goethe's Werther, "the voice of the World's Despair"?

A negative answer must be given to the question whether Levinas falls into this category of Romanticism, which is still teleological because it is the expression of disappointment at the apparent failure of teleology. Levinas cannot be deemed a Romantic of this kind if the words "Woe is me" that express it are taken to be the expression both of an unhappy consciousness and of the pre-principial ethicality which, according to him, disconcerts ethics based on the principle of the moral law. For that pre-principial ethicality is prior also to any natural law and to any field explicable or describable in terms of laws of nature, including the field of consciousness. It is prior both to the sphere of psychology and to the field of pure consciousness which transcendental phenomenology sets out to describe. A parable that brings out why this is so is told prior to and beyond the verse, Isaiah 6:5, in which the prophet laments "Woe is me, because I am undone." The word here translated as "undone" is *nidmeyti*. But this word can also mean "cut off" and, as though it were one's tongue that is cut off, "made silent." Isaiah is not simply expressing a state of mind. That he is also referring to the state of objective wretchedness that gives rise to that state of mind is indicated by the fact that in the preceding chapter there is a series of verses culminating in three consecutive ones in which he calls down woe upon those people of Jerusalem and Judea who follow certain specified evil ways. When this crescendo culminates in the declaration of his own woe, then, woe still means the opposite of weal. What he laments is that despite having spoken up against wrongoing, he has not spoken up often enough (hence the Vulgate's *quia tacui* instead of "because I am undone"), and so he is not any more worthy to speak than the other sinners. His guilt makes him unworthy to address them. He too has unclean lips. The verses that follow describe how his lips are cleansed. They are touched by a hot coal from the incense burner. There may be an allusion here to the sacrifice of burnt offering, but what is especially to be noted is that the prophet's lips are not burnt by the hot coal. And it is not their being thus touched that brings about his forgiveness. That would be to make his forgiveness turn on natural magic. What restores him to cleanliness is his recognition "I am a man of unclean lips" and his response "Here I am. Send me" to God's "Whom shall I send? And who shall go for us?" The burning coal touching the prophet's lips symbolizes the placing in his mouth of the word of God, as also the burning bush represents the words spoken to Moses by God. Both Isaiah and Moses respond "Here I am. Send me." They are prophets. They speak for Israel the word previously put in their mouths by God, even if they themselves do not understand it. For the word here is the foreword, the *dire* before those words that convey an understandable content, a message, something *dit*.

For Levinas, the Hebrew prophet and the special responsibility of Israel represent the special responsibility of every human being. But how can every human being have a special responsibility? Levinas remarks that where everything is divine or holy nothing is divine or holy. This does not exclude, as he seems to think, that, provided not everything is divine or holy, the scope of what is divine or holy might be wider than he thinks. However, it must not be forgotten that by "holy" or "divine" Levinas means separated from and elevated above (*kadosh*). What is separated from and elevated above is separated from and elevated above something else. Holiness is a relational notion. This does not mean that it is a relational property. It is the Relation or Rapport that makes relations and properties possible, nothing less than what he calls the face to face. The face to face is not special in the sense of something bearing a quality or relational property that differentiates it from everything else. Its specialty is not specific, and therefore does not raise the Leibnizian question as to whether there can be two things that differ from each other only numerically. If the statement that everything is special is self-contradictory (and there are ways of interpreting it according to which it is not), this is because it is a statement, something said, a proposition with truth conditions defined by the principle of non-contradiction. But the face to face is precisely what cannot be contained in such a statement. It belongs to that previously mentioned space of diction as saying that cuts across (*contra*) contradiction defined by truth tables or dialectical negation.

This is why Levinas is not trapped in the contradiction in which Kant is trapped on the reading of him given above, the contradiction of the self that is doubly bound both to and not to further its own happiness as an end. That contradiction arises because of the symmetry between myself and others implied by the moral law. If a law of a system of nature conceived as an organic whole is the typical analogy for a realm governed by the moral law, the latter is a system as viewed by God or from nowhere. It is this "German Romantic" totalization through universalization which forestalls the defense (promised or threatened two sections ago) that although willing the universalization of the maxim "Promote the happiness of others" does promote my own, it does not will it under that description. Nor is the contradiction avoided if the relevant maxim is "Promote the happiness of others, not your own." For when that is universalized and addressed by me to you, as the transitivity of the categorical imperative requires, the words "not your own" do not apply to my happiness. My happiness now falls under the description "happiness of the other." Kant cannot reconcile that third personal view with the different standpoints of the second and first persons. His attempt to incorporate second and first personality into the symmetricality and transitivity of the third person panorama necessitates the universalization of a contradiction.

Kant's difficulty is a consequence of his teaching that persons attract moral respect only as bearers of the moral law. This teaching and its consequence is what is called into question by Levinas's doctrine of face-to-face asymmetry. According to this doctrine, the anarchic origin of ethics is my being more responsible than any other, to the point of being responsible for the other's responsibilities. That is something that it makes sense only for me to say. Where being toward my death is according to Heidegger what singles me out from the anonymity and impersonality of the one, *das Man,* according to Levinas what singles me out is my being elected to a responsibility to substitute myself for the other, and that is a responsibility in which no one else can be substituted for me.

But, it will asked, how does Levinas avoid being trapped like Kant by this self-contradiction regarding the self's own happiness? Whether one begins with the third personality and attempts to fit the first and second person into it, like Kant, or with first and second personality and attempts to adjust the third person to it, if the former procedure leads to inconsistency, so too will the latter. Indeed it will, but the latter procedure is not Levinas's. Although his doctrine of the ethical is beset by difficulties, they arise not, like Kant's, in the space of formal logic and its application to practice, but at the intersection of the logic of diction as what is said and diction as saying. This is indeed the intersection of the pronouns "you" and "he" and "He," but their intersection across the intersection of saying and what is said. In your face the face of the third party already looks at me and addresses me. The "he" of the third party and the "He" of illeity are not, as they would be for Sartre, origins of a panoramic view in which I figure merely as an object. And although, conversely, the asymmetry of your facing me requires that I acknowledge the symmetrical relationships among all third parties, I cannot acknowledge that this symmetrical relationship includes me. Only others can acknowledge that. It is only thanks to them that I have rights. It is only *grâce à Dieu,* as Levinas says, that I can expect to be happy.

How safe are your expectations of happiness from the danger of unhappiness thanks to and caused by me, even if I am conscientiously concerned with your welfare? Conscientiousness demands that I be concerned not only with your welfare, but also with that of the third party, the other other who is always from the start present in your eyes, the one for whom you are a third party in turn. Derrida brings out how this complicates the promise, tacit or explicit, which I make to you. Although Levinas appears not to say so in so

219

many—or so few—words, and appears not to use the words *parjure*, "betrayal," and *serment*, "oath," it follows from what he does say that the word of honor spoken to the other from the beginning or before any beginning is at the same time a word that threatens betrayal. This "quasi-transcendental fatality of betrayal" (T 108, Ad 66ff.) is a solemn oath in good faith that amounts to an oathing, a cursing, as though in swearing on my honor to assist my neighbor I swear at him. For my answearability to you is an answearability at the same time to the third party.

Is this a trap, an impassable aporia? Or is it a dilemma that can be resolved? What if we recall that in my responsibility I am responding to the command of another? But which other? If it is you that commands on your own behalf "Thou shalt not kill" I may be able to obey only by killing the third party. If it is the third party that commands on his own behalf, I may be able to obey only by killing you. But the third party is already there in your looking and speaking to me. That is to say, you command me also not to harm him, and he commands me not to harm you. Otherwise said, the source of the command is not just you or the third party, he in the lower case, but He in the upper case, the He of Illeity, Infinity, God. This must not be taken to be equivalent to saying that the source of the command is reason, as in Kant. That would entrap Levinas in the self-contradiction of the self's happiness to which Kant is exposed. Levinas can escape that only by insisting that although third personality interrupts the directness of the interruption effected by the asymmetrical face to face of you and me, the third personality remains in touch with the second and the first across the dictive difference between the saying and the said, one calling for the other and the other calling for the one unendingly.

IN TOUCH

The asymmetry of the face to face and the third party's presence there jointly guard against the risk of the ethical relation becoming lost in the impersonality of systematic legality. They guard also against the risk of intimacy of the I-thou, such as is exemplified par excellence in the voluptuosity of erotic desire. The verses cited from Isaiah tell us that the prophet's lips are touched but not burnt by the hot coal which the seraph presses on them. It is as though they are touched and not touched. As though the climax of ethical responsibility when the prophet's tongue receives the word of God is anticipated by an erotic caress where, according to Levinas, contact is not possession, but a grazing or gracing tact whose temporality is less that of presence than of promise: the temporality expressed by the adverb "presently," the time of the impending gift, the gift of time itself, and therefore the gift of death. But also the gift of what is beyond my death, beyond the face, when I am no longer on the scene, beyond my possibility. This beyond possibility and beyond the face presupposes the face. As does the violence of murder and the threat of death, where the "of" is double and where death is not, as it is for Heidegger, the possibility of impossibility within which all other possibilities of the human being are ordered. For Levinas, death is the impossibility of possibility in the face of which I may fail to respond to the face of the other human being which says to me "Thou shalt not kill." The sting of death is the ontical possibility of my indifference to that command, my doing what is ethically impossible. Not my death, but the other's death and my contributing to it is what is primarily at stake in ethics. But death puts in an appearance before the ethical is fully articulated. In what way?

After sections making a transition from the previous chapter to this one, it was asked at the outset of the section entitled "Teleology and Deontology": if Amen is the foreword, to what does it look forward? Without closing that question, the verses from Isaiah brought us to the question: what is before this foreword? In the order of exposition of *Totality and Infinity*, before the word that says ethics, before the word that is the saying that is before the saying that is correlative with the said, are the "sweet nothings" that are murmured as an accompaniment to the caress that postpones engagement, transcending possibility toward a future more future than any possibility. But the insignificance of the murmured syllables presupposes the significance that presupposes semioethical saying, the signifying face. Erotic voluptuosity, between explicit concept and guarded secret—"Les derniers dons, les doigts qui les défendent"[5]—is the expression of the refusal to express (TeI 238, TaI 260). So, here is an equivocity which is not that of something said, not conceptual ambiguity, but an equivocality of saying—or "saying"—between speech and the renunciation of speech. (Levinas sometimes writes the word between inverted commas when he is speaking of "feminine" saying.) Hence the conditional clause of Derrida's question: "We still need to know where the line is drawn, if there is one, between the beyond possibility which exceeds the caress, while yet making it possible as caress, and the beyond possibility which opens and makes ethics possible"? Of this question Derrida poses the further question:

> What does our question mean? It asks after what, in the tender tending (*le tendre*) of the caress, comes to tend toward the beyond possibility. Does this movement of transcendence not tend already toward the ethical? Or must one rather interrupt the tender tenderness of the caress in order to tend toward the ethical, of a beyond possibility toward the other—beyond possibility? (T 107)

Two sayings, one discrete, one indiscrete. Two desires, erotic desire and ethical Desire, corresponding to an inscribed erotic *dire* or "dire" and an inscribed ethical *Dire*. Two nudities, that of the bodies caressed and that of the frankness of the face. Ultimately two deaths, the one declared ethically impossible in "Thou shalt not kill" and the one referred to when Levinas says of the caress that "It loses itself in a being that dissipates as though into an impersonal dream without will and even without resistance, a passivity, an already animal or infantile anonymity, already entirely at death" (TeI 236, TaI 259). A mortal evanescence whose passivity is beyond the opposition of activity and passivity within the terms of which is framed the philosophy of, say, Immanuel Kant. Suffering without suffering, the caress "dies with its death and suffers with this suffering." Its "intentionality" is not that of movement toward the meaningful. Its voluptuosity "goes without going to an end," without going either toward light or toward happiness. Its voluptuosity is suffering transformed into happiness.

Given these pairings of types and prototypes along the path of Levinas's genealogy of ethics from the impersonality of the *il y a* to the personality of *illéité*, and given the emergence of this happiness of voluptuosity, one is led to assume a happiness with which it too is paired. But if the feminine face is encountered in the linear exposition of this genealogy somewhere near the midpoint between ilyaity and illeity, and if the saying, desire, nudity, and death intimate with it are paired with Saying, Desire, Nudity, and Death in the direction of Illeity, one can expect a pairing of each of these latter with a prefiguration in the direction away from the ethical extreme and away from the intermediate feminine face toward the extreme of ilyaity. And the same expectation would hold for happiness. These expectations are met in a reading of *Totality and Infinity* which finds that each of the masculine versions intimated by each of the equivocal expressions of femininity corresponds also with each member of another series of which one is saying as representation. Before we go on to list the other members, note that the structure of the overbrimming of world-constituting Kantian representation by the infinity of the ethical (and by God according to the third of the *Meditations* of Descartes) is reflected in the overwhelming of the same world-constitutive representation by alimentation (TeI 101, TaI 128). To come now to the second member of this new series correlated with the feminine-erotic series and the masculine-ethical series; corresponding in particular with ethical Desire, and intermediately with erotic desire which is not possessive, but has a future beyond the future of the realization of possibility, is desire for the possession of the fruits of the earth from which we live. Thirdly, corresponding with death as the death of the other whose life I threaten, is my death threatened by the other and by the scarcity of the fruits of the earth. Fourthly, the nudity of the other's face corresponds with the nudity of my own body at birth and for as long as it needs nourishment and clothing or a shroud.

But what about happiness?

HAPPINESS

The happiness of my enjoyment of that from which I live is coupled with the happiness of voluptuosity, the happiness of coupling. But with what do these correspond at the maximally and masculinely ethical end of the scale—if indeed this is one?

Let us go back to the one who speaks forward and for, back to the prophet Isaiah. His woe is an unhappiness not over the distance he finds himself from satisfaction, contentment, or sensible wholeness. It is over the distance he finds himself from holiness. Levinas says from time to time in his later work that he had come to realize that the ethical, his chief concern, is the holy, *le saint, kadosh,* meaning by that the separate. The holy is wholly separate from the natural, and therefore from happiness at least as happiness is understood by Kant. It is responsibility for the happiness of others, meaning by that most urgently the responsibility for attending to their needs. As we have seen, Levinas is in agreement with Kant that I am under no obligation to secure my own happiness. He disagrees, however, with Kant's doctrine that justice demands that I can hope for personal happiness commensurate with worthiness to be happy in what he calls the kingdom of God, an expression Kant uses in apposition to the expression *summum bonum.* But how can the kingdom of God be the *summum bonum* when this is defined as "the worth of a person and his worthiness to be happy."[6] That would be the highest good only for a single person. How could that be the highest good in comparison with happiness commensurate with virtue for all persons, "the *summum bonum* for a possible world" (ibid.)? Presumably by my virtue being incomplete unless it includes obedience to the command to further the happiness of all persons. We are members one of another, and not just through natural sympathy, but through practical reason expressed in the moral law. Kant begins his discussion of the highest good with the highest good "for one person" (*in einer Person*) because that is the topic of the Stoic and Epicurean accounts of the relation between virtue and happiness to which he wishes to present an alternative.

The fundamental logical difference between his alternative and their accounts is that whereas in the latter virtue and happiness are connected analytically, by identity, in his they are connected synthetically, via a moral-theological postulate. For the Epicurean, virtue is consciousness that the maxim of one's action leads to personal happiness; for him virtue is prudence. For the Stoic, consciousness of one's virtue is happiness. Since both the Epicurean and the Stoic define happiness as consciousness, neither their notion of virtue nor their notion of happiness can be a part of what Levinas means by the ethical. Nor can happiness when this is defined as consciousness of pleasure by Kant, who writes:

> The moral disposition is necessarily connected with a consciousness of the determination of the will directly by a law. Now the consciousness of a determination of the faculty of desire is always a ground for satisfaction in the resulting action; but this pleasure, this satisfaction with one's self, is not the determining ground of the action; on the contrary, the determination of the will directly by reason alone is the ground of the feeling of pleasure, and this remains a pure practical determination of the faculty of desire, not a sensuous one.[7]

Kant goes on to describe what he calls the illusion that the determination or motive to morality is sensuous. But in this passage he does say that in both sensuously determined action and in intellectually determined action consciousness of the achievement of the desired end is satisfaction with one's self, and a pleasure. He goes on further to distinguish sensuous pleasure (*Lust*) and bliss (*Glückseligkeit*) from intellectual contentment or satisfaction (*Zufriedenheit*). This last is not some special sensible feeling ("'intellectual feeling' being a contradiction in terms"). Nor, however, can it be respect (*Achtung*) for the moral law, since that is the moral action's motive, not a state of mind consequent upon the thought that one has acted from that motive. That state of mind cannot be the end at which action performed out of respect aims. If it were, ethics would not be autonomous, as Kant insists that it is. It would be heteronomous, as Levinas insists that it is, though his rational heteronomy is not the heteronomy of natural sensibility that is opposed to the autonomy of reason by Kant. In these paragraphs of the *Critique of Practical Reason*, Kant blurs the distinction between the motive of respect and the state of mind consequent upon reflection that one has acted out of respect. But he is quite clear that self-satisfaction (*Selbstzufriedenheit*) is the best word to distinguish the satisfaction (*Wohlgefallen*) with one's existence supervenient upon this reflection from the sensuous or supersensuous gratification or enjoyment (*Genuss*) indicated by the word "bliss" (*Glückseligkeit*).

No more than the *summum bonum* as described by the Epicurean, the Stoic, or Kant, can either of these forms of satisfaction be any part of that anarchic moment of the ethical which Levinas calls the face to face. This cannot be construed as or as involving any kind of satisfaction. It is the subversion of all doctrines of ethics founded upon satisfaction or contentment, however noble and Stoically heroic the virtue that gives satisfaction may be. Consciousness of one's virtue is irrelevant because both consciousness and virtue are irrelevant, they being terms from the vocabulary with which human nature and its dispositions or capacities are described. The ethics of the other human being is not an ethics of human nature, not even of natural benevolence or of the rationality that differentiates the nature of the human from the nature of the animal according to Kant, Aristotle, and so on. The rationality of absolute responsibility as described by Levinas is more like Aristotelian *nous*, which comes into the understanding from outside. But this coming into the understanding from outside is difficult to understand; it is an aporia, because, like and unlike Hegelian reason, it is bound to slip through the fingers of the understanding that tries to grasp it. It deconstitutes the constitutive understanding, because it calls into question the classical distinction between inside and outside. It's coming in is the "Come" of a welcome of the other where this second "of" is both "subjective" and "objective," and where the welcome in both directions is at the same time a threat to the other, a threat-promise, as observed in remarks of Derrida referred to above.

Levinas's doctrine of the ethical is relentlessly and restlessly austere. But what about the "austere happiness" we referred to at the end of the discussion of the question "What is orientation in thinking?" Catherine Chalier cites from Psalms 1: "Blessed is the man that walketh not in the counsel of the ungodly. . . . his delight is in the law of the Lord"; and from *Zohar* 243a: "Happy is the lot of him who devotes himself to the Torah fittingly, happy in this world and in the world to come."[8] She explains that to study the Torah "fittingly" is not to adhere slavishly to what it most apparently says, but to interpret it in ways that renew and enrich, taking those who receive it along paths hitherto untrodden by them. (Note 38 of chapter 5 records her point that *ashrei,* meaning happy, is cognate with *asher,* meaning to walk.) She paraphrases the further sentences of Zohar which say that when fittingly interpreted the words please God and God regards with pleasure the godly who interpret them in this way. "This divine happiness and regard constitute the highest recompense of a human life."

Risks are run in making these citations, the same as are threatened in my own citation of Isaiah earlier in this chapter, and in Catherine Chalier's appeal earlier in her book to the "permanent *saying* of the Bible," "*dire* permanent de la Bible."[9] Of course, what for me may seem threatened risks—*Mes chances,* to cite the title of an essay by Derrida—may for others seem promises and welcome opportunities. Or, as we have seen, for me and for others they may be both promises and threats. For me and Catherine Chalier and Jacques Derrida and Emmanuel Levinas and others. The risk is identified by Levinas as that of citing confessional texts as though they were premises in an argument that purports to be philosophical. He says "I would never, for example, introduce a Talmudic or biblical verse into one of my philosophical texts, to try to prove or justify a philosophical argument."[10] He would never because he could never, not unless "introduce . . . into" is allowed the complexity we earlier remarked in the Come and the coming, partially constatative and partially performative, of the Reason that comes in from outside like a God, as Aristotle says, and as Levinas says after him. The word "God," extraordinary in the ordinary language of every day, is repeated more and more frequently in what Levinas describes as his "Greek" philosophical texts. It represents there what cannot be represented there. It is introduced only in the way that one person may be introduced to another, presented but remaining as separate as the ego enjoying its existence "atheistically." For for all I know, there may have been no one there when I thought I heard someone approaching and knocking at my door, asking to come in from outside. But it is precisely what I cannot know or be conscious of or want or will that is traced non-theologically in "God," "illeity," and the words cited in the philosophical texts from the confessional scriptures. Moreover, since the *saying* of the other human being is the inspiration of the "*saying* of the Bible," there is a sense in which the latter inspires what I can know, be conscious of, want, or freely will or indeed desire, whether that be enjoyment or the wisdom of which philosophy is the love. That love of wisdom, that desire, freedom, and knowledge or wisdom is invested in the wisdom of a love which is unpossessive, as according to Levinas erotic love already is.

If the sayings most densely cited and interpreted in Levinas's Talmudic readings are the expression of the "experience" without context or horizon of the other human being, they are not out of place in the philosophical texts, no more or less out of place there and untimely than the "out of joint" time of saying as such (SM 42ff., 101, 122, 243, 276, SM tr. 18ff., 58, 72, 149, 174). Where those sayings have the syntax of such pronouncements as "Happy is the lot of him who devotes himself to the Torah" and "Blessed is the man that walketh not in the counsel of the ungodly," they appear to be spoken from the point of view of God, third-person illeity or *sub specie aeternitatis,* points of view assumed in the *Science of Logic* of Hegel and in the *Ethics* of Spinoza. Still, their meaning springs from the daily occurrence of a you facing a me. Hence when Levinas writes immediately before the section of *Totality and Infinity* he entitles "Conclusions," maybe in recollection of Kierkegaard's *Concluding Unscientific Postscript,* that a certain problem concerning eternity "exceeds (*déborde*) the framework of this book," it is not perhaps the book, but the framework of the book, its *Gestell,* its structure, that cannot contain the problem, as an idea cannot contain the idea of God but is overbrimmed by it. Derrida suggests that Levinas is here parodying the rhetoric of academic publications. (TEL 43, Ps 183, RRL 31, ED 191, WD 130). One could say also that the problem in question, the question in question, exceeds itself insofar as questions that expect answers, as even some philosophical ones do, are put by questioners with infinite answerability (ED 117–18, WD 79–80).

As . . . as . . . as. Catherine Chalier writes that when in a purportedly philosophical text Levinas seeks to describe the force of the third person pronoun *Il,* he makes a comparison, a *comme-paraison,* it might be said, in which someone is summoned to appear, to *com(me)paraître,* face a charge. He says "as in Chapter 13 of Exodus," where it is written that "God spake to Moses face to face."[11] Levinas, she says, is not here using the word *comme* to draw an analogy. He is using it to say that, as in Exodus the word of God is expressed through the mouth of the prophet Moses, so too the trace of *Il* breaks through the morphemes uttered by the human being, exceeds them. As Derrida writes of the face, "The face is neither the face of God nor the figure of man: it is their resemblance. A resemblance which, however, we must think before, or without, the assistance of the Same" (ED 161, WD 109). As Levinas himself writes, what surfaces in the face, as tangential as a caress, is the as as such, the *comme tel,* the in-itselfness of the human being that is otherwise than being and beyond the essence which Greek calls *kath' auto.*

What is the problem of which Levinas writes that "it exceeds the framework of this book"? It is a problem concerning eternity, infinity, and time. So it is a problem that exceeds his book at least in the sense that it arises in books written by others, for instance the aforementioned Kierkegaard,

Hegel, and Spinoza, and Kant, of whom Levinas writes in a later book of his own that in the fourth antinomy of the *Critique of Pure Reason* he shows that "The *otherwise than being* cannot be situated in any eternal order extracted from time that would somehow command the temporal series" (AE 10, OB 9). Not commanding time, eternity nonetheless triumphs, but as the triumph *of* time both over history and the judgment of history that would forget the so-called "subjectivity" of the singular human being and over the "tedium, fruit of the mournful incuriosity that takes on the proportions of immortality,"[12] that is to say, over the fake eternity of a continuous, perpetual time in which the isolated heroic ego seeks salvation for itself (TeI 284, TaI 307). Eschatology, the day of judgment, conceived otherwise than as the revealed opinion of dogmatic religions (TeI XII, TaI 23), is the judgment of every resurrected moment in time that leaves an opening for truth even after my death. Across death I am affiliated with generations to whom my words and deeds remain infinitely open to judgment that defeats the judgment of fate, history, and the state. This eschatology is without end. In particular it is without the happy teleological end of Christianity and the Kantian highest good. And, if, as Levinas says, eschatology has to be distinguished from the revealed opinion of dogmatic religions, it has to be distinguished from "the world to come" of *Zohar* 243a, unless this is not interpreted as a revelation of a dogmatic religion, but as the expression of a *religio* that is not a revealed *doxa* or *epistêmê* about a world that transcends human experience and time, but is the expression of the experience of being bound to the other human being which is the pre-original source of time.

There is no happy ending, then, because, unlike Heideggerian Dasein, who exists endingly, for the Levinasian human being there is no ending. This does not mean that there is no happiness. Levinas goes as far as to say that "The dream of a happy eternity, which subsists in man alongside his happiness, is not a simple aberration" (TeI 261, TaI 284). The happiness alongside which this dream of a happy eternity subsists is the happiness of the self as isolated ego or with other egos enjoying the fruits of the earth, culture, and civilization in his place in the sun. It is the happiness without which he has nothing to sacrifice and therefore that which it is ethically impossible for him to be without: at the very least the happiness of the enjoyment of the place in the sun which may be the thing he is called to sacrifice at the very last without the expectation of gratitude or grace. This does not mean that the good things of life are good only as means to achieving the good of another. On the contrary, insofar as my free indulgence in enjoyment of them is to be invested in service to my neighbor, they must be goods which I continue to enjoy for themselves. This is why Levinas employs the image, knowing well how distasteful readers may find it, of giving to the other the bread (I do not say wafer) that is already in my mouth. The bread that is enjoyed for itself is also the staff of life, mine and yours, and the activities and experiences of higher civilization, while valued for themselves, are in addition to be cultivated by the individual as Kant says for the ethical reason that the individual is thereby enabled to be of greatest assistance to others.

So much for the happiness along with which Levinas says that the dream of a happy eternity subsists. What about this dream, the dream of which Levinas says that it is not an aberration? If it is a dream, what is dreamt of may be a figment. We have already observed that insofar as it is not either a figment or irrelevant to Levinas's doctrine of ethically metaphysical religion, the happiness of the happy eternity is not that of the Kantian *summum bonum* or Christian immortality. More positively, the relevant eternity here referred to is not outside time. Whether or not it is a new structure of time is part of the question of which Levinas says that it exceeds the framework of his book *Totality and Infinity*. But it is a time. Messianic time, he calls it, a time that is completed, *achevé*. What does this mean? This completion of time, he says, is not death. It is time's being sealed by truth. Truth, he says, requires both an infinite time and a sealed time. Why this is so begins to become clear only if it is understood that the truth of which Levinas is here speaking is not that cognate with theoretical or speculative opinion or knowledge, *epistêmê*, nor the opening, *Lichtung*, which according to Heideggerian phenomenological ontology is the primordial truth presupposed by that truth of coherence, correspondence, and adequacy; it is the still more originary anarchic truth of respondence whose synonyms are veracity, sincerity, respect, and justice where one person is faced by another to whom he is forever inadequate. For this truth of troth before contract there must be both infinite time and completed time. Infinite time is necessary to this truth because it is the time of fecundity heralded by the time of erotic desire for what exceeds possibility beyond the face, beyond my death, and so beyond the happiness of my enjoyment of the fruits of nature and culture. Without this truth there would be only either the universal truth of the state and historical fate, the *fatum* that silences the *fari* (*for*) of prophetic speaking for the other singular human being, or the truth based on the subject's freedom of will, his *vouloir dire,* which, because it is based only on the subject's freedom of will, is, and Hegel would agree, arbitrarily willful. Why, as well as infinite time, is completed time required by this truth, by truth as justice, by, that is to say, the truth of the third party in the contextless context of the other's face? Completed time is required because completion here means the supplement of the seal—of the signature then, of apposition. But, as Derrida writes, "It is always necessary that the other sign and it is always the other that signs last. In other words, first" (FL 1036, 1037). Ultimately and initially, the other beyond my death and the other beyond the death of the other. This is why in the happy (*ashrei*) contact at the heart of the chiasmus of Jacques Derrida and Emmanuel Levinas, the paths along which each of them walks (*asher*) are, like the midrashic imagination and the multiplication of our interpretations of their works, without end.

POLITICS AFTER

The paths along which Derrida and Levinas walk cross only because they diverge. They diverge too from the path followed by Kant. But the difference of orientation is difficult to distinguish. We have remarked in this book (chapter 12) on the journey Levinas makes from the distinction made in the *Phaedrus* (the "common root" on which draw so many of the leaves of Levinas's and Derrida's writings) between speaking and writing, where the former is given priority over the latter, to a readiness to give priority over them both to what sounds or reads like "a certain rehabilitation of writing" when in the last sentence of *Otherwise than Being* he refers to the trace as an "unpronounceable writing," as though in response to Derrida's question in "Violence and Metaphysics" "Is not the 'He' whom transcendence and generous absence uniquely announce in the trace more readily the author of writing than of speech?" (ED 151, WD 102). We have also noted in this book (chapter 4) how when Derrida responds to Levinas he betrays an awareness that he is often not using precisely the same words as the latter. After all, how could he hand back the same? In order to be faithful to Levinas's teaching he must betray it. However much, as reader of Levinas, Derrida is indebted to him, a discontinuity marks any "family resemblance" between them due to the "fecundity in general" (TeI 283, TaI 306) of the relationship of non-biological filiation here. That is how it is with any relationship between teacher and pupil, which, because it is non-biological, has nothing to do with relative age. That is how it is with biological fecundity and filiation. Paternity and sonship, biological or theological or otherwise, disrupt the one-ship taught by Father Parmenides.

One such place at which in discussing Levinas Derrida advises his reader that he is bending his words is the later part of "The word of welcome" where that word is turned in the direction of that great city, holy Jerusalem, the eternal city, the house of peace, wherever that may be. Locating what he says as "between Kant and Lévinas," he is continuing there discontinuously the discussion toward the end of *Specters of Marx* of what he calls "messianicity in general" to denote a structure of experience, rather than messianism as a belief of a particular religion (SM 266, SM tr. 167–68, Ad 121). It is also not a particular religion but what we might call religion in general that Levinas is discussing when in the last pages of *Totality and Infinity* he picks up again the references to messianic peace made in the first pages of his preface. The biological family is but a synecdoche for the family, for which the state may reserve a framework which the family overflows (TeI 283, TaI 306). Similarly, "religion" is the word that dogmatic, revealed religions borrow from where it is uncannily at home, *heimlich-unheimlich*, at the threshold between hospitality and hostility where I am not equal to the stranger, the asylum-seeker and the Romany (SM 267ff. SM tr. 168ff., Ad 105–106, 192–93, Ap 120, Ap tr. 67). The inequality of hospitality is necessary if rights are not to silence justice in the political state in which the recognition of equality secures general happiness.

From this question of happiness within a political state, whether in history or at the end of history, we are obliged to return to a question regarding happiness that we left in the air, the question of the happiness of eternity the dream of which, Levinas tells us, is not a simple aberration. It is not an aberration when the happiness dreamt of is not peace of mind or contentment (*Zufriedenheit*) nor peace understood politically, but, in the words of "Politics after!" the peace that "exceeds (*déborde*) purely political thinking" (ADV 228, BV 195). This is not the peace achieved by treaties that end wars, for they remain based on the idea of empires and nations and individuals in self-centered warlike competition. The *pax* achieved by such pacts is one of enlightened self-interest. Even if political peace is brought into harmony with morality by being founded on the transcendent idea of right, as Kant argues in the second part of "Zum ewigen Frieden," that morality of right and equality calls to be tied somehow to a justice anarchically inspired by the initial inequality in the triangulation of the first, second, and third persons singular.

In the triangulation produced by his writing, as he says, "between Kant and Lévinas" (Ad 175), Derrida alludes to the little joke Kant enjoys when he gives his essay a title that could be and indeed has been the name of an inn near a cemetery, a *Friedhof,* namely "At the Sign of Eternal Peace." Staying with Kant, we have just reminded ourselves that his word for contentment is *Zufriedenheit.* So the happiness of the eternity of the dream which Levinas says is not a simple—nor a complicated—aberration, is the peace (*Friede*) of the pure triumph of messianism. This triumph is pure because, unlike the infinite time of fecundity which remains exposed to the threat of the triumph of totality, of "politique d'abord," messianism is extreme vigilance. The happiness of its eternity, therefore, cannot be Kant's contentment (*Zufriedenheit*), much less his self-contentment (*Selbstzufriedenheit*) and pleasurable satisfaction (*Wohlgefallen*—or, to return to the inn, *Zum Wohlgefallen*) with one's existence that he says is supervenient upon the thought that one has acted from respect for the moral law. Messianic peace is a difficult peace, the dream of which is not a simple aberration. But it is complicated by being neither peace of mind, a state of consciousness, nor a state of unconsciousness, sleep, but rather eternally vigilant insomnia. This complication is reflected in the question stating the problem which Levinas says exceeds the framework of the book *Totality and Infinity:* "Is this eternity a new structure of time, or an extreme vigilance of the messianic consciousness?" Insofar as this question asks about structure and consciousness, it should be possible to answer it within the framework of a philosophical, "Greek," book. Insofar as, at the same time, it is unanswerable unless it invokes and is invoked by answerability as responsibility, the question overflows its own frame. It is framed, structured, and destructured by being posed and deposed in the contact at the heart of the chiasmus between the author and the reader, be they those whose apposed names are Emmanuel Levinas and Jacques Derrida.

NOTES

INTRODUCTION

1. Edmund Husserl, *Ideen zu einer reinen Phänomenologie und phänomenologischen Philosophie*, vol. 1, Husserliana 3, ed. Walter Biemel (The Hague: Nijhoff, 1950); *Ideas*, trans. W. R. Boyce Gibson (London: Allen and Unwin, 1931), §117.

2. Martial Gueroult, *Descartes selon l'ordre des raisons* (Paris: Aubier, 1953), vol. 1, p. 229.

3. Ibid., p. 224.

4. The translation erroneously has "with."

5. Jean-Paul Sartre, *L'être et le néant* (Paris: Gallimard, 1943), pp. 125–26, 135–36; *Being and Nothingness*, trans. Hazel Barnes (London: Methuen, 1969), pp. 83, 92.

6. Ibid., pp. 24f, 31–32, pp. xxxivf, xl–xli.

7. See also Levinas, EeI 45f.; EaI 47f.

8. Sartre, *L'être et le néant*, pp. 315–18; *Being and Nothingness*, pp. 257–60.

9. Husserl, *Ideas*, §24; Jacques Derrida, VP, SP.

10. Husserl, *Ideas*, §117.

11. Cited at ED 226, WD 152.

12. Other examples are cited at ED 208, WD 141.

13. Maurice Merleau-Ponty, *Phénoménologie de la perception* (Paris: Gallimard, 1945), p. VIII; *Phenomenology of Perception*, trans. Colin Smith (London: Routledge and Kegan Paul, 1962), p. xiv.

1. RESPONSIBILITY WITH INDECIDABILITY

1. John P. Leavey, Jr., *GLASsary* (Lincoln and London: University of Nebraska Press, 1986), pp. 17–18.

2. Tom Stoppard, *The Dog It Was That Died and Other Plays* (London and Boston: Faber and Faber, 1983), p. 44. Read on. The plot thickens.

3. F. P. Ramsey, *The Foundations of Mathematics* (London: Kegan Paul, Trench, Trubner and Co., 1931), p. 20.

4. John Austin, *How to Do Things with Words,* ed. J. O. Urmson (Oxford: Clarendon Press, 1962), p. 67.

5. Ibid., p. 68.

6. Jean-Luc Marion, *Dieu sans l'être* (Paris: Communio/Fayard, 1982).

7. Jean-Luc Marion, *L'idole et la distance* (Paris: Grasset, 1977), pp. 290–93.

8. Ibid., p. 294.

9. Ibid., pp. 318–19.

10. Martin Heidegger, *Die Grundbegriffe der Metaphysik—Welt—Endlichkeit—Einsamkeit* (Frankfurt am Main: Klostermann, 1992); *The Fundamental Concepts of Metaphysics: World, Finitude, Solitude,* trans. William McNeill and Nicholas Walker (Bloomington: Indiana University Press, 1995).

11. Victor Farias, *Heidegger et le nazisme* (Lagrasse: Verdier, 1987). See also Hugo Ott, *Martin Heidegger: Unterwegs zu seiner Biographie* (Frankfurt am Main and New York: Campus Verlag, 1988).

12. Philippe Lacoue-Labarthe and Jean-Luc Nancy, eds., *Les fins de l'homme à partir du travail de Jacques Derrida* (Paris: Editions Galilée, 1981), p. 476.

13. Ibid., pp. 476–77.

14. Austin, *How to Do Things with Words,* pp. 74, 76.

15. Jacques Derrida, "Like the Sound of the Sea Deep Within a Shell: Paul de Man's War," trans. Peggy Kamuf, *Critical Inquiry,* 14 (1988), 639.

16. For amplification of what is said here on responsibility, classification, schematism, and critique, see Jacques Derrida, "The Politics of Friendship," *Journal of Philosophy* 85 (1988), 632–48; *Politiques de l'amitié* (Paris: Galilée, 1994); *Force de loi: le fondement mystique de l'autorité* (Paris: Galilée, 1994); "Force of Law: The 'Mystical Foundation of Authority,'" trans. Mary Quaintance, in *Deconstruction and the Possibility of Justice* (New York: Cardozo Law Review, 1990).

For special assistance in the preparation of this chapter I am grateful to Howard Llewelyn, Howell Oakley, David Wood, and the late Nelly Demé.

2. DERRIDA, MALLARMÉ, AND ANATOLE

1. Jacques Derrida, "Mallarmé," in *Tableau de la littérature francaise: De Madame de Staël à Rimbaud* (Paris: Gallimard, 1974), pp. 368–79.

2. Friedrich Nietzsche, *The Will to Power,* trans. Walter Kaufmann and R. J. Hollingdale (London: Weidenfeld & Nicolson, 1967), pp. 371–72.

3. On these questions of pleasure and/or pain, life and/or death, see Derrida, *La carte postale de Socrate à Freud et au-delà.*

4. Gilles Deleuze, *Nietzsche et la philosophie* (Paris: Presses Universitaires de France, 1962), p. 213.

5. See "Ja, ou le faux-bond," p. 111: "Il faut qu'au-delà de l'infatigable contradiction du *double bind,* une différence affirmative, innocente, intacte, gaie, en vienne *bien* à fausser compagnie, échappe d'un saut et vienne signer en riant ce qu'elle laisse faire et défiler en double bande. Lui faisant d'un coup faux-bond, ne s'expliquant soudain plus avec la double bande. C'est ce que j'aime, ce faux-bond, celui-ci (à ne pas confondre avec les rendez-vous manqués, ni avec aucune logique du rendez-vous), tout ce que j'aime, c'est l'instant du '*ungeheure unbegrenzte Ja,*' du 'oui prodigieux et sans limite' qui vient à la fin de *Glas* (système de la D.B.), du 'oui qui nous est commun' et depuis lequel 'nous nous taisons, nous nous sourions notre savoir,' dit Zarathoustra."

6. Translations are my own unless stated otherwise.

7. Henri Cazalis (Jean Lahor), *Melancholia* (Paris: Alphonse Lemerre, 1868). The poem entitled *La voie lactée* contains a line which in this edition runs: "Ils vont par l'infini faire des cieux nouveaux." Mallarmé has "Ils vont par l'Infini faire des lieux nouveaux." See Stéphane Mallarmé, *Correspondance 1862–1871* (Paris: Gallimard, 1959), p. 273. Of this line Mallarmé writes to Eugène Lefébure that it is "Un bien beau vers, et qui fut toute ma vie depuis que je suis mort." With reference to the question asked by Ruben Berezdivin mentioned above, it may be noted now that one of Mallarmé's favorite words is *ennui* and that the first entry for that word given by Littré (1863) begins: "Tourment de l'âme causé par la mort de personnes aimées. . . ."

8. Nietzsche, *Ecce Homo,* in *On the Genealogy of Morals* and *Ecce Homo,* trans. Walter Kaufmann and R. J. Hollingdale (New York: Knopf and Random House, 1969), p. 221.

9. Robert Greer Cohn, *L'oeuvre de Mallarmé: Un Coup de dés* (Paris: Librairie des Lettres, 1951), p. 422, citing *L'amitié de Stéphane Mallarmé et de Georges Rodenbach* (Geneva: Pierre Cailler, 1949), p. 120.

10. Stéphane Mallarmé, *Oeuvres complètes* (Paris: Gallimard, 1945), p. 379: in the section "Le Livre, Instrument Spirituel" of *Quant au Livre.*

11. Mallarmé, *Pour un Tombeau d'Anatole* (Paris: Seuil, 1961), leaflet 128.

12. Ibid., leaflet 14.

13. Ibid., leaflets 15 and 79.

14. Ibid., p. 65.

15. Ibid., leaflet 130.

16. Ibid., leaflet 77.

17. Henri Mondor, *Vie de Mallarmé* (Paris: Gallimard, 1941), p. 801.

18. Mallarmé, *Pour un Tombeau d'Anatole,* leaflet 117.

19. Mallarmé, *Oeuvres complètes,* p. 664

20. Mallarmé, *Mimique, Oeuvres complètes,* p. 310.

21. Jacques Scherer, *Le "Livre" de Mallarmé* (Paris: Gallimard, 1957), leaflet 93(A). Derrida, *La dissémination,* p. 255, *Dissemination,* p. 226. "Each session of play being a game, a fragmentary show, but sufficient at that unto itself . . . "

22. Scherer, ibid., leaflet 191 (A).

23. Mallarmé, *Oeuvres complètes,* p. 378.

24. Jean Hyppolite, "Le coup de dés de Mallarmé et le message," *Les études philosophiques* 13 (1958), 463–68.

25. As I forgot until reminded by Geoff Bennington. I thank him and all the other participants in the workshop on Philosophers, Writers, and Poets held in July 1985 at the University of Warwick, where a version of this paper was first read, and Stephen Houlgate for spotting the unintended malapropisms.

26. Mallarmé, *Oeuvres complètes,* p. 663. Emphasis added.

27. Ibid., p. 684. Mallarmé's emphasis.

28. Mallarmé, *Correspondance 1862–1871,* p. 208. Letter to Cazalis of the end of April 1866.

29. Mallarmé, *Oeuvres complètes,* p. 663.

30. Letter of February 1889 to Odilon Redon cited at Cohn, *L'oeuvre de Mallarmé,* p. 124, and Henri Mondor, *Vie de Mallarmé,* pp. 452–53. Cf. Mallarmé's "ce devait être très beau" in his "Recommandation quant à mes papiers," cited by Mondor at p. 801, and the following comment of Jean-Pierre Richard, *L'univers imaginaire de*

Mallarmé (Paris: Seuil, 1961), p. 437: "Tout l'oeuvre de Mallarmé doit ainsi se lire en même temps à l'indicatif et au conditionnel: il faut voir en elle comment cela *est* beau, mais aussi, pour reprendre la si juste parole testamentaire de Mallarmé, comment '*cela devait être très beau*'." A double reading.

31. Derrida, "Forcener le subjectile," *Le Matin,* 26 July 1985, p. 25, fragments of the preface of a collection of drawings and paintings by Artaud to be published by Gallimard in 1986. I am grateful to the late Nelly Demé for forwarding the cutting to me. Derrida, D 308, D tr. 276. Mallarmé, *Oeuvres complètes,* p. 901: "Les mots, dans le dictionnaire, gisent. . . ."

32. Nicolas Abraham (and Maria Torok), *L'écorce et le noyau* (Paris: Aubier-Flammarion, 1978), p. 236 of Maria Torok, "Maladie du deuil et fantasme du cadavre exquis," pp. 259–73 of Abraham and Torok, "Deuil ou mélancolie, Introjecter-incorporer."

33. Among these other sources, according to L.-J. Austin, may have been Edmond Scherer, "Hegel et l'hégélianisme," *Revue des deux mondes,* 15 February 1861, vol. 31, 812–56; "Mallarmé et le rêve du 'Livre'," *Mercure de France* 1073 (1 January 1953), 81–108, cited by Gardner Davies; *Vers une explication rationelle du Coup de dés* (Paris: Corti, 1953), p. 33.

34. Mallarmé, *Oeuvres complètes,* p. 657. "La Littérature, d'accord avec la faim, consiste à supprimer le Monsieur qui reste en l'écrivant, celui-ci que vient-il faire, au vue des siens, quotidiennement?" Cited by Philippe Sollers, "Littérature et totalité," in *Logiques* (Paris: Seuil, 1968), p. 116.

35. Mallarmé, *Oeuvres complètes,* p. 364.

36. Mallarmé, *Correspondance 1862–1871,* p. 242. Letter to Cazalis of 14 May 1867. Cf. p. 249, letter to Lefébure of 17 May 1867: ". . . me sentir un diamant qui réfléchit, mais qui n'est pas lui-même . . . "

37. Mallarmé, *Oeuvres completes, p.* 663.

38. Maurice Blanchot, *L'espace littéraire* (Paris: Gallimard, 1955), p. 136.

39. *Pace* Leo Bersani, *The Death of Stéphane Mallarmé* (Cambridge: Cambridge University Press, 1982), p. 63.

40. Julia Kristeva, "Poésie et négativité," in *Semeiotikè* (Paris: Seuil, 1969), p. 212. Robert Magliola, *Derrida on the Mend* (West Lafayette: Purdue University Press, 1984), p. 89 and other pages listed in the index under "*Sūnyāta.*"

41. Mallarmé, *Oeuvres complètes,* p. 439. In the first letter referred to in note 36 Mallarmé writes: "j'ai encore besoin, tant ont été grandes les avanies de mon triomphe, de me regarder dans cette glace pour penser et que si elle n'était pas devant la table où je t'écris cette lettre, je redeviendrais le Néant'."

42. Abraham (and Torok), "'L'objet perdu—moi.' Notations sur l'identification endocryptique," in Nicolas Abraham (and Maria Torok), *L'écorce et le noyau,* pp. 295–317.

43. Jacques Derrida, "Entre crochets," *Digraphe* 8 (1976), 108.

44. Ibid., 105, 107.

45. Derrida, "La pharmacie de Platon," in *La dissémination.*

46. Abraham (and Torok), *L'écorce et le noyau,* p. 259.

47. See note 32.

48. Mallarmé, *Oeuvres complètes,* p. 373.

49. A. R. Chisholm, *Mallarmé's Grand Oeuvre* (Manchester: Manchester University Press, 1962), p. 130.

50. Mallarmé, *Oeuvres complètes, p.* 1580.

51. Ibid., p. 364. Cf. Mallarmé, *Correspondance 1862–1871*, p. 154, Letter to Lefébure of February 1865: "Le peu d'inspiration que j'ai eu, je le dois à ce nom, et je crois que si mon héroïne s'était appelée Salomé, j'eusse inventé ce mot sombre, et rouge comme une grenade ouverte, Hérodiade."

52. Ibid., p. 953.

53. Ibid., p. 948.

54. Ibid., p. 855.

55. Derrida, "Entre crochets," p. 105.

56. Mallarmé, *Oeuvres complètes*, pp. 399–400.

57. Derrida, "Mallarmé," p. 371.

58. Mallarmé, *Oeuvres complètes*, p. 857. On p. 56 (*Prose pour des Esseintes*) *iridées* rhymes with *Idées*.

59. Scherer, *Le "Livre" de Mallarmé*, leaflet 2.

60. Mallarmé, *Oeuvres complètes*, p. 69: *Sonnet* (*Pour votre chère morte, son ami*).

61. Mallarmé, *Oeuvres complètes*, p. 296.

3. THE ORIGIN AND END OF PHILOSOPHY

1. Martin Heidegger, "Building Dwelling Thinking," in *Martin Heidegger: Basic Writings*, ed. D. F. Krell (London: Routledge & Kegan Paul, 1978), pp. 323–39.

2. Paul Valéry, *Cahiers*, 29 vols. (Paris: Centre National de Recherche Scientifique, 1957–61); *Oeuvres*, vols. I and II (Paris: Gallimard, 1957). These publications are referred to in the text as C and O.

3. Sir Arthur Eddington, *The Nature of the Physical World* (the Gifford Lectures given at the University of Edinburgh in 1927) (London: Dent, 1935), p. 6.

4. L. Susan Stebbing, *Philosophy and the Physicists* (London: Penguin Books, 1944), pp. 49–50. All quotations are from her chapter 3.

5. Sir Isaac Newton, *Opticks*, 4th ed. reprinted (London: Bell & Sons, 1931), bk. I, pt. II, pp. 124–25, cited at Stebbing, p. 54.

6. Compare Eddington, pp. 8–9: "It is true that the whole scientific inquiry starts from the familiar world and in the end it must return to the familiar world; but the part of the journey over which the physicist has charge is in foreign territory. Until recently there was a much closer linkage; the physicist used to borrow the raw material of his world from the familiar world, but he does so no longer. His raw materials are aether, electrons, quanta, potentials, Hamiltonian functions, etc., and he is nowadays scrupulously careful to guard these from contamination by conceptions borrowed from the other world."

4. IN THE NAME OF PHILOSOPHY

1. *De generatione animalium* 736b28 and *De anima* 430a10. At 1248a 25 of the *Eudemian Ethics*. Aristotle draws an analogy between *nous* and the divine first mover.

2. "Our own project is much indebted to him." Emmanuel Levinas, "Énigme et phénomène," in *En découvrant l'existence avec Husserl et Heidegger* (Paris: Vrin, 1982), p. 206n; "Phenomenon and Enigma," in *Collected Philosophical Papers*, trans. Alphonso Lingis (The Hague: Nijhoff, 1987), p. 63n.

3. Vladimir Jankélévitch, *La philosophie première. Introduction à une philosophie du "presque"* (Paris: Presses Universitaires de France, 1954), p. 54.

4. See also Adriaan T. Peperzak, Simon Critchley, and Robert Bernasconi, eds., *Emmanuel Levinas: Basic Philosophical Writings* (Bloomington: Indiana University Press, 1996), p. 188: "'A fine risk' (*le beau risque*) alludes to Socrates's phrase 'Kalos

gar ho kindunos' ['for the venture is well worth while (noble, glorious, fair, just)'] in Plato's *Phaedo* 114d." See further Paul Davies "A fine risk: Reading Blanchot Reading Levinas," in Robert Bernasconi and Simon Critchley, eds., *Re-Reading Levinas* (Bloomington: Indiana University Press, 1991), pp. 201–36.

5. Vladimir Jankélévitch, *Le je-ne-sais-quoi et le presque-rien* (Paris: Seuil, 1981), vol. 1, p. 71.

6. Richard Kearney, ed., *Dialogues with Contemporary Continental Thinkers: The Phenomenological Heritage* (Manchester: Manchester University Press, 1984), p. 64. In substituting "for love of" for "for the sake of" I am following the French version of this dialogue published in *Esprit* 234, July 1997.

7. Jacques Derrida, *Adieu à Emmanuel Lévinas* (Paris: Galilée, 1997), pp. 61, 66, 110. (On this last page the word is written thus: "illéité," between inverted commas.) It may not be irrelevant that a French accent is given to the name of the person to whom in bidding him good-bye this book—a book in which one of the questions treated is that of political and national hospitality—also offers the word of welcome. Whether responsibility for the variation should be attributed to Derrida or his publishers or both, the accent is not given in most of Derrida's earlier uses of the name. In "Donner la mort" it is sometimes given, sometimes not. Jacques Derrida, "Donner la mort," in Jean-Michel Rabaté and Michael Wetzel, eds., *L'éthique du don. Jacques Derrida et la pensée du don*, Colloque de Royaumont, December 1990 (Paris: Métailé-Transition, 1992); *The Gift of Death*, trans. David Wills (Chicago: University of Chicago Press, 1995). In both cases a crossing of frontiers is at stake.

8. Ibid., pp. 54, 66, 67, 68, 91, 118, 119.

9. Emmanuel Levinas, "Aimer la Torah plus que Dieu," in *Difficile liberté: essais sur le judaïsme* (Paris: Albin Michel, 1976); "Loving the Torah More Than God," in *Difficult Freedom: Essays on Judaism,* trans. Seán Hand (Baltimore: Johns Hopkins University Press, 1990).

10. Marie-Anne Lescourret, *Emmanuel Levinas* (Paris: Flammarion, 1984), pp. 217–18.

11. P. Hadot, *Plotin ou la simplicité du regard* (Paris: Études augustiniennes, 1963), p. 73.

12. Jankélévitch, *La philosophie première,* 176.

13. Ibid., 244.

14. For further developments see John Llewelyn, *The HypoCritical Imagination: Between Kant and Levinas* (London: Routledge, 2000).

15. Richard Kearney, ed., *Dialogues with Contemporary Continental Thinkers,* p. 56.

16. I am grateful to Adriaan Peperzak for pointing out the allusion to Claudel. See Paul Claudel, *L'œil écoute,* in *Oeuvres en prose* (Paris: Gallimard, 1965), p. 176.

17. Emmanuel Levinas, "La conscience non intentionnelle," in Catherine Chalier and Miguel Abensour, eds., *Emmanuel Levinas* (Paris: L'Herne, 1991), p. 118.

18. Jankélévitch, *La philosophie première,* pp. 172, 254, 260, 264. Emmanuel Levinas, "Dieu et la philosophie," in *De Dieu qui vient à l'idée* (Paris: Vrin, 1982), p. 127; "God and Philosophy," trans. Alphonso Lingis and Richard Cohen, revised, in *Basic Philosophical Writings,* ed. Adriaan T. Peperzak, Simon Critchley, and Robert Bernasconi (Bloomington: Indiana University Press, 1996), 148. Winking and diachrony are here attributed to what Levinas calls the enigma, a term used technically in *Charmides* 161a–162b, *Apology* 27a, *Theaetetus* 152c, *Republic* 332b, 479c. See Jean-Michel Charrue, *Plotin lecteur de Platon* (Paris: Société d'édition Les Belles Lettres, 1978), p. 25, citing A. Eon, "La notion plotinienne d'exégèse," *Rev Int de Phil,* 24, 1970, 274. Jankélévitch, *La philosophie première,* pp. 172, 254, 260, 264.

19. Compare Levinas, *Autrement qu'être*, p. 200, *Otherwise than Being*, p. 157: "The third party introduces a contradiction in the saying whose signification before the other until then went in one direction."

5. WHAT IS ORIENTATION IN THINKING?

1. Immanuel Kant, "What Is Orientation in Thinking?," in *The Critique of Practical Reason and other Writings in Moral Philosophy*, trans. Lewis White Beck (Chicago: University of Chicago Press, 1949), pp. 293–304, p. 294.

2. Emmanuel Levinas, *Entre nous: Essais sur le penser-à-l'autre* (Paris: Grasset, 1991), p. 125.

3. On Kant's caution and incaution see Lewis White Beck, *A Commentary on Kant's Critique of Practical Reason* (Chicago: University of Chicago Press, 1960), p. 166, note 10. The incaution is not an accident. It is, as Kant himself might have said, transcendental. It has a parallel in what Levinas says about the enigmatic ambiguity manifested in the oscillation between the trace and the sign. See "Énigme et phénomène," in Emmanuel Levinas, *En découvrant l'existence avec Husserl et Heidegger* (Paris: Vrin, 1967); "Enigma and Phenomenon," trans. Alphonso Lingis, revised by the editors, Adriaan T. Peperzak, Simon Critchley, and Robert Bernasconi, in *Emmanuel Levinas: Basic Philosophical Writings* (Bloomington: Indiana University Press, 1996).

4. Virginia Woolf, *The Second Common Reader* (New York: Harcourt Brace Jovanovich, 1932), pp. 56–58.

5. Daniel Defoe, *The Life & Strange Surprizing Adventures of Robinson Crusoe of York, Mariner* (Oxford: Blackwell, 1927), vol. I, pp. 1–2 (hereinafter *RC*).

6. See the interview with Michel Tournier in Lise Andries, ed., *Robinson* (Paris: Editions Autrement, 1996).

7. Ian Watt, *The Rise of the Novel: Studies in Defoe, Richardson, and Fielding* (Berkeley and Los Angeles: University of California Press, 1957), p. 63.

8. Maximillian E. Novak, *Economics and the Fiction of Daniel Defoe* (Berkeley: University of California Press, 1962), p. 49.

9. Bram Dijkstra, *Defoe and Economics: The Fortunes of Roxana in the History of Interpretation* (London: Macmillan, 1987), p. 166.

10. Novak, p. 44.

11. Watt, p. 37.

12. J. Paul Hunter, *The Reluctant Pilgrim: Defoe's Emblematic Method and the Quest for Form in "Robinson Crusoe"* (Baltimore: Johns Hopkins University Press, 1966), pp. 5–6, note 12.

13. Ibid., p. 14.

14. On the significance of Rochester for Defoe see John McVeagh, "Rochester and Defoe: A Study of Influence," *Studies in English Literature* 14 (1974), and Virginia Ogden Birdsall, *Defoe's Perpetual Seekers: A Study of the Major Fiction* (Lewisburg: Bucknell University Press, 1985).

15. *RC*, vol. I, p. 177.

16. Friedrich Nietzsche, *Thus Spoke Zarathustra*, in Walter Kaufmann, ed. and trans., *The Portable Nietzsche* (New York: Viking Press, 1968), Fourth Part, §10, p. 387.

17. Michael Seidel, *Exile and the Narrative Imagination* (New Haven: Yale University Press, 1986), pp. 35–36.

18. Emmanuel Levinas, *L'humanisme de l'autre homme* (Montpellier: Fata Morgana, 1972).

19. Seidel, *Exile and the Narrative Imagination*, p. 36.

20. *RC*, vol. I, p. 108.

21. Ibid., vol. I, p. 111.

22. Ibid. vol. II, pp. 30–31.

23. Immanuel Kant, *Groundwork of the Metaphysic of Morals*, trans. H. J. Paton, in *The Moral Law* (London: Hutchinson, 1956), p. 90.

24. *RC*, vol. I, p. 180.

25. Daniel Defoe, *A Collection of Miscellany Letters, Selected out of Mist's Weekly Journal*, The First Volume, London 1722, pp. 192ff., cited in Robert James Merrett, *Daniel Defoe's Moral and Rhetorical Ideas* (British Columbia: University of Victoria Press, 1980), pp. 25–29.

26. The phrase cited explains why traces of the middle voice are detected in the teaching of Levinas and not only in that of Heidegger according to John Llewelyn, *The Middle Voice of Ecological Conscience: A Chiasmic Reading of Responsibility in the Neighbourhood of Levinas, Heidegger and Others* (London: Macmillan; New York: St Martin's Press, 1991).

27. Immanuel Kant, "What Is Enlightenment?," pp. 286–92 in *The Critique of Practical Reason and other Writings in Moral Philosophy*, p. 290.

28. Immanuel Kant, *Critique of Pure Reason*, trans. Norman Kemp Smith (London: Macmillan, 1968), p. 9.

29. See John Llewelyn, *The HypoCritical Imagination: Between Kant and Levinas* (London: Routledge, 2000), chapter 7, "Levinas's Critical and HypoCritical Diction," *Philosophy Today* 41, Supplement (1997).

30. "Die Welt ist alles, was der Fall ist." Ludwig Wittgenstein, *Tractatus Logico-Philosophicus*, trans. D. F. Pears and B. F. McGuinness (London: Routledge & Kegan Paul, 1961), proposition 1.

31. At the same time as it requires the asymmetry of a me face to face with a you, ethical justice according to Levinas requires a "just economy" (Levinas, *Difficile liberté*, p. 36; *Difficult Freedom*, p. 20). Made concrete, earthed, applied to "terrestrial morals" (Levinas, *Entre nous*, p. 42), the blank check written out for ethical humanity in the Kantian idea of a kingdom of accountable ends demands to be "cashed" as economic humanity, "realized" as countable money, notwithstanding the power this would confer upon Israel to sell the righteous for silver (Amos 2:6) or upon Crusoe to sell his boy Xury for sixty pieces of eight, twenty fewer than he accepts for his boat. The injustice of an economy wherein people are bought and sold can be overcome, Levinas maintains, only by an economy of a higher kind, an economy of the totality of humankind; but this, however shocking it may seem, is still one which calls for the quantification of the human being. Without this quantification there is no justice, because there is not the possibility of injustice which is the misappropriation of what someone has "made," his or her money or product (ibid., pp. 42–43). Mutual respect is a relation among equals, but it is sham, according to Levinas, unless this equality is economic, translated into money. Granted that questions of justice may be irrelevant to someone "on a desert island, without humanity, without third parties," it may not be entirely fanciful to see an acknowledgment at least of the economic condition of society—if not of money as the condition of justice and exchange-value as the inevitable corollary of use-value—in the "Second Thoughts" Crusoe has at that delicate moment when he is not sure whether he will be alone on his island and records that on revisiting the wreck to collect whatever might come in handy, "I discover'd a Locker with Drawers in it, in one of which I found two or

three Razors, and one Pair of large Sizzers, with some ten or a Dozen of good Knives and Forks; in another I found about Thirty six Pounds value in Money, some European coin, some Brasil, some Pieces of Eight, some Gold, some Silver. I smil'd to myself at the Sight of the Money, O Drug! Said I aloud, what art thou good for, Thou art not worth to me, no not the taking off of the Ground, one of those Knives is worth all this Heap, I have no Manner of use for thee, e'en remain where thou art, and go to the Bottom as a Creature whose life is not worth saving. However, upon Second Thoughts, I took it away . . ." (*RC*, vol. 1, p. 64).

32. *RC*, vol. I, p. 111.

33. See also Levinas, *Difficile liberté*, pp. 39, 107; *Difficult Freedom*, pp. 22, 78: "The more just I am, the more severely I am judged." I thank Catherine Chalier, Rabbi René Gutman, Peter Hayman and Rabbi David Sedley for identifying the "Talmudic text" Levinas refers to as probably Yebamoth 121b and Bava Kamma 50a. The latter version reads: "R. Aha, however, said: Nevertheless . . . [thus bearing out what the Scripture says], 'And it shall be very tempestuous round about him,' which teaches that the Holy One, blessed be He, is particular with those round about Him even for matters as light as a single hair. R. Nehonia derived the same lesson from the verse, 'God is greatly to be feared in the assembly of the saints and to be had in reverence of all them that are about Him.'" See also Ps 50:3: "Our God shall come, and shall not keep silence: a fire shall devour before him, and it shall be very tempestuous round about him." As it was round about Robinson Crusoe.

34. Martin Heidegger, *Sein und Zeit* (Tübingen: Niemeyer, 1953), *Being and Time*, trans. John Macquarrie and Edward Robinson (Oxford: Blackwell, 1967), trans. Joan Stambaugh (Albany: State University of New York Press, 1996), pp. 281–99. My references are to the pages of *Sein und Zeit* and correspond to the references given in the margins of the English editions.

35. For accounts of the various forms see Vincent Hope, *Virtue by Consensus: The Moral Philosophy of Hutcheson, Hume, and Adam Smith* (Oxford: Clarendon Press, 1981), and John Mullen, *Sentiment and Sociability: The Language of Feeling in the Eighteenth Century* (Oxford: Clarendon Press, 1988), especially chapter 1.

36. Plato, *Timaeus*, 52. For the stimulus of many exchanges concerning the *Timaeus* I thank Charles Bigger.

37. For more on this see John Llewelyn, *The HypoCritical Imagination*.

38. For a sharply focused study of aspects of the relation of Levinas's thinking to that of Kant, see Catherine Chalier, *Pour une morale au-delà du savoir: Kant et Levinas* (Paris: Albin Michel, 1998), especially chapter VII on the topic of what Levinas refers to as austere but glorious *bonheur*. One of many thought-provoking observations she makes is that the Hebrew word for "happy," *ashrei*, suggests a stage on a journey, *asher* meaning to go, to go straight ahead. So, on this revised conception, happiness is to be always underway, *immer unterwegs* as Heidegger would say—not, however, in the same direction as he goes, not in the direction of the same, but in another direction, in another's direction.

39. This is connected with Levinas's argument for the non-possessive and open-ended nature of erotic desire. For that argument see especially the subsection of *Totality and Infinity* entitled "Phenomenology of Eros." For complications of that argument and further references, see John Llewelyn, *Emmanuel Levinas. The Genealogy of Ethics* (London: Routledge, 1995), pp. 98–99, 120–24. For a searching reflection upon the nature of the disquiet mentioned in this paragraph, see Catherine

Chalier, *De l'intranquillité de l'âme* (Paris: Payot, 1999). See too Michael Ignatieff, *The Needs of Strangers* (London: Vintage, 1944).

40. Immanuel Kant, *Religion within the Limits of Reason Alone,* trans. Theodore M. Greene and Hoyt H. Hudson (New York: Harper & Row, 1960).

41. And perhaps of another contemporary, Rabbi Eliyahu of Vilna, aspects of whose teachings re-emerge in Rabbi Hayyim of Volozhyn, *L'âme de la vie. Nefesh Hahayyim* (Paris: Verdier, 1986), a work on which Levinas draws. I thank Robert Bernasconi and Melvyn New for comments on an earlier version of this chapter and bibliographical information.

6. Amen

1. Franz Rosenzweig, *Der Stern der Erlösung,* 2nd ed. (Frankfurt am Main: Kauffmann, 1930), p. 477; *The Star of Redemption,* trans. William W. Hallo (Notre Dame, Ind.: University of Notre Dame Press, 1985), p. 380.

2. Friedrich Nietzsche, *Ecce Homo, Kritische Gesamtausgabe,* ed. Giorgio Colli and Mazzino Montinari (Berlin: De Gruyter, 1967 ff), 6.3.333.

3. ". . . so umschreibt die Bejahung des Nichtnichts als innere Grenze die Unendlichkeit alles dessen, was nicht Nichts ist. Es wird ein Unendliches bejaht: Gottes unendliches Wesen, seine unendliche Tatsächlichkeit, seine Physis" (Rosenzweig, *Stern* 36, *Star* 26–27).

4. Robert Gibbs, *Correlations in Rosenzweig and Levinas* (Princeton: Princeton University Press, 1992), pp. 32–33.

5. Rosenzweig, *Stern,* p. 36; *Star,* p. 27.

6. Ferdinand de Saussure, *Cours de linguistique générale* (Paris: Payot, 1971), p. 37; *Course in General Linguistics,* trans. Jonathan Culler (London: Fontana-Collins, 1974), pp. 18–19.

7. Jacques Derrida, "En ce moment même dans cet ouvrage me voici," in *Psyché* (Paris: Galilée, 1987), p. 187: "At this very moment in this work here I am," in *Re-Reading Levinas,* ed. Robert Bernasconi and Simon Critchley (Bloomington: Indiana University Press, 1991) pp. 34–35.

8. John Austin, *How to Do Things with Words* (Oxford: Clarendon Press, 1962), Lecture XI.

9. *Aussprache mit Martin Heidegger an 06/XI/1951,* Vortragsausschuss der Studentenschaft der Universität Zürich, Zürich, 1952. This is reproduced in part with acknowledgment to Jean Beaufret by Jean-Luc Marion, *Dieu sans l'être* (Paris: Communio/Fayard, 1982), p. 93, and translated by Jean Greisch in *Heidegger et la question de Dieu,* ed. Richard Kearney and Joseph Stephen O'Leary (Paris: Grasset, 1980), pp. 333–34, and by D. Saatdjian and F. Fédier in *Poésie* (Paris) 13 (1980), 60–61.

10. Martin Heidegger, *Sein und Zeit* (Tübingen: Niemeyer, 1953), *Being and Time,* trans. John Macquarrie and Edward Robinson (Oxford: Blackwell, 1967), trans. Joan Stambaugh (Albany: State University of New York Press, 1996), p. 192.

11. "I prefer the word *épreuve* to *expérience* because in the word *expérience* a knowing of which the self is master is always said. In the word *épreuve* there is at once the idea of life and of a critical 'verification' which overflows the self of which it is only the 'scene.'" Interview in Salomon Malka, *Lire Lévinas* (Paris: Cerf, 1984), p. 108.

12. "Yes," according to James Joyce, as well as being "the most positive word in the human language," is also "the female word." See Richard Ellmann, *James Joyce* (Oxford: Oxford University Press, 1983), pp. 522, 501.

13. Maurice Blanchot, *L'écriture du désastre* (Paris: Gallimard, 1980). Martin Heidegger, *Aus der Erfahrung des Denkens* (Pfullingen: Neske, 1954), p. 7: "Auf einen Stern zugehen, nur dieses . . ."

7. THE IMPOSSIBILITY OF LEVINAS'S DEATH

1. See John Llewelyn, "The 'Possibility' of Heidegger's Death," *Journal of the British Society for Phenomenology*, vol. 14, no. 2 (1983), 127–38, reproduced in this volume as chapter 8, but some readers may prefer to read it before continuing with the present one.

2. Emmanuel Levinas, *La Théorie de l'intuition dans la phénoménologie de Husserl* (Paris: Alcan, 1930), *The Theory of Intuition in Husserl's Phenomenology*, trans. A. Orianne (Evanston: Northwestern University Press, 1973).

3. Edmund Husserl, *The Phenomenology of Internal Time Consciousness*, trans. J. S. Churchill (The Hague: Nijhoff, 1964), p. 15.

4. G. W. F. Hegel, *Philosophy of Right*, trans. T. M. Knox (Oxford: Oxford University Press, 1967), p. 57 (§70).

5. See John Llewelyn, *The HypoCritical Imagination: Between Kant and Levinas* (London: Routledge, 2000).

6. In *Dieu, la mort et le temps* at least one thesis of Ernst Bloch's work of this title is endorsed by Levinas. See also "Sur la mort dans la pensée d'Ernst Bloch," in *De Dieu qui vient à l'idée*.

8. THE POSSIBILITY OF HEIDEGGER'S DEATH

1. Paul Edwards, "Heidegger and Death as 'Possibility'," *Mind* 84 (1975), 560. Also Paul Edwards, *Heidegger on Death: A Critical Evaluation, Monist* Monograph Number 1 (La Salle: The Hegeler Institute, 1979), p. 35. 1 shall refer to these as HDP and HD.

2. HDP, p. 558, HD, p. 33.

3. Martin Heidegger, *Sein und Zeit* (Tübingen: Niemeyer, 1952), *Being and Time*, trans. John Macquarrie and Edward Robinson (Oxford: Blackwell, 1962), trans. Joan Stambaugh (Albany: State University of New York Press, 1996), p. 258. My references, abbreviated below as SZ, are to the pages of *Sein und Zeit* and correspond to the references given in the margins of the English editions.

4. SZ, p. 258: "der eigenste Möglichkeitscharakter des Todes: gewiss und dabei unbestimmt, das heisst jeden Augenblick möglich." Compare Martin Heidegger, *Prolegomena zur Geschichte des Zeitsbegriffs* (Frankfurt am Main: Klostermann, 1979), p. 433: "Ich bin nämlich dieses 'Ich kann jeden Augenblick sterben'." *History of the Concept of Time: Prolegomena*, trans. Theodore Kisiel (Bloomington: Indiana University Press, 1985), p. 313: "For I am this 'I can die at any moment.'"

5. My "un-closedness" is an attempt to reflect the idea that *Ent-schlossenheit* is a distinctive mode of *Erschlossenheit*, dis-closedness (SZ, pp. 297 and 299f.). My "resolvedness" is an attempt to mark the difference between it and the ontic state of will called resolution of which *Ent-schlossenheit* is the enabling ontological condition. Since Heidegger often writes the name for this condition without the hyphen, John Macquarrie and Edward Robinson are prepared to run the risk Heidegger himself runs in using a single word, "resoluteness," with a dual purpose.

6. SZ, pp. 247–48.

7. Søren Kierkegaard, *Concluding Unscientific Postscript*, trans. David F. Swenson and Walter Lowrie (Princeton: Princeton University Press, 1941), pp. 154–55. It

may not be entirely irrelevant in the context of discussion of Heidegger's analysis of *Sein zum Tode* to recall that the title of the translation of another of Kierkegaard's books is *Krankheit zum Tode.*

8. SZ, pp. 322–23.

9. SZ p. 235, note vi.

10. Paul Edwards, "Heidegger and Death: A Deflationary Critique," *The Monist* 59 (1976), 180. HD, p. 23.

11. SZ, p. 258.

12. SZ, p. 245.

13. SZ, p. 247.

14. I am grateful to the late Magda King for suggesting this locution.

15. SZ pp. 247–48.

16. SZ, p. 259.

17. Martin Heidegger, "Was ist Metaphysik?," in *Wegmarken* (Frankfurt am Main: Klostermann, 1976), p. 120; "What is Metaphysics?," in *Pathmarks,* trans. William McNeill (Cambridge: Cambridge University Press, 1998), p. 95; *Existence and Being* (London: Vision, 1949), p. 377; *Basic Writings,* ed. David Farrell Krell (London: Routledge and Kegan Paul, 1978), p. 110.

18. Whereas "Everyday concern makes definite for itself the indefiniteness of certain death by interposing before it those urgencies and possibilities which can be taken in at a glance, and which belong to the everyday matters that are closest to us" (SZ, p. 258).

19. Martin Heidegger, *Prolegomena zur Geschichte des Zeitbegriffs,* p. 433; *History of the Concept of Time,* p. 313.

20. SZ, p. 54. Compare Martin Heidegger, *An Introduction to Metaphysics* (New York: Doubleday, 1961), pp. 58ff., and "Bauen Wohnen Denken," in *Vorträge und Aufsätze* (Pfullingen: Neske, 1967), vol. II, pp. 19ff.

21. Martin Heidegger, "Das Ding," in *Vorträge und Aufsätze,* vol. II, p. 51, and *Poetry, Language, Thought,* trans. Albert Hofstadter (New York: Harper, 1971), p. 179.

9. sELECTION

1. This is a slightly modified excerpt from a statement reported in Irving Greenberg, "Lessons to Be Learned from the Holocaust," a paper read at the International Conference on the Church Struggle and the Holocaust, Hamburg, 8–11 June 1975, reproduced from Alice L. Eckardt and A. Roy Eckardt, *Long Night's Journey into Day: A Revised Retrospective on the Holocaust* (Detroit: Wayne State University Press; Oxford: Pergamon Press, 1988), p. 134.

2. Elie Wiesel, *Night* (London: Penguin, 1981), pp. 76–77.

3. Israel W. Charny, *How Can We Commit the Unthinkable? Genocide—The Human Cancer* (Boulder: Westview Press, 1982), p. x.

4. Alan Milchman and Alan Rosenberg, *Postmodernism and the Holocaust* (Amsterdam and Atlanta: Rodopi, 1998).

5. An older inmate of Auschwitz records, "I bite deeply into my lips: we know well that to gain a small, extraneous pain serves as a stimulant to mobilize our last reserves of energy." Primo Levi, *If This Is a Man* (London: Penguin, 1979).

6. André Schwarz-Bart, *The Last of the Just,* trans. Stephen Becker (New York: Bantam, 1960).

7. David Farrell Krell, *Of Memory, Reminiscence and Writing: On the Verge* (Bloomington: Indiana University Press, 1990). Jacques Derrida, *Glas* (Paris: Galilée, 1974,

Paris: Denoël-Gonthier, 1981); *Glas,* trans. John P. Leavey, Jr., and Richard Rand (Lincoln: Nebraska University Press, 1986).

8. George Steiner, "Dying as an Art," in *Language and Silence: Essays 1958–1966* (London: Faber and Faber, 1967), p. 330.

9. Emmanuel Levinas, "As If Consenting to Horror," trans. Paula Wissing, *Critical Inquiry,* 15, 1989, 487.

10. Sylvia Plath, *The Collected Poems,* ed. Ted Hughes (New York: Harper-Collins, 1992), p. 223.

11. Eckardt, Alice A., and Eckardt, A. Roy, *Long Night's Journey into Day,* p. 150.

12. Eliezer Berkovits, *Faith after the Holocaust* (New York: Ktav, 1973), pp. 67–68.

13. For further discussion of Levinas's enigmatic *peut-être* see John Llewelyn, *Emmanuel Levinas. The Genealogy of Ethics* (London and New York: Routledge, 1995), chapter 12.

14. See Levinas, "'A l'image de Dieu,' d'après Rabbi Haïm de Voloziner," in *L'au-delà du verset: lectures et discours talmudiques* (Paris: Minuit, 1982), pp. 182–200, and his preface to Rabbi Hayyim de Volozhin, *L'âme de la vie (Nefesh Hahayyim)* (Paris: Verdier, 1986).

15. Rabbi Hayyim of Volozhin, *L'âme de la vie,* p. 44.

16. For an exegesis of Levinas in which "He" turns itself into "(S)he," see John Llewelyn, "En ce moment même: . . . une répétition qui n'en est pas une," in *Le passage des frontières. Autour du travail de Jacques Derrida,* Colloque de Cerisy (Paris: Galilée, 1994), pp. 245–48 (translated in chapter 11 in this volume).

17. *Song of Solomon* 5:6.

18. Gillian Rose, *Judaism and Modernity. Philosophical Essays* (Oxford: Blackwell, 1993), p. 8.

19. Levinas, "The Trace of the Other," trans. Alphonso Lingis, in Mark Taylor, ed., *Deconstruction in Context* (Chicago: University of Chicago Press, 1986), p. 357.

20. Manès Sperber, as cited in a book review by Jakob J. Petuchowski, *Conservative Judaism* 31, nos. 1–2 (1976–77), p. 96, as cited by Eckardt and Eckardt, *Long Night's Journey into Day,* p. 93.

21. Eckardt and Eckardt, *Long Night's Journey into Day,* p. 94.

22. Eckardt and Eckardt, *Long Night's Journey into Day,* p. 90, citing Eliezer Berkovits, "The Hiding of God of History," in Israel Gutman and Livia Rothkirchen, eds., *The Catastrophe of European Jewry: Antecedents—History—Reflections* (Jerusalem: Yad Vashem, 1976), pp. 694, 704; Berkovits, *Faith after the Holocaust* (New York: Klav, 1973), pp. 99, 131.

23. Lucy S. Dawidowicz in "The Holocaust as Historical Record," in *Dimensions of the Holocaust,* Lectures at Northwestern University (Evanston: Northwestern University, 1977), p. 32.

24. Emil L. Fackenheim, "The Human Condition after Auschwitz: A Jewish Testimony a Generation After," *Congress Bi-Weekly* 39, no. 7 (28 April 1972), 6–10; no. 8 (19 May 1972), 5–7, cited by Eckardt and Eckardt, *Long Night's Journey into Day,* p. 66.

25. Hannah Arendt, letter to Karl Jaspers, 4 March 1951, in Lotte Koehler and Hans Saner, eds., *Hannah Arendt, Karl Jaspers Briefwechsel, 1926–1969* (Munich: Piper, 1985), no. 109, paraphrased by Dagma Barnouw, *Visible Spaces: Hannah Arendt and the German-Jewish Experience* (Baltimore: Johns Hopkins University Press, 1990), p. 350.

26. Graham B. Walker Jr., *Elie Wiesel: A Challenge to Theology* (Jefferson: McFarland, 1988), p. 104.

27. From a letter cited by Lucy S. Dawidowicz in "The Holocaust as Historical Record," in *Dimensions of the Holocaust*, p. 28.

28. Symposium on "Le scandale du mal. Catastrophes naturelles et crimes de l'homme," *Les Nouveaux Cahiers* 22, no. 85 (1986), p. 17.

29. Edmond Jabès, as reported by Elisabeth de Fontany in her introduction to the symposium on "Le scandale du mal. Catastrophes naturelles et crimes de l'homme," *Les Nouveaux Cahiers* 22 (1986), no. 85, p. 5.

30. Arthur A. Cohen, *The Tremendum: A Theological Interpretation of the Holocaust* (New York: Crossroads, 1981).

31. Richard Rubinstein, *After Auschwitz: History, Theology and Contemporary Judaism* (Baltimore: Johns Hopkins University Press, 2nd ed. 1992), p. 192. For a concise review of these and other alternatives see Dan Cohn-Sherbok, *Holocaust Theology* (London: Lamp, 1989).

32. Catastrophe is a topic in chapter 15 of the book referred to in note 13.

10. JEWGREEK OR GREEKJEW

1. G. W. F. Hegel, *The Phenomenology of Spirit*, trans. A. V. Miller (Oxford: Clarendon Press, 1977), p. 102.

2. See *The Philosophy of Martin Buber*, ed. P. A. Schilpp and M. Friedman (La Salle, Ill.: Open Court, 1967; London: Cambridge University Press, 1967), p. 723.

3. Martin Heidegger, *Sein und Zeit* (Tübingen: Niemeyer, 1953), *Being and Time*, trans. John Macquarrie and Edward Robinson (Oxford: Blackwell, 1962), trans. Joan Stambaugh (Albany: State University of New York Press, 1996), p. 199, 300.

4. Ibid, p. 122.

5. Emmanuel Levinas "Le mot je, le mot tu, le mot Dieu," *Le Monde*, 19–20 March 1978, p. 2. l am grateful to Gustave Calamand for sending me a cutting of this.

6. Martin Heidegger, *Holzwege* (Frankfurt am Main: Klostermann, 1972), p. 310; *Early Greek Thinking*, trans. David Farrell Krell and Frank A. Capuzzi (New York: Harper and Row, 1975), p. 26.

7. I am grateful to Adriaan Peperzak for a shrewd comment on this question.

8. Heidegger, *Holzwege*, p. 311; *Early Greek Thinking*, p. 26.

9. Martin Heidegger, *Platons Lehre von der Wahrheit, mit einem Brief über den "Humanismus"* (Bern: Franke, 1954), pp. 84–85; "Letter on 'Humanism,'" in *Wegmarken* (Frankfurt am Main: Klostermann, 1976), p. 338; *Pathmarks*, ed. William McNeill (Cambridge: Cambridge University Press, 1998), pp. 257–58; *Martin Heidegger: Basic Writings*, ed. David Farrell Krell (New York: Harper and Row, 1977; London: Routledge and Kegan Paul, 1978), p. 217.

10. Ibid., p. 60, p. 319, p. 243, p. 199.

11. Heidegger, *Holzwege* p. 310; *Early Greek Thinking*, p. 25.

11. AT THIS VERY MOMENT . . . A REPETITION THAT IS NOT ONE

1. "ELoHiM, Elohim, God. In fact this word is in the plural; it means 'the gods.' Maybe this is a plural become generic name: Genesis 1:1." Armand Abécassis, *La pensée juive* (Paris: Minuit, 1982), vol. 1, p. 335. Compare Emmanuel Levinas, *L'au-delà du verset: lectures et discours talmudiques*, p. 147 (BV 119): "The word designating divinity is precisely the word Name, a generic term in relation to which the different names of God are individuated." "Illéité" and "Elléité" would be ways of saying distributively generic pronominality, despite the final syllable which, like that al-

ready of "altérité," would put them "under the authority of a category, of an essence, of a being once more" (TEL 29, Ps 167, RRL 18). It is to be noted further that from the point of view of English, "ELoHim" or "EloHIM" could serve as a hypomnemonic of a complicity of sex and genre, therefore of passage between "il" or "Il" and "elle" or "Elle" in my text.

12. LEVINAS AND LANGUAGE

1. "Name" here translates *nom*, which can also mean "noun," as in "Pro-noun."

2. Ferdinand de Saussure, *Course in General Linguistics*, trans. Wade Baskin (London: Fontana-Collins, 1974).

3. Jean-Paul Sartre, *L'existentialisme est un humanisme* (Paris: Nagel, 1946).

4. Martin Heidegger, *Basic Writings*, ed. David Farrell Krell (London: Routledge, 1978), p. 239.

5. Martin Heidegger, *Sein und Zeit* (Tübingen: Niemeyer, 1953), *Being and Time*, trans. John Macquarrie and Edward Robinson (Oxford: Blackwell, 1962), trans. Joan Stambaugh (Albany: State University of New York Press, 1996), p. 165. My references are to the pages of *Sein und Zeit* and correspond to the references given in the margins of the English editions.

6. Ibid., pp. 276, 285, 300.

7. Ludwig Wittgenstein, *Philosophical Investigations*, trans. G. E. M. Anscombe (Oxford: Blackwell, 1953), 11.

8. Martin Heidegger, "Der Weg zur Sprache," in *Unterwegs zur Sprache* (Pfullingen: Neske, 1975), p. 254; "The Way to Language," in *On the Way to Language*, trans. Peter D. Hertz and Joan Stambaugh (New York: Harper and Row, 1975), p. 124.

9. Ibid., p. 265; p. 134.

10. John Austin, *How to Do Things with Words* (Oxford: Clarendon Press, 1962).

11. Paul Ricoeur, "Culpabilité, éthique et religion," in *Le conflit des interprétations: essais d'herméneutique* (Paris: Seuil, 1969), pp. 416–30.

12. W. V. Quine, *From a Logical Point of View: Logico-Philosophical Essays* (Cambridge, Mass.: Harvard University Press, 1953), pp. 8, 167.

13. The anecdote is due to Michaël Levinas.

14. Martin Heidegger, *On Time and Being*, trans. Joan Stambaugh (New York: Harper and Row, 1972), pp. 1–24.

15. G. W. F. Hegel, *Phenomenology of Spirit*, trans. A. V. Miller (Oxford: Clarendon Press, 1979), p. 65.

16. Gottlob Frege, "On Concept and Object," in P. T. Geach and Max Black, eds., *Translations from the Philosophical Writings of Gottlob Frege* (Oxford: Blackwell, 1960), pp. 45–48.

17. Hegel, *Phenomenology*, p. 60.

18. Jacques Derrida, "La pharmacie de Platon," in *La Dissémination* (Paris: Seuil, 1972); "Plato's Pharmacy," in *Dissemination*, trans. Barbara Johnson (Chicago: University of Chicago Press, 1981), pp. 61–171.

19. See Robert Bernasconi, "The Third Party: Levinas on the Intersection of the Ethical and the Political," *Journal of the British Society for Phenomenology* 30 (1999), 76–87.

20. Saussure, *Course*, chap. IV. See also Jacques Lacan, "L'instance de la lettre dans l'inconscient ou la raison depuis Freud," in *Écrits* (Paris: Seuil, 1966), pp. 493–528.

21. Edmund Husserl, *The Phenomenology of Internal Time Consciousness*, trans. James S. Churchill (The Hague: Nijhoff, 1964).

22. Plato, *Republic* 359–60.

23. Martin Heidegger, *Unterwegs zur Sprache,* p. 215; *On the Way to Language,* p. 108.

24. See, for example, Noam Chomsky, *Topics in the Theory of Generative Grammar* (The Hague: Mouton, 1966), pp. 11–12.

13. THRESHOLDS

1. See John Llewelyn, *The HypoCritical Imagination: Between Kant and Levinas* (London: Routledge, 2000), chapter 2. References to Hegel are to the *Enzyklopädie* (Enc); *Wissenschaft der Logik* (WL); and *Phänomenologie des Geistes.* I have used the following translation of these works of Hegel: *Encyclopaedia Logic,* trans. W. Wallace (Oxford: Clarendon, 1975), *Hegel's Science of Logic,* trans. A. V. Miller (London: Allen and Unwin, 1969), and *Phenomenology of Spirit,* trans. A. V. Miller (Oxford: Clarendon, 1977). The translations of quotations from Derrida are my own.

2. *Hegel's Introduction to Aesthetics,* trans. T. M. Knox (Oxford: Clarendon, 1979), p. 88.

3. Ibid.

4. Jean Hyppolite, "Structure du langage philosophique d'après la 'Préface de la Phénomenologie de l'esprit' de Hegel," in *Figures de la pensée philosophique* (Paris: Presses Universitaires de France, 1971), vol. 1, pp. 351–52. See also *The Language of Criticism and the Science of Man,* ed. Richard Macksey and Eugenio Donato (Baltimore and London: Johns Hopkins University Press, 1970).

5. Alexandre Koyré, *Etudes d'histoire de la pensée philosophique* (Paris: Gallimard, 1971), p. 168.

6. This manuscript may be as lost as the notes from which Hyppolite spoke about absolute knowing at his seminar on Hegel at the Collège de France. When the proceedings of this seminar were published after his death the volume contained six papers, including Derrida's "Le puits et la pyramide," but nothing by the convener himself. See the *Avertissement* to *Hegel et la pensée moderne,* ed. Jacques d'Hondt (Paris: Presses Universitaires de France, 1970).

14. SEMIOETHICS

1. Thomas A. Sebeok, Alfred S. Hayes, and Mary Catherine Bateson, eds., *Approaches to Semiotics,* Transactions of the Indiana University Conference on Paralinguistics and Kinesis (The Hague: Mouton, 1964). Otherwise than Marion's "*the* call as such," the call neither is nor has an *as* or a *such.* See Jean-Luc Marion, *Réduction et donation. Recherches sur Husserl, Heidegger et la phénoménologie* (Paris: Presses Universitaires de France, 1989), p. 295. See also Jacques Derrida, *Donner le temps, 1, La fausse monnaie* (Paris: Galilée, 1991), pp. 72–74.

2. Ferdinand de Saussure, *Cours de linguistique générale* (Paris: Payot, 1971), p. 98; *Course in General Linguistics,* trans. Wade Baskin (London: Fontana, 1974), p. 66.

3. Dorian Cairns, *Guide for Translating Husserl* (The Hague: Nijhoff, 1973). Edmund Husserl, *Recherches logiques,* trans. Hubert Elie, Arion L. Kelkel, and René Scherer (Paris: Presses Universitaires de France, 1959–64). Edmund Husserl, *Logical Investigations,* trans. J. N. Findlay (London: Routledge and Kegan Paul, 1976).

4. In what follows the hyphen is dropped except in the nominal form.

5. Edmund Husserl, *Ideen zu einer reinen Phänomenologie und phänomenologischen Philosophie,* vol. 1, Husserliana 3 (The Hague: Nijhoff, 1950), p. 312; *Ideas,* trans. W. R. Boyce Gibson (London: Allen and Unwin, 1931), p. 355.

6. Ibid., pp. 305, 347.

7. In "The Meaning of a Word," John Austin conducts what he would be ready to call linguistic phenomenology in order to show that sentences, but not words, have meaning (in *Philosophical Papers*, ed. J. O. Urmson and G. J. Warnock (Oxford: Clarendon Press, 1979), pp. 55–75). Supposing he is right, we can still make the distinction on which much that is said in the first part of the present chapter turns, the distinction between the meaning of a sentence and what someone means in uttering it or a word. See Derrida, *Memoires for Paul de Man*, trans. Cecile Lindsay, Jonathan Culler, and Eduardo Cadava (New York: Columbia University Press, 1986), pp. 112ff., MPM 113ff.

8. J. N. Mohanty, "On Husserl's Theory of Meaning," *Southwestern Journal of Philosophy* 5 (1974), 229–44.

9. Husserl, *Ideas*, §4, §70.

10. Paul de Man, "Sign and Symbol in Hegel's *Aesthetics*," *Critical Inquiry*, 8, 1982, 761–75, especially 768–69.

11. G. W. F. Hegel, *Phänomenologie des Geistes* (Frankfurt am Main: Suhrkamp, 1970), pp. 83, 90, 92; *Phenomenology of Spirit*, trans. A. V. Miller (Oxford: Clarendon Press, 1977), pp. 59, 65, 66; *Phenomenology of Mind*, trans. J. B. Baillie (New York: Harper and Row, 1967), pp. 150, 158, 159–60.

12. G. W. F. Hegel, *Phänomenologie des Geistes*, p. 91; *Phenomenology of Spirit*, pp. 65–66; *Phenomenology of Mind*, p. 159.

13. Hegel, *Phänomenologie des Geistes*, p 92; *Phenomenology of Spirit*, p. 66; *Phenomonology of Mind*, p. 160.

14. See Robert Bernasconi, "The Trace of Levinas in Derrida," in *Derrida and Différance*, ed. David Wood and Robert Bernasconi (Evanston, Ill.: Northwestern University Press, 1988), pp. 13–29.

15. Emmanuel Levinas, "La substitution," *Revue philosophique de Louvain* 66, no. 1 (1968), 487–508.

15. NO HAPPY ENDING

1. Are there also allusions to "the number of his name" of Revelations 13:17; to the Book named Numbers which tells of God's addressing Moses in the Tabernacle of the Presence; and to *Nombres* by Philippe Sollers? Derrida writes of Sollers: "Numbers begins by putting the signer's name in an umbra. . . . No longer answerable to anyone, unjustifiable. . . . (*Ne répond plus devant personne, injustifiable. . . .*)" (D 329, D tr. 296).

2. Jacques Derrida, *Le problème de la genèse dans la philosophie de Husserl* (Paris: Presses Universitaires de France, 1990). See p. 179, note 4, referring to Husserl's ontology and the account of it given by Levinas in *La théorie de l'intution dans la phénoménologie de Husserl:* "Besides, this ontology is 'monotypical.' Human 'existence' and empirical 'existence' are not essentially different. Both can be 'objectivated' by a theoretical intuition. But this ontology is above all one of the first moments of phenomenology. It is also difficult to agree with Levinas that the whole of Husserl's thinking is motivated by such an ontological presupposition. Furthermore, M. Levinas's thesis is supported only by texts earlier than the *Cartesian Meditations*. An unequivocal ontology is nuanced already by certain statements in *Ideas I* on the topic of the originarily 'evaluating' and 'practical,' even 'ethical' attitude of the subject. . . ."

3. *Otherwise than Being or Beyond Essence* is dedicated "To the memory of those who were closest among the six million assassinated by the National Socialists, and of the millions on millions of all confessions and all nations, victims of the same hatred of the other man, the same anti-semitism." On the same page is written, in Hebrew, a list of the names of those who were closest, followed by the acronym for "May your soul be bound up in the bundle of life" (1 Samuel 25:29).

4. Abbott's translation sometimes confuses the *supremum* with the *summum*.

5. Paul Valéry, "Le cimetière marin," *Poésies* (Paris: Gallimard, 1942), p. 192.

6. Immanuel Kant, *Critique of Practical Reason,* trans. Lewis White Beck (New York: Liberal Arts Press, 1956), p. 115.

7. Ibid., p. 121.

8. Catherine Chalier, *Pour une morale au-delà du savoir: Kant et Levinas* (Paris: Albin Michel, 1998), p. 175.

9. Ibid., p. 105.

10. Dialogue with Richard Kearney in Richard A. Cohen, ed., *Face to Face with Levinas* (Albany: State University of New York Press, 1986), p. 18.

11. Catherine Chalier, *Pour une morale au-delà du savoir,* pp. 145–46.

12. Quand sous les lourds flocons des neigeuses années

L'ennui, fruit de la morne incuriosité,

Prend les proportions de l'immortalité.

Charles Baudelaire, "Spleen," "J'ai plus de souvenirs . . . ," in *Oeuvres complètes* (Pléiade) (Paris: Gallimard, 1961), p. 69.

INDEX

Abraham, 114; and Isaac, 139; and Ulysses, 115
Abraham, N., 48
accusative, 3, 4, 109, 114
activity. *See* passivity and activity
affirmation, 39–40, 98
aging, 116
Akedah, 139
allergy, 7, 89, 108, 184
almost (*presque*), 70, 74
alterity, absolute, radical, 8, 11, 14, 16, 30, 146
alternation, 78
amen, 94–104 passim, 162, 209, 212, 213
anarchy, 12, 71, 171, 211
and, 9
answearability, 220, 226
antihumanism, 165–66
anti-Semitism, 138
apposition, xiii, 228
Arendt, H., 140
Aristotle, 10; distinctivness of sense, 63; *nous,* 224; *phronêsis,* 55
art, 77, 76, 179
ashes and dust, 114–15
asymmetry, 88, 159, 220
atheism, 95
Aufhebung, 8, 63, 178, 181, 186, 187, 206

Auschwitz, 130–32, 138, 141
Austin, J., 22–23, 25, 30, 34, 36, 42, 100, 168, 200
authenticity, 122, 126, 129

Bachelard, G., 2, 187, 189
Bachelard, S., 196
Baillie, J. B., 201
Barth, K., 32
Bass, A., 58, 192, 193
Bataille, G., 13, 186–87, 189
Baudelaire, C., 47
beautiful, 73
being, 7, 12, 134, 143, 151; beyond, 12, 16, 105, 113; house of, 166; way of, 13, 101, 168
being-with, 2, 88, 206
Bentham, J., 90
Berezdivin, R., 39
Bergson, H., 68, 69, 73, 74, 116
Berkeley, G., 31, 146
Berkovits, E., 139
Bernasconi, R., xiv
Betti, E., 2
biology, 115–16, 145
Blanchot, M., 28, 70, 212
blasphemy, 131, 133, 136
bliss, 224
Boehme, J., 96
Brentano, F., 8, 193

249

John Llewelyn has been Reader in Philosophy at the University of Edinburgh, Visiting Professor of Philosophy at the University of Memphis, and the Arthur J. Schmitt Distinguished Visiting Professor of Philosophy at Loyola University Chicago. Among his publications are *Beyond Metaphysics? The Hermeneutic Circle in Contemporary Continental Philosophy; Derrida on the Threshold of Sense; The Middle Voice of Ecological Conscience; Emmanuel Levinas: The Genealogy of Ethics;* and *The Hypo-Critical Imagination: Between Kant and Levinas.*